The

SCIENTIFIC
100

The
SCIENTIFIC
100

---

*A Ranking of
the Most Influential
Scientists,
Past and Present*

John Simmons

k

Citadel Press
Kensington Publishing Corp.
www.kensingtonbooks.com

CITADEL PRESS books are published by

Kensington Publishing Corp.
850 Third Avenue
New York, NY 10022

All Kensington titles, imprints, and distributed lines are available at special quantity discounts for bulk purchases for sales promotions, premiums, fund-raising, educational, or institutional use. Special book excerpts or customized printings can also be created to fit specific needs. For details, write or phone the office of the Kensington special sales manager: Kensington Publishing Corp., 850 Third Avenue, New York, NY 10022, attn: Special Sales Department, Phone: 1-800-221-2647

Kensington and the K logo Reg. U.S. Pat. & TM Off.
Citadel Press is a trademark of Kensington Publishing Corp.

First printing 2000
Printed in the United States of America
10 9 8 7 6 5 4 3 2 1

The Library of Congress has cataloged the Citadel edition as follows:

Simmons, John G., 1949–
    The scientific 100 : a ranking of the most influential scientists, past and present / John Simmons.
        p.   cm.
    "A Citadel Press book."
    ISBN 0–8065–2094–9 (pbk.)
    1. Scientists—Rating of. 2. Scientists—Biographt—Chronology. 3. Science—istory.
Q148.S55 1996
509.2'2—dc20
[B]   99–31181
                                                           CIP

for Clayton & Jocelyne

CONTENTS

ACKNOWLEDGMENTS

It is my privilege to extend thanks to the individuals whose expertise played a key role in compiling the list of scientists profiled in this volume. At the New York Academy of Sciences, Irwin Gittelman, Marguerite F. Levy, Louis Muschel, Margaret A. Reilly, David G. Black, and Sylvia Slote all reviewed the growing roster and made valuable suggestions. I also wish to thank the academy's development officer, Craig Purinton, who was unfailingly helpful and courteous. I owe special thanks to Adnan Waly, the experimental physicist, who provided advice and valuable insight, based on both his own wisdom and personal acquaintance with the major figures of twentieth-century physics.

Where possible, I offered contemporary scientists an opportunity to correct factual mistakes in their respective profiles. For their courteous help my thanks are due to Hans Bethe, Noam Chomsky, Francis Crick, Gertrude Belle Elion, Claude Lévi-Strauss, Lynn Margulis, Ernst Mayr, Frederick Sanger, Edward Teller, and Edward O. Wilson. Individual chapters were also reviewed by David Cassidy, Gale Christianson, Bruce Chandler, Jeff Cohlberg, Sue Massy, Alan Rocke, K. C. Wali, and Deborah Weir. A sensitive reading of the entire manuscript by Donald J. Davidson was invaluable. I am grateful to all, and add that the errors which remain are mine alone.

During early work on this project I was inspired by reading Stephen G. Brush's *History of Modern Science: A Guide to the Second Scientific Revolution* as well as by his illuminating article, "Should the History of Science Be Rated X?" Professor Brush kindly reviewed the list for this volume and made important suggestions. My gratitude is also due Keith Benson of the History of

Science Society at the University of Washington. The veteran science writer Stephen S. Hall also made valuable recommendations, as did Iain Boal and Lawrence Creshkoff. For photo research I am grateful to Jocelyne Barque as well as Inge King. For her patience and skill in shepherding the manuscript through production, I thank Arline M. Cooke. My thanks and appreciation, as well, to Fred Korndorf and to my colleagues at the Writers Room.

For over fifteen years at *Current Biography* I have had the pleasure to work with Judith Graham as well as with her predecessor, Charles Moritz, and take this opportunity to thank them for introducing me to a great variety of interesting people, scientists among them.

Finally, I could not have found a better editor anywhere in publishing than James Ellison.

INTRODUCTION

Profiled in this volume are the scientific figures whose influence in shaping the contemporary world is pervasive and inescapable. They formulated the laws of motion, discovered how electricity works, and illuminated the structure of the atom. They broke down chemicals into elements and found them in the sun, the moon, and stars as well as on Earth, down to its deep core. Investigating fossils of plants and animals, they emerged with a theory of evolution. With the help of green peas, white-eyed fruit flies, and X-rays, they came up with a theory of heredity that had a cellular, then a molecular basis. Into this was plugged evolution and now, after a few centuries of poking into the microworld, they showed how one-celled creatures are descended from bacteria, and both are ancestral to human beings. And, not least, they discerned in human discourse a hidden dimension of unconscious motivation and cognitive structure—clarifying the nature of emotional development, language, and the basic elements of cultures all over the globe.

Those are only a *few* of the things they did.

And apart from a couple of intellectual discoveries which go back to the Greeks and Babylonians, they accomplished it all in several hundred years.

Science is theory supported by experiment, and most of the scientists found here preferred one or the other. The chemist August Kekulé disliked working at the laboratory bench, but one night, dozing aboard a London omnibus, he had a dream from which derives all of organic chemistry. Creating the first atomic pile, Enrico Fermi was happy to get his hands dirty, but his friend Leo Szilard couldn't be bothered and preferred to sit around discussing nuclear physics. Stephen Hawking disliked looking at stars through a telescope, but has become the most influential cosmologist of his generation. However, virtually all would agree with Richard Feynman, a great theorist who could fix everything from a washing machine to a particle accelerator, that *"The sole test of the validity of any idea is experiment."* The potency of this notion has given the physical sciences an important cachet in the present world, which can be seen in the way theories are formulated and evaluated even in anthropology and psychology. And its impact is reflected throughout this book.

The scientists chosen for this volume are distinguished for discovering new things about nature, but not for manipulating it for other ends. This common and useful distinction leaves out of *The Scientific 100* the great inventors and engineers. The tremendously productive Thomas Edison, inventor of the electric light, is absent because his achievements did not contribute to basic science. The single scientific discovery credited to him—the Edison effect, from 1883—he could demonstrate but not explain. The same holds true for Nicola Tesla, the innovator in electric power, and Robert Fulton, who designed and built the first steamboats. Influential as these individuals were for the everyday modern world, they belong to another realm and deserve a volume of their own.

Brief biographies are an attractive way for a nonscientist to understand how science developed because they contain messages that everyone can understand. People are born, become educated, develop certain personal relationships as well as interests, beliefs, and ideas. This is true of everybody in *The Scientific 100,* and the major difference between these individuals and the rest of us is the significance of their ideas. Ernest Rutherford bombarded a piece of foil with alpha rays and when a few of those particles ricocheted, it was "as if you had fired a fifteen-inch shell at a piece of tissue paper, and it came back and hit you." Part of the message was contained in the atomic particles, and another, crucial part consisted in all the things Rutherford already knew about them. When he put the two together, it became a profound scientific discovery which led to a new understanding of the atom. Many great discoveries of science have come from this marriage of experiment or observation, and synthetic weave of concept and experience. And they can be more readily understood if you know a little about the individuals involved, what they endured, and the social context of their work.

The title of a famous article on science and prosopography—the study of collective biography—is aptly entitled "Who the Guys Were." Although there are several women among the *Scientific 100,* the overwhelming majority are white males of European descent. In addition, perhaps surprisingly, most of the individuals in *The Scientific 100* are not self-made. With a couple of exceptions—the best-known being Michael Faraday—none of the scientists in this volume was born to an impoverished background. Rather, they came from striving families or cultivated homes in which intellectual pursuits were highly valued. Most of them were prized and encouraged by their parents, and as children went about collecting insects, looking at birds, learning algebra and calculus, and building things. A few of them, such as Paul Dirac, came from excruciatingly painful home environments, and it shows. After his father died, Dirac wrote, "I feel much freer now." But he was an exception, as was Isaac Newton. If genius is in any measure genetic, *The Scientific 100* suggests that the best way to stifle it is through grinding poverty or an inconstant, hateful parent.

In developing the list of scientists to be included in *The Scientific 100,* a major consideration was to provide the general reader with a sense of the overall breadth and diversity of scientific discovery. This is indicated by the first six figures: Newton, Einstein, Bohr, Darwin, Pasteur, and Freud. Although the physical sciences take precedence, I have made an effort not to neglect the impact of science on humanity, culture, and the human body. As Gerald Holton observes, apropos the work of such people as Franz Boas in combating racism, "One tends to forget that not all the desirable applications of science look like VCRs or pills."

Ordering the scientists according to overall influence enables this volume to conform with others in Citadel's "100" series; but a fuller explanation is in order. Ranking scientists is an enterprise which dates at least to the nineteenth century, when the American psychologist James McKeen Cattell counted the inches of space allotted to the great scientific figures in various encyclopedias. In *The Scientific 100* there is no such pretension to an objective measure. The final order is mine alone, and I made decisions based, insofar as possible, on recent assessments of individual scientists. Sometimes I briefly justify or explain the relative status of an entrant; more often, I leave it to an authority. The scientists were chosen for their positive accomplishments and the significance of what they did. It must be noted they are ranked in the same manner. Position on the list does not reflect the devaluation of any scientist because his or her viewpoint turned out to be somehow erroneous.

Although the final order is, as one eminent scientist wrote me, "bound to be in large degree arbitrary," this limitation should also be fairly obvious. It seems transparently useless to argue the relative significance of NIELS BOHR [3] and CHARLES DARWIN [4]. And it is more appropriate to say that the influence of the two nineteenth-century scientists GUSTAV KIRCHHOFF [57] and HERMANN VON HELMHOLTZ [63] was of the same order than to argue that one was better than the other. The chief claim for the list is general and simple: The order is essentially irreversible. Perhaps ARCHIMEDES [100] could become [1], but it would never do for WILHELM WUNDT [99] to become [2], or for NIELS BOHR [3] to become [97]. The list is not meant to be rigid, and is more flexible toward the middle than at the ends.

Finally, the list is "rounded" by history. Scientists whose discoveries are recent—over the past fifty years or so—are more likely to be found toward the end of the book. This is also the case with a few entrants whose positive influence is cautionary or diminishing. The Russian, TROFIM LYSENKO [93], is the clearest example, but his value to science, as an example of what it ought not to be, was great; his stature bought him a place in the authoritative *Dictionary of Scientific Biography* as one of the most controversial of modern figures. ALEXANDER FLEMING [97] is here as well, even though the glory heaped upon him was disproportionate to his scientific ability or real accomplishment.

In the bibliographic reference work *Prominent Scientists*, over 10,000 names are listed. Clearly, when restricted to one hundred, many of the greatest scientists must be left out. With contemporary figures the problem is compounded by the collaborative nature of much research. Murray Gell-Mann and Sheldon Glashow both find a place here as representatives of recent developments in physics; but lack of room made it impossible to include a profile, for example, of Steve Weinberg. A number of such scientists are mentioned in "Inexcusable Omissions, Honorable Mentions, and Also-Rans" at book's end.

With exceptions, most of the people in this book were awarded many honors, and some were covered with glory before they died. Thirty-one were awarded the Nobel Prize once, and three others won it twice. The number of laureates would be much higher if there were an award for biology or if the dead could be brought back to life and sent to Stockholm. As a consequence, great scientists have no further need of commendation. Encomiums on the order of "It was a bold move" and "This was one of the most dramatic and marvelous discoveries in human history" have been kept to a relative minimum. At the same time, every effort has been made to put their discoveries into historical and scientific context, the better to allow a clear notion of what they accomplished.

Finally, although *The Scientific 100* is not a unified history, the entrants as ensemble strongly reflect the evolving unity of the physical sciences and the expanding range of science in investigating language, psychology, and human culture. "Sooner or later," wrote the great historian of science, George Sarton, long ago, "[science] will go out to conquer other fields and to throw floods of light into all the dark places where superstition and ignorance are still rampant." At the end of the twentieth century, one is apt to reply, "Were it only so." Yet it remains that almost all the hundred profiled here represent the still-habitable outposts on just such a venture.

The
SCIENTIFIC
100

1

Isaac Newton
and the Newtonian Revolution

1642–1727

Isaac Newton is the most influential figure in the history of Western science. He was considered a great intellectual hero in his lifetime, and adulation within the scientific community continues today, scarcely diminished after three hundred years. The reason is straightforward: When Newton came into it, the physical world was poorly understood, while by the time he died, on account of his works, it was known to be governed by mathematical laws of great accuracy. Newton did not initiate the scientific revolution, which was already well under way when he was born; his achievement was rather to give shape and provide the basic intellectual instruments of the modern science of physics. To

3

Newton are owed the three basic laws of motion and the law of gravity, by which all the physical phenomena on Earth, as in the heavens, become predictable, orderly, and in principle amenable to reason and manipulation by technology. Only in the twentieth century, when scientists began to deal with the smallest of magnitudes—the nature of the atom—did the validity of Newton's laws come into question.

Isaac Newton was born on December 25, 1642, in a small hamlet in Lincolnshire, England.* His yeoman father died before he was born, and his mother left him in the care of a grandmother when he was about three years old, to wed and live apart with Barnabas Smith, her second husband, a preacher and stepfather whom Newton detested. It is not surprising, given the experiences of his early childhood, that Newton as an adult evinced tendencies toward paranoia and violent rage. More interesting, perhaps, was his ability to countenance some of the aggression he felt: In a youthful catalogue of his sins Newton included "Threatening my father and mother Smith to burne them and the house over them." It should be recorded that Newton made his first important calculations—leading to the calculus—in the blank pages of his dead stepfather's commonplace book.

As a child Newton showed great curiosity and mechanical ability, and clearly he was not destined to become a farmer. In 1661 he matriculated at Trinity College, Cambridge. The university curriculum was largely weighted to Aristotelian philosophy; but within two years Newton had lost his appetite for *Nicomachean Ethics*. On his own initiative he began to read and make notes on the works of Francis Bacon, René Descartes, and other early scientific figures; and he conceived a passion for both mathematics and celestial phenomena. *Amicus Plato amicus Aristoteles magis amica veritas*, he wrote in his notebook. "Plato and Aristotle are my friends. But my best friend is Truth."

In 1664 Newton was selected to be a scholar at Trinity, a status which would have left him free to work on his own after taking his bachelor of arts degree the following year. But the

---

* This is Newton's birth date according to the Gregorian calendar introduced by papal decree in Europe in 1582 and used everywhere today. But in England, Newton's date of birth was recorded by the old-style Julian calendar as January 6, 1643.

Great Plague intervened. The university closed its doors in 1665, and Newton returned to stay with his mother, who was now widowed. There he remained two years, during which, as he described it later, "I was in the prime of my age for invention & minded Mathematicks & Philosophy more than at any time since." Indeed, building upon the geometry of Descartes, Newton invented an elementary calculus—that branch of mathematics which provides tools for computing the rate of change. Newton's "method of fluxions" became indispensable for solving problems raised anew, for the first time in hundreds of years, with the erosion of Aristotelian physics. During this early period Newton also conceived, at least in partial form, the universal law of gravitation and investigated the nature of light by experimenting with prisms. But although he composed his papers with great care—almost compulsively—he did not publish his findings for some years. The founder of modern science reworked his data constantly, for reasons which were surely emotional though not entirely clear, and long remained silent.

Returning to London in 1667, Newton was elected a fellow of Trinity College, University of Cambridge. In 1669, he took the position of Isaac Barrow—the first to recognize his genius—as the Lucasian Professor of Mathematics. He constructed the first reflecting telescope, which created a considerable stir, and which, in 1672, caused him to be elected to the Royal Society. However, when he offered an article, "New Theory About Light and Colours" to the Society, he was attacked by the eminent Robert Hooke. Wounded, Newton withdrew to continue his research in intellectual isolation.

In 1684 Newton received a visit from Edmond Halley, the great astronomer and mathematician, who discussed with him the then current problem of the motion of the planets. Hooke, for example, had proposed that planetary motion could be explained by the inverse square law, but he could not say why. The answer—that the planets move in elliptical orbits—Newton had effectively discovered years earlier by using his calculus. He returned to these questions now, publishing his *De motus corporum* in 1684, and over the next several years completed the more complete text, the *Philosophiae naturalis principia mathematica*. In this work, supported by a multitude of observations, Newton formulates the three laws of motion and the law of universal gravitation, to wit:

1. A body in motion moves with constant velocity unless acted upon by some force; a body at rest remains at rest unless acted upon by some force. This is the law of inertia.

2. An object's acceleration is in direct proportion to the force which acts upon it and inversely proportional to the object's mass. This may be expressed as the equation, *F*orce is equivalent to *m*ass multiplied by *a*cceleration, $F = ma$.

3. Every action evokes an equal and opposite reaction.

Newton's law of gravity states that *between any two bodies, the gravitational force is proportional to the product of their masses, and inversely proportional to the square of the distance between them.*

Published by Edmond Halley in 1687, the *Principia* was a great triumph which signaled the peak of Newton's career as a scientist, and the culmination of the scientific revolution.

Although Newton attained great prominence with the *Principia* and became a living symbol of the new science, his subsequent career was filled with contradictions. Beginning in 1689, after the English Revolution, he had a brief and undistinguished career in Parliament. In 1696 he was appointed warden of the Royal Mint, and three years later became master of the Mint, a position from which he was able to prosecute counterfeiters—as he did with great assiduity. He was elected president of the Royal Society in 1703 and held that office until his death, on March 31, 1727. In 1704, with the death of nemesis Robert Hooke, Newton published his *Opticks*. His authority was by then so great that his corpuscular theory of light was dominant for the next century in spite of certain flaws. He was the first scientific figure to be knighted, by Queen Anne, in 1705.

At his death, Newton left a huge trove of unpublished papers, which included over a million words on the esoteric and mystical study of alchemy. He had conducted studies over many years and in great depth, doing experiments by which he hoped, for example, to change base metal into philosopher's mercury. His alchemical researches, which share the diligence but not the careful rationalism of his physics, have long disturbed scholars. John Maynard Keynes, who purchased and studied the alchemical papers, ended by calling Newton a "magician" rather than a scientist—which is an interesting verdict coming from an economist. It is likely that the religious component in alchemy attracted Newton, as did its overarching goals; one of his

At his death Newton left a trove of alchemical research, at odds with his discoveries in physics, which has long baffled scientists and historians.

biographers, Gale Christianson, has suggested, for example, that Newton was aiming at a great synthetic understanding of the universe.

Newton's life is marked by a series of conflicts which can render him to modern eyes an unsympathetic figure. He was given to violent rages and unnecessarily rancorous disputes with contemporaries, such as Leibniz and Hooke. He seems to have had his strongest relationship with Nicolas Fatio de Duillier, a young admirer, the rupture of which likely contributed to a brief but wrenching mental breakdown. Newton never married—indeed, he was barred as a Cambridge fellow from doing so—and passed his adult life almost wholly in the company of men. He seldom laughed, although an anecdote that comes down to us is touching and revealing. When a friend said that he could not see how any use could come from studying Euclid, the Greek mathematician, Newton broke into merry laughter. For Erasmus Darwin, *Newton Explored in Nature's scenes the effect and cause, / And, charm'd, unravelled all her latent laws.* But more elegant is the couplet by Alexander Pope, written upon Newton's death and engraved in the room where he was born at Woolsthorpe Manor. *Nature and Nature's Laws lay hid in Night. / God said,* Let Newton be! *and all was* Light.

2

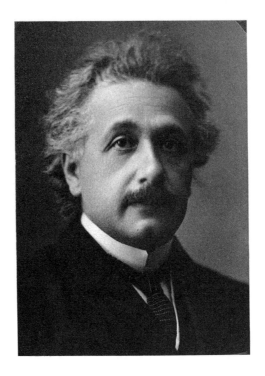

Albert Einstein
and Twentieth-Century Science

1879–1955

The work of Albert Einstein forms the source of twentieth-century physics. His special and general theories of relativity provide a new basis for understanding fundamental laws of nature and the concepts of space, mass, and energy. The special theory of relativity, proposed in 1905, turned out to be necessary for a detailed grasp of the interactions of atomic and subatomic particles. A decade later, the general theory of relativity created the possibility of a modern cosmology.

"The imprint of Einstein's work on the different areas of physical science is so large and varied," writes Gerald Holton in a recent assessment, "that a scientist who tries to trace it would be hard put to know where to start." Indeed, like ISAAC NEWTON [1], Einstein's theories undergird an immense manipulation of nature through technology. Transistors, electron microscopes, computers, and photoelectric cells are only a few examples of the vast augmentation of the yield of invention, information, and communication to which the Einsteinian revolution gave birth.

Albert Einstein was born in Ulm, Germany, on March 14, 1879, the son of Hermann Einstein and Pauline Koch Einstein. The family moved to Munich the following year. As a child Einstein was taciturn and regarded as unusual rather than gifted. At the Leopold Gymnasium, which he attended from age ten, he disliked the rigid German discipline and was not enthusiastic about Latin and Greek. His introduction to science came through mathematics and was stimulated by his uncle, Jakob Einstein, an engineer. At about age twelve Einstein taught himself geometry and, in an unusual instance of an adolescent dream destined to be fulfilled, decided that he would one day solve the riddles of the world.

Einstein's secondary education was as problematic as his elementary school education. In 1894, the Einsteins moved to Milan, Italy, where his father reestablished himself following a reversal in business. Left behind to finish school, Albert quit the gymnasium without a degree in order to rejoin his family. At age seventeen, he was admitted to the Swiss Polytechnical Institute, a year after failing his first entrance exam. Here he realized that physics rather than mathematics would be his field, and he studied the works of HERMANN VON HELMHOLTZ [63], JAMES CLERK MAXWELL [12], and others. But he was not an ideal student, felt constrained in school, and wrote later that it is "nothing short of a miracle that modern methods of teaching have not yet entirely strangled the sacred spirit of curiosity and inquiry." He graduated in 1900.

Beginning in 1902 Einstein took a position as a junior patent examiner in the Swiss Patent Office, which leads to the hypothesis that his work there—scrutinizing and clarifying applications for devices of all sorts—stimulated his thinking about space and time. Certainly, it was an important period during which Einstein was isolated from the physics community but at the same time was aware of contemporary developments in the field.

In 1905—often called Einstein's *annus mirabilis*—he published three crucially important papers in volume XVII of

Annalen der Physik, and his genius, as Emilio Segrè wrote, "flamed with unsurpassed brilliance." Each of the three papers is concerned with a different topic:

1. In an article on "Brownian motion," Einstein showed that the zigzag dance of particles suspended in liquid is a measurable and predictable function of molecular kinetics. This served as a virtual proof of the existence of molecules, still disputed in some quarters, and experiments several years later confirmed Einstein's calculations.

2. In his first contribution to quantum theory, Einstein showed that a fundamental process in nature is at work in the remarkable mathematical equation which had resolved, several years previously, the problem of "blackbody radiation." Light itself, Einstein showed, may be shown to be a stream of particles with a computable energy using the number known as Planck's constant. (The term *photon*, a particle of light, was coined later.) Experimental confirmation came within a decade for visible light, and it was for this paper that Einstein received the Nobel Prize, in 1921.

3. Both these papers, and particularly the latter, were revolutionary, but neither more so than the third, "On the Electrodynamics of Moving Bodies." This paper contains Einstein's first expression of what came to be known as the special theory of relativity.

The special theory of relativity bears upon physical mechanics but, in certain respects, is seriously counterintuitive with respect to our ordinary notions of time and space. Briefly, Einstein states as a postulate, in considering motion in space, that the speed of light may be taken as a constant value in *all* frames of reference—*independent* of the light's source or its detector. In other words, the speed of light, which had indeed been calculated, does not change depending on the velocity of the observer. But if this is the case, no two observers, traveling at different speeds, will agree on the occurrence in time of a particular event. Time and space, given the speed of light as a constant, become a united frame of reference.

It is easy to see why Einstein's special theory of relativity was revolutionary, for it leads to a situation in which common sense and philosophical notions yield to a new scientific concept—that is, one which can in principle be demonstrated. More difficult, perhaps, is to understand why it won fairly ready acceptance by physicists.

When Einstein proposed it, special relativity bore directly upon serious problems besetting the rapidly advancing science of electrodynamics. A generation earlier, James Clerk Maxwell had developed equations which suggested that electromagnetic waves moved through space at the speed of light. To explain the mechanics of this—how the waves are propagated through space at some particular speed—an invisible *ether* was postulated. But the ether had never been detected, in spite of extensive efforts, leaving a highly successful theory in physics disturbingly incomplete. The theory of special relativity dispenses with the ether, an important simplification. Indeed, it explained certain experimental results, such as the increase of mass of objects traveling at high speeds, which had already been adumbrated by Hendrik Lorentz, a Dutch physicist.

Another, broader reason for the success of relativity was the advent, in 1900, of quantum theory. The theory of special relativity would eventually be applied, as Newtonian physical laws could not be, to predict certain effects on a subatomic level. MAX PLANCK [25], one of the founders of quantum theory, immediately recognized the significance of special relativity—he compared it to the Copernican revolution—as did NIELS BOHR [3]. Relativity explained that, as Einstein stated, "The mass of a body is a measure of its energy-content" and he soon published a more comprehensive account, in which he brought forward his famous equation: $E = mc^2$—a mass m can be expressed as an amount of energy E when multiplied by the speed of light, c, squared.

In 1909, as he became known to physicists and as word of his 1905 papers spread, Einstein left the Swiss Patent Office for a university career. He went to the University of Zurich in 1909 and then taught briefly, in 1911, at the University of Prague, where he was unhappy with the anti-Semitic tenor of Austria. He returned to teach in Zurich in 1912. Appointed to a special post at The Prussian Academy of Science with a concurrent appointment at the University of Berlin in 1914, Einstein was thereafter able to devote much of his time to research.

What is today known as the *general theory of relativity* bears upon the notion of gravity and corrects certain problems in Newtonian physics. It was developed by Einstein from 1907 until its publication in 1916. The general theory is effectively an extension of the special theory to systems in accelerated motion, such as bodies in space. From the general theory of relativity issues all of twentieth-century cosmology—from an explanation of the "red shift" that indicates the universe is expanding, to the notion of black holes.

To understand the general theory, one begins with Einstein's *equivalence principle*. As Galileo had famously noticed, objects fall to Earth with a constant acceleration independent of their mass. In this sense, whether great or small, falling objects are "weightless"; their weight changes nothing in response to gravitation. Indeed, astronauts in orbit around the earth are constantly "falling" toward it—and they feel weightless. If their spacecraft leaves orbit, however, and shoots off toward a distant star, they can feel their full weight (and more) as the rate of acceleration changes. Acceleration, not gravity, is responsible. Einstein suggested that gravitational force and the "inertial" force of a system in accelerated motion are *indistinguishable*.

The great consequence of this principle is that gravitation is *not* simply the force in nature by which all objects are attracted to each other. It is rather the "warping" of space and time by physical mass. The existence of mass shows that space must be "curved"—non-Euclidian in shape and measurable, given the speed of light. Although general relativity and classical laws give basically the same results in the ordinary world, Einstein's theory not only can describe the elliptical orbits of the planets, but corrects certain Newtonian anomalies, such as the orbit of Mercury around the sun.

Astronomical observation verified the general theory of relativity several years after Einstein proposed it. Einstein had predicted, as early as 1911, that light from a star passing close by a large body such as the sun would be bent by the sun's great mass. He subsequently realized that the amount of curvature was calculable. Thus, the star would have a true position and, viewed from the earth, an apparent position on account of the warping of space caused by the sun's mass. Classical physics, viewing space as flat, would give a different value for the bending of light, half that of general relativity.

A solar eclipse would provide an occasion to view the stars and compare the Newtonian and Einsteinian values. Several unsuccessful efforts were made before 1919, when at the instigation of astronomer ARTHUR EDDINGTON [37], two expeditions were mounted, one to Brazil, another to Principe Island off the coast of West Central Africa. The results were not ambiguous: when the photographs were analyzed, the position of the stars was in consonance with the general theory of relativity. Einstein became, virtually overnight, a great public celebrity. On November 7, 1919, the London *Times* announced: "Revolution in Science / New Theory of the Universe / Newtonian Ideas Overthrown." The *New York Times* followed with its own story two days later.

Einstein's later work, in search of a unified field theory that would unite the theories of gravitation and electromagnetism, was inconclusive. He held out hope for a full grasp of some ultimate reality in spite of limitations imposed by the quantum theory that his 1905 paper on the photoelectric effect (and much other work besides) had helped to found. He conducted a long debate on the philosophical implications of quantum theory with Niels Bohr, writing that, "I still believe in the possibility of a model of reality—that is, of a theory which represents things themselves and not merely the probability of their occurrence." After about 1928, with the full flowering of quantum theory, Einstein ceased to dominate physics.

In 1933 Einstein's were among the books burned by the Nazis in Berlin, and his property was confiscated. Einstein, who was already teaching in the United States, never returned to Germany. He received an appointment for life at the Institute for Advanced Study at Princeton University. He was inspired by the rise of Hitlerism to give up some of his pacifist convictions, and in 1939, reluctantly, he signed a letter to Franklin Roosevelt recommending the development of an atomic bomb. He did not further participate in the development of the bomb, however, in part because he was considered a security risk with left-wing sympathies. After the war Einstein was an advocate of nuclear disarmament. He did not become an American patriot, and he opposed the congressional hearings on so-called un-American activities in the 1950s. In 1952, he refused an offer to become president of Israel, a ceremonial position.

Einstein's later career largely reflected his tremendous prestige. A public figure in great demand as a speaker, Einstein's anthologies *The World as I See It*, from 1934, and *Out of My Later Years*, in 1950, have often been reprinted. They contain articles on a diverse array of topics, including the nature of science, socialism, black-white relations, Zionism, and moral decay. Like Freud, with whom he corresponded, Einstein's political and social opinions embody the wisdom of nineteenth-century liberalism, and remain worth reading today. Although Einstein is often quoted as saying that "God does not play dice" with respect to quantum statistics, in religion he was an agnostic. Asked whether he believed in God, he once replied, "One may not ask that of someone who with growing amazement attempts to explore and understand the authoritative order in the universe."

It is difficult to characterize Einstein's personality, especially in his later years, when he led a largely solitary life. He was not given to articulating his feelings for other people, though he was quite capable of expressing his deep devotion to humanity. He had experienced a difficult divorce from his first wife, Mileva Marić, at the height of his fame. With her he had two sons, one of whom became a prominent professor of mechanical engineering; the other became schizophrenic. A third child, born before their marriage, was given up for adoption. Einstein subsequently married a first cousin, Elsa Löwenthal, who left him a widower in 1936.

On April 11, 1955, Albert Einstein signed a pacifist, anti-nuclear manifesto being circulated by the philosopher Bertrand Russell. Several days later he suffered the rupture of an aortic aneurysm but did not succumb immediately. He refused an operation, saying, "I want to go when *I* want. It is tasteless to prolong life artificially." Albert Einstein died, peacefully, in Princeton, New Jersey, on April 18, 1955.

3

Niels Bohr
and the Atom

1885–1962

Quantum mechanics constitutes the essential framework for twentieth-century physics. Providing a means for understanding the microworld, it has led to a host of major new technologies, including the transistor, the silicon chip, and nuclear energy. It has provided a far more comprehensive explanation of the chemical bond and brought about new ways of understanding biological phenomena and so lies at the root of a multitude of new methods of manipulating nature. Today, even cosmology depends upon quantum ideas, and apart from changing the mechanics of everyday life, quantum theory also lies behind broad shifts in philosophical thought. Of all those who developed quantum theory, the most eminent was the Danish physicist Niels Bohr.

Bohr's importance is doubly manifest, through his own work and through his overarching influence upon theoretical physics in the first quarter of the twentieth century. Beginning in 1913, his proposal of a highly influential model of the atom laid the basis for quantum mechanics as it finally emerged at the end of the 1920s. Bohr also examined the larger implications of the theory, which entails a radical break with determinism and common-sense notions of cause and effect; and his "Copenhagen interpretation" of the quantum world remains dominant today. With Niels Bohr there comes an end to mainstream efforts to discover some "ultimate" reality. "It is wrong to think that the task of physics is to find out how nature *is*," according to Bohr. "Physics concerns what we can *say* about nature."

Niels Bohr was born in Copenhagen on October 7, 1885, the son of Christian Bohr, a professor of physiology, and Ellen Adler Bohr. The Bohrs were a close-knit, unusually sophisticated and intellectual family, and Niels grew up in a highly propitious milieu. His mother was warm and intelligent, and his father, as Bohr himself later recalled, recognized "that something was expected of me." The family was not at all devout, and Bohr became an atheist who regarded religious thought as harmful and misguided. From 1891 he attended the Gammelholms Latin og Realskole, where he was remembered as a good pupil, big for his age, and apt to use fisticuffs, but also somewhat shy. As he recollected himself, he was passionately drawn to science "owing to the influence of my father." He entered the University of Copenhagen in 1903, where he majored in physics and remained until he received his master's degree in 1909 and his doctorate in 1911. His father died that year, and Niels married Margrethe Norlund.

In 1911 the revolution in understanding the structure of the atom was already under way. Indeed, Bohr's doctoral thesis concerned the theory of electrons, which had been discovered about a decade earlier by JOSEPH J. THOMSON [31] and were known to be universal constituents of all matter. Thomson had also suggested that the number of electrons in an atom corresponded to its weight, accounting for the variety of different stable atoms. And ERNEST RUTHERFORD [19] had made the crucial discovery that the atom possessed a compact, massive nucleus. This led physicists to abandon the theory that the atom was a sort of "plum pudding"—a nucleus studded with raisin-like electrons—in favor of Rutherford's model of electrons orbiting a tiny nucleus.

In 1913, while in England and working with Rutherford, Bohr published three papers that concern atomic structure. They effectively changed the course of physics. Although Rutherford's model of the atom solved certain important problems, the crucial question remained why the orbiting electrons—evidently attracted to the nucleus—were not destined to be absorbed into it. In brief, the model did not account for the stability of the atom, which is one of its central features.

Bohr perceived that classical Newtonian mechanics could not explain the behavior of matter at atomic scale. He was inspired to turn to quantum physics, which MAX PLANCK [25] had proposed to solve the problem of "blackbody radiation" at the turn of the century and ALBERT EINSTEIN [2] had employed several years earlier to explain the particle-like behavior of light. During a relatively brief period of intense work in 1912, Bohr examined how a hydrogen atom radiated light and developed a theory which had an exceptionally close fit with observable facts. He assumed that the electron radiated light only when it changed orbits, and so identified the emission of a "quantum" with the "jump" of an electron from one orbit to another. Einstein, upon learning of Bohr's results, commented with characteristic laconic certitude: "This is an enormous achievement."

The Rutherford-Bohr model of the atom, as it came to be known, was a fundamental advance, and soon was used to gain a new understanding of the atomic structure of all the known elements. One of Bohr's accomplishments in 1913 was to identify the quantum jumps of electrons with the X-ray spectra.* In the next year, following Bohr's lead, the British physicist Harry Moseley brought a new, definitive order to the periodic table, subjecting each of the chemical elements to X-ray spectral analysis and assigning to each an atomic number. Over the next several years Bohr managed a number of technical achievements which, as Abraham Pais wrote, "In retrospect…are all the more fabulous and astounding because they are based on analogies—

---

*Light spectroscopy in the nineteenth century had enabled scientists to analyze the various elements. With much shorter wavelengths than visible light, X rays could provide more fundamental information on an atomic scale. In this volume see GUSTAV KIRCHHOFF [57] and MAX VON LAUE [56].

atomic orbits similar to the motions of the planets around the sun, and spin similar to the rotation of the planets while orbiting—which are in fact false." Bohr was awarded the Nobel prize in physics in 1922.

Indeed, Bohr's model of the atom turned out to have several significant flaws. What sometimes is called the "first quantum revolution" did not resolve certain problems with the behavior of more complex atoms. Although the theory was developed in various ways between 1913 and 1925, it accumulated serious problems, which would ultimately lead to what is known as the "second quantum revolution."

During the 1920s Bohr was a key figure in helping to resolve the crisis in physics generated by defects in the atomic structure he himself had proposed. Returning to the University of Copenhagen in 1916, he became professor of theoretical physics and participated in the opening, five years later, of the Institute for Theoretical Physics. In this way Copenhagen became a magnet for physicists, with Bohr the central figure. The "second quantum revolution" gave birth to a purely mathematical model of the atom which effectively acknowledged the limitations of human perception of subatomic events. It was epitomized by Erwin Schrödinger's wave mechanics, Heisenberg's matrix mechanics, and the famous Uncertainty Principle, which acknowledges restrictions upon direct knowledge of physical systems.

In the late 1920s Bohr evolved two principles to help guide the quantum revolution to a successful rebirth. In a famous lecture in 1927, "The Philosophical Foundations of Quantum Theory," he first discussed the concept of "complementarity." This is the idea that, although subatomic systems may be measured by contrasting, exclusive models—as waves or as particles—both are needed for a full description of the phenomena. Intrigued by the philosophical implications of this idea, Bohr eventually argued that the complementarity principle might be applied to the problem of free will and to the basic life processes. Perhaps the more important yield of this idea was that quantum theory was subsequently taken to offer a basically complete description of nature that would not be altered by future discoveries: There is no "deeper" reality lying behind quantum measurements. Although this notion has often been challenged in various ways, it remains the bedrock of the "Copenhagen spirit"—various thought experiments, the "mind of God," and theories of multiple universes notwithstanding. This doctrine was never wholly accepted by Albert Einstein, Max Planck, or a number of other physicists, but it endures, basically unchanged, to the present.

During the 1930s Bohr began investigating the expanding field of nuclear physics and in 1934 suggested the "liquid drop" model for the nucleus of the atom; it proved important for understanding nuclear fission. In 1936 he provided a summary theory of the atomic nucleus that became a general guide for physicists over the next decade. In Bohr's theory, neutrons and protons were tightly knit together in the nucleus by the "strong force." Although energy would clearly be released if this compound nucleus were disturbed, at this time the effects of splitting the atom were by no means clear.

After the onset of World War II, Bohr initially remained in Denmark, which was invaded by the Nazis in 1940. Because of his stature, he was able to help some of his colleagues escape persecution, and he refused to cooperate with Nazi war aims. But in 1943, after rumors convinced him that he was soon to be imprisoned, he and his family escaped to Sweden, then to England and the United States. He soon joined the Manhattan Project, where he was given the security alias "Uncle Nick." Bohr's importance to the project was more symbolic than substantial. He was not in favor of dropping the atomic bomb, and in the course of the war met with Roosevelt and with Churchill, who repudiated his proposal to forestall a nuclear arms race by openly sharing information with the Soviet Union.

Returning to Denmark after the war, Bohr was active until the end of his life, retiring from the University of Copenhagen in 1955. A committed scientist who remained opposed to the production of atomic weapons, Bohr wrote a famous "open letter" to the United Nations in 1950 and received, among many other honors, the Atoms for Peace award in 1957. He was also active in promoting international cooperation in physics and helped found the European Center for Nuclear Research (CERN) in Geneva. On November 17, 1962, he gave an interview, which was to be his last, on the history of quantum theory. The next day, he took his usual nap after lunch, had a heart attack, and died. He is buried in the family tomb in Copenhagen.

Highly collaborative in his approach to physics—rather unlike Einstein in this respect—Bohr was often the subject of lavish praise by colleagues, just as he was adored by his family and friends. According to Victor Weisskopf, Bohr created the "Copenhagen Style" and "We see him, the greatest among his colleagues, acting, talking, living as an equal in a group of young, optimistic, jocular, enthusiastic people, approaching the deepest riddles of nature with a spirit of attack, a spirit of freedom from conventional bonds, and a spirit of joy that can hardly be described." His happy marriage to Margrethe produced six sons, and one of them, Aage Bohr, also became a theoretical physicist and Nobel laureate.

Although Niels Bohr was by no means alone in developing a new theoretical edifice for understanding the physical world, he holds a place in the history of science that is unique and more or less uncontested. Richard Rhodes puts it simply: "Bohr's contributions to twentieth-century physics would rank second only to Einstein's."

4

Charles Darwin
and Evolution

1809–1882

With Charles Darwin the new relationship between man and nature, born of science and industry, takes a dramatic and secular turn. In 1859 Darwin published his *On the Origin of Species* and, twelve years later, *The Descent of Man*. Conflicting with dogmatic views of immutable species and a unique place for human beings in the natural order, Darwin's theories of evolution and natural selection have had an exceptionally direct influence in Western culture. Although Darwinism created controversy from the beginning, its full impact was not felt until well into the twentieth century, when it was empowered by further advances in the physical sciences. Genetics and microbiology, together with a more sophisticated evolutionary theory, form the twentieth-century heritage of Charles Darwin. "Darwin is arguably the best-known scientist in history," write his recent biographers, Adrian Desmond and James Moore. "More than any modern thinker—even Freud or Marx—this affable old-world naturalist from the minor Shropshire gentry has transformed the way we see ourselves on this planet."

Charles Robert Darwin was born on February 12, 1809, the fifth child and youngest of two sons, to Robert Waring Darwin, a physician, and Susannah Wedgwood. His paternal grandfather was Erasmus Darwin (1731–1802), a well-known physician, poet, philosopher, and inventor; his mother's father was Josiah Wedgwood, the famous pottery and ceramics manufacturer. When he was eight years old, Darwin's mother died of a gastrointestinal illness, probably a cancer. Darwin later recounted that his sisters forbade him to talk about his mother after her death, and so he recalled little about her. Sent to Shrewsbury School, a prestigious private school run by Samuel Butler, Charles did not enjoy the curriculum, with its strong emphasis on classics; he did not learn languages easily. However, outside the classroom, he had developed an interest in natural history and in collecting plants and animals. "The passion for collecting," wrote Darwin in his *Autobiography*, "which leads a man to be a systematic naturalist, a virtuoso or a miser, was very strong in me, and was clearly innate, as none of my sisters or brother ever had this taste."

Darwin recalled his father, the leading physician in Shrewsbury, with admiration, although others found him a somewhat overbearing if benevolent tyrant. Like Robert Darwin, Charles initially planned to study medicine when he began attending Edinburgh University in 1825. The following year he joined the Plinian Natural History Society and came under the influence of Robert Grant, a well-known physician and zoologist. As for his medical studies, however, Darwin did not like them. He particularly detested anatomy—to his later regret, because he never learned to dissect. It also became apparent that he was sensitive to human suffering; he could not bear to observe operations, which were performed in those days without anesthetic.

Darwin's ambivalence about his choice of careers led to an unusual and pivotal result in the history of science. When his father learned of Darwin's reservations about the study of medicine, he suggested that Charles become a clergyman. Darwin obediently left Edinburgh in 1827 and enrolled in Christ's College, Cambridge University. Here his time was wasted, as he later said; however, he collected beetles, studied with botanist John Steven Henslow, and graduated in 1831. Soon after, he was offered a position as a naturalist to ship out on a voyage around the world. The young captain of the *H.M.S. Beagle*, Robert FitzRoy, wanted a young, well-bred companion on what promised to be a long and sometimes tedious trip. Its purpose was to survey the coast of Tierra del Fuego and the shores of Chile and Peru and to visit the South Sea Islands and the Indian Archipelago. Darwin's name was put forward by his teacher, Henslow, as "amply qualified for collecting, observing and noting." Overcoming his father's objections, Darwin was on board the *Beagle* when it left port on December 27, 1831. It would not return to England for five years.

In the popular literature of science, Darwin's voyage aboard the *Beagle* has a special place. Sometimes it is recounted as an exciting expedition in which Darwin is portrayed as "a man physically vigorous, adventuresome and courageous in spirit, inventive and resourceful when faced with difficulties, and constantly driven beyond the limits of his known environment and by some nameless impulse." Indeed, the *Beagle* set anchor in Montevideo when it was in the throes of revolution, and Darwin crossed the pampas on horseback and wrote his sister, "I am become quite a Gaucho, drink my Matee & smoke my cigar & then lie down & sleep as comfortably with the Heavens for Canopy as on a feather bed." Darwin was also plagued by seasickness throughout the voyage, and experienced considerable homesickness as well.

Most significant, Darwin took advantage of an unusual opportunity to absorb raw material in the context of historic intellectual ferment in the natural sciences. Initially, his prime interest was in geology, and his great influence was CHARLES LYELL [28], whose recently published *Principles of Geology* he read assiduously during the voyage. Darwin also made collections of both flora and fauna. He kept field notebooks to record observations, which he expanded in the form of a journal. He noted with interest the slight variations among populations of birds and tortoises on neighboring islands in the Galápagos Islands, and was also aware of his growing competence in scrutiny. "I have always felt that I owe to the Voyage the first real training or education of my mind," he wrote later. "I was led to attend closely to several branches of natural history, and thus my powers of

The theory of common descent caused great discomfort.

observation were improved, though they were already fairly developed." The *Beagle* returned to England on October 2, 1836.

In 1837, still intellectually fresh from his voyage, Darwin set out to sketch the theoretical yield from a mass of observations, and in 1838, while reading Malthus, he conceived the idea of natural selection—the conservation of traits through their adaptability to conditions of life. He did not publish his theory at this time, however, but continued to accumulate data. He published three scientific works on his observations of coral reefs, volcanic islands, and other geological formations. These assured Darwin a solid professional reputation.

At Down House, outside London, where Darwin lived from 1842 on, he spent the years 1846 until 1854 engaged in systematic research on the structure of barnacles, the pesky crustaceans which became widely distributed around the world by attaching themselves to ships. He made a third sketch of his theory in 1856, but even at the urging of Charles Lyell—now a personal friend— he refused to publish it. Although Darwin was anxious to establish priority for his scientific ideas, he believed that only a theoretical presentation buttressed by a huge array of facts was appropriate.

In 1858 Darwin was compelled to bring his ideas to light after Alfred Wallace, an amateur naturalist who had also traveled to South America, sent him a clear exposition of the theory of speciation. In that same year separate papers by Darwin and Wallace were read to the Linnaean Society, and Darwin's precedence was established. The following year saw the publication of *On the Origin of Species by Means of Natural Selection; or, the Preservation of Favoured Races in the Struggle for Life*.

The *Origin* had an immediate and controversial impact on scientists, general readers, and theologians. Most famously, at a meeting of the British Association, the Bishop of Oxford, who was ignorant of Darwin's theory, nevertheless ridiculed it. The bishop was reduced to silence by Thomas Huxley—sometimes called "Darwin's bulldog"—who said that, for himself, he would "rather be related to an ape than to a man of proven ability who used his brains to pervert the truth."*

As was the case with the Copernican revolution and Freud's hypothesis of the unconscious mind, Darwin's theory was so powerful that it became highly influential well ahead of experimental proof. Indeed, Darwin's reluctance to publish *Origin* is understandable in that not even the rules of inheritance, much less the mechanisms, were clear at the time. If traits were blended, as biologists then supposed, why would individual adaptations not be diluted and disappear over several generations? This problem so plagued Darwin that he was led to adopt a quasi-Lamarckian solution—known as *pangenesis*—toward the end of his life.† A physical explanation of inheritance and natural

---

*The bishop was not humiliated, as is often stated; he reprinted his speech. He is only embarrassed by history.

†Pangenesis involved the notion that cells throughout the body all contribute instructions to the reproductive cells. This could enable acquired traits to be passed on to offspring, as LAMARCK [69] had suggested. A speculative idea, it was soon abandoned.

selection awaited the discovery of chromosomes, the rediscovery of GREGOR MENDEL [60], and the work of geneticists. A half century separates the publication of *Origin* and the explanation of genetic inheritance by THOMAS HUNT MORGAN [62].

Following the appearance of *On the Origin of Species*, Darwin went on to publish ten books concerning the theory of natural selection. These include *The Descent of Man* in 1871, *The Expression of the Emotions in Man and Animals* in 1872, and the *Power of Movement in Plants* in 1880.

Darwin's personal life has been often studied and his idiosyncrasies much debated. In 1839 he married a first cousin, Emma Wedgwood, and fathered ten children, seven of whom lived to adulthood. For much of his later life Darwin suffered from some kind of malady, the diagnosis of which is far from clear and may have been psychosomatic. When he wrote the *Origin,* Darwin was a theist in religion; he later became an agnostic. At his death, on April 19, 1882, he was buried in Westminster Abbey, not far from ISAAC NEWTON [1].

Charles Darwin "by reason of his immense influence on human thought, must be classed with the greatest men of science —with Aristotle, Galileo, Newton, Lavoisier, and Einstein." So wrote A. E. E. McKenzie in his classic history, *The Major Achievements of Science,* and nothing has occurred to change that view. Like Freudian thought, Darwinism provides a more painful probe of personal and social preconceptions than does physics. The theory entails a gamut of social consequences, and controversy has become one of its constant and evolving features. Nevertheless, Charles Darwin, writes George Gaylord Simpson, is the "genius who, though fallible as all of us are, revolutionized scientific scrutiny and knowledge of our origins, and of our physical relationships to nature and the universe."

5

Louis Pasteur
and the Germ Theory of Disease

1822–1895

The theory that diseases are caused by microorganisms, not demons or the miasma, is not much more than a century old. Proposed during the Renaissance by the Italian physician Fracastorius, who gave syphilis its name, the contagion theory had its defenders over the following two centuries but could not be definitively established. Not until the second half of the nineteenth century did this begin to change, both with isolated observations by physicians and the systematic work of such figures as British surgeon Joseph Lister. But the science of bacteriology, which became immensely successful, is commonly credited to the genius of Louis Pasteur.

Although recent studies bring Pasteur down to earth—like Sigmund Freud, he has frequently been revered beyond reason—it is difficult to avoid the conclusion, already drawn during his lifetime, that he belongs with the greatest scientists of history. Trained in chemistry, Pasteur turned to practical problems of fermentation in vinegar, wine, and beer after early discoveries in crystallography. During the last and most important phase of his career, he studied the causes of infectious illnesses in humans and animals and developed vaccines against anthrax and rabies, spawning much successful research to combat a host of other diseases. Pasteur's exceptional capacity to draw solid theoretical conclusions from his ceaseless experiments led to sweeping innovations in medicine. In principle, they have saved millions of lives and led to profound changes in everyday life around the world. It should be no surprise that Pasteur became a figure of legendary renown in his own time, or that today, with more critical attitudes toward great figures in science, his accomplishments are being subjected to more intense scrutiny.

Louis Pasteur was born on December 27, 1822, in Dôle, in eastern France. His father, Joseph Pasteur, had been a sergeant in Napoleon's army, was a tanner by profession, and had a strong positive influence on his son. As a young man, Louis was a promising painter—his surviving portraits show exceptional talent—but he abandoned artistic ambitions at age nineteen to pursue a scientific career. Following his graduation from the *collège* at Besançon, he and his family decided that he would continue his education in Paris at the École Normale Supérieure, which was then, as it is today, dedicated to turning out college professors in the arts and sciences. It is a mark of Pasteur's diligence, perfectionism, egotism, and eccentricity that, in 1842, when he ranked fairly low on the entrance exams—including a "mediocre" in chemistry—he refused to matriculate. He studied another year, retook the exam, and entered only after he had scored close to the top. He studied physics and chemistry, qualifying as a professor when he passed his *agrégation* in 1846. He defended two theses, one in physics, the other in chemistry, the following year.

Pasteur's earliest discovery came in 1848 in the field of crystallography—then a field of considerable activity—and showed his obstinacy, powers of observation, and ability to formulate a general theory. Chemists were attracted to certain crystals, formed from tartrates, that are chemically the same but exhibit different optical properties—that is, some deflect light but others do not. The term *isomers* had been coined by J. J. Berzelius to describe such compounds of equal parts, but how this could be was not clear. Using a hand-lens tweezers, Pasteur showed, through tedious observations that were extraordinarily precise, that the two forms of the same crystal were, in fact, mirror images of one another. According to legend, Pasteur's solution to the mystery led him to shout what became a well-known quotation, *Tout est trouvé!* He had resolved, as he recognized, not simply the structure of tartaric acid, but had discovered dissymmetric molecules, a whole new class of substances. The study of how the arrangement of molecular structure affects the properties of a chemical became known as stereochemistry.

In 1854 Pasteur accepted the chair of chemistry at the University of Lille. It was there that he turned his interest to the study of fermentation. At the urging of a local industrialist who could not understand why certain lots of his beet juice did not convert to ethyl alcohol, Pasteur studied the problem. He broadened his inquiry to include both lactic and alcohol fermentation. Known to involve the production of alcohol from sugar, fermentation was believed by JUSTUS LIEBIG [36] and other chemists of the period to be a chemical process.

Pasteur, however, came to the much different conclusion that fermentation is a biological process, involving the multiplication of yeast. In 1857 he published a brief paper entitled "Mémoire sur la fermentation appelée lactique" (Note on so-called Lactic Fermentation), which may be considered one of the foundation stones of microbiology. Although Pasteur's theory was not entirely correct, it was highly fertile, leading him to suggest "that there is a category of creatures whose respiration is active enough to obtain oxygen from certain compounds which are...subjected to a slow and progressive decomposition." Pasteur had discovered anaerobic organisms and given a scientific basis to a process that had been used for centuries to make beer and wine. The industrial use of yeast today comprises not only food and alcohol production but also the manufacture of vitamins, antibiotics, and hormones.

Returning to Paris in 1857, Pasteur became director of scientific studies at the École Normale. The study of fermentation had raised for Pasteur the problem of spontaneous generation—

the ancient belief that certain life forms arise from nonlife. This highly plausible notion (worms and flies, for example, emerge from the soil) was consistently being undermined by organic chemistry, and now Pasteur carried out an impressive variety of ingenious experiments. He showed that atmospheric air always contains microorganisms, and that living things can always be found in substances such as sugar water when exposed to air. He heated swan-neck glass flasks to boiling, and in them no organism appeared—until air was introduced. At one point Pasteur went to the Jura Mountains, climbed Mont Poupet, opened his flasks there, and showed that such inhospitable regions were relatively uncontaminated. René Dubos writes that, "After Pasteur had done his work, there was no longer any reason to believe that spontaneous generation ever occurs—under ordinary conditions at least."

Over the course of a decade, from about 1863, Louis Pasteur had a tremendous influence on French industry, and his reputation became international. In 1863, at the direction of Napoleon III, he undertook to study the diseases of wines, which for unknown reasons sometimes turned to vinegar or became bitter or were otherwise spoiled. Pastuer was able to show that bacterial decomposition was responsible for these effects. Although he initially considered introducing some sort of antiseptic into the wine, he discovered that heat treatment was a better solution— indeed, a method already employed by peasants in certain regions of Spain and elsewhere. After France was defeated by Germany in 1871, Pasteur applied similar principles to the study of beer, a gesture more or less patriotic. The pasteurization process—heating beer or wine for a short time at 50 to 60° C— was soon applied to a wide variety of foods, especially milk and other dairy products.

Diseases of silkworms were another of Pasteur's preoccupations during the 1860s, and he was able to save the French silk industry from catastrophe through control of the breeding process to eliminate diseased eggs.

By 1873 Pasteur had achieved great eminence, and his work on infectious diseases in the last twenty years of his life was closely followed by an ever-growing and admiring public. In 1880 Pasteur made his first effort to create a vaccine after isolating the organism that causes cholera in fowls. Perhaps to avoid competition, he kept to himself the explanation of how he created the vaccine—which was simply through attenuation of the microbe when exposed to air. Pasteur grasped that the reduced potency of the organism was responsible for the animals' resulting immunity after being injected.* Recognizing this as a general principle, Pasteur began the most important, heroic phase of his career.

Initially, Pasteur's success with chicken cholera led him to attack the problem of anthrax, a disease which afflicts livestock and can be transmitted to humans. After an elaborate investigation, Pasteur established the microbe responsible and suggested that it was transmitted from the carcasses of animals buried in the pastures. In 1881 Pasteur gave a dramatic public demonstration of his anthrax vaccine, which he claimed to have developed from an attenuated virus. He infected fifty sheep with virulent culture. The twenty-five animals that had not been inoculated all died; the vaccinated animals all lived. These were controversial experiments which Pasteur had been challenged to perform. He carried them out with great flair, and they were widely reported in the press.

Pasteur's experiments in nascent immunology culminated with his celebrated rabies vaccine, developed during the 1880s. On account of its dramatic symptoms and mortal outcome, rabies was a particularly mystifying and frightening disease. In the laboratory, Pasteur succeeded in protecting dogs by injecting them with an attenuated form of the culture; then he challenged them with a culture at full strength. He had not tried this vaccine on humans, and he was not tempted to until a young boy, Joseph Meister, was brought to him in 1885 after being bitten by a rabid dog. Since the boy was presumed to be doomed without the vaccine, Pasteur, not without reluctance, injected the boy with a series of inoculations. Young Meister lived, and Pasteur was covered with glory.† This final success enabled Pasteur to raise funds through public subscription to build the medical institute that today bears his name.

Louis Pasteur married Marie Laurent in 1849, and they had four children, two of whom survived to adulthood. He was a paragon of bourgeois respectability, and was characterized as

---

*Edward Jenner (1749–1823) had developed a method of inoculation against smallpox, but had no means to understand how it worked.

†Meister subsequently was made gatekeeper at the Pasteur Institute. In 1940, according to René Dubos, he killed himself rather than submit to the invading Germans' demand that he open Pasteur's elaborate tomb.

patriarchal, authoritarian, and humorless. In 1868, Pasteur suffered a stroke which left him impaired in gait, speech, and dexterity for the rest of his life; but he continued to work tirelessly for the next quarter century. He died in St. Cloud on September 28, 1895, and received a state funeral as a national hero. He is buried with his wife in a crypt in the Pasteur Institute.

It is not surprising to learn that Pasteur was endowed with a great capacity for work and an exceptional memory. More important, perhaps, he combined an ability to penetrate details with a faculty for broad and accurate generalization. This ability—which is clear from the range and clarity of his writing—he shares with ISAAC NEWTON [1], ALBERT EINSTEIN [2], NIELS BOHR [3], CHARLES DARWIN [4], and SIGMUND FREUD [6]. Like several of these figures, he could be unfair and antagonistic. He engaged in petty hostilities with CLAUDE BERNARD [13] and he was a pious patriot and a devout Catholic who refused to consider Darwinism. But these failings pale beside what Jacques Nicolle calls "his remarkable talent for incidental observations which opened subject after subject to later workers—as a river irrigates large tracts of country without losing its way to the sea."

More seriously, like other great scientists whose work has been intensively studied, Pasteur has not lived up to the claims made by his early biographers. Recently, historian and biographer Gerald L. Geison, in an exceptional work, has documented how Pasteur's anthrax vaccine depended not on attenuation, as he claimed, but on a technique developed by a rival; and similar deceptions existed with regard to his rabies vaccine. Acknowledging that "Pasteur's scientific work was enormously important and fertile, and some of his principles continue to guide us today," Geison has attempted to deflate the unnecessary aspects of what is known as the Pastorian legend. "That image was forged in a context that has lost much of its meaning for us—a context in which heroic biographies were used to transmit widely accepted moral verities, and in which science was seen as straightforwardly useful and 'positive' knowledge. Even in an age in need and search of heroes, we need no longer accept that image at face value."

6

Sigmund Freud

and Psychology of the Unconscious

1856–1939

By the late nineteenth century, advances in science, technology, and medicine had come to promise enormous consequences for the subjective, interior lives of men and women in Western civilization. The industrial revolution, urbanization, and new and complex forms of social life, including the rise of a substantial middle class, expanded the range of human personality and strongly affected interpersonal and sexual relationships. It is less than surprising that in 1900, the same year that MAX PLANCK [25] divined the secret of blackbody radiation, Sigmund Freud published *The Interpretation of Dreams*. Freud is the single most significant scientific figure associated with a new understanding of the self and its transformations. He aroused considerable antagonism in his time, as he does today, and the "continuing extremes of hostility," writes the historian of science, I. Bernard Cohen, "may be taken as an index of the profound impact of the Freudian revolution."

Sigmund Freud was born on May 6, 1856, in Freiburg, East Moravia, a town which then belonged to the Austro-Hungarian Empire and which today, as Príbor, lies within the Czech Republic. His parents were Jacob Freud, a relatively unsuccessful wool merchant with scholarly interests, and his third wife, twenty years his junior, Amalie Nathanson. Sigmund was the first of eight children, and when he was three the family moved to Vienna. He received some schooling at home and was an exceptional student at the gymnasium, from which he graduated at age seventeen. He considered studying law but wrote a friend in 1873 that "I have determined to become a natural scientist." For a student from modest circumstances, that meant medicine. Later that year Freud entered the University of Vienna and graduated in 1881. His first scientific work dates from this period. A paper on male river eels published in 1877 reflects his interest in physiology, which he studied from 1876 to 1882 at the institute directed by Ernst Brücke. Although he might have continued his research there, he had a financially more auspicious future in medicine. This was important because in 1882 Freud became engaged to Martha Bernays, whom he married in 1886.

For three years, from 1882 to 1885, Freud acquired clinical experience at the Vienna General Hospital, where he also undertook some of the first research on cocaine. For a time, he became a proponent of the drug, and on his account a friend discovered its usefulness in eye surgery. In 1885 Freud spent a brief but important six months on a scholarship in Paris, where he was strongly influenced by Jean Charcot. One of the most important neuropathologists of the era, Charcot was interested in hysteria, a psychological disease analogous to today's anorexia nervosa, in that it created severe symptoms but had no clear physical or hereditary cause. Hysteria was widely considered to be a uniquely female disease, but Charcot thought otherwise. Once back in Vienna, Freud lectured on male hysteria but met with opposition from some of his colleagues. Theodor Meynert, a well-known psychiatrist, excluded Freud from his laboratory of cerebral anatomy. "I withdrew from academic life," Freud wrote later, "and ceased to attend the learned societies."

In his private practice as a neuropathologist, Freud attempted to use such commonly prescribed methods as massage and electrotherapy, and the early stages of psychoanalysis reflect his disappointment as well as early efforts to find a new, ultimately broader explanation for "nervous" disorders. With Josef Breuer, a well-known generalist and researcher, Freud, using hypnotism, explored the case of a young female hysteric, known as Anna O.; their *Studies in Hysteria* was published in 1895. In Breuer's technique of "abreaction"—emotional discharge to ease intrapsychic conflict—Freud recognized that symptoms might be due to the sexual content of repressed fantasies.

From this insight Freud developed the fundamental notion that neurotic behavior involves a psychological defense against unacceptable ideas. Over time, he put forth a series of tentative theories that situated sexual problems at the root of neurosis and explained dissatisfaction with sexual life as leading to symptoms of anxiety and hysteria. All these ideas, including the notion that childhood sexual trauma engendered neurosis, he later refined. Meanwhile, beginning about 1895, a largely epistolary friendship with Wilhelm Fliess, a Berlin physician, gave Freud the unique opportunity to examine many of his own emotional conflicts and to test a number of theoretical ideas. From this period dates what Freud would later call a "self-analysis" as well as an important "Project" to give psychology a neurophysiological basis. Although the analysis cannot be described as a thorough success, and the "Project" was abandoned, the period was exceptionally productive. Psychoanalysis received its name in 1896.

In 1900 Freud published *The Interpretation of Dreams*, which forms both the culmination of his earlier work on psychoneuroses and a new departure toward a general psychology. Freud's major thesis, that dreams have decipherable meanings relating to unconscious conflict, had a universal applicability which he further examined over the next four decades. In general, Freud elaborated a model, rooted in Darwinian and neurological terms, of sexual and aggressive drives seeking satisfaction. In 1904 he published *The Psychopathology of Everyday Life*, an analysis of slips of the tongue and other mistakes of psychological motivation, and a year later, his *Three Essays on Sexuality* provided a groundbreaking view of emotional development, in which adult conflicts are linked to the novel notion of infantile sexuality and what came to be called the Oedipal conflict. The discovery of the strong relationship between the body and emotional and cognitive growth is one of Freud's most significant generalizations.

Psychoanalysis as a theory was tremendously successful, in spite of criticism, and its influence was soon widely felt. Not only a treatment of neurotic mental disorders, psychoanalysis revealed the meaning of small acts of speech, provided an explanation for the details and overall significance of custom and ritual, and illuminated infantile motivation behind widely held beliefs. Recognition of the existence of aggressive and sexual feelings and fantasies in children eventually led to widely adopted, if diffuse, changes in child-rearing techniques and an entirely new way of understanding childhood.

As a method of treatment, psychoanalysis is more difficult to assess. From the beginning it lacked any clearly definable, reliable, or desirable criteria for cure such as can be found in medicine for specific diseases; frequently, its most successful cases were individuals with relatively mild problems. However, the robust character of the theory was apparent from the way that Freud and other analysts—who began to adhere to the "movement" after 1900—developed a variety of durable techniques and conceptual tools for grasping the psychoanalytic situation or "talking cure." *Free association* was the basic rule by which the patient was asked to verbalize all that came to mind; the analyst, by contrast, generally kept silent, save for carefully dosed interpretations. *Resistance*, expressed in a variety of ways, impeded treatment, but was inevitable in a patient's *working through* of conflicts and coming to a more textured, nuanced, and honest understanding of the self and emotional conflicts. Perhaps the most important analytic concept is *transference*, by which Freud referred to the feelings of both tender attachment and anger that the patient holds toward the analyst—in principle, for no good reason.* Psychoanalysis could provide, as no other psychological theory, plausible investigations, through language, of the minutiae of fantasy and the subtleties of emotional experience.

---

*A marvelous example of transference is provided by the late psychoanalyst Helene Deutsch. In analysis with Freud, she found herself one afternoon looking in a shop window near his home and weeping as she wondered, "What will the Professor's poor wife do now?" She was imagining that Freud was about to leave his wife and marry her.

During the early decades of the twentieth century, Freud's theory developed in a variety of directions, both clinically and theoretically. A number of schools of analysis sprang up based on new hypotheses (such as Otto Rank's "birth trauma") or rejection of some part of the evolving theory. Toward the end of the 1920s, clinical psychoanalysis shifted emphasis from exposing patients' repressed conflicts to examine their means of psychic defense. Freud introduced, in place of a "topography" of unconscious and conscious, a rather more clinically fruitful tripartite division, functionally defined, of the mind. In Freud's structural theory, from an infantile, undifferentiated *id* evolves an *ego*, in which resides the conscious personality, and a punitive *superego*. (In English these terms sound technical and miss Freud's attempt, as physicists had done with *work* and *force*, to put ordinary words to scientific use.) The task of psychoanalysis then became, in its broadest terms, an attempt to modify the harshness of the superego.

Under the Nazis in Germany, psychoanalysis was banned and, as was the case with physicists, an important migration to the United States resulted. After the Nazis invaded Austria in 1938, Freud—old and suffering from cancer—finally was persuaded to leave, but he was extricated only with difficulty. He resettled in England in midsummer, and died in London the following year, on September 23, 1939.

So much has been written and fantasized about Freud's personality that efforts to describe it briefly are bound to be insufficient. Although capable of feeling depressed, Freud was essentially even-tempered and cordial. His relationships, especially with men, were sometimes intense and conflictual, partly because of his own unresolved feelings of omnipotence. An excellent speaker and raconteur, he enjoyed telling jokes, and even wrote a book, *Jokes and Their Relation to the Unconscious*. He lived a conventional middle-class life with Martha Bernays, and they had five children, one of whom, Anna, became an eminent psychoanalyst. In religion he was a militant atheist. With his sons he was apparently a good father, though not as emotionally expansive as with his daughters and grandchildren.

Freud's legacy is as complex as that of CHARLES DARWIN [4], and his thought has been the source of much rancorous dispute. Although scientific evidence can be adduced to support or contradict the various psychoanalytic hypotheses, these have not yet been refined either by progress in brain science or by any

The Freud Museum in Vienna.

measurable amelioration of everyday life. Psychoanalysts themselves are much to blame for longstanding suspicion by some scientists of both the profession and the theory. The psychoanalytic establishment long failed to develop a consensus on basic tenets which would be consonant with contemporary science. Even worse, continuing reliance among some of its most important figures on "instinct theory"—which at present has all the scientific status of phlogiston—and, more generally, on a medical model of disease, has strongly affected its overall status. In the 1960s, dogmatism and disorder in the field prevented MURRAY GELL-MANN [45], the theoretical physicist, from attempting to put analytic theory on a firmly scientific footing.

Problems in assessing Freud himself come from without and within the profession. In the United States, a whole generation of college students learned that psychoanalysis was unscientific—from behaviorists whose own project is now largely discredited. At the same time, one of Freud's most persistent problems was always the tremendous reverence settled on him by colleagues. Describing Freud from a 1926 etching, K. R. Eissler wrote of "an inscrutable face, from which the eyes look out keen, wise and understanding; a face which does not flinch from the tragic eventualities of this world; a face which can never again know fear, and which, despite the expression of sadness, is a stranger to despair; a controlled face, with a slight suggestion of those Olympian gestures that Goethe so loved to show to the world." This sort of ennoblement is not unknown in science—ALBERT

EINSTEIN [2] was widely spoken of in similar terms—but it is an uncomely attitude in an endeavor that seeks to unmask the emotional roots of such extravagance.

In the late twentieth century, debunking Freud has become highly problematic, as his influence outlives both his overzealous imitators and his harshest critics. Historians and philosophers of science, who view the scientific enterprise with more humility than a generation ago, are today less apt to exclude psycho-analysis.* One will always be able to say that Freud was not a scientist—FRANCIS CRICK [33], for one, believes he merely "wrote well," and the great immunologist Peter Medawar called psycho-analysis "the most stupendous intellectual confidence trick of the twentieth century." But as Robert Holt points out, "It would be no trick for a pathologist to find statements in the writings of RUDOLF VIRCHOW [17] that are false by contemporary standards, or for a physiologist to do a hatchet job on CLAUDE BERNARD [13]." The emotionally provocative content of Freud's work has determined much of his vulnerability.

If it were unfruitful, Freud's influence should logically have diminished a half century after his death; but, much like Coper-nican theory, psychoanalytic concepts have instead continued to evolve. One cannot read the object relations theorists, such as W. R. D. Fairbairn, without recognizing that Freudian theory can be treated scientifically. The scientific basis and value of the developmental theories of Margaret Mahler and René Spitz, among others, is difficult to deny. Freud's overall impact has continued to spread, and the breadth of his influence in Euro-american culture explains his position in this volume. "It is a commonplace," writes Peter Gay, "that we all speak Freud today whether we recognize it or not."

One can deny the basic propositions of psychoanalysis, just as millions of people continue to reject the evolution of species and the descent of man. But such willful negligence does not belong to science. "Sigmund Freud," wrote the physicist and Nobel laureate Eugene Wigner, "was clearly a genius. Alone, he had founded a new science—and how many men have ever done that?"

---

*The literature about Freud and psychoanalysis is vast, and several recent works deserve mention. Peter Gay's exceptional *Freud* is the most judicious portrait ever to appear. A fully informed discussion of the scientific status of psychoanalysis is Robert R. Holt's *Freud Reappraised*. Those who prefer to see Freud as a pseudoscientist, albeit highly influential, will be encouraged by reading E. Fuller Torrey's *Freudian Fraud*.

7

Galileo Galilei
and the New Science

1564–1642

Galileo remains one of the most fascinating of early scientific figures, and his life and work have inspired a multitude of historians and critics. His achievements are many. He provided an early account of classical mechanics, and his descriptions of the night sky with a telescope laid the foundation of physical astronomy. But perhaps most significant, Galileo epitomized a new scientific outlook. By his rhetoric, supported by mathematical reasoning, and the force of his personality, Galileo helped to establish the Copernican model of the solar system as a revolution in science. Entirely aware of the philosophical implications of his new discoveries, he became a controversial and highly visible figure who was an embarrassment to the authority and dogma of the Catholic Church. Critics have long argued over the nature of his spirit of scientific inquiry; but Galileo's influence, in historical terms, is enormous.

Galileo Galilei was born in Pisa, Italy, on February 15, 1564, the son of Vincenzio Galilei, a musician and tradesman, and Giula Ammannati. (The first-name repetition of the surname was a Tuscan custom.) His family, which was not wealthy, moved to Florence when he was a child, and Galileo attended a Jesuit monastery school, but after becoming a novice at age fifteen, he was forced to withdraw by his father. In 1581 he entered the University of Pisa, planning to study medicine, but did not like it and acquired a reputation as disputatious. He soon transferred his interest to mathematics, and after leaving the university in 1585, without a degree, he returned to Florence to teach. In 1592, after the death of his father, he moved to Padua, where he continued teaching and invented, among other things, a military compass. He lived well; he acquired a mistress, Marina Gabba, and, to the distress of his aging mother, sired several illegitimate children.

Galileo's most significant early work, *De motu*, concerns the dynamics of motion and reflects his skepticism about the reigning—but crumbling—principles of scholastic science. According to Aristotle, an object in motion requires a constant mover; a ball, for example, is said to be propelled by air pushing behind it. This was a vulnerable point in Aristotelian physics, and it became an early locus of Galileo's interest. In all probability, Galileo was influenced by ballistics engineers, some of whom realized that a moving bullet appears to be pulled down to earth. Galileo recognized the importance of such observations. Experimenting on his own with a ball rolling off a table, he discovered a general law. Projectiles make a curved path as they fall. And, as a mathematician profoundly influenced by ARCHIMEDES [100], he summarized this discovery in a simple mathematical formula, described first in a letter dated 1604. (Mistakes in Galileo's calculations have given rise to considerable speculation among philosophers of science as to his intended line of reasoning.)

A new and important phase in Galileo's career began in 1609, when he learned of the invention of the telescope. He constructed his own model, which brought objects as much as one thousand times closer than they appeared to the naked eye. This he trained upon the moon. According to the old science of the cosmos, heavenly bodies were perfect in shape; Galileo found that Earth's satellite was pockmarked. He saw peaks and valleys and what he thought were seas. Looking out farther into the night sky, he discovered that the Milky Way consisted, so it seemed, of a multitude of stars—a far cry from the pristine night sky of Ptolemaic astronomy.

Indeed, the publication in 1610 of *Siderus nunicus (The Starry Messenger)* was a sensation; and historian J. R. Ravetz has called the slight book "perhaps the greatest classic ever of popular science, and also a masterpiece of subtle propaganda for the Copernican system." Learned men everywhere bought and read *The Starry Messenger*, and within five years there was even an edition in Chinese, translated by a Jesuit. Perhaps the most intriguing and remarkable of Galileo's discoveries was that four objects seemed to be circling the planet Jupiter, changing their position from night to night. To Galileo these were clearly satellites and resembled a Copernican scheme in miniature.

The success of *The Starry Messenger* put Galileo on the path to further discoveries, as well as on a collision course with the Catholic Church. However, he had first of all become a famous man, and his 1611 audience with the Pope was encouraging and friendly. Soon Galileo acquired a powerful patron in a former student, Cosimo II, the Grand Duke of Tuscany, who appointed Galileo his chief mathematician and philosopher. In 1612 Galileo's *Discourse on Floating Bodies* established hydrostatics, and the following year he published a series of letters in which he discussed his observations of sunspots. Here Galileo explicitly approved of COPERNICUS [10] and made an initial formulation of the principle of inertia. But by now, Galileo had aroused the wrath of church figures, and when in 1616 he visited Rome, he was admonished not to teach Copernicus's heliocentric views, against which a formal decree was issued. Galileo was not charged with heresy, however, and so may have taken a characteristically optimistic assessment of the situation. The historical record is a source of much debate.

When in 1623 Galileo published *The Assayer*, a polemic concerning the nature of comets, he dedicated it to Urban VIII, the new pope who (as Mafeo Barberini) had been an early supporter. Galileo hoped that the 1616 decree would be lifted, but his patron, Cosimo II, having died, Galileo was more vulnerable than before. He also received mixed messages from his old friend, who as pope was proving more the militarist than friend to science.* However, obtaining permission to discuss the systems of the world so long as he came to the right conclusion, Galileo wrote his *Dialogue Concerning the Two Chief World Systems*, which was published in 1632. In this work, a masterpiece of science, it is hard not to see Galileo's strong identification with his father, the author of a *Dialogue on Ancient and Modern Music*. Psychologically, this conceivably prevented Galileo from realizing the gravity of his undertaking.

The *Dialogue* was a great success when published in March 1633, but within six months the Inquisitor had stepped in. The *Dialogue* was banned, and Galileo was soon summoned once again to Rome, where he was technically imprisoned. Galileo's famous audience with Pope Urban VIII, and his grilling by the Inquisitor, have been the subject of much discussion over the years. The main issue was Galileo's disobedience of the 1616 admonitions. He has sometimes been taken to task for being less than courageous in face of these trials; in fact, he was a political prisoner, old and ill, and he was literally threatened with torture at a time when heretics were regularly, with cautionary fanfare, burned at the stake. In the end, the church prohibited and consigned the *Dialogues* to the flames, disgraced Galileo in a grand public spectacle, and refused to make him a martyr. He was imprisoned in fairly congenial circumstances.

It is a testament to Galileo's personal strength that the church's condemnation did not finish him by any means. His *Discourse on Two New Sciences*, published in Leyden in 1634, reprised his earlier experiments and discussed the properties of solids and the motion of falling bodies and projectiles. In 1637 he made his last scientific discovery: the wobbling of the moon. Although the *Dialogues* had been banned, it was soon known throughout Protestant Europe. Galileo was visited by the poet John Milton and the philosopher Thomas Hobbes, and his final letters, in which he professes faith in Aristotelian physics, may be read as ironic. At the end of his life Galileo was blind, apparently from cataracts, and he died on January 9, 1642.

Three and a half centuries after Galileo's death, Pope John

---

*Several years ago the scholar Pietro Redondi found documents at the Vatican suggesting that a Jesuit, Orazio Grassi, whom Galileo had ridiculed in *The Assayer*, was responsible for the trial which followed.

Paul II, who had served as Archbishop of Cracow and liked to refer to himself as the "Copernican Canon," conceded on behalf of the Catholic Church that Galileo had been unjustly treated. This admission, made in 1992, seems to have had a public relations angle. It was accorded a wry headline in the *New York Times*: "After 350 Years Vatican Says Galileo Was Right: It Moves." Three years earlier, in October 1989, the *Galileo*, a space probe, was launched from the space shuttle *Atlantis*. In 1995, the probe reached Jupiter, whose four moons Galileo had first viewed 385 years earlier.

Galileo was the great transitional figure in the history of science, and his work is formalized in that of ISAAC NEWTON [1]. However, the nature of Galileo's influence has been the subject of much scholarly debate over the past half century. In 1939 Alexandre Koyré described Galileo's great importance to science as primarily conceptual and philosophical and downplayed his use of experiment. This ignited considerable interest and led the scholar Stillman Drake to a more recent, painstaking reevaluation of Galileo's notes and manuscripts. Drake concluded "that a coherent depiction emerges of [Galileo] as a recognizably modern physical scientist" who made pioneering investigations on the nature of gravity. In either event, Galileo remains, together with JOHANNES KEPLER [9], the most significant figure in the scientific revolution before Newton.

8

Antoine Laurent Lavoisier
and the Revolution in Chemistry

1743–1794

The founder of modern chemistry was Antoine Lavoisier, and both his works and fate reflect the revolution in thought and everyday life taking place in Europe at the end of the eighteenth century. Among many other accomplishments, Lavoisier explained how combustion involves oxygen, developed the concept of the element as a basic substance, and laid down the principle of the conservation of matter in chemical reactions. In his *Traité élémentaire de chimie*, he did for chemistry "what Newton had done for mechanics a century earlier, in the *Principia*," as Douglas McKie has observed, and his work lies at the base of the rise of industry. Like the other founders of major scientific disciplines,

Lavoisier recognized the importance of quantitative analysis and so spent great sums of money on precision instruments. In 1793, in the bitter days of the French Revolution, the *bonnets rouges* came to arrest Lavoisier, and found him, according to an apocryphal story, performing an experiment on respiration and perspiration upon an assistant wrapped in a silken bag with only an airhole for breathing. Lavoisier was put on trial during the Terror and guillotined.

The eldest son of Jean-Antoine Lavoisier, a lawyer, and Émilie Punctis, Antoine-Laurent Lavoisier was born on August 26, 1743. His mother, who came from a wealthy family, died in 1746, and Antoine was thereafter raised by an adoring aunt, Clémence Punctis. Antoine grew up in Paris, and for nine years he attended the prestigious Collège Mazarin, which was renowned for its courses in science. But he also studied law, and in 1763 he received a degree in jurisprudence. His legal training had an important influence on his rhetorical abilities, which were considerable, and made him skeptical of contemporary scientific theories. In addition, he was endowed with great personal ambition.

While still in school, Lavoisier had become interested in science, learned basic botany at the Jardin du Roi, and around 1762 began attending the lectures on chemistry given by Guillame-François Rouelle. He also studied such sources as the article on chemistry in Diderot's encyclopedia, prepared under the influence of Newton's *Principia*. And in 1763 Lavoisier accompanied geologist Jean-Etienne Guettard, a close friend of his family, on a long trip through France with the mission of cataloguing its minerals. This investigation of natural resources reflected the French monarchy's apprehension at the birth of the industrial revolution in England. Indeed, Lavoisier's whole career, up to his death, is intimately bound up with the foundations of industry and capitalism and the disintegration of the old order in France.

In 1765 Lavoisier presented a report to the French Academy on the nature of gypsum, which was used to make plaster of Paris. The following year, he received a gold medal from the French Academy for his theoretical treatment of the best way to light the streets of Paris. About this time, he also became financially independent, receiving a large inheritance, and joined the Ferme Générale, the private share company which collected taxes for the king. The *fermiers* were widely detested on account of abuse and corruption, and although politically a liberal, Lavoisier would later suffer from his association with them. In 1771 he married Marie-Anne-Pierrette Paulze, a fourteen-year-old who eventually became his assistant in the laboratory, an illustrator of his work, and a translator of articles by English scientists. They enjoyed a happy although childless marriage and were well known in French intellectual society; the painter Jacques Louis David made a famous painting of them.

Lavoisier was formally admitted to the French Academy in 1768, and over the next two decades, he undertook numerous studies on a wide variety of issues, including the problem of food adulteration, the nature of animal magnetism, and the condition of prisons. How dyes work, how metals rust, how water might be stored aboard ships on long voyages, and how glass manufacture could be improved were just a few of some two hundred reports in which Lavoisier participated over the next quarter century. In 1775, when he was appointed to the Gunpowder Commission, he moved to the Arsenal, near the Bastille, where he installed an elaborate laboratory.

The extent of Lavoisier's scientific genius, and its strong connection to social history, is apparent from his practical studies, such as the potability of Parisian water. Asked to study whether water brought to Paris in an open canal was acceptably pure, he analyzed it through evaporation and by examining the solid content which remained. But in doing so, Lavoisier recognized that water could contain impurities, and so was forced to dispute the theory that it could be simply "transmuted" into earth. By 1772 Lavoisier was suggesting that all matter has three possible states: solid, liquid, and gas. By recognizing the importance of the gaseous state, which implied the conservation of matter in chemical reactions, Lavoisier had an important theoretical probe.

Indeed, the most significant and famous of Lavoisier's achievements was a new understanding of combustion and, as a consequence, the discovery of oxygen. In the seventeenth century *phlogiston*, a hypothetical substance, had been proposed to explain how things burn, and later was invoked to interpret many different chemical reactions. All flammable substances were said to contain phlogiston, given off in smoke and flame when they burned. Charcoal, for example, was said to be composed mainly of phlogiston, which was imparted to ore during smelting. Contradictory evidence, such as the fact that metals gain weight (through oxidation) when they burn, was ignored or given a roundabout explanation.

After experiments with sulphur, phosphorus, and other chemicals, in 1772, Lavoisier, in a note deposited with the French Academy to establish priority, offered a new hypothesis: Combustion does not entail giving off phlogiston but, rather, things that burn absorb and require air. This was not quite correct, but Lavoisier was now inspired to investigate the considerable work which other (mainly British) chemists had already done on the various "airs." They had discovered such substances as (so we call them today) carbon monoxide, nitrogen, and hydrogen chloride. As Lavoisier wrote in 1773, he planned to repeat earlier experiments "in order to link our knowledge of the air that goes into combustion or is liberated from substances, with other acquired knowledge, and to form a theory." In 1774 the yield of these researches was published as *Opuscules physiques et chimiques*.

Lavoisier was led to oxygen in 1778, after four more years of experiment, and with the help of the work of Joseph Priestley, who had recognized the special properties of "dephlogisticated air," which was produced in heating calx of mercury. While Priestley clung to the theory of phlogiston, Lavoisier was able to identify "the healthiest and purest part of air" as oxygen.* The context of Lavoisier's work was the interpretation of acidity, and so he called the substance oxygen, which means "acid-former." Though rather a misnomer, as it turned out, the name remained. More important, Lavoisier recognized that oxygen reacted with metals to form oxides, and with non-metals to form acids. Rusting metal, decaying animal and vegetable matter, and burning wood are all examples of oxidation. And, as Lavoisier showed, combustion is a basic chemical process in respiration, in which oxygen from the air is absorbed while carbon dioxide is expelled.

Lavoisier is sometimes also given credit for the discovery of the composition of water. The discovery is mired in claims of priority among British scientists Joseph Priestley, Henry Cavendish, and James Watt—who had noticed that oxygen and hydrogen could be transformed into a sort of dew when an electric

---

*Lavoisier did not appropriately credit Priestley for his work on oxygen. But neither this nor Lavoisier's careful establishment of priority, nor the dispute over the discovery of water, should give the impression of a solitary and jealous scientist. Frederic Lawrence Holmes has pointed out that "an important source of Lavoisier's success was his capacity to engage in creative collaborations." One of his collaborators was PIERRE SIMON DE LAPLACE [29].

spark brought them together. The dew seemed to be—and it was—nothing but water. Lavoisier was the first to correctly identify the elements which compose it.

As should be apparent from the foregoing, Lavoisier had an overarching, highly ambitious program and viewed his discoveries as establishing an entirely new field of science. He recognized the importance of rhetoric, and to further his ends, he initiated a review, the *Annales de Chimique*, which is still published today. In his *Méthode de nomenclature chimique*, published in 1787, he created the system of naming chemicals which recalls their important properties or constituents, and he devised a system of symbols. In spite of initial opposition from British and German scientists, this system has survived, little changed, to the present.

In 1789, Lavoisier's *Traité élémentaire de chimie* set forth basic principles and a theory of how chemical compounds are formed from the elements. Most important, Lavoisier's postulating the conservation of matter during chemical reactions marks the *Traité* as a fully modern work, as does his view of science, when he states, "We must trust to nothing but facts. These are presented to us by Nature and cannot deceive. We ought in every instance, to submit our reasoning to the test of experiment...." Lavoisier at the same time recognized the limits imposed by instruments and techniques. He did not propose that his elements, for example, were eternally simple substances, but only that they could not be further broken down by "the present state of our knowledge."

Lavoisier would have expanded the *Traité*, which is relatively short and easily read, had it not been for the French Revolution. An Enlightenment figure who supported the initial aims of the Revolution, he had nevertheless profited from the old regime as a *fermier générale* and, in addition, during the terror of 1793, his enemy Jean-Paul Marat came briefly to power. Lavoisier was arrested late that year and tried the following spring, together with thirty other tax farmers. He was judged guilty, and when his scientific accomplishments were brought to the attention of the court, Judge Coffinhal (later himself executed) was said to have replied: "The Republic has no need of scientists." This remark, according to George B. Kauffman, is apocryphal. But after Antoine Lavoisier was guillotined on May 8, 1794, the mathematician Joseph Louis de Lagrange did say, "It took a mere instant to cut off that head, and yet a hundred years may not produce another like it."

9

Johannes Kepler
and Motion of the Planets

1571–1630

To Johannes Kepler are owed the laws of planetary motion and the founding of celestial mechanics. He is the pivotal and culminating figure in the revolution in astronomy which took place at the beginning of the seventeenth century, when the heliocentric universe proposed by Copernicus, half a century earlier, was supported by the discoveries and rhetoric of Galileo. Although highly religious and desirous of celebrating God in astronomy and a Lutheran who lived in the midst of the Reformation and Counter-Reformation, Kepler's mystical attachment to harmony was balanced by a commitment to observation. He was able to abandon unproductive hypotheses and to seek mathemati-

50

cal laws. "I have attested it as true in my deepest soul," he wrote of the solar system as he viewed it, "and I contemplate its beauty with incredible and ravishing delight."

Johannes Kepler was born in Weil, a town in the former German state of Würtemburg, on December 27, 1571. His father was a soldier who was personally eccentric; Kepler himself was sickly as a child and hypochondriacal as an adult. He attended the University of Tübingen, where he became a student of Michael Mästlin, a convinced Copernican. Initially Kepler intended to become a theologian, but after graduating in 1591, he accepted a teaching post at Graz, a city in the state of Styria in the Austrian Empire. As professor of mathematics and morals he was not notably successful and had few students; he spent his free time casting horoscopes—he believed in astrology but with diminishing credulity—and studying astronomy.

In 1597 Kepler published his *Mysterium Cosmographicum*, in which he supported Copernicus's view of a heliocentric cosmos. Notably, Kepler brought Pythagorean ideas to bear on the notion of a sun-centered universe, taking seriously the special ontological status which the ancient Greek accorded to mathematics. ("All is numbers," Pythagoras is supposed to have said.) Kepler attempted to show that the orbits of the six known planets were spaced apart by the five geometrical solids which the ancient Greeks had discovered. Within the celestial sphere of Saturn, for example, was a cube; within that of Mercury an octahedron. It is not surprising that Galileo, to whom Kepler sent his book, replied with a friendly but essentially cautious letter.

In 1600, to avoid possible persecution as a Lutheran during the Counter-Reformation, Kepler moved from Graz to Prague. There he worked for a brief but important time as assistant to the great astronomer TYCHO BRAHE [22]. The two men must have had a difficult relationship, for Brahe hoped that celestial measurements gathered during a lifetime's work—which he guarded jealously—would support his own system of the universe. However, upon Brahe's death the following year, Kepler inherited this mass of observations, including remarkable data on Mars. Using this information, and sharing Brahe's respect for precision, Kepler made his most important discoveries over the next eight years.

Kepler's signal break with traditional astronomy was to invoke the concept of force, and to propose laws which would

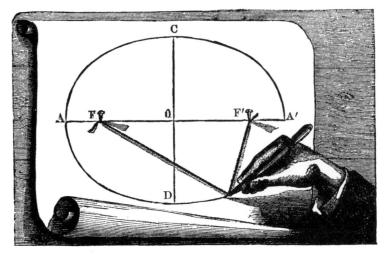

The ellipse is defined as a closed curve by two foci from which the sum of their distances from every point is equal. An important curve in the physical world, Kepler discovered its significance for the solar system.

explain the motion of the planets. Astronomy down to and including Copernicus had no such concept, and had essentially aimed at allowing predictions of the comings and goings of planets. Recognizing that the Martian orbit fit *neither* Ptolemaic nor Copernican schemes, Kepler at length abandoned something which the two systems shared: the ancient and philosophical certainty of perfectly circular orbits. At the same time, he gave up the assumption that the planets moved at uniform speed. His data told him that all the planets moved faster when close to the sun, and slower as they moved further away. Through trial and error, Kepler discovered the law which governs this motion. An imaginary line, the radius vector, from Sun to planet, sweeps out equal areas in equal times. This became known as Kepler's second law.

Having discovered the second law within a Copernican framework, the true shape of the orbits of the planets remained to be clarified. After considerable work Kepler came to realize the advantage of an ellipse, a shape which had been known to the ancients. It fit the predictions of arc with great precision and became Kepler's first law: The orbits of the planets are elliptical, with the sun at one of the foci.

Kepler's first two laws were given in his *Astronomia Nova*, published in 1609. Like Galileo, although he did not discover the universal law of gravitation, he had come close. He was aware of a force at work between planetary bodies which is proportional to their mass, but he suggested that it was magnetic. The key significance of *Astronomia Nova*, however, is its fundamental reorientation of the aims and methods of astronomy. Celestial geometry was subordinated to a new celestial physics, which operated by laws which could be discovered and understood.

In 1619, when *Harmonice mundi (Harmony of the World)* was published, Kepler considered it his masterpiece. Filled with illustrations and musical examples—each planet is ascribed its own range of sounds—*Harmonice mundi* is a sometimes delirious work which exemplifies Kepler's view that notions of mathematics provide a means for knowing the universe, and this view of the world is something which mankind can share with God. Even though it is frequently mystical, the book includes a basic scientific discovery: Kepler's third law of planetary motion—the square of the time a planet takes to circle the sun is proportional to the cube of its average distance from the sun. This allows computation of the distances of planets from the sun during their orbits.

In addition to his principal works, Kepler was the author of two important treatises on optics. His *Epitome astronomiae (Epitome of Copernican Astronomy)* was published between 1619 and 1621, and quickly found its way onto the list of books prohibited by the Catholic Church. In 1627 he published his tabulation of the known stars, the *Rudolphine Tables*, based on Brahe's work; the tables were used for a century afterward.

By all accounts, Kepler's later life in Counter-Reformation Europe was not easy. His efforts to publish Tycho's data embroiled him with the astronomer's family, and his salary was not always paid on time. Both his wife and son died in 1611, and the next year his patron, the Emperor Rudolph, abdicated after a revolt and left his chief astronomer jobless. Kepler soon moved to Linz, where he worked as a mathematician, and about 1625 went to Ulm, again to escape religious persecution. Returning to Prague in 1627, he was received with honors and employed by the Duchy of Sagan as an astrologer. In this capacity, Kepler may have been given to skepticism, and he finally left to search for a new job. He died in Bavaria on November 15, 1630.

One digression is in order: Johannes Kepler is the only

scientist of *The Scientific 100* compelled to defend his mother against charges of witchcraft. Although the details are not clear, it is certain that Katharina, Kepler's mother, was publicly accused of being a witch. She sued for slander, but during the Reformation and in its aftermath there was a surfeit of witches and much belief in their powers. A strong case was mounted against her. In 1617 Kepler wrote petitions on his mother's behalf and requested her name be cleared, but in 1620 she was arrested one night, at the age of seventy-four, and carried out of her home inside a linen chest. She was threatened with torture on the rack before being freed; she died in 1622.

Some of his mother's ordeal, strangely enough, Kepler may have caused himself, by writing a manuscript, circulated about 1610, in which he described his mother as being in touch with demons from the moon. This incident is thought to be at the root of his posthumous *Somnium (Dream)*, a brilliant allegory, and in part a disguised autobiography. Kepler imagines a voyage to the moon, which turns out not to be a utopia, but a nightmarish world, parching hot in some places, freezing in others, inhabited by an enormous race of serpentine creatures, some winged and others who crawl.

Somnium testifies to the fertility of Kepler's scientific imagination, as well as to the intellectual conflicts that he engendered. Kepler is not only a pivotal but a contradictory figure in the history of science. He was devout and wrote "I take religion seriously, I do not play with it." However, the effect of his works was to help topple forever the secular authority of the church, whether Catholic or Protestant.

"Kepler was one of the few who are simply incapable of doing anything but stand up openly for their convictions in every field," wrote ALBERT EINSTEIN [2], who admired the man who liberated himself from "the intellectual traditions into which he was born. This meant not merely the religious tradition, based on the authority of the Church, but general concepts on the nature and limitations of action within the universe and the human sphere, as well as notions of the relative importance of thought and experience in science."

10

Nicolaus Copernicus
and the Heliocentric Universe

1473–1543

The notion of a stationary Earth at the center of the universe was supported by a mathematical system devised by the brilliant Greek astronomer Ptolemy. To his book, known to the Middle Ages as *Almagest*, we owe the description of the various constellations of stars such as the Big Dipper, still used today to describe the night sky. The Ptolemaic system was powerful and convincing for hundreds of years, and was, most important, the linchpin of a whole way of looking at the real world.* It was

---

*Ptolemy's brilliance as an astronomer and great influence should not be doubted. Only lack of space prevents his inclusion in *The Scientific 100*.

central to explanations of falling bodies and of the movements of stars and clouds, as well as to a whole theological interpretation of the place of human beings in the universe.

By the sixteenth century, however, with voyages of discovery bringing evidence of a more diverse world and with the authority of the Roman church faltering, Ptolemy's system began to crack. The posthumous publication in 1543 of *De revolutionibus orbium coelestium* (*On the Revolution of the Heavenly Bodies*), by Nicolaus Copernicus, eventually brought about its downfall. "The Earth," wrote Copernicus, "carrying the Moon's path, passes in a great orbit among the other Planets in an annual revolution around the Sun." Although not an accomplished fact for almost a century to come, the Copernican Revolution had begun.

Nicolaus Copernicus was born to prosperous circumstances on February 19, 1473, in Toruń, in the Kingdom of Poland. His father, Niklas Koppernign, was a merchant, and his mother, Barbara Watzenrode, was from an established and wealthy family. After the death of his father when he was ten years old, Nicolaus was raised by his maternal uncle, an academic and churchman who had become the bishop of Ermland in 1479. Nicolaus received an exemplary education. In 1491 he began attending the respected University of Cracow, then a center of natural philosophy. In 1496 Nicolaus moved to the University of Bologna, continuing his studies in Greek, mathematics, philosophy, and astronomy. About this time, he came under the influence of Domenico Maria da Novara, an astronomy professor who was an early critic of the Ptolemaic system, and on March 9, 1497, the two men witnessed together an eclipse of the moon. Copernicus studied at the University of Padua in 1501, then took a degree in law in 1503 from the University of Ferrara before returning to Padua for a course in medicine.

By 1506 Copernicus had completed his education—as a linguist, mathematician, and physician—and he returned to Poland, where he would remain until his death. He had been elected a canon in 1497 while he was a student abroad, and after several years as medical adviser to his uncle, upon the latter's death, he took up his duties as the canon of the Frauenburg Cathedral in newly established East Prussia. This was a church position with no religious duties, and Copernicus does not seem to have had any religious motivation in his life. He worked as a general administrator, judge, tax collector, and physician. In his spare time he was an astronomer, and in 1513 he constructed a tower to observe the stars.

Little is known about the genesis and development of Copernicus's thought, but he was by no means in a hurry to publish. He circulated a summary manuscript of his views on the cosmos as early as 1514 (it was not published until the nineteenth century), and he completed his great work in 1530. A decade later an admirer, George Joachim Rheticus, wrote a summary of the unpublished volume, entitled *Narratio prima*. When this book did not excite the animosity of the church—its implications were not immediately clear—Copernicus's objections may have been over-come. *De revolutionibus orbium coelestium* was published in Nurem-burg in 1543, just as he died.

Copernicus strongly and persistently objects in *De revolu-tionibus* to Ptolemy's arguments for an immobile Earth. Reasoning on a physical basis with a prejudice toward harmony, Copernicus undermines the idea that Earth must be at the center of the universe. He points out, for example, that the stars do not always appear to be at the same distance from Earth. Efforts to explain such effects using epicycles—small circular orbits—were un-satisfactory and introduced awkward complications. For lack of physical theory, Copernicus ultimately developed a conception of the solar system which is a mixture of ancient and modern. He was aware of problems of acceleration and falling bodies, but had no solution. Without a modern conception of force, he retained the model of celestial spheres, not the notion of planets hurtling through space.

Eventually *De revolutionibus* found its way into the hands of learned men throughout Europe. Early readers of the book were at the very least fascinated by its mathematics, underscoring their growing dissatisfaction with the limitations of Ptolemaic astron-omy. Religion did not object to the book, for during this era of the Reformation, the Catholic Church had bigger fish to fry. Not until 1616, and owing to Galileo's success, was Copernicus's book prohibited by the church.

The "Copernican Revolution" is an eminently useful term, although its actual content has been much discussed and dis-puted since it was first employed by Immanuel Kant two cen-turies ago. The term should be understood as referring to Copernicus's break with Ptolemaic astronomy and to his priority in developing a Sun-centered model. He did not accomplish it alone. It has long been understood that, as astronomer J. L. E. Dreyer wrote, "Copernicus did not produce what is nowadays meant by 'the Copernican system.'" And historian of science I. Bernard Cohen concludes, "If there was a revolution in astronomy, that revolution was Keplerian and Newtonian, and not in any simple or valid sense Copernican." This is not to gainsay Copernicus's influence but only to put it in the context of his real achievement. "One can easily argue that Copernicus was not the equal of Ptolemy or of Kepler in mathematics, although for his day he stood well above his contemporaries," argues Owen Gingerich. "Yet as a sensitive visionary who precipitated a scientific revolution, Copernicus stands as a cosmological genius with few equals."

Of the man himself, relatively little is known. His friend Rheticus's purported biography has been lost, as have most of his letters. According to legend, Copernicus received a copy of *De revolutionibus* on his deathbed. He had suffered a stroke, and could make no emendations but had the opportunity to handle the book before his death, which came on May 24, 1543. There remains the famous image—a man of honesty and devotion, high cheekbones and a penetrating gaze—which has come down to us in a handful of portraits. He did translate, from Greek into Latin, some eighty-five brief poems by the Byzantine poet Theophylactus Simocatta. Some of these *Epistles* are moral, others pastoral, and still others ribald. Fred Hoyle, the twentieth-century cosmologist, is grateful for the latter, for otherwise, he wrote, "I cannot hear Copernicus laugh."

11

Michael Faraday
and the Classical Field Theory

1791–1867

Michael Faraday stands at the nineteenth-century frontier of a great transformation of physics, finally triggering new and fundamental theories of electricity, magnetism, and light. The consummate experimentalist with a visionary's sense of the unity of nature, Faraday was the first to conceptualize the electromagnetic field, which JAMES CLERK MAXWELL [12] would later quantify, and his broad array of accomplishments gives him a preeminent place in the history of both physics and chemistry. Indeed, he resembles the biblical character Moses, who leads his people to, but not into, the promised land, for, mathematically illiterate, Faraday could not himself hope to provide a sophisticated quantitative theory.

The early life story of Michael Faraday has the quality of a fairy tale set in the industrial revolution. He was born on September 22, 1791, in Newington Butts, Surrey, which is now Elephant and Castle in London. His father, James Faraday, was a blacksmith, ailing and scarcely able to feed his wife and four children. The family was close and nurturing, loving but stern. His mother, born Margaret Hastwell, was Faraday's stronger parent, and, after her husband died in 1809, his only one. In 1804, at age thirteen, after minimal schooling, Michael became a newspaper boy for a French émigré to whom he was later apprenticed as a bookbinder. Over the next seven years he began to develop the dexterity which made him a great experimenter; and during this time, the books on which he sewed covers aroused his intellect. He was particularly influenced by the *Encyclopaedia Britannica* and a self-help text entitled *The Improvement of the Mind*. In 1810 he began attending lectures at the local City Philosophical Society, and two years later at the far more prestigious Royal Institution.

In 1813 Faraday became assistant to Sir Humphry Davy, to whom he had introduced himself at the Royal Institution, and began an unusually productive apprenticeship. Davy, himself from a poor background, was an important early scientist—also remembered for discovering how one can be, as the poet Robert Southey put it, "turned on" by nitrous oxide. Faraday accompanied Davy on a voyage to Europe in 1813, during which he met the important men of science of the period, including Alessandro Volta, André Ampère, and the chemist Joseph Gay-Lussac. He subsequently became active in Davy's research, helping to develop the safety lamp for miners and doing experiments of a primitive kind of low-temperature physics. Indeed—although Davy took credit—in 1823 Faraday succeeded in liquefying some of the important gases, including carbon dioxide and chlorine. This was a major step, for it was not until then clear that a gas could have more than a single state. Two years later Faraday isolated benzene from whale oil; forty years later it would become a key to the development of organic chemistry. He worked on improving glass used for lenses and discovered what came to be called the Faraday Effect—the rotation of a beam of light as it passes through a magnetic field. In brief, Faraday's discoveries during

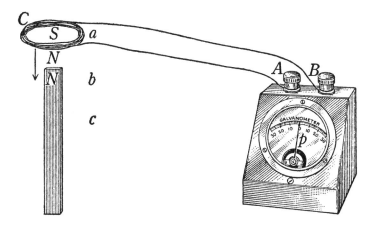

Electrical induction using a bar magnet.

the 1820s were extraordinary achievements of central importance, and it is not surprising that he was elected a member of the Royal Society in 1824.

Although electrical phenomena interested early scientists of the eighteenth century, and Alessandro Volta's invention of a simple battery in 1799 was a turning point, the great experiment was Hans Christian Oersted's demonstration, in 1819, of a relationship between electricity and magnetism. This created a flurry of activity over the next decade. In 1821, Faraday showed that a bar magnet could be made to rotate around a wire which carried an electrical charge; and by the same token, a suspended, electrically charged wire would turn around a fixed bar magnet. This was actually the first demonstration of the conversion of electrical into mechanical energy. Nine years later, in 1830, having succeeded Davy in the chair of chemistry, Faraday returned the focus of his interest to electricity and magnetism and made his greatest discoveries.

Faraday's demonstrations of electromagnetic induction in the fall of 1831 "altered the history of the world," as one typically understated recent article suggests, and "changed the lot of mankind." It involved many experiments, two of which can be singled out as crucial. In the first, in August 1831 Faraday wrapped two separate strands of wire around an iron core. One strand he passed by a magnetic compass, and when he connected the other to a battery, the resulting shift in the needle of the compass, as he wrote, "continued for an instant only." But Faraday had recognized the principle of the transformer, and his statue at the Royal Institution portrays him holding the induction coil in his hand.

For a continuous current to exist, Faraday recognized the necessity of motion in an electrical field, which he described as consisting of "tubes of force," and he succeeded not long after in developing a disk generator. To do this, he attached a fixed wire at the center of a copper disk and a sliding wire along its edge. Connecting the wires to a galvanometer, and placing the disk between a horseshoe magnet, he was able to generate a steady current. Just as, in 1821, he had shown how electrical energy could be turned into mechanical energy, so, in October 1831, he demonstrated the reverse. This was the first dynamo, or generator, which, about a half century later, became the principal means of delivering electrical energy to the world. Faraday went on to build primitive dynamos and motors for his experiments. The story is told that when the British prime minister visited his laboratory and asked the purpose of one of his generators, Faraday replied, "I know not, but I wager that one day your government will tax it."

The discovery of electromagnetic induction led Faraday to perform a vast number of experiments and to lay the foundation of subsequent research. In 1832 Faraday effectively founded electrochemistry, in which an electric current is used to break down chemical compounds. He developed the laws which govern electrolysis, which bear his name, showing the fundamental connection between electricity and the composition of the elements. With William Whewell, Faraday also developed the basic language of electricity: *Electrolyte, electrode, anode, cathode, ion,* and many other terms derive from his work. Faraday's research was collected in the three volumes of *Experimental Researches in Electricity, 1839–1855,* and his *Experimental Researches in Chemistry and Physics* was published in 1859.

Just as significant as Faraday's experimental demonstration of electrical induction and his laws of electrolysis are his theoretical contributions. He showed that all the various electricities which had been discovered over the preceding generation—thermochemistry, static electricity, magneto-electricity, volta-electricity—were the same. As a consequence, he recognized the possibility that from electrical phenomena might emerge an understanding of the underlying unity of nature. He was virtually convinced, he wrote, "that the various forms under which the forms of matter are made manifest have one common origin: in other words, are so directly related and naturally dependent that they are convertible as it were into one another and possess equivalents of power in their action." His "Thoughts on Ray Vibrations," dating from 1846, became the touchstone for James Clerk Maxwell's further development of the fundamental laws of electromagnetism and the theory of the electromagnetic field.

In 1839 Faraday fell prey to a serious illness—perhaps from fatigue though post-hoc diagnoses are legion—and never entirely recovered his health. He suffered from headaches and, as he grew older, was plagued by an unreliable memory. Nevertheless, in his later years he was showered with honors, became an adept consultant on various scientific-related matters for the government, and was provided a Grace and Favor Residence by Queen Victoria, whose children used to attend his annual Christmas lectures. Such was his renown that Lady Lovelace, daughter of Lord Byron, once offered to duplicate his experiments.

Faraday married Sarah Barnard in 1821. She was said to be a warm and cheerful person whose maternal feelings were pressed on her nieces and her husband, for the couple was childless. In religion Faraday was devout, belonging to the Sandemanians, a religious sect. His pious adherence to simplicity made it impossible for him to be buried at Westminster Abbey, near Newton and other great scientific figures. He died on August 25, 1867, at Hampton Court, in Middlesex, and was laid to rest in Highgate Cemetery.

12

James Clerk Maxwell
and the Electromagnetic Field

1831–1879

"The most significant event of the nineteenth century," writes RICHARD FEYNMAN [52], "will be judged as Maxwell's discovery of the laws of electrodynamics." Mathematical in content, these laws involve complex differential equations, but their importance is easy to grasp: They unify electricity and magnetism as a single, measurable force. In addition, they suggest—a fact obviously of enormous consequence—that light is part of this electromagnetic field and the visible portion of a much broader spectrum. For all this, as well as for his work on the dynamics of gases, James Clerk Maxwell most clearly prefigures twentieth-century physics. His research led directly to the technology associated with radio and television, and some of his work prefigures cybernetics. Maxwell is frequently ranked alongside Isaac Newton and Albert Einstein, and it would be difficult to overestimate his influence.

James Maxwell was born in Edinburgh, Scotland, on June 13, 1831, the only child of John Clerk Maxwell and Frances Kay. When his mother died of cancer in 1839, eight-year-old James was led to cry, "Oh, I'm so glad! Now she'll have no more pain." His father was laird, or landed proprietor, of an estate at Glenlair, Kircudbright, as well as a lawyer and a part-time inventor.

Maxwell's childhood was something of a model for a future scientist. He was close to his father, was endowed with an exceptional memory, and had a fascination with mechanical toys which he retained all his life. He won the math medal at Edinburgh Academy in 1841 and soon thereafter began accompanying his father to meetings of the Edinburgh Royal Society. His precocity was such that he was only fourteen when the Society published his paper on drawing ellipses using pins and thread. After attending the University of Edinburgh beginning in 1847, Maxwell entered Trinity College, Cambridge, three years later. He graduated in 1854 and returned to teach at Marischal College in Aberdeen, Scotland. In 1857 he studied the rings of Saturn, describing them in a way which was corroborated, over a century later, by the *Voyager* space probe.

In 1860 Maxwell returned to King's College in London, where he spent the most fruitful decade of his life. He formulated a theory of color in 1855, and in 1861 created the first color photograph—of the Scottish tartan ribbon. That year he was elected to the Royal Society. A decade later he organized the Cavendish Laboratory and became its first director.

Maxwell's work on electromagnetism derives from his predecessor MICHAEL FARADAY [11], and represents a quantification of it. Neither Faraday nor Lord Kelvin, Maxwell's contemporary, could easily visualize how electricity works unless they had a mechanical model of some sort. In Faraday's terms, for example, tubelike "lines of force" explain the apparent "action at a distance" in magnetic phenomena. Much as Isaac Newton had provided equations to explain the mechanics of moving bodies, however, Maxwell replaced a machine-like model with one which computed and predicted electrical phenomena. Electricity is no longer thought of as gadgetry that can be pictured in the mind.

As early as 1855 Maxwell had attempted to understand how

Faraday's ideas might be given mathematical form. Maxwell's famous account, "A Dynamical Theory of the Electromagnetic Field," was read before a largely perplexed Royal Society in 1864. Here he brought forth, for the first time, the equations which comprise the basic laws of electromagnetism. They show how an electric charge radiates waves through space at various definite frequencies that determine the charge's place in the electromagnetic spectrum. Maxwell was able to predict the existence of the entire electromagnetic spectrum—now understood to include radio waves, microwaves, infrared waves, ultraviolet waves, X rays, and gamma rays.

But, in addition, Maxwell's equations deliver their most profound consequence by giving the speed of electricity at about 300,000 km/sec—quite close to the experimentally derived speed of light.* "The velocity is so nearly that of light," wrote Maxwell, "that it seems we have strong reason to conclude that light itself...is an electromagnetic disturbance in the form of waves propagated through the electromagnetic field according to electromagnetic laws." The full significance of Maxwell's work, which was expanded as *Treatise on Electricity and Magnetism* in 1873, was not immediately grasped. This was largely because an understanding of the atomic nature of electromagnetism was not yet at hand.

During the 1860s Maxwell also took up the problem of quantifying the composition of gases and the physical properties of molecules. In general, Maxwell describes mathematically the movement of molecules in a gas at a given temperature. Maxwell first considered the problem in the 1850s while studying the rings of Saturn, and soon other physicists had developed the doctrines of the conservation of energy and entropy—the laws of thermodynamics. In addition, a mass of experimental material on the behavior of gases made possible further theoretical advances. In 1860 Maxwell hit upon the notion of using statistics to describe the way gas molecules behave. With his 1867 paper "On the Dynamical Theory of Gases" the properties of known gases were shown to correspond with those predicted by theory, and in 1870 Maxwell published his textbook *Theory of Heat*. The theory

---

*The speed of light had been first measured about 1676 by the Dane Olaus Roemer, with a remarkable estimate from the eclipses of Jupiter's moons. In 1862 Jean Foucault made more precise measurements and showed that light's speed slowed as it moved through water.

became a "cornerstone of the nineteenth century view of matter," writes Maxwell's biographer Ivan Tolstoy, adding, "One may say that where Maxwell's theory of electromagnetism gives a true measure of his genius, his work on molecular theory is a monument to his profound physical insight."

One final contribution of Maxwell's needs to be noted for its contemporary interest. His paper "On Governors" is one of the foundations of the theory of feedback established in the mid-twentieth century, most closely associated with Norbert Wiener. Indeed, Wiener's *cybernetics*—derived from the Greek word for steersman—is an allusion to Maxwell's term.

James Clerk Maxwell was married to Katherine Mary Dewar in 1858. The couple remained childless, and although biographers sometimes say that it was an exemplary union, his wife was not well liked by Maxwell's colleagues. She was said to be less good-humored than he, telling him at parties, "James, you're beginning to enjoy yourself; it is time we go home." Maxwell did not have the advantage of a long life. He died of the same disease, abdominal cancer, as his mother, on November 5, 1879, at the age of forty-eight.

At his death, Maxwell's reputation was uncertain. He was recognized to have been an exceptional scientist, but his theory of electromagnetism remained to be convincingly demonstrated. About 1880 HERMANN VON HELMHOLTZ [63], an admirer of Maxwell, discussed the possibility of confirming his equations with a student, Heinrich Hertz. In 1888 Hertz performed a series of experiments which produced and measured electromagnetic waves and showed how they behaved like light. Thereafter, Maxwell's reputation continued to grow, and with the Viennese LUDWIG BOLTZMANN [24], he may be said to have prepared the way for twentieth-century physics.

Claude Bernard
and the Founding of Modern Physiology

1813–1878

The founder of experimental medicine and a key figure in the history of physiology, Claude Bernard discovered, wrote one of his pupils, "as others breathe." The vital importance of the pancreas for digestion, how the liver regulates blood sugar, how the vasomotor nervous system contracts and expands blood vessels—all these discoveries, which lie at the foundation of modern medicine, owe first of all to Bernard. But in addition, and arguably his outstanding achievement, were the basic dictums of physiology which he derived from experimental data. Bernard grasped the nature of the organism as a self-regulating system and, in doing so, created a fruitful structure for medical research. Today's concepts of homeostasis, stress, and physiological feedback all touch on ideas first enunciated by Bernard, and he remains a figure of constant reference. "His philosophy," writes Nobel laureate Rosalyn S. Yalow, "provides the basis for interdisciplinary research which has become increasingly important in modern science as the boundaries between the various disciplines appear to merge."

Claude Bernard was born on July 12, 1813, near Saint-Julien, in the department of the Rhône, in the region of France known for Beaujolais wine. His father, Pierre François Bernard, was a winegrower and sometime schoolmaster, and his mother, whom he adored, was Jeanne Saulnier. Bernard attended a Jesuit-run school in Villefranche, near his home, and for a time was a student at the Collège de Thoissey, where he did not study science and was undistinguished academically. At age eighteen, Bernard was compelled to withdraw from school to help his financially strapped father, and he took a position as a pharmacist's apprentice. He came to wonder whether many of the medicines whose ingredients he mixed were of any use whatever, a first sign of the skepticism which he would subsequently exhibit, in matters pertaining to the body, throughout his life.

Following an unusual route to a scientific career, Bernard first became involved in the theater and, before he was twenty, had written a play, *The Rose of the Rhône*, which was produced in Lyons. Encouraged, he migrated to Paris, arriving in 1834. He showed his work to Saint Marc Girardin, a well-known critic, who advised him to seek another line of work. Bernard soon earned his baccalaureate and enrolled in the School of Medicine of the University of Paris.

Bernard did not excel in his medical studies; he graduated toward the bottom of his class, twenty-sixth out of twenty-nine. However, pivotal to his future were lectures he attended by François Magendie, a renowned physiologist and neurologist. Bernard immediately appreciated Magendie, who was a determined investigator highly skeptical of theory, and offered his services as an unpaid lab assistant. From this period onward Bernard's notebooks indicate the extent to which he questioned contemporary medical knowledge.

Bernard received his medical degree in 1843 but never practiced medicine. Like many later researchers, he had not the slightest interest in curing people of illness. In Bernard's case this proved to be an initial complication, because at this point in his career he was also unsuited to becoming an academic. Consequently, he remained as Magendie's assistant—he became exceptional at dissection—while undertaking research into the process of digestion and the functioning of the nervous system.

An early focus of Bernard's interest was the digestive process. In 1848 he showed that the pancreas digested fats, and he demonstrated that its absence led to death. Bernard took excellent practical advantage of William Beaumont's famous experiments upon Alexis St. Martin, a man whose digestion could be observed after a gunshot wound left a hole in his side and stomach. Using animals as subjects, Bernard created fistulas, or artificial passages, for purposes of observation—a method which, although it did not fail to anger nineteenth-century antivivisectionists, was highly useful. In this way, Bernard discovered that not only the pancreas but the small intestine was involved in digestion. In general, Bernard extended the work of LAVOISIER [8], who had recognized combustion in the process of respiration. Bernard was the first to consider digestion within the larger context of assimilation of nutrients through metabolism, viewing combustion as taking place throughout the body, in all tissue.

In 1848 Bernard discovered that the liver normally secretes glucose, a form of sugar, into the blood; and over the next decade he isolated glycogen, the stored form of glucose. These discoveries are generally considered his great achievements. "They had the greatest impact on his contemporaries," observes Joseph Fruton, "and on the later development of physiology and biochemistry." In the years 1855 and 1856 Bernard published the first edition of his two-volume *Leçons de physiologie expérimentale appliquée à la medicine.*

Bernard also made major discoveries concerning the nervous system. His description of the ear included an explanation of the cranial nerve, and he delineated the action of the vasomotor nervous system, which controls the expansion and contraction of the blood vessels. Other research into the nervous system brought him to experiment with toxic substances, showing how carbon monoxide and strychnine cause death. From this work emerged some understanding of the mechanism of curare, a poison which became important in anesthesia. For this work, Bernard is also known as a founder of experimental pharmacology.

About 1857 a new and mature phase of Bernard's career

began, in which he developed the general principles of physiology that undergird his discoveries. His *Introduction to the Study of Experimental Medicine* appeared in 1865, and two years later he published a tract that offered a unified theory of physiology based on the idea of the *milieu intérieur* (internal environment). Here Bernard makes the great generalization that the body, as a living organism, protects itself from the outer world by creating a stable inner environment regulated by the nervous system. Although he did not have the idea of chemical neurotransmitters nor was he aware of the endocrine system, Bernard's *milieu intérieur* prefigures homeostasis, as developed by Walter Cannon in the twentieth century. HANS SELYE [86], who developed the concept of stress, was also consciously in Bernard's debt; he wrote that it was Bernard who "clearly pointed out that the internal environment...of a living organism must remain fairly constant, despite changes in the external environment."

Later in life Bernard was showered with honors. He joined the Legion of Honor in 1867 and was elected a member of the Académie Française in 1869. In the same year he became a senator under Napoleon III, serving as a rubber stamp for the government's policies. As a consequence he was forced to flee Paris in 1870 during the Franco-Prussian War.

Claude Bernard's personal life was fairly disastrous. In order to continue his research, he made a marriage of convenience to a well-off woman, Marie Françoise Martin, in 1845. His two sons died in infancy, and his two daughters became estranged from him, as did their mother, in part on account of their disgust at his experiments with animals. At the end of his life he formed a platonic relationship with Marie Raffalovich, the wife of a Parisian banker, which provided him comfort and companionship in his last years. An agnostic, he was given last rites, against his wishes. When he died on February 10, 1878, he was the first French scientist to be given a state funeral.

14

Franz Boas
and Modern Anthropology

1858–1942

The founder of modern anthropology, and its outstanding figure to the mid-twentieth century, is Franz Boas. Immensely prolific over a career that spanned six decades, Boas put an end to anthropology as travelogue and developed a vision of a scientific enterprise operating with carefully collected data and broadly humanist aims. A consummate relativist and anti-authoritarian, his work stands as one of the basic statements of science on the issue of race. In addition, Boas's recognition of the importance of language to culture gives him relevance today in the developing cognitive sciences. Boas "was one of these nineteenth-century titans," writes CLAUDE LÉVI-STRAUSS [79], "whose output demanded respect not only for its quantity but for its diversity: physical anthropology, linguistics, ethnography, archaeology, mythology, folklore, nothing was foreign to him. His work covers the entirety of the anthropological domain. All of American anthropology issues from him."

Franz Boas was born on July 9, 1858, in Minden, Westphalia, then a province of Prussia and today a part of Germany. He was the only son of six children, three of whom survived to adulthood; his father was Meier Boas, a fairly prosperous merchant, and his mother, Sophie, née Meyer, was a socially active woman who founded the local Froebel-style Kindergarten. Raised in a liberal, freethinking Jewish household, Franz was a somewhat fragile and sickly child. Beginning in 1877 he attended the universities of Heidelberg, Bonn, and Kiel, from which he graduated in 1881 with a degree in physics. His dissertation, in the domain of "psychophysics," concerned a problem in color perception.

While a student, Boas recognized in himself a desire to travel and explore, not unlike his early nineteenth-century compatriot Alexander von Humboldt. In 1883, following army service, Boas undertook an expedition among the Eskimos on Baffin Island, in the Canadian Arctic. His original purpose was to develop improved maps of the region, but by the time he returned, the focus of his interest had greatly expanded to the culture as a whole. As he had earlier been attracted to the study of perception as "the intelligent understanding of a complex phenomenon," he wrote later, now he was interested in the behavior of people. "When from geography my interest was directed to ethnology," he wrote, "the same interest prevailed." Several years later, in 1888, he published *The Central Eskimos*.

A sojourn in New York following his Arctic voyage made a favorable impression on Boas; he found the freedom of intellectual life stimulating by contrast with German academia and not so restricted by anti-Semitism. As a consequence, in 1887, after a period spent teaching in Germany, he accepted a position to work for the magazine *Science*, for which he became a prolific journalist. For several years Boas combined popular scientific writing with his professional research.

During the 1890s Boas began to formulate the overall aims of his career, moving into academia to establish anthropology as a discipline. For four years, from 1888 to 1892, he held a teaching position at Clark University, and in 1894 he was appointed curator at the Field Museum in Chicago. He became assistant curator of the American Museum of Natural History in 1896 and curator in 1901. While there, he directed the ambitious Jessup North Pacific Expedition, which had as its overall goal an improved understanding of the relations between language, culture, custom, and race.

In 1899 Boas was appointed professor of anthropology at Columbia University, where he was to remain for the next thirty-eight years. From this post, he was able to exercise considerable influence in developing the scientific status of anthropology. Boas was intent on excluding self-styled amateurs just as, within the field, he opposed both scientism and "evolutionary" anthropology, which viewed European peoples as the end point and high point of civilization. And while Boas demanded quantifiable data, he recognized that anthropology would never meaningfully provide the sort of precision found in the physical sciences.

In 1888 Boas had begun what turned into a lifetime of fieldwork with Kwakiutl Indians of the North Pacific Coast—eventually, he made thirteen trips to study them in British Columbia. Although he never produced a definitive work on the ethnography of the Kwakiutl, he wrote about them extensively and developed an important model for anthropological research. According to Boas, primitive tribes ought to be studied in detail, with careful collection of artifacts and every aspect of culture, including history, language, customs, and physical environment. Boas advocated a comparative method, in addition, with studies of neighboring tribes for tracing the formation of cultural differences. This persistent and extensive accumulation of material was to be followed by the articulation of more general statements from which would emerge laws of cultural evolution. Boas was sometimes criticized for the vast amount of material which he gathered but did not analyze. Yet his insistence on detail had strong impact on his students, among them Margaret Mead, Ruth Benedict, and Ralph Linton.

In 1911 Boas published *The Mind of Primitive Man*, developed from a landmark series of lectures in which he attacked the notion of "inferior" races by pointing to the instability of features that were claimed to distinguish one race from another. "More than any other anthropologist," writes Marshall Hyatt, "[Boas] was responsible for a fundamental shift in science away from

The idea that the shape of the head bears some importance for temperament is very old. Franz Boas debunked it in the early twentieth century.

social Darwinism to support of equal rights. No longer could pseudo-scientists monopolize science to prove their theories of black inferiority. His reasoned assault on racism, and his defense of Afro-Americans, were characteristic of the nexus between Boas's social activism and his professional work."

Coincident with his study of American blacks, Boas made an investigation in the field of physical anthropology concerning the supposedly "smaller-brained races" which were immigrating from Europe to the United States amid opposition from nativists. Highly race conscious Americans had drawn science into the fray, and at the request of the United States Immigration Commission, Boas studied families of European immigrants. Employing common tools used by scientists of the period to measure supposed differences among races, Boas found among immigrant groups considerable plasticity, which changed physically within a generation of migration. Boas measured the cranium, for example, finding that immigrants with long heads produced children with shorter heads after arriving in the United States. Although none of Boas's measurements showed great differences among races in the first place, he could say that "not even those characteristics of a race which have proved to be most permanent in their old home remain the same under new surroundings." His report, *Changes in Bodily Form of Descendants of Immigrants*, was published by the U.S. government in 1911.

Anthropology became a diverse field even during Boas's lifetime, and numerous other methodologies and enterprises have since competed for attention. But Boas's general influence, and his role in developing anthropology as a scientific discourse, are perhaps most evident today in his emphasis on linguistic analysis. His *Handbook of American Indian Languages* was first published in 1911, and his views were exceptionally fruitful; Leonard Bloomfield credits him with forging "almost single-handed, the tools of phonetic and structural description." Boas "marked a transformation," according to George W. Stocking, "in the framework of American linguistics methods and assumptions, and the starting point of the modern tradition in descriptive linguistics."

Boas's life and career were not without conflict. Kind and personable, he was married to Mari Krackowizer, with whom he had six children, two of whom died before reaching adulthood. Mari herself was killed in an automobile accident in 1929. During World War I Boas's reputation was damaged when he refused to support the entry of the United States into the war. He lost the presidency of the American Anthropological Association as a consequence, and for a time was expelled as a member, later to be reinstated.

On December 21, 1942, Boas attended a luncheon at the Columbia Faculty Club for Paul Rivet, a French anthropologist who had fled Nazi-occupied France. The guests included Ruth Benedict and Ralph Linton. Claude Lévi-Strauss, who also attended, remembered that Boas arrived wearing "an old fur hat that must have dated from his expeditions among the Eskimos sixty years earlier." In the midst of a pleasant discussion, Franz Boas came to a sudden end. He pushed himself away from the table and died.

15

Werner Heisenberg
and Quantum Theory

1901–1976

In the mid-1920s physicists abandoned efforts to visualize the atom while, using quantum numbers, their mathematical models became highly successful. In 1925 Werner Heisenberg became one of the main architects of a new quantum theory and two years later proposed the "uncertainty principle," which sets limits upon all efforts to measure subatomic particles. With NIELS BOHR [3], during the 1930s Heisenberg became one of the main exponents of what came to be known as the "Copenhagen doctrine" of quantum theory, gaining for it the full measure of acceptance which largely abides today. During the Nazi era Heisenberg did not join the exodus to the United States but chose to remain in

Germany. There, during World War II, he worked on fission research, the ultimate purpose of which has been a source of considerable debate in recent years. "Werner Heisenberg, born at the dawn of the twentieth century," writes his biographer David Cassidy, "became one of its greatest physicists. He is also among its most controversial."

Werner Heisenberg was born on December 5, 1901, in Würzburg, Germany, to August Heisenberg, a professor of Byzantine studies at the University of Munich, and Anna Wecklein Heisenberg. As a youth, Werner had a close relationship with his mother, and he developed an outwardly tranquil but inwardly driven disposition which both contrasted with and reflected his father's strong personality and academic ambitions. In September 1911, Werner entered the Maximilians-Gymnasium—a prestigious institution directed by his maternal grandfather—from which he graduated nine years later. He participated in the German youth movement after World War I and actively supported suppression of the Communist-led worker's revolt in Bavaria in 1919. Thereafter, in general, Heisenberg attempted, with dubious results, to remain aloof from political involvement.

Heisenberg came to physics at a propitious time, entering the University of Munich in 1920. In 1922, the year he began to study with MAX BORN [32], Heisenberg met Niels Bohr at the University of Göttingen. The two men took a walk over the Hain mountain, and Bohr said afterward of Heisenberg, "He understands everything." Heisenberg took his Ph.D. from Munich in 1923 and the next year went to Copenhagen to continue his work at Bohr's Institute for Physics. In 1925 Heisenberg developed matrix mechanics—a discovery considered a key turning point in modern physics.

By the early 1920s serious problems had developed with the new Rutherford-Bohr model of the atom; in spite of its success, it could not account for a variety of experimental phenomena. In 1924 Heisenberg began considering the possibility of a theory in which measurable and observable quantities, such as light intensity and frequency, would be the only variables. Just as ALBERT EINSTEIN [2] had decided to treat as fictions the infinities implicit in Newtonian laws, so Heisenberg forced the admission that electrons could not be individually measured with certainty. "They adhered," writes David Cassidy of Heisenberg and his colleagues "to such essentials as the existence of quantum jumps and discontinuities within atoms and rejected the idea of *an-schaulich*, or visualizable, atomic models."

Soon after Heisenberg developed matrix mechanics—so called because it used matrix algebra to describe the electron—the Austrian physicist ERWIN SCHRÖDINGER [18] proposed another model, called wave mechanics. At first there was no ready agreement about which theory was correct. They were later shown to be mathematically equivalent in spite of the fact that one theory characterizes the electron as a particle, the other as a wave. Heisenberg interpreted this apparent contradiction with a famous paper published in 1927. In "On the Intuitive Content of Quantum Kinematics and Mechanics," he proposed the concept that became closely associated with his name: the "uncertainty principle." This states simply that it is not possible to calculate with perfect accuracy both the position and momentum of a subatomic particle. Effectively, the more certainty with which a subatomic particle's speed is measured, the less accuracy can be assigned to its position. The uncertainty principle gave full weight to an idea that had been known to physics for several years: namely, that ordinary language cannot describe the atom. The atom can only be measured, and into these measurements is built inherent uncertainty due to the limitations of human perception.

In the years that followed, Heisenberg became a major proponent of this new "Copenhagen interpretation" of quantum mechanics. Together with Niels Bohr and others, he became tremendously influential both in Europe and in the United States, which he visited in 1929, delivering an important series of lectures at the University of Chicago. From 1927 to 1941 Heisenberg was professor of physics at the University of Leipzig, where he worked with Wolfgang Pauli and others to develop quantum electrodynamics and quantum field theory, laying the groundwork for research into nuclear and high-energy physics. Together with Erwin Schrödinger and PAUL DIRAC [20], he was awarded the Nobel Prize, for the year 1932, in 1933.

Heisenberg's unwillingness to leave Germany under Hitler, and his work on the potential of nuclear energy during World War II, have received a good deal of scrutiny over the years. His political decisions reflected both his patriotism and belief, common among non-Nazi Germans, that Hitler would emerge victorious from World War II. Heisenberg himself was attacked on ideological grounds by Hitler's SS in 1937, but he was exonerated by the organization's leader, Heinrich Himmler. According to Heisenberg's wife, Elisabeth Schumacher, Heisenberg saw politics as a "game of chess, in which the feelings and passions of people are subordinated to the charted course of political events, just as the chess figures to the rules of the game." He refused to leave Germany for good when he had the opportunity during a 1939 lecture trip to the United States; instead, he returned to Germany to purchase a country retreat and decided to "do my bit as best I personally could."

In 1942 Heisenberg was appointed director of the Kaiser Wilhelm Institute for Physics in Berlin. He worked on nuclear fission and directed Hitler's uranium project. Although it has been suggested that Heisenberg may have deliberately helped forestall Germany's development of an atom bomb, the issue is far from clear. In a 1941 visit with Niels Bohr, not long before the latter fled to the United States, Heisenberg discussed nuclear reactions and may have drawn a picture of a reactor. Heisenberg's intentions—whether as a warning, a boast, or an avowal of peaceful intentions—remain unclear to this day.

At the end of World War II, Heisenberg was arrested by the Allies and was interned with other German scientists for about six months in England. In 1946 he was allowed to return to Germany, where he was named director of the Kaiser Wilhelm Institute for Physics in Göttingen, later known as the Max Planck Institute. Heisenberg, quite young when he made his great discoveries, had a long postwar career. As a public scientist, he headed the German delegation to the European Council for Nuclear Research and was deeply involved in issues of science policy. He wrote several books, including *The Physicist's Conception of Nature*, and an autobiography, *Physics and Beyond*. In 1970 he resigned his position at the Max Planck Institute. Six years later, on February 1, 1976, he died of cancer. His death occasioned, on the part of colleagues and friends, a candlelight procession to the door of his home.

In old age, Heisenberg became disenchanted with particle physics, believing that there was a conceptual problem with the notion of elementary particles such as quarks, and he worked on a version of a unified field theory. "We will have to abandon the philosophy of Democritus and the concept of fundamental elementary particles," he wrote in *Tradition in Science*. "And we should accept instead the concept of fundamental symmetries, which is a concept derived from the philosophy of Plato." Indeed, at the end of his life he returned to the Platonism he had learned as a youth, the fused legacy of his family and education.

16

Linus Pauling
and Twentieth-Century Chemistry

1901–1994

The specific qualities and interactions of the multitude of chemical substances—both organic and inorganic, natural and synthetic—were described but never adequately explained by nineteenth-century chemistry. What accounts for such palpable differences among things (hard and soft, sweet and sour, for instance), not to mention the myriad of chemical reactions that occur among a handful of elements? Well into the twentieth century, chemical theory was more or less mute. But by the 1930s, deriving new methods of analysis from the mature theory of quantum mechanics, a new picture of the chemical bond began to emerge. It culminated not only in a new facility to analyze properties of the elements and predict chemical reactions but has vast and ongoing consequences in molecular biology and the biochemical interpretation of life. The first major figure in this transformation was an American, Linus Pauling.

Linus Pauling was born on February 28, 1901, in Oswego, Oregon, the son of Lucy Isabelle Darling Pauling and Herman William Pauling. The Paulings were an unusual family; Linus had an aunt, Stella "Fingers" Darling, who was a well-known safecracker, and another of his relatives was a spiritualist. Herman Pauling, a pharmacist (he once advertised "Pauling's Pink Pills for Pale People") died at a young age from a gastric ulcer; this was in 1910, soon after he had written a letter to a local newspaper asking how to encourage his son's exceptional intellectual talents. After her husband's death, Belle Pauling ran a rooming house in the small, one-horse town of Condon, Oregon. Linus, who had not been interested in chemistry while his father was alive, at age twelve began conducting experiments with chemicals appropriated from an abandoned smelting operation.

Although Pauling left high school in 1917 without a diploma—the degree was awarded to him in 1962, after he won his second Nobel Prize—he was able to enroll in Oregon Agricultural College, where he studied chemical engineering. His college education was notably self-willed, for his mother would have preferred that he work to provide financial help to the family. After receiving his bachelor's degree in 1922, Pauling began graduate studies at the California Institute of Technology, which happened to have an extraordinary chemistry department and whose president was Robert Millikan, the eminent physicist whose simple "oil drop" experiment first calculated the charge on an electron. At Caltech, Pauling's major area of interest was physical chemistry, and he soon came under the influence of Roscoe Dickinson, who was developing a way of using X-ray diffraction, discovered a decade earlier by MAX VON LAUE [56], to study the composition of complex crystals. In collaboration with Dickinson, Pauling described the structure of molybdenite, a mineral, and went on to publish a number of papers. Pauling received his doctorate summa cum laude in 1925.

The advent of a new quantum theory in the mid-1920s provided a better understanding of the atom and set the stage for new perspectives in chemistry as well. Pauling went to Europe in 1926, spending time in Munich with Arnold Sommerfeld, whom he had met two years earlier, and also meeting ERWIN SCHRÖDINGER [18] in Zurich, NIELS BOHR [3] in Copenhagen, and WERNER HEISENBERG [15] and MAX BORN [32] in Göttingen. Pauling's acquaintance with the major figures of quantum mechanics was emblematic of the new links being forged between chemistry and physics. When he returned to Caltech in 1927, he was one of the few chemists alive with a good grasp of quantum theory. He became a full professor at Caltech in 1931, and he also taught at the University of California, Berkeley, from 1929 to 1934.

In 1928, moving beyond his early work on crystals, Pauling brought quantum theory to bear on the chemical bond. He showed how the specific properties of various atoms are related to their electrons as interpreted by wave mechanics. Pauling developed a series of rules that systematically laid out the formation of chemical bonds. Generalizing from their mathematical form, the rules relate to the pairing and spin of electrons and to where these may be found in the atom's orbitals.* The interaction of orbitals determines physical relationships and, on a large scale, the various qualities associated with chemicals. "If one wished to wax poetic," write Ted and Ben Goertzel in their lucid biography of Pauling, "one might say that atoms reach out to each other, distorting the quantum wave functions of their electrons in precisely the most effective way to "grab" each other. In this way atoms join together to make molecules, the basic elements of matter."

In 1931 Pauling's most influential and significant paper, "The Nature of the Chemical Bond," was published in the *Journal of the American Chemical Society.* The paper proved to be the first in a series of seven classic papers published in the early 1930s. Pauling's achievement did not go unnoticed; he became renowned for his work in scientific circles and was celebrated in the media as a rising young American scientist and potential Nobel Prize winner. Pauling was equal to this attention, for he was an excellent speaker who went out of his way to explain his theories and findings, providing exceptional context and imagery leavened with humor. In 1931, delivering a lecture after his reception of the Langmuir Prize, he continued speaking with scarcely a

---

*Orbitals represent the region where electrons may be found around the atomic nucleus, derived from the original concept of electrons in fixed orbits. Orbits are Newtonian: orbitals are quantum wave mechanical.

pause when, by chance, the electricity failed and the hall went dark. In 1939 Pauling published the first edition of *The Nature of the Chemical Bond*, one of the twentieth century's most significant works in chemistry.

"By 1935," wrote Pauling, "...I felt I had an essentially complete understanding of the nature of the atomic bond." Thereafter, he broadened his horizon to include the study of more complex, organic molecules. He had become interested in biology as early as 1929 when geneticist THOMAS HUNT MORGAN [62] arrived at Caltech; Pauling became aware of the importance of chemistry for understanding life processes.

Pauling's biochemical research had repercussions in several specific areas, including medicine. His earliest studies involved attempts to unravel the structure of hemoglobin, a protein that transports oxygen in the blood and is responsible for its red color. He was not initially successful but was led, some years later—in a burst of insight while having dinner at the Century Club in New York City—to discover the chemical basis of sickle-cell anemia. As a consequence, it was soon confirmed that this blood disease had a molecular basis, was transmitted by Mendel's laws of inheritance, and was a genetic adaptation to protect against malaria, which explains its prevalence in blacks.

Pauling's discovery of the chemistry of sickle-cell anemia was a landmark in biogenetics; it also led him to study serological reactions in more detail and to investigate the structure of antibodies and their relationship to invading antigens. Inspired and encouraged by KARL LANDSTEINER [81], the most prominent researcher in immunology at the time, Pauling developed an influential theory, although not finally correct, of antibody-antigen interaction, and he was involved in producing the first synthetic antibodies in 1942.

But Pauling's most influential accomplishments in biochemistry were his studies of proteins and amino acids, which laid much of the groundwork for further advances in molecular biology. Proteins are ubiquitous in the biological microworld and, since early in the twentieth century, were believed to be the key to understanding living systems; but by sheer numbers and complexity, they long resisted analysis. In addition to using conventional techniques, Pauling adopted what became a famous method of building scale models of molecules while gathering clues from X-ray diffraction studies. Pauling's work began in

1937, and by the late 1940s he was ready to throw overboard the notion that the large molecules would obey some variety of symmetry in their repeated connections. Rather, Pauling realized—through a leap of scientific imagination—that a helical shape represented "the *general* relation between two asymmetric but equivalent objects in space." Long molecules tend to this shape, and with Robert Corey, Pauling published a key paper on helical structures in 1950.

The structure of DNA, the long thin double-helical molecule which encodes genetic information and directs the synthesis of proteins, is the most famous breakthrough to emerge from Pauling's insight. Indeed, it is conceivable that Pauling himself might have made the discovery but for the meddling of the U.S. government. Although he was working on the problem, Pauling did not have access to new, high quality X-ray diffraction photographs taken by Maurice Wilkins at King's College, Cambridge. He planned to view them during a trip to England in 1952. However, because of Pauling's liberal political views, the U.S. State Department, acting on the advice of the House Un-American Activities Committee, declined to renew his passport. As a consequence, Pauling remained in the United States. In early 1953 he published a paper that described a triple helix model for the DNA molecule—which was mistaken. Two months later an explanation of the correct double-helical structure was announced by JAMES WATSON [49] and FRANCES CRICK [33].

The later career of Linus Pauling was distinguished in great part by his political activism. During the 1930s he had been a supporter of Upton Sinclair's remarkable, though failed, socialist campaign to become governor of California. After World War II, Pauling became a strong opponent of cold war politics and an influential advocate of a nuclear test-ban treaty. He was investigated as a left-wing radical during the 1950s: The American Legion described him as one of the "abettors of the Communist line," and when he won the Nobel Prize for peace in 1963 the *New York Herald Tribune* called him a "placating peacenik." During the Vietnam War, Pauling generally supported New Left politics and he became one of its spokespersons, but by no means was he a political thinker.

Caltech's scant notice of Pauling's second Nobel prize led him to move to the Center for the Study of Democratic Institutions in 1963. In 1967 he joined the University of California at San

Diego, and from 1969 to 1974, when he retired, he worked at Stanford University.

In the last quarter century of his life, from about 1966, Pauling became involved in an effort to demonstrate the importance of Vitamin C in avoiding the common cold and many other diseases, from herpes to cancer. He could not provide convincing evidence of the efficacy of the megadoses which he and his wife, Ava Helen, took each morning, apart, perhaps, from his own longevity. With a Christian fundamentalist, Arthur Robinson, Pauling founded the Institute of Orthomolecular Medicine in 1974, which is currently the Linus Pauling Institute of Science and Medicine in Palo Alto, California.

Pauling's personal life was outwardly calm but not without internal conflict. He was wed to Ava Helen Miller, one of his students, in 1922, and they had three sons and a daughter in the course of a long and happy marriage. Although an atheist, he and his wife joined the Unitarian church because, he said, it "accepts as members people who believe in trying to make the world a better place." Pauling's participation in two studies of scientists using Rorschach methods for assessing personality revealed his own narcissistic tendencies, strong ambition, and considerable imagination as well as feelings of emptiness. Pauling would seem to have needed to withhold his emotions and employed a good deal of effort to control them. He himself felt he had been less than excellent as a father. Of his four children, he was closest to his daughter, Linda Pauling Kamb.

In his last years, Pauling was widely admired. His appearance on a national talk show after his wife's death brought numerous solicitous letters from women. In 1990 he was diagnosed with prostate cancer, which later spread to the intestines. Linus Pauling had never claimed that his ten daily grams of Vitamin C would confer immortality. He died on August 19, 1994.

17

Rudolf Virchow
and the Cell Doctrine

1821–1902

Until the mid-nineteenth century, *cells* in the European mind were mainly the sparce domiciles of monks. When Robert Hooke observed "a great many little Boxes" in slices of cork in 1665 through his compound microscope, he compared them to honeycomb and chose a name connoting an empty enclosed space. The teeming interior of the cell and its fundamental role in living organisms remained unguessed for the next two hundred years. Only in 1838 and 1839, with improved optics and theories advanced by botanist Matthias Schleiden and zoologist Theodor Schwann, came suggestions of its broader significance. But the genius of cell theory is the German physician and anatomist Rudolf Virchow, the founder of cellular pathology.

One of the most famous physicians of his time, Virchow achieved great influence through his capacity, not unlike Pasteur's, to attack problems of fundamental importance, derive a general theory from experimental data, and fight for its acceptance. Virchow was a politically involved scientist and radical politician who believed that physicians ought to be "the natural attorneys of the poor," and at his death, writes his biographer, Erwin H. Ackerknecht, "Germany would complain of having lost four great men at once: her leading pathologist, her leading anthropologist, her leading sanitarian, and her leading liberal."

Rudolf Ludwig Carl Virchow was born on October 13, 1821, in the town of Schivelbein, today a part of Poland but then in the Prussian province of Pomerania, on the Baltic Sea. His father, Carl Christian Siegfred Virchow, was a farmer, unsuccessful businessman, and the town treasurer, and his mother was Johanna Maria Hesse Virchow. Leaving home to attend a gymnasium at age fourteen, Rudolf excelled academically, developing a lust for learning and aiming to possess an "all-embracing knowledge of nature from the Deity down to the stone." In 1838 he won a scholarship to study medicine at the Friedrich-Wilhelms Institute in Berlin, where he was inspired by Johannes Peter Müller, whose works on physiology were making important new advances in microscopic and pathological anatomy. Virchow received his medical degree in 1843.

Virchow became an intern at Berlin's Charité Hospital, a site of considerable intellectual ferment in medicine. Initially he served as prosector of pathology, performing dissections for anatomical demonstrations. In 1847 he became a *Privatdozent*, which enabled him to teach; and in the meantime he had begun his first research.

Virchow's early work concerned phlebitis, the inflammatory disease of the veins, which was then thought to play a causal role in pathology. Analyzing fibrin, the chief protein in blood clots, Virchow showed its importance to coagulation, and he coined the terms *embolism* and *thrombosis*. He demonstrated that clots which caused phlebitis were not local causes of inflammation but only packages of degenerated cells transported from other sites. Similarly, he showed that pus was made up of white blood cells. Virchow's observations on the formation of leukocytes led him to describe the disease of leukemia.

By no means immune from the social unrest characteristic of

the 1840s, Virchow became politically engaged after investigating a typhus epidemic in Upper Silesia, home to an oppressed Polish minority in Prussia. As part of a commission formed by the government following revelations in the press, Virchow traveled to the region and issued a report which found that the fundamental causes of the epidemic were social. This was the first of Virchow's political thrusts, and he prescribed for the epidemic "democracy, education, freedom, and prosperity." He asked rhetorically a question that resonates no less clearly today than in the nineteenth century: "Are the triumphs of human genius to lead only to this, that the human race shall become more miserable?"

In Berlin for the 1848 revolution, Virchow was an activist—albeit ineffective, he confessed, on the barricades—and moved to reform the German medical establishment. He published a radical weekly journal, *Die Medizenische Reform*, in which he promulgated the view that physicians have a duty to serve the poor. He was also elected to the Prussian Diet but was not allowed to serve because of his youth. For his abrasive antiroyalist as well as agnostic views, Virchow was made to suffer in the subsequent period of political reaction; his meager salary was cut off and he was effectively dismissed from Charité. He was also compelled to leave Berlin—and when he returned to be married, in 1849, local authorities saw to it that he left town as soon as the ceremony was over. But Virchow's reputation was already made, and at the University of Würzburg he was named to a chair of pathological anatomy.

Indeed, by 1847, with his establishment of an important journal, *Archiv für pathologische Anatomie und Physiologie*, Virchow had become the major force in Germany—as CLAUDE BERNARD [13] was in France—behind the new primacy of experimental physiology in medicine. "Experiment," he wrote, "is the ultimate court of the science of pathologic physiology." He established the study of normal structures as key to understanding pathological ones, performed systematic research, and published numerous monographs. It was during the early 1850s that he developed the cell doctrine and the fundamental principles of cellular pathology.

Although Theodor Schwann had developed an important cell theory in 1839, it was incomplete, and Virchow corrected and extended it both conceptually and in a great number of details. He demonstrated that muscle and bone are comprised of cells just as as tissue is, and he made a number of anatomical discoveries. He showed the presence of connective tissue intermingled with nerve cells in the spinal cord and brain; and he also developed a basic classification of cellular tissue.

As early as 1845 Virchow called the cell the fundamental unit of life, and in 1852 he hypothesized the process of cell division to account for reproduction, rejecting Schwann's notion of a generative substance called blastema. Famously, Virchow formulated what came to be known as the cell doctrine: *Omnis cellula e cellula* (Every cell arises from another cell). Virchow understood that chemical processes were at work within cells, and he recognized the importance of the nucleus. "Development cannot cease to be continuous," he wrote, "because no particular generation can start a fresh series of developments. We must reduce all tissues to a single simple element, the cell." Recognizing the cell as the basic unit of life, he wrote that it is "the ultimate irreducible form of every living element, and...from it emanate all the activities of life both in health and in sickness."

In 1856 Virchow was lured back to Berlin, and it is a measure of his prestige that he could assure, as a condition for his return, the construction of a new Pathological Institute, of which he became director. His highly influential *Cellular-pathologie*, drawn from a series of lectures he gave at the Institute, was published in 1858 and translated into English within two years. "What Virchow accomplished in *Cellular Pathology*," writes physician and author Sherwin Nuland, "was nothing less than to enunciate the principles upon which medical research would be based for the next hundred years and more." With the cellular hypothesis, Virchow expanded the research horizons of biochemistry and physiology and had great influence in the broader field of biology, where the cell doctrine eventually evolved into molecular biology as genetics evolved and reproduction became better understood. "It is too often overlooked," comments Elof A. Carlson, "that the cell doctrine came into being at about the same time (1858) as Darwin's *Origin of Species* (1859)."*

It has not escaped the notice of historians that Virchow's development of the cell theory might bear some relation to his political stance. The physician in favor of "unrestricted democracy" was the same one who developed a theory of cells which, as

---

*In this regard it is ironic to note that Virchow had two notable scientific misses. Focused on cellular pathology, he did not accept the germ theory of disease as proposed by LOUIS PASTEUR [5]. And while not rejecting the theory of evolution, he was suspicious of it.

Erwin Ackerknecht wrote, "showed the body to be a free state of equal individuals, a federation of cells, a democratic cell state." Virchow remained politically active throughout his life. He was elected to the Prussian parliament in 1862, where he became a leader of the opposition. One of his political enemies, Otto Bismarck, challenged him to a duel in 1865, which Virchow refused with sarcastic derision. Elected to the Reichstag in 1880, where he remained until 1893, Virchow also came into conflict with the anti-Semitic Christian Social Party. Although Virchow did not succeed either in stemming Bismarck's rise or the disastrous consequences of German patriotism, he was an effective civic leader, helping bring to Berlin decent sewage and drainage systems and a potable water supply.

One of the outgrowths of Virchow's political thought as he grew older was his interest in archaeology and the new science of physical anthropology, which dominated his activity after 1870. Firmly opposed to the increasingly popular notion of racial superiority, he undertook a census of schoolchildren which invalidated the claims of a single German race. He excavated skulls in his native Pomerania and accompanied Heinrich Schliemann to the ruins of Troy in 1878. He showed, in effect, that great civilizations had flourished while primitive German tribes were still living in caves. In an appreciation, FRANZ BOAS [14] wrote, "Physical anthropology and prehistoric archaeology in Germany have become what they are largely through Virchow's influence and activity."

Not surprisingly, but unlike other great German scientists of the nineteenth century, Virchow refused the title of nobility and the addition of *von* to his name. Although he rejected communism, Virchow was a revolutionary left-wing socialist throughout his life. "Our society," he wrote, "like blind Oedipus, stumbles deeper and deeper into its regrettable darkness, and in producing and strengthening its enemies and pushing them eventually towards extreme measures, that again are insane, it creates its own destruction. Thus it fulfills the prophecy of the oracle."

Fully cognizant of his importance to medicine, and an activist in the full sense of the term, Virchow lectured widely on general problems of science and of politics and was by the end of his life showered with honors of every kind. He died, following complications from a fall from a tram which broke his femur, on September 5, 1902.

Erwin Schrödinger
and Wave Mechanics
1887–1961

Erwin Schrödinger has had a signal importance for both twentieth-century physics and biology. During the 1920s he created one of the two separate but equal equations describing the electron's behavior around the atomic nucleus. The first was Heisenberg's matrix mechanics; the second was Schrödinger's wave equation, which MAX BORN [32] described as one of the "most sublime" in all physics. In addition, like NIELS BOHR [3], Schrödinger was deeply interested in the philosophical implications of the new advances in theoretical physics. He was the author of *What Is Life?* a brief book but arguably one of the most influential in the twentieth century, for it encouraged a number of physicists to study the basic mechanisms of biology. "Everybody read Schrödinger," writes Horace Freeland Judson. "The fascination lay in the clarity with which Schrödinger approached the gene not as an algebraic unit but as a physical substance that had to be almost perfectly stable and yet express immense variety."

Erwin Schrödinger was born in Vienna on August 12, 1887, the only child of Rudolf Schrödinger and his wife, Georgine. Adored by his mother, pampered by an aunt, and strongly influenced by his father, Schrödinger had a virtually ideal upper middle-class childhood. Proprietor of a linoleum business, Rudolf Schrödinger was also an amateur botanist, published articles on plant genetics, and cultivated an interest in Italian painting; he became to his son "friend, teacher, and tireless partner in conversation." After private tutoring to age eleven, Erwin attended the famous humanities-oriented Akademisches Gymnasium, beginning in 1898. Here he received a classical and secular education, studying literature and philosophy. Schrödinger's maternal aunt Minnie was from Britain, and so he also learned fluent English in addition to French, Spanish, and classical Greek and Latin. While on quiet walks to Innsbruck, his mother forced him to practice his English, telling him, "Now we are going to speak English to each other the whole way—not another word of German." Although reluctant, Schrödinger "only realized later how much I profited from it to this day."

Entering the university in 1906, a year after Albert Einstein [2] had published his famous series of papers, Schrödinger soon began to study physics in earnest. He received his doctorate from the University of Vienna in 1910 and remained there to teach. During World War I he served as an artillery officer, earning citations for bravery. Like many of his generation, Schrödinger was strongly affected by the war and so developed an interest in philosophical studies, including Indian philosophy. In 1925 he wrote a reprise of his personal convictions entitled *My World View*. It is clear that Schrödinger was at once spiritually inclined and antireligious, unconventional, and influenced by Arthur Schopenhauer, the nineteenth-century German pessimist. And perhaps more than any of the great scientists save SIGMUND FREUD [6] and ALFRED KINSEY [96], Schrödinger also nurtured a considerable interest in sexual experience, which he conceived as a means of attaining transcendence.

In 1921 Schrödinger took an academic post in Zurich, where he continued early work on the statistical mechanics of gases, the theory of color, and atomic theory. He also kept abreast of advances in quantum theory, which had accumulated important problems and inconsistencies since Niels Bohr had begun to apply it, in 1913, to the behavior of electrons. A major advance came, as it turned out, in 1924, when LOUIS VICTOR DE BROGLIE [75] suggested that, just as Einstein had shown that light waves behave as particles, under certain conditions subatomic particles might behave like waves. This was an important impetus to Schrödinger, who was inspired by a seminar he gave on de Broglie. By the mid-1920s Schrödinger was poised to make his own major contribution to quantum theory.

Schrödinger's wave equation was invented during the Christmas holidays in 1925, and it is interesting to record the emotional context: Schrödinger's wife was having an affair, and to console himself he had a liaison of his own with an old friend—whose identity remains a mystery—at a skiing resort in the Swiss Alps. There he conceived the rudiments of a formula which he knew, once solved, would be "very beautiful," and he began a yearlong quest which culminated in one of the most important differential equations in the history of mathematical physics.

Schrödinger effectively cast de Broglie's hypothesis into a mathematical formula, viewing an electron not as a *point* at various locations around the nucleus of an atom but as a *standing wave* which washes around and about the nucleus at definite energy levels. His series of six papers explaining the concept of wave mechanics was published in 1926, and its importance was immediately recognized. "The power of Schrödinger's wave mechanics was awesome," writes historian of science David Cassidy, "its advantages obvious, its profound importance loudly proclaimed."

Approximately at the same time as Schrödinger developed the wave equation, WERNER HEISENBERG [15] had developed matrix mechanics, which also describes the behavior of subatomic particles. To overcome problems associated with "quantum leaps," this formula pictured the electron as an array, or matrix, of numbers. With respect to Schrödinger's equation it was somewhat more unwieldy to use. However, matrix mechanics and Schrödinger's wave theory of matter are mathematically equivalent, as was soon shown—by PAUL DIRAC [20], among others. And MAX BORN [32] suggested probability as an explanation for the electron's apparent wavelike behavior. A new and durable quantum theory had come to life.

Unlike Niels Bohr, who already believed that subatomic particles could not be entirely described, Schrödinger at first thought that his theory might lead to a complete explanation of the atom. Like Einstein, he continued to hope for a unified theory in which the ordinary concept of causation was not abandoned in favor of statistics. Soon after his theory of wave mechanics was published, he visited Bohr in Copenhagen and held a long series of personal discussions on the philosophical implications of quantum theory. He told Bohr that, if the notion of quantum leaps were necessary, "I should be sorry that I ever got involved with quantum theory."

Bohr replied, "But the rest of us are extremely grateful that you did; your wave mechanics has contributed so much to mathematical clarity and simplicity that it represents gigantic progress over all previous forms of quantum mechanics."

In 1927, Schrödinger moved to the University of Berlin, where he was chosen to succeed to the prestigious chair of theoretical physics vacated by the retiring MAX PLANCK [25]. In 1933, with the rise of Nazism, Schrödinger became one of the first scientists to leave Germany, but his antifascism was passive and his exile not due to any active opposition to Hitler's becoming chancellor. Later that year, Schrödinger won the Nobel Prize in Physics, which he shared with the English physicist Paul Dirac. In 1936, after three years at Magdalen College, Oxford, Schrödinger returned to Austria to teach at the University of Graz. Soon the *Anschluss* of 1938 led to serious consequences for Schrödinger, who came under Nazi surveillance. He eventually wrote a "confession"—for which he was severely criticized by colleagues and which he later regretted—supporting "the will of the Führer." This did not appease the Nazis, however, and Schrödinger was dismissed from his post. Belatedly convinced that he could not remain in Austria, Schrödinger and his wife fled the country with ten marks in their pockets. After a brief period in Italy and the United States, he was invited to Dublin's School of Theoretical Physics, recently founded by the Irish political leader Eamon de Valera. Here Schrödinger remained until 1956.

Inspired to some extent by the later philosophical work of the astronomer ARTHUR EDDINGTON [37], Schrödinger had what

C. W. Kilmster has called "a second flowering of his genius" beginning about 1935. At Dublin he wrote *What Is Life?*, in which he provided a possible explanation of cellular function according to the laws of thermodynamics. Schrödinger viewed the genes as controlling the entropy, or disorder, which builds up in any system, and he took the view that the basis of life could therefore be fully understood through its chemical and physical properties. *What is Life?*, writes Roger Penrose, "represents a powerful attempt to comprehend some of the genuine mysteries of life" and is "among the most influential of scientific writings in this century." Although wrong in important respects, it was an influence upon both FRANCIS CRICK [33] and JAMES WATSON [49], and thus an intellectual component in the discovery of the function of the DNA molecule.

After World War II, Schrödinger was inclined to return to Austria and finally repatriated in 1956, when he accepted a position at the University of Vienna. He soon became ill, however, and in his last years did little work. He had a notable personality: highly cultured, articulate, nonconformist, and somewhat rakish.* In 1920 Schrödinger had married Annemarie Berthel, a considerate woman whom he treated like a domestic, according to his biographer, Walter Moore. Although sexually incompatible, they remained together, each conducting affairs in the interwar atmosphere of enlightened Zurich. Erwin Schrödinger died on January 4, 1961 and is buried in the village of Alpach.

Schrödinger is one scientist whose work lends itself to fascinating speculation about where exactly he belongs among others in terms of influence. It may be remembered that Schrödinger's wave theory was developed with the express intention of avoiding "quantum jumps" (which were inevitable), and he remained philosophically attached to older notions of an underlying reality. And the central idea of *What Is Life?*—that living things are characterized by "negative entropy"—is today considered mistaken.

Do these "mistakes" detract from his influence? The answer is: No, not in any way. Schrödinger only represents a clear case of how scientists may evolve fruitful ideas for the wrong reason. The

---

*Not long before his death Schrödinger commented that, were he to write something more than a brief autobiographical sketch, "I would have to leave out a very substantial part of this portrait, i.e., that dealing with my relationships with women."

fact remains that Schrödinger's wave equation was a crucial step in quantum mechanics, was relatively easy to employ, and had far-reaching practical benefits. The significance of his *What Is Life?* cannot be doubted, either, among a whole generation of molecular biologists. That Schrödinger's influence abides is a lesson in the nature of scientific advance.

19

Ernest Rutherford
and the Structure of the Atom

1871–1937

Equilibrium and stability characterize atoms, and for Democritus in ancient Greece as for physicists in the nineteenth century, atoms were solid and indivisible. This view was disrupted about 1900, after the discovery of unstable radioactive elements offered an invaluable window on atomic structure; and thus, the establishment of the modern atom may be traced to the mysterious X rays detected by Wilhelm Röntgen in 1895 and the discovery of radioactivity by Pierre and MARIE CURIE [26]. But it is to the New Zealand physicist Ernest Rutherford that we owe the first great explanation of the structure of the atom. Rutherford developed a model of the atom as a small, tightly packed nucleus surrounded by orbiting electrons. In doing so, he initiated nuclear physics, explained radioactive decay, and helped rectify the periodic table of elements. He is frequently classed with MICHAEL FARADAY [11] as one of the greatest experimentalists in the history of science. Upon his death he was eulogized as the "Newton of atomic physics."

Ernest Rutherford was born on August 30, 1871, in Spring Grove, New Zealand, the fourth of twelve children (nine of whom survived to adulthood) born to James and Martha Rutherford. James Rutherford had several careers—as flax farmer, wheelwright, mill owner—and was frequently away from home. Rutherford was closer to his mother, a schoolmistress. He read his first book on physics at age ten. He proved to be an excellent student at Nelson College, which he attended on a scholarship, beginning in 1887. He went on to Canterbury College, Christchurch, at the University of New Zealand, taking his bachelor's in 1892 with "firsts" in mathematics and physics. He received his master's degree in 1893 and his B.Sc. in 1894. When notification of his scholarship to study in England came in 1895, he was at work on the family farm. He let down his shovel and said to his mother, "This is the last potato I have dug in my life."

Rutherford's arrival in Cambridge coincided with the serendipitous discoveries of X rays by Wilhelm Röntgen in 1895 and mysterious uranium emissions by Henri Becquerel. Their unusual properties caused tremendous excitement in the scientific world. Soon Rutherford was studying them with JOSEPH J. THOMSON [31], director of the Cavendish Laboratory. Thomson had showed that X rays would cause a gas to conduct electricity. However, the conductivity was destroyed if the gas was forced to pass through glass wool or if it was passed between electrically charged plates. This suggested that X rays consisted of particles, and Rutherford was certain of their physical existence, as "jolly little beggars so real that I can almost see them." Ionization similar to that known to exist for over sixty years in water was now shown to be occurring in a gas.* This codiscovery, with Thomson, established Rutherford's reputation in 1896.

---

*An *ion* came to be understood as a charged atom: positively charged (a *cation*, with electrons missing), or negatively charged (an *anion*, with a surplus of electrons). Michael Faraday coined the term in the context of electrochemistry in the 1830s; in 1887 Svante August Arrhenius suggested that ions were electrically charged atoms. This concept was not accepted until Thomson's discovery of the electron and the investigations of radioactivity.

At the end of his life, Rutherford said that the most important decision of his career, taken in 1897, was to study radioactive phenomena. In 1898 he distinguished two forms of radioactive emanations from uranium, which he called alpha rays and beta rays. Alpha radiation (afterward discovered to consist of helium nuclei) was strongly ionizing but had little ability to penetrate and could be stopped by air. Beta rays (later found to be high-energy electrons) were not very ionizing but far more invasive, able to pass through thick sheets of metal. Although still mysterious, alpha and beta rays became in Rutherford's hands experimental probes of exceptional importance for discovering the nature of the atom.

In 1898 Rutherford accepted an appointment at McGill University in Montreal, where he had the benefit of a well-equipped laboratory and a stock of rare, expensive radium bromide. He also met Frederick Soddy, a chemist who for several years became his chief collaborator. Together, Rutherford and Soddy performed basic experiments which "laid down the fundamental principles of radioactivity," wrote A. S. Eve some years ago. In particular, they showed how the radioactive element thorium decayed at a fixed rate over time into a series of other elements, finally stabilizing as a form of lead. This led to the concept of "half life." As early as 1904 Rutherford discussed the possibility of using radioactivity for dating the earth. In view of the common precept at the turn of the century, that atoms were indestructible, this kind of transmutation of elements seemed heretical to many scientists. When Rutherford and Soddy published their theory in 1905, they engendered both astonishment and considerable criticism.

The still greater generalization to emerge from the study of radioactivity was the structure of the atom itself. Returning to England in 1907, Rutherford accepted a chair in physics at the University of Manchester, where he directed a team of students which included Hans Geiger and Ernest Marsden. Experimenting on a hunch, Rutherford and his associates bombarded a thin piece of gold foil, surrounded by screens of zinc sulfide, with alpha particles from radon. Most of the alpha particles passed through the foil, as expected. But an occasional particle clearly ricocheted, and caused a visible spark when it hit the zinc sulfide. It was "as if," Rutherford said later, "you had fired a fifteen-inch shell at a sheet of tissue paper and it came back and hit you."

Rutherford had discovered that an atom was not the "nice hard fellow" as had been widely thought since the days of JOHN DALTON [74]. Rather, the atom was a point of concentrated electrical charge "surrounded by a uniform spherical distribution of opposite electricity equal in amount." Thus, while most alpha particles possessed such mass and velocity as to pass through the gold foil's atoms, occasionally one would pass close to a nucleus and be deflected. Rutherford was able to calculate the size of the central particle as some ten thousand times less than the circumference of the whole atom. Rutherford publicly announced his discovery at a meeting of the Manchester Literary and Philosophical Society on March 7, 1911.

Rutherford thus developed the model of the atom as miniature solar system made up of a tiny but dense nucleus orbited by much smaller electrons. In 1914, Rutherford thought that the nucleus itself was comprised of negatively charged electrons and "positive electrons," which he later called protons. The Rutherford atom (also called the Rutherford-Bohr atom) had important defects and was subsequently greatly modified with the advent of quantum mechanics. But it is a linchpin in the history of modern physics. It also formed the theoretical basis for a necessary correction of the periodic table.*

Rutherford's last great contributions came during World War I, when he embarked on an experimental course that was an alchemist's dream. He had already shown how atoms are not indivisible and that radioactive elements can decay into other elements. Now he reasoned that it should be possible to transmute one kind of atom into another if one or more particles could be liberated from its nucleus. To this end he bombarded atmospheric nitrogen with alpha particles, which led to the emission of hydrogen nuclei. Having conducted some of his experiments during World War I, Rutherford apologized to the British officials for his absence from the defense effort, writing, "If, as I have reason to believe, I have disintegrated the nucleus of the atom, this is of greater significance than the war." As was

---

*Two numbers are associated with each element in the periodic table. The atomic weight gives the relative mass while the atomic number gives the number of protons in the nucleus. Hafnium, for example, has an atomic weight of 178.49; its atomic number, relative to the other elements, is 72. Arranging the elements by atomic numbers avoids anomalies that come about when they are arranged by weight.

subsequently understood, this experiment produced the first instance of deliberate atomic fission.

Although he continued working over the next seventeen years, Rutherford had accomplished his final work having great significance. He subsequently moved from Manchester to Cambridge University, succeeding J. J. Thomson as head of Cavendish Laboratory in 1919. Rutherford died on October 19, 1937, after an unfortunate accident led to the infection of an umbilical hernia. He is buried in Westminster Abbey.

Ernest Rutherford was covered with honors in his lifetime. He was awarded the Nobel Prize in 1908—oddly, for chemistry, which led to jokes about the physicist who was "instantaneously transmuted" into a chemist. He was knighted in 1914, served as president of the Royal Society from 1925 to 1930, and was made a peer in 1931.

One of the quintessential great men of science, Rutherford has been the object of much adulation. Friendly and outgoing, he was married to Mary Georgina Newton, an intelligent, well-read, down-to-earth woman. He maintained a warm, if long-distance relationship with his mother, who remained in New Zealand. When he was made a peer, he wrote her, "Now Lord Rutherford; more your honour than mine, Ernest." He was much disturbed by her death in 1935. Politically a liberal, Rutherford was not religious. He was an excellent writer on scientific topics, but Rutherford's biographer David Wilson found that "when he came to write about himself he became unutterably boring." A powerful personality, "He was always full of fire," wrote E. N. da C. Andrade, "and infectious enthusiasm when describing work into which he had put his heart and always generous in his acknowledgment of the work of others."

20

Paul Dirac
and Quantum Electrodynamics

1902–1984

"Enter Dirac," writes Abraham Pais of a historical juncture in physics during the 1920s, when Paul Dirac became a central figure in the development of quantum mechanics. Just as WERNER HEISENBERG [15] and ERWIN SCHRÖDINGER [18] developed equations which explained subatomic behavior, in 1927 Dirac proposed a "field theory" which describes the nature of light as it interacts with matter—a tremendous achievement in the history of science. And in 1928 he discovered, using relativistic principles, an equation for predicting the behavior of an electron, which was a major first step in developing the modern theory of quantum electrodynamics (QED). Dirac was also led to predict the existence of the positron, the positively charged counterpart to the negatively charged electron. The positron was in fact detected in 1932—the first of many essentially massless "antiparticles" prophesied by quantum theory. Dirac's influence on physics has been profound but expressed wholly through abstract equations; he lacked the passionate interest of NIELS BOHR [3], Heisenberg, and Schrödinger in the philosophical implications of the new physics.

Paul Adrien Maurice Dirac was born in Bristol, England, on August 8, 1902, the son of Charles Adrien Ladislav Dirac and Florence Hannah Dirac, née Holten. Dirac's relationship with his father, who was of Swiss origin and an instructor of French, was considerably strained by the latter's strict discipline, and the family environment was full of psychological pain. Dirac, a notably silent personality as an adult, later explained that when he was a child, his father saw scant value in social contact and had moreover insisted that Paul speak to him only in French, a language he scarcely knew. "The result was that I didn't speak to anybody unless spoken to. I was very much an introvert, and I spent my time thinking about problems in nature." When his father died, in 1935, Dirac wrote to his wife, Margit, "I feel much freer now."

Attending Merchant Venturer's College, the secondary school where his father was a teacher, Dirac proved exceptional in mathematics. At the local Bristol College, he studied electrical engineering though he had little interest in the subject and received his bachelor of science degree, with first-class honors, in 1921. When he was unable to find work following graduation—because of high unemployment in England—he was granted a dispensation to continue reading mathematics at Bristol. His outstanding abilities were noticed, and in 1923 he obtained a scholarship to become a research student at St. John's College, Cambridge, and while there he learned atomic theory and met Niels Bohr.

Dirac's great importance to quantum mechanics is historically due to circumstance, for he arrived at Cambridge at a point of high crisis in quantum theory. Although the Bohr-Rutherford atom had been established with the help of quantum mechanical ideas, the new theory could not predict the electron's behavior around any but the simplest atom, hydrogen. Examining particles whose diameter was less than one-billionth of an inch, physicists had reached past the limits of human perception. Matrix mechanics and wave mechanics, the two quantum mechanical solutions, were essentially mathematical and more counterintuitive than classical physics. They were developed separately by Werner Heisenberg and Erwin Schrödinger in 1925 and 1926—and it is at this point that Dirac appears on the scene.

In 1925, Dirac made his initial contribution to quantum theory when he saw a draft of Heisenberg's first paper on matrix mechanics. Dirac recognized in the mathematics some similarity with an obscure classical formulation from the nineteenth century, and he derived an equivalent formula and wrote to Heisenberg, causing considerable excitement in Göttingen. And when, several months later, equations by Schrödinger showed that the electron could be also viewed as packets of waves around the atomic nucleus, Dirac was able to link these, too, to older classical formulations. In effect, Dirac was able to show that classical mechanics could be considered a special case of quantum mechanics.

Dirac's work on Heisenberg's matrix mechanics became his thesis, and he received his doctorate in physics from St. John's College, Cambridge, in 1926. In the spring of that year he left England to meet and collaborate with Heisenberg in Germany as well as with Niels Bohr in Copenhagen. By the fall he had produced a "transformation theory" which united Heisenberg's matrix mechanics and Schrödinger's wave mechanics in a single, abstract equation. In 1927 this theory was presented at the Fifth Solvay Conference in Brussels, where it was much discussed. In general, physicists found Dirac both compelling—and hard to follow. Erwin Schrödinger, for one, complained to Bohr that Dirac "has no idea how *difficult* his papers are for the normal human being."

One of the limitations of the new quantum theory was that while it nicely described electrons when they were moving slowly, it failed when electrons move at or near the speed of light, as they frequently do. And although wave and matrix mechanics might give accurate results for atoms in simple states, what happens when light, for example, bounces off a wall? To describe these events, Einstein's theory of relativity must be employed, and in late 1926 Dirac began working on an equation which would describe these sorts of events. The result was a "field theory" and a famous paper, "The Quantum Theory of the Emission and Absorption of Radiation."

The importance of having a quantum mechanics which obeyed the principles of relativity was now fully apparent, and Dirac continued to work on a means of fully explaining the behavior of the electron. Several years earlier, it had been suggested that electrons possess "spin" as they move, a concept which solved certain problems in viewing the various X-ray spectra of the elements. Dirac now incorporated this idea into a single equation to describe an electron's motion and, more generally, resolved its behavior with greater elegance and depth than before.

The Dirac equation, as it came to be called, did not assign an electron a point in space but rather, in consonance with quantum theory, gave a *range* of possible locations chartered by probability. The theory predicted a magnetic field around the electron and suggested, for example, that the four "quantum numbers" required to calculate its movement reflect the four dimensions of space-time. The equation was, as Dirac said later, "a self-consistent theory which fits the experimental facts as far as is yet known."

But the equation's most extraordinary aspect was that it concretized a suspected view of the atom as awash in a sea of "virtual" or massless particles. "Dirac," write Robert P. Crease and Charles C. Mann, "had set down the beginnings of the modern theory of electromagnetism—the first solid piece of the standard model—but he had also unwittingly let loose an onslaught of conceptual demons that would change our views of space and matter." Dirac's theory, they add, "exposed a frightful chaos on the lowest order of matter. The spaces around and within atoms, previously thought to be empty, were now supposed to be filled with a boiling soup of ghostly particles."

Indeed, Dirac predicted in 1930 the existence of an elementary particle which was effectively the counterpart of the electron, but of a positive charge. To some, at the time, it sounded outlandish, but experimental physicists had recently discovered "cosmic rays" bombarding the earth's atmosphere from outer space.* And at the California Institute of Technology, a powerful cloud chamber, built to study such radiation, detected tracks of

---

*Cosmic rays consist of nuclei of common elements, as well as electrons, positrons, and other elementary particles. They were detected as early as 1911, named in 1925; but their origin is not certain.

certain particles that were indeed the *same weight* as electrons but of a *positive* charge. These were positrons, found in 1932—the first form of "antimatter." In 1933 Paul Dirac was awarded the Nobel Prize for physics.

Elected a Fellow of St. John's College in 1927, Dirac remained there to teach, and in 1932 he became Lucasian Professor of Physics at Cambridge. He retained this position until 1969, though he frequently taught and lectured abroad. In the late 1960s he moved to Florida, and from 1972 until 1984 served as professor of physics at Florida State University. Dirac's wife was Margit Wigner, sister of the great Hungarian physicist Eugene Wigner, with whom he had two daughters.

A famous personality in physics, although eccentric, Dirac was widely liked and admired, described by a newspaper as "shy as a gazelle and modest as a Victorian maid." He seems to have resorted often to what psychologists would call concrete thinking, which was amusing to colleagues. "Very windy today" as a conversation starter once led Dirac to leave the dinner table, open the front door, return to the table and say, "Yes." When Wolfgang Pauli wanted to lose weight, he asked Dirac how many lumps of sugar he ought to use in his coffee. Dirac replied, "I think one is enough for you." A moment later, he generalized by specifying, "I think the lumps are made in such a way that one is enough for anybody."

Dirac was somewhat left wing in politics, and his contact with Soviet science led to his being denied a visa to the United States during the cold war. His fairly complete lack of interest in art or literature, given his background, recalls that of RICHARD FEYNMAN [52], who further developed quantum electrodynamics. In the latter part of his career Dirac emphasized an idiosyncratic conception of "mathematical beauty," and his biographer, Helge S. Kragh, believes that it is one of the reasons that "the mid-1930s marked a major line of division: all of his great discoveries were made before that period, and after 1935 he largely failed to produce physics of lasting value." None of this detracts from the fact that it was Dirac who brought quantum theory to "definitive form," writes John C. Taylor, "creating a theory as compelling as Newton's mechanics had been."

Paul Dirac died on October 20, 1984.

21

Andreas Vesalius
and the New Anatomy
1514–1564

The great medical authority in the late Middle Ages was Galen, a Greek physician of the second century A.D. A brilliant doctor and prolific writer, Galen was taken up by the church as the main arbiter in medicine, especially as concerned anatomy, much as the scholastics adopted Aristotle in physics. For a long time, this posed few problems, not least because the spiritual conception of the human body in the Middle Ages was not favorable to a systematic understanding of it. But as a new secular appreciation evolved—vividly expressed, for example, in the paintings and drawings of Leonardo da Vinci—this medieval grasp faltered. To Andreas Vesalius it then fell to establish the groundwork of modern anatomy. "I could have done nothing more worthwhile," he said of himself, "than to give a new description of the whole human body, of which nobody understood the anatomy."

Andreas Vesalius was born to a distinguished medical family on December 31, 1514, in Brussels, then part of the Hapsburg Empire. His father, Andreas, was apothecary to Emperor Charles V; his mother was Isabel Crabbe. The location of the family estate provided a view of the city gallows, where criminals were executed and their bodies left, for days afterward, to be picked at by birds. As a child, Vesalius began to dissect small animals, not excluding the unfortunate stray cat or dog.

After attending the university in Louvain, Vesalius studied medicine from 1533 until 1536 at the prestigious University of Paris, then a bulwark of conservative thinking. There Vesalius learned, he later said, nothing of much importance. After helping his teacher, Guinter of Andernach, bring to press a book on anatomy, he remarked that the latter was, with respect to the structure of the human body, an ignoramus. While in Paris, Vesalius hunted for bones in the Cemetery of the Innocents and examined the corpses of criminals after they were hanged at Montfaucon, where he was once, as he wrote late, "imperiled by the many savage dogs."

The war between France and the Holy Roman Empire forced Vesalius to leave Paris in 1536 and return to the University of Louvain, where he received his bachelor's degree in medicine. He then went on to the University of Padua in Florence, where he was awarded his doctoral degree magna cum laude in 1537. This university, where NICOLAUS COPERNICUS [10] had studied and GALILEO GALILEI [7] would later teach, also became the stage for Vesalius's major achievements. In 1537, just after receiving his degree, he was appointed professor of surgery and anatomy.

Dissection of corpses was not forbidden in medical schools; it had been common since the fourteenth century. But it was done in a scholastic fashion: Students watched from the gallery while a barber cut open the body and a professor read from Galen's text. As Vesalius later put it, "Everything is wrongly taught, days are wasted in absurd questions, and in the confusion less is offered to the onlooker than a butcher in his stall could teach a doctor."

Vesalius therefore began dissecting cadavers himself in front of students and within a short time had acquired a considerable reputation. In 1538 he published the *Tabulae anatomicae sex (Six*

Anatomical Charts) which, although they fit into the Galenic framework, indicated the direction of his work. The plates were beautifully executed by Flemish artist Jan Stephen van Calcar, a student of Titian. Two years later, when Vesalius was asked to give a lecture and demonstration in Bologna at the Church of San Francesco, he pointed out a variety of errors and embarrassed and angered the Galenist professor Matteo Corti.

De humani corposi fabrica (*On the Structure of the Human Body*) appeared in 1543, a textbook of anatomy such as had never been seen before and a landmark of medicine. It should be said that Vesalius did not directly attack Galen, whom he admired, but he corrected numerous errors—showing, for example, that the human thigh bone was not curved like a canine's, and that men and women possessed the same number of ribs. Much of Galen's work was based on observations of animals, and so Vesalius also put an end to such structures as the liver with five lobes and the horned uterus.

De fabrica is designed to be studied and consulted and to be used as a how-to manual by students, who are clearly encouraged to discover the interior of the human body for themselves. "When the remaining organs of the thorax have been thrown into the vessel," writes Vesalius, "turn the cadaver into the prone position and as far as possible clean the flesh from the rest of the neck, back, and whole thorax, but take care not to break any of the ribs, which are fragile, nor to damage any of the processes by dissecting too closely. You must be even more careful when you proceed shortly to free the individual ribs from the thoracic vertebrae." Vesalius was aware of variation among individuals, and wanted his students to search for differences in structure.

De fabrica was a great success, but Vesalius, who could be abrasive to colleagues, came under considerable attack. In 1551 Jacobus Sylvius published *A Refutation of the Slanders of a Madman Against the Writings of Hippocrates and Galen.* "I urge you," wrote Sylvius, in one of his milder statements, "to pay no attention to a certain ridiculous madman, one utterly lacking talent, who curses and inveighs piously against his teachers." But there soon became no question as to the great influence of *De fabrica.* It propitiously appeared within a week of *De revolutionibus* by Nicolaus Copernicus—indeed, it excited as much immediate interest as the latter and established its revolutionary impact within a shorter time. "By the beginning of the seventeenth century," writes

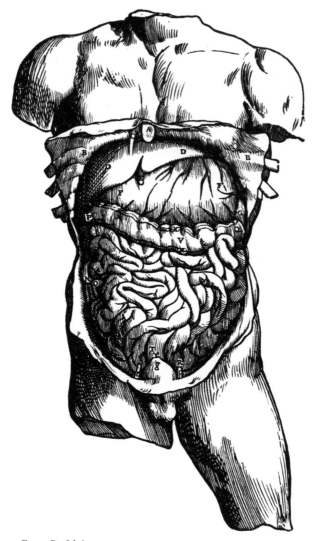

From *De fabrica.*

Vesalius' biographer, C. D. O'Malley, "with the exception of a few conservative centers such as Paris and some parts of the Empire, Vesalius anatomy had gained both academic and general support."

Soon after the publication of *De fabrica,* for reasons not entirely clear, Vesalius accepted an offer to become personal physician to Emperor Charles V, who was then fighting his long and ultimately unsuccessful battle to hold together the Holy

Roman Empire. From a family with a long history of royal service, this was perhaps not surprising. He was an eminent and much esteemed physician, and although he did not again make anatomy his central interest, he revised *De fabrica* as late as 1555 and often visited medical schools. He remained to serve the emperor even after Charles abdicated in favor of his son Philip II of Spain in 1556. The details of his end are unclear, but in 1564 Vesalius, returning from a voyage to the Holy Land, was caught in a shipwreck and died on the island of Zante, off the coast of Peloponnesus.

In the twentieth century Andreas Vesalius has been the victim of an interesting and egregious example of character assassination by psychobiography. In 1943, on the five hundredth anniversary of *De fabrica*, the *Bulletin of the History of Medicine* published a special number devoted to Vesalius. Included were the praises of Ludwig Edelman, for example, who honors Vesalius as wearing the "robe of the humanist." But from the pen of psychiatrist Gregory Zilboorg a psychoanalytic article attempts to dissect the mentality of Vesalius, showing him to be a schizoid and pathologically depressed individual who might have become a butcher. Zilboorg portrays Vesalius as "no fighter" and a man who "reacted very little to the problems of his day" and wrote that "he did not stay to fight it out with his opponents." These views, which have little basis, are possibly due to the fact that, when Zilboorg was writing, the United States, as well as his native Russia, was in the midst of World War II. One of their enemies was Italy and another was Germany. Vesalius was effectively born in one and schooled in the other.

Physicians today all know of Vesalius, and in 1932 one of them, Louis Bragman, penned several less than immortal lines of adulation in *A Rhymed History of Medicine,* which deserve repeating:

> *Dissection gained a good repute,*
> *And helped the ancient wrongs refute.*
> *Vesalius, iconoclast,*
> *Untrammeled by authority*
> *Grave doubts on Galen's dictums cast,*
> *And made a new anatomy.*

22

Tycho Brahe
and the New Astronomy

1546–1601

The Danish nobleman Tycho Brahe is a romantic figure in the history of astronomy. Abrasive and arrogant and the first to sight the supernova of 1572, he became famous and built an observatory and castle on an island in the Danish sound. He did not hold with NICOLAUS COPERNICUS [10] that the earth turns round the sun, but fortunately he chose for his successor JOHANNES KEPLER [9], who did. These three, with GALILEO GALILEI [7] overturned the ancient Ptolemaic system and dislodged the earth from the center of the universe. Brahe is the conservative among them; and his genius lay rather in his patient, and modern, pursuit of careful observation and accurate data about the stars. "If Coper-

114

nicus was the greatest European astronomer of the first half of the sixteenth century," writes Thomas Kuhn, "Tycho Brahe...was the preeminent astronomical authority of the second. And, judged purely by technical proficiency, Brahe was the greater man."

Tyge (later Latinized to Tycho) Brahe was born on December 14, 1546, in Skåne, a section of what was then Denmark and today belongs to Sweden. Born to the highest nobility, he was one of ten children of Otto Brahe and Beate Bille; but he was raised by his father's brother, Jörgen Brahe and his wife, who were themselves childless. At age thirteen, after some private tutoring, Tycho began attending the Lutheran University of Copenhagen. To be provided with an education in the liberal arts, he followed the trivium (courses in rhetoric, logic, and grammar) and the quadrivium (astronomy, arithmetic, music, and geometry), preparatory to the study of law, as his uncle wished.

However, after viewing the eclipse of the sun which was predicted for August 21, 1560, Brahe was taken up with the study of astronomy. This could not have pleased his family, for in 1562, when he moved on to the University of Leipzig, a tutor was employed to hold him to the study of law. During this period Brahe studied science in secret, and given his age—he was still an adolescent—it is entirely plausible that, as the tale is told, he would sneak outside to study the stars while his mentor slept. More important, following an observation of the conjunction of Saturn and Jupiter in August 1563, Brahe became aware of considerable errors of calculations in then current astronomical tables. He wanted to correct them, and from this motivation developed the man whom Kepler called the "Phoenix of astronomers."

Returning to Copenhagen in 1565, when his uncle died, Brahe began studies in astronomy at the University of Wittenberg. In 1566 he engaged in a duel which cost him part of his nose. Brahe subsequently wore a metal prosthesis, and it is intriguing to note that centuries after his death, when his body was disinterred in 1901, the bone around his nasal passage was found to be dyed a bright green patina. This was due to corrosion and showed that his replacement prosthesis, although long thought to be of gold and silver, must have contained copper.

After sunset on the clear night of November 11, 1572, Brahe wrote, "I noticed that a new and unusual star, surpassing the other stars in brilliancy, was shining almost directly above my head." Tracking the star with a sextant throughout the winter and carefully recording the positions of the sun, moon, and planets, Brahe found that he could not make a parallax measurement for it. This indicated that it could not be located near the moon. In addition, because it did not move, it was not a comet, nor could it be attached to any of the revolving planetary spheres. Therefore, it belonged to the eighth sphere of fixed stars; and indeed, it twinkled like a star. But how was it that something new appeared in heavens which were supposed to be perfect and changeless? Tycho's Star, as it came to be known after he published his brief book *De nova stella* (*On the New Star*), was the first such addition to the heavens observed since the time of the ancient Greek Hipparchus. It was tracked by astronomers and learned men throughout Europe, who generally recognized that some accommodation would have to be made, even after the star disappeared from view the following spring.*

In 1576 Brahe accepted an offer of pension and fief from Frederick II, the King of Denmark, to occupy the island of Hven, off the Danish Sound. Here Brahe established Uraniborg (Castle of the Heavens) and later built a second observatory, Stjerneborg (Castle of the Stars), where he lived and worked for the next twenty years. Though lacking a telescope, which was not to be invented for another generation, Brahe, with the help of a number of assistants, made great use of a remarkable array of calibrated instruments, including oversized quadrants, circumferential wheels, and a huge, revolving armillary sphere. In 1577, the year in which he received a clock with a second hand, a comet with a long tail passed through the skies. It inspired a good deal of commentary—and fabulous prognostications of coming disasters. As it crossed the heavens, it provided still more evidence that the ancient Ptolemaic system needed revision. Brahe showed that the comet must be far more distant than the moon, and so could not be passing within the earth's atmosphere. Just as important, the comet did not sketch an orbit, which meant it broke through the crystalline celestial spheres. Eventually, Brahe published a work in which he argued the implausibility of such invisible spheres.

---

*Brahe had discovered what today would be called a supernova—a star that explodes and grows much brighter before fading from view. About a half dozen have been observed over the past millennium.

Although the comet of 1577, as well as those he noted subsequently, could have been counted as support of Copernicus's theory of a heliocentric solar system, Brahe continued to support a geocentric model. Eventually he constructed the Tychonic system, in which Earth and Moon are at the center while the other planets revolve around them. Although it was quite wrong, mathematically it could fit the known facts about as well as Copernicus's theory.

With the death of King Frederick in 1588, Brahe lost his patron. He quarreled with Frederick's successor, King Christian I, and as a consequence lost his home and his job. In 1597, not without resources, though unsettled and under the weight of his instruments, he left Hven and reached Prague two years later. There he came under the protection of Rudolph II, the Holy Roman emperor who courted intellectuals, and received a new castle and another pension.

It was fortunate that in 1600 Brahe took as his assistant Johannes Kepler, for Tycho was not to live long. In 1601, Brahe suffered a stroke while having dinner, and he died ten days later, on October 24. On his deathbed he bequeathed his data on the stars, and especially his work on the planet Mars, which he had carefully guarded, to Kepler, with the injunction to complete his work and publish it. Kepler edited and published, in 1603, Brahe's *Astronomae instauratae progymnasmata (Introduction to the New Astronomy)*, which contained a catalogue of 777 stars. Kepler used Brahe's data to create the larger *Rudolphine Tables* (named after the king) in 1627.

Buried in Prague, Brahe's remains now lie in a crypt outside a church in the Old Town Square. And today, on the island of Hven, which came to belong to Sweden and is now called Ven, is the site of another memorial. A museum was established in 1930, but all that remains of Uraniborg, the Castle of the Heavens, are stones marking the site.

23

Comte de Buffon
and l'Histoire Naturelle

1707–1788

In 1749 the first volume of *l'Histoire naturelle* was published, written by King Louis XV's superintendent of the royal gardens, Comte Georges-Louis Leclerc de Buffon. Forty-three more volumes followed over the next four decades, the last eight appearing after their author's death. Although not generally based on original research, and laced with speculation, *l'Histoire naturelle* establishes Buffon as a key figure in the development of the biological sciences. He adopted a Newtonian outlook, developing a view of the world based on physical causation and devoid of miracles and biblical chronology. Buffon brings under scientific scrutiny the great themes of natural science, questioning received wisdom on a wide variety of issues, from the age of the cosmos to the development of animal species. Biology, zoology, geology, anthropology, and cosmogony can all be found within Buffon's purview. He was, in addition, a great stylist, and his work has considerable literary value. His oft-repeated proverb, "Genius is only a great aptitude for patience," echoes ISAAC NEWTON [1].

George-Louis Leclerc Buffon was born on September 7, 1707, in Montbard, Burgundy, to Benjamin François Leclerc and Anne Cristine Marlin. The Buffons were prosperous members of the emerging bourgeoisie; Benjamin François became the Lord of Buffon and Montbard, owing to his wife's inheritance, and served as counselor to the Burgundian parliament. George-Louis was sent to a Jesuit school in Dijon, where he was not a particularly distinguished student, although he was captivated by mathematics. His father intended that he study law, but Buffon's interests, by his late teens, lay in scientific matters. In 1728 he matriculated at the University of Angers, where he studied medicine, mathematics, astronomy, and botany.

In 1730, after involvement in a duel, Buffon cut his studies short and left France for a time. He traveled to Switzerland, Italy, and England, where he was impressed and influenced by British science. Returning to France upon the death of his mother, Buffon found to his dismay that his father claimed properties at Montbard which were supposed to have been passed on to him. Although Buffon emerged victorious from the subsequent legal battle, his relationship with his father ended, and the two never spoke again. This outcome was fateful to Buffon's career, for his scientific pursuits could only have been undertaken by a man of independent means.

In the early 1730s Buffon published studies on the tensile strength of timbers used in making warships, and in an application of probability theory using Newton's calculus, he wrote an essay on the French lottery. His stature grew, and in 1834 he was elected an adjunct to the Académie Royale (he eventually became a full member); six years later he was made a member of the British Royal Society. But his most significant advance came in 1739, when he was appointed director of the Jardin du Roi, which included supervision over the royal museums, gardens, and animal menageries. It was from this position that Buffon embarked on his most ambitious project.

L'Histoire naturelle, générale et particulière, a tremendous publishing success in its time, ranks with Diderot's encyclopedia as a cornerstone of Enlightenment thought. The first volume, *Discours sur la manière d'étudier et de traiter l'histoire naturelle*, stated Buffon's intention to examine the whole of the natural world, from the formation and development of the earth to every sort of animal which inhabits it. Importantly, Buffon segregated natural history from religious inquiry and resisted, even while he speculated, solutions requiring supernatural or divine explanation. In this respect, he deliberately emulated Isaac Newton. Excluding God and teleological thought from natural history was a necessary step for a scientific understanding of the world.

Of all the issues broached by Buffon, several stand out today for their relevance. One is his definition of an animal species as "a group that breeds among itself," a criterion he developed through experiment; it is close to the definition used in twentieth-century evolutionary biology. Buffon was an opponent of CARL LINNAEUS [76], the Swedish botanist whose system of classification he regarded as artificial. The interesting aspect of Buffon's theory of species is that he arrived at it gradually, giving up his early nominalist notion that nature was a vast mélange, which people sorted out by attaching labels.

Another aspect of Buffon's thought which retains its interest today is his view of the age of the earth and his cosmological speculations. After first suggesting an age for the earth of 75,000 years, much older than allowed by biblical tales, he later speculated (according to his manuscripts) that 3,000,000 years was an appropriate figure. He developed a cosmological theory that the earth had formed from a gaseous state, and he adduced a series of epochs by which it attained its present state. Animal life appeared before the continents formed, Buffon claimed, and as evidence he cited fossil remains.

One must be cautious in viewing Buffon as a precursor of modern geology or biology. Large parts of his work draw upon the observations and theories of others, and he did not have Darwin's eye for detail. But he performed experiments—some of which, recently replicated, clearly show his scientific intentions. His influence on science and on the popular understanding of its power was great. In his time, wrote zoologist and historian Janet Browne in a recent assessment, "Nearly all cultivated persons were familiar with his work; nearly all natural scientists and philosophers felt that he had successfully mapped out the route that scientific endeavors should follow through the century." Indeed, his influence is analogous to that of WILLIAM HERSCHEL [27], whose observations have been largely rendered obsolete by others more informed, but whose influence abides in the historic trajectory of science.

Buffon married rather late, in 1752, and became a widower seventeen years later, after his union with the noble Marie-Françoise de Saint-Belin produced two children, including a son, who lost his head to the guillotine. Buffon himself died April 16, 1788.

24

Ludwig Boltzmann
and Thermodynamics

1844–1906

The law of entropy, as the second law of thermodynamics is called, was described by JAMES CLERK MAXWELL [12] as the notion that "if you throw a tumblerful of water into the sea, you cannot get the same tumblerful of water out again." In fact, it has profound consequences in the physical world. The operation of steam engines and the diffusion of gases, as well as chemical and biological processes and the very definition of time, are clarified by entropy. Its discovery and formulation was the work of several nineteenth-century scientists—including Sadi Carnot, Lord Kelvin, Josiah Gibbs, and Rudolf Clausius. But perhaps the most significant and influential figure in this enterprise, owing to his prescient view of its role in nature, is Ludwig Boltzmann, the founder of statistical mechanics.

One of the last of the great classical physicists, a supporter of Maxwell and proponent of the new atomic theory, Boltzmann was, according to MAX PLANCK [25], "the one who grasped the meaning of entropy most profoundly." He saw in the molecular basis of the second law of thermodynamics its macroscopic implications and by his statistical approach built a crucial bridge to twentieth-century physics. "This development," writes Abraham Pais, "one of the great advances in nineteenth century physical theory, is principally due to Boltzmann."

Ludwig Boltzmann was born on a Shrove Tuesday, February 20, 1844, in Erdberg, a suburb of Vienna. His father, Ludwig, was a revenue officer, and his mother, Katharina Pauernfeind, was from Salzburg. Ludwig was initially tutored at home; as a boy he made excursions into the countryside to collect butterflies and beetles. Like his grandfather, a clockmaker, he was an enthusiastic craftsman. He attended the University of Vienna and received his Ph.D. in 1866. Boltzmann's interest in electromagnetism, mechanics, and thermodynamics thus dates from his university career. With the help of an English grammar and a dictionary, he studied Maxwell's electromagnetic theory.

Early in his career, Boltzmann became well regarded by older colleagues. About 1870 he worked with Robert Bunsen, GUSTAV KIRCHHOFF [57], and HERMANN VON HELMHOLTZ [63] at the University of Berlin. He taught at the University of Vienna from 1873 to 1876, then became professor of experimental physics at the University of Graz, where he eventually became vice chancellor. Upon the death of his professor Josef Stefan in 1894, Boltzmann occupied the chair of physics at the University of Vienna. Boltzmann was an exceptional lecturer. Historian of science Gerald Holton writes that Boltzmann's "precise preparation and carefully structured delivery, tempered by his great humor and humanity, made his lecture room always overflow with students and visitors."

In the nineteenth century, there developed the crucial study of heat and temperature known as thermodynamics. It was established that in a physical system, energy was conserved—not created or destroyed—when heat, one form of energy, was converted to motion, another form. Expressed as a physical law, this clarified, after the fact, the operation of such inventions as the steam engine. To the first law of thermodynamics was added a second: Any system—whether solid, liquid, or gas—will tend toward maximum disorder. Energy flows in one direction only, toward thermal equilibrium. This concept developed over the course of several decades, beginning in 1824 with the French physicist Nicolas-Léonard Sadi Carnot and was refined and described as entropy in 1850 by the German Rudolf Clausius. Now, inspired by the work of James Maxwell on gases, Boltzmann brought to bear on the second law of thermodynamics a statistical approach.

The molecular nature of gases was clarified only gradually in the nineteenth century, before the full establishment of atomic theory. James Maxwell's kinetic theory of gases, devised in 1860, aimed at showing that the overall behavior of a gas was a function of its microscopic, invisible constituents—molecules. This theory essentially provided a Newtonian, mechanical perspective on the collision of individual molecules and constituted a considerable advance. However, Maxwell did not explain thermal equilibrium in a gas: the tendency, for example, of hot air from a radiator to diffuse throughout a room.

In 1866 Boltzmann made a first attempt to discuss thermal equilibrium. Several years later he developed the "Boltzmann distribution," a formula for computing the diffusion of gas molecules that became a fundamental feature of thermodynamic calculations.* Initially, this work created the appearance of a paradox. For insofar as the distribution of molecules in a gas was supposed to be Newtonian and mechanical, it ought to be reversible, like a motor that can be run backward. But it is obvious that gas from a flask let into the atmosphere cannot be put back, nor can helium be harvested from a balloon that breaks.

In 1877 Boltzmann met this objection with a proof of entropy that was basically statistical. It has become known as the Boltzmann principle. Using the Boltzmann constant k, the entropy of a system S is related to probability W by a formula $S = k \log W$. This famous equation describes the tendency of any gas to reach a state of equilibrium over time. It was to become the most significant and succinct expression of the law of entropy.

Apart from his contributions to the kinetic theory of gas, Boltzmann wrote on a variety of phenomena; his work includes

---

*Alternatively called the Maxwell-Boltzmann distribution.

papers on mathematics, chemistry, and physics as well as philosophy. Boltzmann was said to be a good experimentalist, though handicapped by poor eyesight. His empiricist bias made him a hostile opponent of German idealist thinkers such as Arthur Schopenhauer and G. W. Hegel. Boltzmann was an early and ardent supporter of the theories of CHARLES DARWIN [4], and there extends a line of influence from Boltzmann to another Viennese, ERWIN SCHRÖDINGER [18], to the assumptions underlying the discovery of the structure of DNA. Boltzmann was an atomist who recognized, at the same time, the possibility of a subatomic world. He wrote: "We are ready to drop immutability [of atoms] in those cases where a different assumption would better represent the phenomena." He is one nineteenth-century physicist who would have felt comfortable in the world of quantum mechanics as well as biology. "Modern molecular biologists like Francis Crick and Jacques Monod," writes Walter Moore, "would have felt perfectly at home with Ludwig Boltzmann."

However, during the 1890s Boltzmann was forced to defend the existence of atoms, and the conflict is sometimes thought to have contributed to his death. Challenged by such eminences as Ernst Mach, whom he detested, and Wilhelm Ostwald, Boltzmann took the part of atoms in a debate which was sometimes unusually bitter and which struck at the heart of his life's work. But Boltzmann was also plagued by ill health. At the end of his life he suffered from asthma, migraines, and near blindness. And in a hagiographic memoir, Engelbert Broda writes that, "Despite his great success in scientific work, his enjoyment of the beauties of Nature and art in full measure, and his optimism and humor, he suffered from depressions."

In 1904 Boltzmann visited the United States, where he delivered lectures at the St. Louis World's Fair and visited California. His humorous article on his travels for the German press was entitled "A German Professor in Eldorado." Back in Europe, in 1906, he took a vacation trip to Trieste, in those days part of the Austro-Hungarian Empire. On September 4, while his wife and daughter were bathing in the lovely Bay of Duino, Boltzmann took the occasion to hang himself.

He was buried in Vienna's Central Cemetery. Upon his marble tombstone is a sculpted bust and the equation:

$$S = k \log W.$$

25

Max Planck
and the Quanta

1858–1947

The work of Max Planck initiated quantum theory at the turn of the twentieth century and thereby changed forever the fundamental framework of physics. So extraordinary was Planck's basic achievement that he is sometimes classed with ISAAC NEWTON [1] and ALBERT EINSTEIN [2]. The latter wrote that Planck's work "has given one of the most powerful of all impulses to the progress of science." He is indeed a chief figure in the history of physics and an icon curiously attractive to scientists: Orthodox by nature, Planck was yet willing to seek a radical solution to a seemingly insignificant but theoretically crucial problem. "A firm conservative," wrote physicist and historian Emilio Segrè, "he found himself compelled by the strength of factual evidence and logical rigor to promote one of the greatest revolutions in natural philosophy."

Max Karl Ernst Ludwig Planck was born on April 23, 1858. His birthplace was Kiel, a port on the Baltic Sea. Kiel belonged to Denmark but in 1866 became part of Prussia. Of German ancestry, Planck's father was Johann Julius Wilhelm von Planck, a well-known professor of constitutional law who helped write the Prussian Civil Code; his mother was Emma Patzig. Educated at the Maximilians-Gymnasium in Munich, Planck was an excellent but not outstanding student. He became interested in physics, entered the University of Munich in 1874, and received his Ph.D. in 1879. His doctoral dissertation concerned the second law of thermodynamics and indicates Planck's fascination with fundamental problems. The prospect that the outside world was something "absolute" challenged him, and he wrote, "the quest for the laws which apply to this absolute appeared to me as the most sublime scientific pursuit in life." After a period of teaching at the universities of Munich and Kiel, Planck became a professor at the University of Berlin in 1889. There he did the bulk of his work, and there he remained until 1928.

The discovery of the quantum is related to the problem of "blackbody radiation," which vexed physicists in the late nineteenth century—and interested Planck just because of its fundamental significance. In 1859 GUSTAV KIRCHHOFF [57] had discovered that the quality of heat radiated by any object was dependent only on temperature and wavelength and *not* on the nature of the object itself. Some universal function was therefore at work. Examining how a "blackbody" would emit radiation, physicists came upon a disturbing result. By classical law, radiation from something which absorbed all radiation *ought* also to radiate heat and light in infinite amounts, with greatest intensity at the shortest, invisible, ultraviolet wavelengths. But experiment showed this was not the case.

Light emitted from a heated cavity—a furnace, for example—gives off a spectral range of colors, from bright yellow to red to blue-white and to the hottest, "white heat." Classical physics could not predict this spectrum. Sometimes called the "ultraviolet catastrophe" because of the wide disagreement of prediction to experiment at the shortest wavelengths, the problem of blackbody radiation was not a minor issue in nineteenth-century physics. It posed a challenge to the first law of thermodynamics, which describes heat as a form of energy and states that, like mechanical energy, thermal energy is conserved, not created or destroyed.

After several false starts beginning in 1897, Planck succeeded in finding a formula predicting blackbody radiation. Essentially, he gave up the underlying classical notion that light and heat would be emitted in a steady stream. Rather, energy is radiated in discrete units, or bundles. Planck discovered a new universal constant, which could be used to compute the observed spectrum. Although Planck's mathematics was solidly founded on physical theory, "Planck's constant," as this number became known, was the result of intense effort and a "fortunate guess." A very small number h—representing a tiny quantity of energy multiplied by an infinitesimal amount of time—Planck called an "elementary quantum of action." It allowed for theoretical equations which agreed with the observable range of spectral phenomena. Effectively, the gathering vibrations in a heated cavity radiate heat only at certain, definite energies, of which the quantum is the smallest unit. There are no fractional quanta—no $h/2$, for example. Planck published his first paper on the quantum in December 1900, inaugurating quantum physics.

The significance of Planck's constant proved to be fundamental when it was generalized as the law of blackbody radiation. Although it violated classical physics and baffled physicists, it was accepted because it agreed with experimental results. Then in 1905, Einstein used the quantum as a theoretical tool to explain the photoelectric effect, showing how light can sometimes behave as a stream of particles. And not long thereafter, in 1913, NIELS BOHR [3] took advantage of the larger implications of Planck's approach in developing his model of the atom. Instead of applying classical principles which conceived of the atom as a sort of miniature solar system, Bohr's model of the atom would now be viewed as a system in which electrons operated only in orbits with certain values, quantitized by using Planck's constant.

In 1919 Planck was awarded the Nobel Prize for Physics, and he had become, by then, a prominent figure. It ought to be added that he was never entirely reconciled with the implications of quantum theory—especially with the uncertainty principle and limitations of causality introduced in the 1920s. These developments, which entailed basic changes in physicists' thinking about fundamental issues, were difficult for him and many others including Einstein, to accept. Planck was, as Abraham Pais has called him, a "transitional figure *par excellence*." In 1928 he left the University of Berlin. Two years later he became president of the Kaiser Wilhelm Society. Although the society was later renamed in his honor, he was forced out of it during the Hitler era, when he courted considerable danger by criticizing the Nazis. During the 1930s he published several works, including *Introduction to Theoretical Physics*, in five volumes, and *Philosophy of Physics*.

Planck was an excellent musician who sometimes was accompanied on the violin by Einstein. His life was not devoid of tragedy. With his first wife, Marga von Hoesslin, Planck had four children. He lost two daughters soon after their marriage, both to complications in childbirth, and one of his sons was killed during World War I. His other son lived to adulthood but was involved in a failed plot to kill Adolf Hitler; he was executed. At the end of World War II, Planck's home and virtually all his papers were destroyed by Allied bombing. He was quite religious, believing to the end of his life in a beneficent Almighty. His second wife, whom he married in 1911, was his first wife's niece. He died on October 4, 1947, not long before his ninetieth birthday.

26

Marie Curie
and Radioactivity
1867–1934

In 1898 Marie Curie, together with her husband Pierre, isolated two new elements, which she called radium and polonium, from the mineral known as pitchblende, found in various regions of the earth. She recognized that its unusual properties—spontaneous glow and capacity to invade other substances—were due to atomic reactions rather than some chemical process. This discovery, which opened the way for the theory of radioactive decay, came in the midst of new findings about the nature of atoms and electromagnetism—the electron had been discovered several years earlier—and was of seminal importance to nuclear physics. Madame Curie was, to quote Abraham Pais, "a driven

driven and probably obsessive personality, who should be remembered as the principal initiator of radiochemistry."

Marie Curie was born Marya Skłodowska, in Warsaw, on November 7, 1867, the youngest of five children of Wladyslaw and Bronislawa Skłodowski. Her father, a member of the declining gentry, was a physics teacher, and her mother was the director of a boarding school before her death from tuberculosis, when Marie was ten years old. The respiratory illness had made Bronislawa wary of displays of physical affection with her children, and, not surprisingly, Marie became herself stoic in bearing and physically distant as a mother. The death of Bronislawa, a devout Roman Catholic, caused in Marie a deep depression and also turned her against religion. She became a lifelong atheist.

The education of Marie Curie is a tale of determination and triumph over all sorts of adversity. Poland was not an independent nation but a province of Russia, which sought to suppress Polish culture. Marie Curie, growing up in this era, was poorly treated at the gymnasium and denied access to higher education, though her academic record was excellent. As a result, after graduating from the gymnasium in 1883, she became associated with the subversive, clandestine, and feminist Floating University. In 1886, at age eighteen, she began working as a governess as part of an agreement with her sister Bronia to complete their education in Paris. In 1891 she moved to France, where she matriculated at the University of Paris. She became the first woman to receive a degree in physics from the Sorbonne, graduating magna cum laude in 1893, and took a degree in mathematics a year later. Naturally timid in a new country, she did not go out of her way to make friends with other students and yet managed even so to attract their attention. When one lovesick, would-be paramour swallowed laudanum to show his affection for her, Marie remarked drily that his priorities were not in order.

Although her original ambition was to return to Poland after completing her studies, a brief trip home in 1894 convinced Marie of the futility of repatriating in hopes of bettering her country. She decided to remain in France. She had already met Pierre Curie. Eight years older than she, Pierre headed the laboratory at the École de Physique et Chimie. "We began a conversation which soon became friendly...," wrote Marie years later. "There was, between his conceptions and mine, despite the difference between our native countries, a surprising kinship...."

They were married in 1895 in a secular ceremony—they did not exchange wedding bands—and for their honeymoon took a bicycle tour of the French countryside.

When he married Marie, Pierre Curie was a well-regarded though poorly compensated chemist. In 1880, with his brother Joseph, he had discovered the piezoelectric effect (how a crystal under pressure produces electricity), and he had also studied magnetism. His doctoral dissertation, on "Magnetic Properties of Bodies at Different Temperatures," was an important contribution. He was admired by Lord Kelvin and devoted to his research. In many ways an admirable character, Pierre seems to have been blind to ambition. Marie later wrote, "One could not enter into a dispute with him because he could not become angry." After their marriage they lived in Paris on rue de la Glacière in an apartment which was sparsely furnished because Marie did not like to keep house.

The discovery of X rays in 1895 by Wilhelm Röntgen, and Henri Becquerel's investigation of mysterious properties of uranium soon afterward, dramatically affected both the trajectory of physics and the life of Marie Curie. In 1897 she decided to study Becquerel's rays as the topic of her doctoral thesis. She set out to measure the properties of uranium and tested a variety of minerals containing it. A sample of pitchblende, a substance which had been mined for a century from the Joachimsthal region in Germany, proved, surprisingly, more active than Becquerel's uranium. When Curie discovered that the element thorium was also radioactive, the mystery deepened. Marie first reported on her research in April 1898, and in another paper published in July, the Curies reported the discovery of a substance they proposed to call polonium. Becquerel's rays were, it seemed, more than a curiosity manifested by a few substances; they were part of a broader phenomenon of nature. The Curies proposed to call it *radioactivity*.

The Curies' labor to extract the new, hitherto unidentified element radium from pitchblende has become part of scientific legend. Working day and night in a leaky shed, Marie wrote later, she and Pierre, were "extremely handicapped by inadequate conditions, by the lack of a proper place to work in, by the lack of money and of personnel." Nevertheless, in spite of the exhausting labor, "we would walk up and down talking of our work, present and future. When we were cold, a cup of hot tea, drunk beside the stove, cheered us. We lived in a preoccupation as complete as that of a dream."

In 1900 the Curies reprised their work in a paper at the International Congress of Physics. They ended by asking the most important question posed by radioactivity: "What is the source of energy coming from the Becquerel rays? Does it come from within the radioactive bodies or from outside them?" A form of energy was being spontaneously emitted by uranium, even when tested in a vacuum, and appeared to come from some *activity within the atoms* themselves; it was not a chemical reaction. This was Marie Curie's fundamental insight, and it is the reason for her high regard among scientists. "From this stark hypothesis," writes one of her biographers, Rosalynd Pflaum, "the mysteries of the structure of the atom were to be exposed as the twentieth century unfolded."

For their work, the Curies received the 1903 Nobel Prize, which they shared with Henri Becquerel. It is altogether to the credit of Pierre that he lobbied intensively on behalf of his wife, for he alone was originally considered for the prize. Husband and wife became wildly famous overnight, but just three years later, in 1906, Pierre was killed in an accident at the Pont Neuf in Paris. On a rainy afternoon, he was knocked to the ground by a young, deadly Percheron, and his skull crushed as the left rear wheel of the horse-drawn cart passed across his head. Grief-stricken, Marie nevertheless took over Pierre's teaching post at the Sorbonne, becoming that university's first female professor. Her initial lecture, given one afternoon after a visit to Pierre's grave, was a great personal torture.

In 1911 Marie was accused in the daily press of an adulterous affair with Paul Langevin, a scientist in the Curies' laboratory who largely shared their political and social beliefs. The ensuing scandal, heightened because of Marie Curie's reputation, gender, left-wing political views, and Polish-Jewish background, reso-nated with the classic reproaches of social reaction, including an animus against science in general. Soon thereafter—and perhaps partly as recompense—Marie Curie was awarded a second Nobel Prize, in chemistry. In her Nobel lecture, she clearly asserted her priority of discovery. "The history of the discovery and isolation of this substance furnished proof of the hypothesis made by me," she stated, "according to which *radioactivity is an atomic property of matter and can provide a method for finding new elements.*" She alone, she stated, had undertaken the task of isolating radium.

During World War I, which decimated a generation of young French males, Marie Curie was highly active and patriotic. She organized the use of X rays for medical and surgical intervention, setting up both mobile and permanent radiology posts and training technicians. After the war she established the Radium Institute of Paris, and was highly prominent in French science. She received tremendous adulation when she visited the United States in 1921 and again eight years later. In 1911 she had been refused admission to the Academy of Sciences, but in 1922 she became the first woman elected to the French Academy of Medicine. She was granted a pension for life in 1923 by the French parliament.

The dangers of radiation were not known when the Curies began their research, and so they were bemused by, and careless of, the new elements they discovered. Pierre carried a test tube containing radium in solution in his pocket, and he suffered contact burns, which he noted healed quite slowly. Marie kept radioactive substances glowing by their bedside. Both manifested symptoms of what is now called radiation sickness, and in later life Marie suffered from health problems that she tended to keep secret. Her laboratory notebooks, even today, are still highly radioactive.

Marie Curie was close to her two daughters, Eve and Irène; she was a perceptive, involved, but undemonstrative mother. Irène became a highly regarded physicist and married Jean-Frédéric Joliot; and in 1935 the Joliot-Curies won the Nobel Prize in Physics for their discovery of artificial radioactivity. Eve took care of her mother during her final illness, and wrote the tender and adoring memoir, *Madame Curie*. On July 4, 1934, Marie Curie died of leukemia associated with radiation poisoning. She is buried in the same tomb with Pierre, in the cemetery at Sceaux.

27

William Herschel

and the Discovery of the Heavens

1738–1822

During the late eighteenth to early nineteenth century, William Herschel explored and cataloged the heavens with the same systematic industry that COMTE DE BUFFON [23] studied plants and animals and CHARLES LYELL [28] investigated the rock formations of the earth. Building the largest telescopes ever to scan the skies, Herschel is remembered as the founder of sidereal astronomy. In addition, he studied the planets, discovered Uranus, found two of its moons, and examined the rings of Saturn. Herschel was the first scientist to fully describe the Milky Way galaxy, and he likened its shape to that of a swirling, disklike bun. Although the value of his great generalizations is today reduced by his limited technical resources, Herschel was undeniably the first modern astronomer.

Friedrick William Herschel was born to a humble household in the electorate of Hanover on November 15, 1738, the son of Isaac and Anna Herschel. Trained to play the violin and the oboe, he joined his father as a member of the regimental band of the Hanoverian Guards in 1753, after a fairly rudimentary education. During an engagement in the Seven Years' War, he precipitously left the battlefield on his father's advice. This later gave rise to rumors that he was a deserter. In fact, he had not technically been a soldier. In 1757 he moved to England (then allied with Frederick the Great) with one of his brothers, Jacob, and he remained there the rest of his life. When he was naturalized in 1793, he took the single name William, by which he is known today.

It is clear that, long before he became an astronomer, Herschel was intrigued both by the night sky and the philosophical implications of the discoveries of eighteenth-century science. Because he was a musician, there is some feeling that the harmonies of the universe appealed to him as they had to JOHANNES KEPLER [9]. As a youth, it is true, as Herschel records in his diaries, he had spent long nights stargazing with his father, who was, in other respects as well, his mentor and model.

Herschel's full dedication to astronomy did not come until he was nearly thirty-five years old. After his arrival in England, he successfully taught and played music for years; in 1766 he became the organist at the Octagon Chapel in Bath. But in 1773 he began to build and acquire telescopes and other instruments. Indeed, he soon turned his whole house into a workshop. His sister Caroline, to whom he was extraordinarily close, recorded that once, when William was polishing a mirror for a telescope, "I was even obliged to feed him by putting the vitals by bits into his mouth." His first telescope had a focal length of six feet; he ultimately made one that was forty feet long, and too cumbersome to be entirely successful. Beginning in 1774, Herschel began devoting all of his nights to observing the heavens. He presented his first papers, including one concerning the mountains on the moon, to the Royal Society in 1780.

On March 13, 1781, Herschel observed a spot in the sky that did not behave like a star. He believed at first it was a comet, but over time its slow movement and orbital trajectory clearly estab-

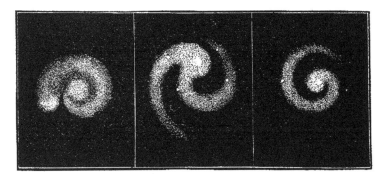

Spiral nebulae.

lished that it was a planet. The object was not unknown to astronomers, but no one before Herschel had recognized its nature. Herschel thus discovered the first new planet since ancient times. Today it is known as Uranus, though Herschel originally named it Georgium Sidus to honor King George III, the British monarch—who in the same year, on earth, lost his North American colonies. Within months, Herschel was elected to the Royal Society, and in 1782 the king appointed him Royal Astronomer. Herschel had become world famous and, no longer obliged to work for a living, began a highly fruitful period of research.

The breadth of Herschel's work and his prodigious output make clear his status as founder of stellar astronomy. Continuing to systematically study and catalog, he published lists of double and multiple stars in 1783. In the same year he began a twenty-year program to search for nebulae, publishing his first catalog in 1786, eventually locating about twenty-five hundred of them. Although severely handicapped by technical limitations, Herschel nevertheless developed an early version of the theory of the origins of the heavenly bodies. Herschel suggested that the stars, once disparate, were gradually drawn to groups of greater density according to the force of attraction, leading to star clusters and nebulae. Herschel's hypothesis was discussed in astronomy textbooks throughout the nineteenth century.

Related to Herschel's work in cataloging the heavens was another long-term effort: to grasp its overall structure. In 1784 Herschel also began to systematically study the shape of the Milky Way. Previously, Galileo had shown it to be composed of large numbers of stars, and earlier speculation considered whether the

Milky Way as a whole was somehow like the Copernican solar system, orbiting around a center. In *On the Construction of the Heavens*, Herschel offered a more or less correct description of the "grindstone" shape of the Milky Way, which supported the speculations of the German philosopher, Immanuel Kant. Although originally he believed that the stars were evenly distributed through the heavens, he eventually concluded "that this immense starry aggregation is by no means uniform." Increasingly aware of the complexity of the heavens, Herschel exhibited a modern willingness to modify his assumptions when observations did not support them.

Although his major achievements were in sidereal astronomy, Herschel also contributed to the study of the solar system and the nature of solar radiation. Using a micrometer, he calculated the height of mountains on the moon (which he felt certain was inhabited). His observations included studies of the known planets: Mercury, Venus, Mars, Jupiter, and Saturn as well as Uranus. Using colored glasses to look at the sun, Herschel noticed that the sensation of heat was not correlated to visible light. This led him to make experiments using thermometers and prisms and to correctly hypothesize the existence of the invisible infrared heat waves.

Throughout his career Herschel was helped by his sister, Caroline, who had come to live with him in 1772 and moved with him to Slough, outside London, in 1786. She assisted him in many ways, performed difficult calculations, and discovered some nebulae and eight comets herself. When in 1788 William married Mary Pitt, the widow of one of his friends, Caroline was bitterly resentful for a time, but she reconciled herself to sharing her brother's affections. She survived William by many years, dying in 1848, at the age of ninety-eight. In 1846 the King of Prussia awarded her his Gold Medal for science.

William Herschel accumulated many honors by the end of his life, including a knighthood. The Prince of Astronomy, as he was sometimes called, died at age eighty-four, on August 25, 1822. His only son by Mary Pitt also became a noted astronomer and man of science and continued his father's work—the celebrated Sir John Herschel.

28

Charles Lyell
and Modern Geology

1797–1875

As early as the Renaissance, new attention was paid to geologic formations. Leonardo da Vinci, for one, was certain that the fossil shells he found in Italy were there because the ocean had once covered the land. But only with the onset of the industrial revolution did there emerge a clear motivation for scientifically understanding—and exploiting—the actual substance of the earth. Thus, the golden age of geology is usually dated from 1780 to 1840, and its most prominent figure is the British scientist Charles Lyell. Lyell's revolution in thinking about the structure and formation of the earth and its physical landscape presages the theory of evolution of CHARLES DARWIN [4].

Indeed, the two men were friends, and the influence was direct. "Lyell must be accorded the secure distinction," writes Loren Eiseley, "not alone of altering the course of geological thought, but of having been the single greatest influence in the life of Charles Darwin."

Born at the family manor in Kinnordy in Angus County, Scotland, on November 14, 1797, Charles Lyell had an English mother and Scottish father. Charles Lyell Sr., a graduate of Cambridge University, was a translator of Dante, kept rare plants, and was an amateur botanist (the plant *Lyellia* is named after him). Young Charles attended private local schools and, at about age ten, during an illness, began collecting insects, which became a regular pastime. Beginning in 1816, he attended Exeter College at Oxford University, where he was interested in scientific pursuits and joined the Geological Society. He studied law, but without great financial motivation to practice, Lyell soon left the bar, with his father's approval, and turned to geology.

By the mid-1820s, Lyell was deeply involved in geological research. He had written a paper on the formation of limestone in 1822 and toured France in 1823, where he made studies of the rocks in Aix-en-Provence and the Auvergne regions. The next year he traveled through Scotland with his teacher, William Buckland. During this early phase of his career, Lyell was a follower of Buckland, who attempted to make a case for the literal truth of biblical creation in his 1823 book *Reliquiae diluvianae*.

At the beginning of the nineteenth century, geological thought was dominated by ideas associated with several versions of catastrophism, which held that the earth's physical structure originated through flood or fire. According to one view, that of the Neptunists—led by a German, Abraham Gottlob Werner—the earth was shaped when the entire planet was under water. This theory, which called for swirling and turbulent oceans as high as the highest mountains, paid considerable attention to the various rock strata, and in this sense made an important contribution. But it failed to see the igneous origin of some rocks, and for years Werner and the Neptunists waged bitter debates with Vulcanists, who underscored the formative significance of volcanoes. In 1785 James Hutton had proposed a theory of uniformatism, which involved constant destruction and creation ("no vestige of a beginning," he wrote, "—no prospect of an end"). But his view was not widely accepted, and catastrophism continued to dominate geological thought.

By the latter part of the 1820s, however, Lyell was at work on his major opus, *The Principles of Geology*. Published in three volumes between 1830 and 1833, the *Principles* proved to be the most influential text on the subject ever written.

Like ANDREAS VESALIUS [21] in human anatomy or ANTOINE LAVOISIER [8] in chemistry, Lyell was fully aware of the importance of his new synthesis. He saw himself as forging a new science. "It cannot easily be created on sound principles," he wrote his publisher, "without making war on many prepossessions with which the public will not part easily. To do this honestly and without getting into a scrape requires much dexterity." In place of bitter controversy, Lyell introduced order and authority. His historical introduction to the topic was what one writer has called "masterly propaganda" which "bore fruit for more than a century." Revised continuously, the *Principles* underwent eleven editions during Lyell's lifetime.

Lyell's major thesis is one of gradualism, the notion that the history of the earth was an "uninterrupted succession of physical events, governed by the laws now in operation." From the beginning of the *Principles*, Lyell demands a cleavage of geology from the biblical theories, and he gives a historical account of the various myths of creation. He also provides a fully researched history of geology to the nineteenth century. Examining the fossil record, such as it existed, Lyell makes a variety of arguments which do not stand up today. But in the third volume of *Principles* he presents a scheme of geological time, including some nomenclature—eocene, miocene, and pliocene—still in use, and so he became known as one of the fathers of the science of stratigraphy.

Lyell was a mentor and friend to and key influence upon Charles Darwin. The first volume of the *Principles* was published a year before young Darwin set out on the *Beagle*; during the voyage he not only studied Lyell's book thoroughly but confirmed its ideas through observation. When he returned to England, the two men became close friends, and Darwin dedicated his *Journal of the Beagle* to Lyell. It is clear that Darwin was most impressed by Lyell's basic stance, that the geological present developed over time as a result of ordinary forces still in operation. And for his own part, Lyell accepted natural selection but was at first unwilling to follow Darwin with respect to the notion of the descent of man. He ultimately did so, writing *The Antiquity of Man* (1863), although the depth of his conversion to the theory of descent is not clear.

Lyell did not court controversy, especially in his later years. He was knighted in 1848 and made a baronet in 1864. In religion he was a deist. He had a pleasant disposition and courtly manners and was at ease in political circles. His marriage in 1832 to Mary Horner led to a honeymoon and geological cruise on the Rhine; the couple was childless. Lyell was a great traveler and quintessential British adventurer. He visited the United States twice, first in 1841; thereafter he wrote *Travels in North America*. While working on a twelfth edition of the *Principles*—despite blindness—he died on February 22, 1875.

29

Pierre Simon de Laplace
and Newtonian Mechanics

1749–1827

The application of mathematics to problems in physics became a primary task for the century that followed ISAAC NEWTON [1]. His work was greatly amplified and elaborated by a host of brilliant mathematical thinkers, and among them the central figure is the Frenchman Pierre Simon de Laplace. With key contributions to celestial mechanics, Laplace's hypothesis concerning the origin of the solar system is still cited today as a precursor to the theory of "black holes." He was a powerful figure, originator of what is called the Laplacian school, and had great immediate influence. "The age of Laplace witnessed the definitive establishment of the discipline of mathematical physics," writes Robert Fox, "with the techniques of mathematics being used to an unprecedented effect in the elaboration of theories that could then be subjected to the control of experiment." Morris Kline calls Laplace simply, "the greatest scientist of the late eighteenth and early nineteenth centuries."

The son of a farmer of moderate means, Laplace was born on March 23, 1749, at Beaumont-en-Auge in Calvados, a region known for its Camembert cheese and apple brandy. One of his uncles, a priest, recognized Laplace's exceptional talent in mathematics while he was a student at the local military school. At age sixteen he began to study at the University of Caen. Two years later he journeyed to Paris, intending to meet the great philosopher and mathematician Jean Le Rond d'Alembert. When he was not received, in spite of his letters of recommendation, he gained d'Alembert's attention by sending him a paper on the principles of mechanics. D'Alembert immediately recognized Laplace's genius, and soon found for him a teaching post at the École Militaire as professor of mathematics.

In 1773, reading a paper before the Academy of Sciences, Laplace asserted the stability of the solar system. Although Newton had been able to mathematically deduce the laws of planetary motion, which JOHANNES KEPLER [9] had formulated, certain problems remained to be resolved. The orbits of the planets around the sun are elliptical but they are not precisely the same year after year. The stability of the heavens and even the law of gravitation were at different times questioned by such eminent figures as Leibniz and LEONHARD EULER [35]. Laplace showed that perturbations among the planets would not change their distances from the sun, even over thousands of years. While this theory has been modified over the past two centuries, John North comments that "the skeleton of his analysis remains, a remarkable testimony to the achievements of Newton's successors in the century following his death."

Indeed, for the next decade after his initial analysis in 1783, Laplace, and the mathematician Joseph Lagrange, contributed a stream of papers on planetary motion. They cleared up the discrepancies of the orbital motions of Jupiter and Saturn, showed how the moon accelerates as a function of the earth's orbit, and introduced a new calculus for discovering the motion of celestial bodies. In 1784, with his *Théorie du mouvement et de la figure elliptique des planètes*, Laplace also introduced a new means of computing planetary orbits, which led to astronomical tables of improved accuracy. Moreover, in 1785 his introduction of a beautiful field equation in spherical harmonics, which bears his name, was found to be applicable to a great many phenomena, including gravitation, the propagation of sound, light, heat, water, electricity, and magnetism.

During the 1780s, Laplace also developed a cosmology. He suggested that the sun created the planets by spinning off successive rings of gaseous matters that then became solid spheres. The Laplace hypothesis, or nebular hypothesis, was a reasonable Newtonian one; it was a staple in astronomy books of the nineteenth century and remains part of broader hypotheses today. Even more impressive, from the standpoint of prescience, is Laplace's suggestion that "the attractive force of a heavenly body could be so large that light could not flow out of it." Though not the only one to have such an idea, which is based on Newton's particulate theory of light, this anticipation of the contemporary theory of "black holes" is very striking. Laplace included it in the first editions of his popular text *Exposition du système du monde*, published first in 1796; he omitted the idea from the final revisions of this work, for reasons which are not known.

In 1799 Laplace began to publish his *Mécanique céleste,* which appeared in five thick volumes over the next quarter century. This work consolidated his reputation, although it is of great mathematical complexity. Beginning in 1829, an American sea captain, actuary, and mathematical astronomer, Nathaniel Bowditch, translated and completely annotated the first four volumes. Laplace liked to shorten his explanations by writing, "It is easy to see that...." Bowditch said that he never encountered the expression "without feeling sure that I have hours of hard work to fill up the chasm."

Laplace also undertook an influential study of probability, publishing *Théorie analytique des probabilités* in 1812 after many years of work. Briefly, he gives a mathematically precise analysis of the notion that probability is a function of favorable outcomes versus all possible outcomes, and he applies it to physical problems. He also introduces the notion of correlation, which would receive a fuller treatment in the works of FRANCIS GALTON [94]. Although CHRISTIAAN HUYGENS [40] had been the first to approach the subject during the seventeenth century, and other mathematicians had contributed to understanding frequency of outcome, the classical theory of probability culminates with Laplace.

Unlike his friend and collaborator ANTOINE LAVOISIER [8], Laplace did not suffer with the coming of the French Revolution. During the revolutionary period he helped introduce the metric system and organize the École Polytechnique and the École Normale. In the reactionary wake of the Thermidor, he presided over a Commission of Five Hundred which issued a report on the progress of science. He subsequently became known to Napoleon, who, when he came to power with a coup d'état on the 18th Brumaire (November 9, 1799), appointed Laplace minister of the interior. This proved an egregious mismatch, and Laplace remained at the post just six weeks. As consolation for his dismissal, he was given a seat in the senate, where he was not particularly effective. However, Laplace continued his impressive ascendancy in the French scientific establishment, which he came to dominate through the first quarter of the nineteenth century. He became the venerated elder statesman for a group of younger, important scientists, including the naturalist Alexander von Humboldt and the chemist Joseph Gay-Lussac. In politics Laplace was not alone in voting for Napoleon's resignation in 1814; under the restorationist regime that followed he was a personage of great prominence. Napoleon having given him the title of count, Laplace was made a marquis by Louis XVIII. Clearly not known for constancy of political commitment, Laplace thus ended his life as an ultraroyalist.

Laplace was married to Charlotte de Courty de Romange in 1788, and they had two children. Many original documents concerning his life have been lost, and gaps in his biography have been filled by myth. Some papers were lost in a fire that destroyed the chateau of a descendant, and others went up in flames when Allied forces bombarded Caen during World War II. Laplace himself died on March 5, 1827, at his home outside Paris, in Arcueil. His last words are famous but disputed. "What we know is trifling; what we know not is immense" is one version; another is "Man follows only phantoms." It is probable that neither is correct.

30

Edwin Hubble
and the Modern Telescope

1889–1953

During the 1920s, in the wake of the revolution in physics and the general theory of relativity put forth by Albert Einstein [2], and with the help of ever more powerful telescopes, Edwin Hubble set the stage for a new cosmology. Astronomers during the nineteenth century had cataloged the stars and discussed the possible evolution of the solar system and origin of the earth—for which *cosmogony* was used as the overall term—but their speculations were limited to the Milky Way. With Hubble, an American Midwesterner working in the huge observatory at Mount Wilson in Southern California, came the recognition of thousands of further galaxies and the hypothesis of a vast, expanding, universe. Hubble's most significant and influential discoveries were, writes historian Robert W. Smith, "a particularly interesting example of the influence of aesthetics in cosmology." His work "helped to breed among astronomers and mathematicians of his day the confidence to discuss and ultimately attempt to explain the entire history of the universe."

Edwin Hubble was born in Marshfield, Missouri, on November 20, 1889, the son of a lawyer and insurance agent, John Powell Hubble, and Virginia Lee James. His family later moved to the Chicago suburb of Wheaton, Illinois, where he went to high school. He was an exceptional all-round athlete and an excellent student. In 1906, he received a scholarship to attend the University of Chicago. Although he studied pre-law at the behest of his father, he became interested in astronomy and took courses with Robert Millikan, the eminent physicist. In 1910 he received a Rhodes scholarship to Queen's College, Oxford. He spent three years there and while in England received his degree in jurisprudence. But, back in the United States, after the death of his father he gave up law. He taught high school Spanish and mathematics for a year in New Albany, Indiana, before returning to the University of Chicago for graduate work in astronomy and receiving his Ph.D. in 1917. Hubble became adept at practical astronomy through research at the university's Yerkes Observatory. His dissertation, a harbinger of work to come, was entitled "Photographic Investigations of Faint Nebulae."

In 1919, following service in World War I, Hubble joined the staff of the Mount Wilson Solar Observatory. The great Hooker reflecting telescope, which boasted a 100-inch mirror, was representative of the growing importance of the larger instruments then being built in the United States. Indeed, the light-gathering capacities of the newer telescopes was changing astronomy. One result was that in the early twenties a pivotal debate arose about the nature of the nebulae—the luminous cloudlike patches discernible in the night sky. According to one view, championed by the eminent Harlow Shapley, the nebulae were clouds of interstellar matter within the Milky Way; another, more radical hypothesis held that they were actually independent galaxies. These two theories represented vastly different conceptions of the content of the cosmos.

In 1922 Hubble published "A General Study of Diffuse Galactic Nebulae" in which he offered a new classification scheme, one that is still in use. More significant still, the following year, on October 4, Hubble resolved several stars within the Andromeda, one of the oldest known nebulae. He initially believed one of those stars to be a nova, or exploding star; but after comparing it with earlier photographs, he recognized that it was a pulsating Cepheid variable instead. As a consequence, Hubble was able to use established techniques to measure the star's distance from Earth. He obtained a figure—some one million light years—which far exceeded what Shapley had suggested was the diameter of the entire Milky Way. Receiving this news from Hubble, Shapley held out the missive to a colleague and said, "Here is the letter that has destroyed my universe."

With this finding and other observations over the next year, Hubble effectively ended the debate: Observable galaxies existed beyond the Milky Way; the universe was vaster than ever imagined.

Hubble's subsequent investigations into the nebulae had yet greater importance because of the potent implications of the general theory of relativity, introduced by ALBERT EINSTEIN [2] in 1916, for a new cosmology. Briefly stated, relativity put into question whether the universe is basically static or dynamic—expanding or contracting. The crucial variable, introduced by the Dutch astronomer Willem de Sitter, was the nature of light emitted by the distant galaxies. If the universe was expanding, this light would be "red-shifted," indicating that the galaxies were receding from Earth. As this debate continued through the 1920s, Hubble and his colleague Milton Humason measured the distant nebulae, and in gathering spectral data they did indeed find a redshift. Hubble's 1929 paper "A Relation Between Distance and Radical Velocity Among Extra-Galactic Nebulae" is a landmark in the history of astronomy.

Measuring the luminosity from these galaxies, Hubble moreover showed that the more distant a galaxy was, the greater its "apparent velocity." Although Hubble himself refrained from saying so directly, his calibrations led to the conclusion that there was a rate of expansion to the universe which could be calculated by what is since known as "Hubble's constant." Derived from this is "Hubble's law," which gives the velocity-distance relation: $V = Hd$, where H is the constant. The precise value of the Hubble constant remains today an interesting question for astronomy.

The notion of an expanding universe met some initial

resistance. Albert Einstein, who for a time believed the universe to be static—he called this the most serious blunder of his career—changed his mind when he visited Hubble at Mount Wilson and the California Institute of Technology in 1931. And the announcement of Einstein's change of heart had the effect of "catapulting Hubble into the eye of international fame," writes his biographer, Gale Christianson. According to a contemporary newspaper account, "The universe, to use a non-scientific expression, [is going] hell-bent for chaos, ignoring the law of gravitation, flying ever outward, faster and faster. It looks as if the whole is breaking up and rushing into a limitless outer void. No good can come of this."

Although Hubble charged with new life the issues that have since become part of contemporary cosmology—in his later career he tried to date the universe—he himself studiously avoided direct entanglement in such debates.* He wrote: "Not until the empirical resources are exhausted, need we pass on to the dreamy realms of speculation." Unlike ARTHUR EDDINGTON [37] in the 1930s or STEPHEN HAWKING [54] today, Hubble was famous without being a great popularizer. However, he did publish *The Realm of the Nebulae* for a lay audience in 1936 and *The Observational Approach to Cosmology* the following year. After his death *The Hubble Atlas of Galaxies* appeared, and *The Nature of Science*, a collection of his essays, was published in 1954. Though he held conservative political views, Hubble was opposed to nuclear weapons. His lecture "The War That Must Not Happen" was a vision of destruction he delivered soon after World War II ended.

Hubble's fame drew numerous visitors to Mount Wilson, and he became acquainted with such intellectuals as Walter Lippmann and Aldous Huxley. He lectured before distinguished audiences at the Carnegie Institution in Washington, D.C., and frequently visited England, where he and his wife, Grace, both Anglophiles, were entertained by the greatest scientists of the era. Among his acquaintances were numerous movie stars and executives from nearby Hollywood, and Hubble and his wife had an

---

*In 1936 Hubble came to the conclusion that the universe was two billion years old, a figure which conflicted with dating methods then in use. Two decades later it was found that Hubble had confounded two types of luminosity of Cepheids, and the figure was revised upward. Today, although the magnitudes of Earth-based and star-based estimates are a better match, the age of the universe remains somewhat uncertain.

enduring friendship with Anita Loos, the author of *Gentlemen Prefer Blondes.*

Not always remembered with great warmth by many of his colleagues, Hubble was considered by some to be arrogant and unpleasant. "Most would admit, but few volunteer," suggests Timothy Ferris, "that he was one of the greatest astronomers who ever lived." On the other hand, he not only encouraged Milton Humason, first hired as a janitor at the Mount Wilson observatory, to work in astronomy, but gave him full credit in the papers they published together.

In 1948 Edwin Hubble became the first to operate Caltech's huge five-meter telescope on Mount Palomar. Five years later, on September 28, 1953, he died of a stroke as he prepared for several nights of observation.

Hubble's name is recalled today not only in the laws of the redshift, but in the space-based Hubble Telescope, launched in 1990. Although initially plagued with technical problems, the Hubble, when repaired, began returning its remarkable images to Earth and continues to peer more deeply into the cosmos than any other instrument yet devised.

31

Joseph J. Thomson
and the Discovery of the Electron

1856–1940

The cathode ray tube is the basis of two omnipresent modern technologies: the television screen and the computer monitor. But originally, in the nineteenth century, the cathode ray tube was an experimental apparatus. In its basic form, it is a glass tube plugged by metal electrodes, with the air evacuated and some specific gas pumped in. When the electrodes are connected to a battery with enough voltage, the cathode rays strike the opposite end of the tube and glow or fluoresce. The rays are streams of electrons, not light rays. And they were the first subatomic particle to be discovered. The discovery of the electron, by Joseph John Thomson in 1897, was the crucial first step in the development of the twentieth-century concept of the atom.

Joseph John Thomson was born on December 18, 1856, at Cheetham Hill, a suburb of Manchester, England. His father, Joseph Thomson, was a publisher and antiquarian book dealer of Scottish origin; his mother was Emma Swindells. The family atmosphere was parochial rather than learned, but James was precocious in school and had an exceptional memory. In 1870, at age fourteen, he began attending Owens College and came under the influence of Balfour Stewart, a physics professor. When his father died in 1873, Joseph received a scholarship which honored the memory of JOHN DALTON [74], the Manchesterian whose work first recast atomic theory in modern form. After graduating Trinity College in 1880 as the "second wrangler" in mathematics, Thomson was elected a fellow and remained at Cambridge for the rest of his life. He worked at Cavendish Laboratory, which had been opened in 1871 and originally headed by JAMES CLERK MAXWELL [12]. In 1884, at an exceptionally young age, Thomson was named Cavendish Professor of Experimental Physics.

Toward the end of the nineteenth century, it became probable that atoms—whose existence was still doubted in some quarters—were not simply impenetrable balls of various weights, but comprised of some underlying structure. The evolving theory of electromagnetism implied that atoms were in some way electrical; and experiments hinted that, possibly, the glowing cathode rays were charged atomic particles. William Crookes, whose improved vacuum tubes were the basis of Thomson's experiments, believed as early as the 1870s that the rays resembled a stream of molecules. Thomson benefited from a great deal of data, which he gathered and pored over for a number of years, as well as from a full theoretical grasp of electromagnetic theory. In addition, he was inspired by the discovery of X rays. His decisive investigations took place from 1896 to 1898.

In the first of several crucial experiments, Thomson placed two metal plates, connected to a battery, inside a cathode tube, creating a magnetic field through which the rays would have to pass. When Thomson found that the presence of this field could deflect cathode rays, he could conclude that they consisted of particles and were not light beams. More significant, Thomson now had the means to derive from the velocity, which was known, the particles' e/m, that is, the ratio between the electric charge and the mass. When Thomson found a very large ratio between charge and mass, he inferred that the particle was very small—

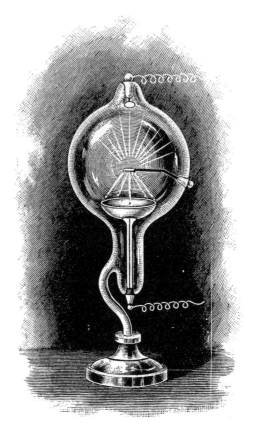

Röntgen's mysterious rays are the starting point of twentieth-century research into the atom.

indeed, at least one thousand times smaller than hydrogen, the lightest known atom.

Thomson tested a variety of materials and gases and achieved for all essentially the same e/m ratio. Continuing his experiments and using a cloud chamber, he was able in 1898 to verify the size of the "corpuscles." His conclusion constitutes one of the true milestones in physics: Cathode rays consist of particles that are elementary and found in all matter. As he put it himself later: "[The] carriers of electricity are bodies…having a mass very much smaller than that of the atom of any known element, and are of the same character from whatever source the negative electricity may be derived."

When Thomson first announced his preliminary discoveries on April 30, 1897, at a Friday evening lecture of the Royal Institute, he was understood by only a few of his colleagues. But so convincing was his series of experiments that recognition was more or less immediate. "The scientific world," according to a contemporary account, "seemed suddenly to awaken to the fact that their conceptions had been revolutionized." Thomson's term for the elementary particle, "corpuscle," was soon replaced by "electron," which had been proposed several years earlier by the Irish physicist, George Johnstone Stoney.

In 1903 Thomson published a summary of his work, *Conduction of Electricity Through Gases*. He developed a "plum pudding" model of the atom, in which electrons studded a uniform sphere. This soon gave way to the solar-system model developed by ERNEST RUTHERFORD [19] and NIELS BOHR [3], which became the last of the visualizable prototypes. Today, neither the atom nor its electrons can be effectively understood through visual representations.

Thomson was a much-beloved scientist and teacher. A number of his students went on to become Nobel laureates. The Cavendish Laboratory was already a mecca for physicists, and it remained so for a long time afterward. It is often remarked, as a foible of Thomson's, that he was a clumsy experimentalist who needed much assistance; but he was highly ingenious at designing and refining instruments. "Thomson's success," wrote A. E. E. McKenzie, "rested on his ability to perceive with clarity a fundamental problem, to formulate an hypothesis, to conceive experimental tests and to marshal a concerted attack from all angles by a team working under him." In 1906 Thomson was awarded the Nobel Prize for physics. After 1912 he reduced his research load and concentrated on administrative duties. He was knighted in 1908; in 1918 he was named to the mastership of Trinity College, a high honor. He resigned from the Cavendish in 1919 and lived, largely in retirement, until August 30, 1940. His remains were cremated and his funeral was held in Westminster Abbey, near the graves of ISAAC NEWTON [1], CHARLES DARWIN [4], and ERNEST RUTHERFORD [19].

Although he disliked philosophy, Thomson was a devout Anglican who prayed privately every day. He was married to Rose Elizabeth Paget, and they had two children. Their son, George Paget Thomson, became a physicist and, like his father, a Nobel laureate, for his work on electron diffraction, a technique used to investigate gas molecules and the structure of solid surfaces.

32

Max Born
and Quantum Mechanics

1882–1970

Speaking generally, it is Max Born who may stand first in line to be blamed for the too-often-quoted remarks by ALBERT EINSTEIN [2] that "God does not play dice" and that "The Lord is subtle but He is not malicious." For Born, who coined the term *quantum mechanics* in 1924, was the first to see that probability, not certainty, governed measurements of the electron. One of the most influential theoretical physicists, Born in the 1920s was at the heart of the interpretation of the new descriptions of the atom. And he became to some extent a model for twentieth-century physics: rigorous in mathematics, not devoid of philosophical understanding, and liberal in spirit. "Born's work was always characterized by full mathematical rigor, in striking contrast to Bohr's patchwork theoretical edifices..." writes John Gribbin. "Both kinds of genius were essential to the new understanding of atoms."

Brought into the world on December 11, 1882, in Breslau, Germany (today Wroclaw, Poland), Max Born was the son of Gustav Born and Margarethe Kauffmann Born. His mother, an excellent pianist from a well-known family of industrialists, died when Max was about four years old. He grew up, however, in an exemplary environment for a German scientist-to-be: urban with a love of nature, intellectual with a penchant for music. And he had a strong relationship with his father. Gustav Born, a professor of anatomy at the University of Breslau, was an amateur botanist. Of him Max later wrote, "I loved to listen to father's fascinating tales about the marvels of life, and to watch tiny creatures in a drop of dirty water out of a pond which he showed us in his microscope." It is interesting that, shortly before his death, Born's father was awarded a gold medal for his work on the development of the embryo.

After attending the Kaiser Wilhelm Gymnasium at the University of Breslau from 1901, Born became interested in mathematics—geometry held first appeal—and then physics. In 1904 Born began to study at the University of Göttingen under an important physicist, Hermann Minkowski, and mathematician David Hilbert, whose assistant he became in 1905. This led Born to study the unsuccessful efforts to discover the "ether," the hypothetical substance through which electromagnetic waves were thought to be propagated. (It was shortly to be proved superfluous by Einstein.) By the time Born received his Ph.D. in 1907, his interests had definitively evolved toward theoretical physics.

In 1908, while at the University of Breslau, Born heard of Einstein's new theory of relativity, which touched on his own interests in the dynamics of electricity and optics. He soon returned to Göttingen, intending to work with his former teacher Minkowski, but the latter died soon after Born's arrival. Born carried on Minkowski's work in relativity and electrodynamics, and in 1915 he was named professor of theoretical physics at the University of Berlin, where the department was under the direction of MAX PLANCK [25]. Here he also became friends with Albert Einstein. Born became well known for the study of the structure and properties of crystals, which laid some of the groundwork for the development, later in the century, of solid-state physics.

In 1921 Born became director of the Institute for Theoretical Physics at the University of Göttingen. There he switched the focus of his interest from crystals to quantum physics. This was a logical, even necessary shift, inasmuch as the quantum theory of the atom had entered its period of crisis. Physicists had discovered that in spite of the theory's clear superiority over classical methods, the electron's behavior could not be predicted merely by resorting to quantum numbers. In mid-1922, following a visit to Göttingen by NIELS BOHR [3], Born stated: "The time is perhaps past when the imagination of the investigator was given free rein to devise atomic molecular models at will. Rather, we are now in a position to construct models with a certain, although still by no means complete certainty, through the application of quantum rules."

This was a call for greater rigor. In pursuit of it Born conducted an important ongoing colloquium—"the high court of Göttingen physics"—in which the latest work was carefully scrutinized and criticized. In early 1923, he made young WERNER HEISENBERG [15] his assistant.

Over the next two years, work by the principal figures at Göttingen and Copenhagen brought quantum theory to its new moment of parturition. In 1924 Born first used the term *Quanten Mechanik*, and in late June 1925 Werner Heisenberg offered an equation that gave certain rules for calculating the position of electrons around an atom. Born recognized in Heisenberg's mathematics the use of "matrix calculus," which together they soon systematized as a general theory of quantum mechanics, applicable to atomic phenomena.

Born also played an important role after ERWIN SCHRÖDINGER [18] published in 1926 his equation for what came to be known as "wave mechanics." Instead of treating the electron as a particle, Schrödinger had given it the status of a wave. Which was it? Schrödinger suggested—in his own defense—that the electron behaved fundamentally like a wave and that it seemed to be a particle only under certain conditions. But this proved not to be the case. Working through Schrödinger's equations, Born realized that the more likely explanation was that the actual representation was a "wave of probability." The electron was neither simply a particle which could be located precisely in three-dimensional space, nor an oceanlike wave of three dimensions. Henceforth the correct results to problems in quantum mechanics would incorporate this statistical, probabilistic notion. Within a year, Heisenberg codified this step as the "uncertainty principle."

As a consequence of these researches, Born's prominence became very great, and for several years Göttingen was an important training ground for physicists in Germany, much like Niels Bohr's Institute at Copenhagen. In 1932 Born was appointed the university's dean of faculty of science. Like many other Germans, he thought Adolf Hitler "simply ridiculous, and we refused to believe that such a mean, low scoundrel could be taken seriously by the 'nation of poets and thinkers', as the Germans used to call themselves." In 1933 Hitler came to power and anti-Semitic laws almost immediately put an end to Born's teaching career in Germany. After a traumatic period, he and his family moved to Great Britain. He remained there in various academic posts until his retirement in 1953.

In the last phase of Born's career, he returned to Germany, resettling near Göttingen. He had published *Atomic Energy and Its Use in War and Peace* soon after World War II, and he continued to be active in the early antinuclear crusade. He was a founder of the Pugwash movement, and a leader of the Göttingen 18, a group of West German physicists who issued a manifesto rejecting any collaboration with government on nuclear weapons. When Born received the Nobel Prize, belatedly, in 1954, he was able to apply enhanced prestige to his new role as statesman of science, examining the social and political consequences of a nuclear world.

Born's involvements in his later years reflect a lifelong interest in the larger problems of science. "I never liked being a specialist," he wrote in his autobiography, *My Life and Views*. "I would not fit into the ways of science today, done by teams of specialists. The philosophical background of science always interested me more than its special results." Throughout his career Born also wrote for a broader audience, and many of his books were translated into English: *Einstein's Theory of Relativity* dates from 1924 and *Mechanics of the Atom* from 1927. His exceptionally popular *Atomic Physics* and *The Restless Universe* were published in 1935. *Physics and Politics* was published in 1962 and *The Born–Einstein Letters* in 1971.

Born married Heidi Ehrenberg in 1913, and they had two daughters and a son. His relationship with his high-strung, demonstrative wife was stormy but enduring. Born was not himself expressively or verbally emotional, which his son, Gustav, suggested was perhaps due to the loss of his mother at an early age. Born was a musician, however, and he enjoyed learning poetry by heart.

Although quantum mechanics involves much mathematics that is obtuse and difficult to understand, one need not be a mathematician to see that momentum p and position q do not add up in the usual way: qp in quantum theory is not the same as pq. The commutative law doesn't apply. When Max Born died on January 5, 1970, he was buried in Göttingen, and his basic, historically strange equation to that effect is etched on his tombstone:

$$pq - qp = \frac{h}{2\pi i}$$

Francis Crick

and Molecular Biology

1916–

In 1953 in collaboration with the American JAMES WATSON [49], British graduate student Francis Crick discovered the structure and function of DNA, the molecule in which is embedded the genetic code. The Watson-Crick hypothesis, developed over the next two decades to explain the basic mechanisms of heredity and cell function, is arguably the most significant development in any field of science since World War II. It has led to a revolution throughout biology, has entirely reshaped the field of genetics research, and is bringing about broad new developments in medicine. "No one man discovered or created molecular biology," Jacques Monod said some years ago. "But one man dominates intellectually the whole field, because he knows the most and understands the most. Francis Crick." In recent years, Crick has turned to neurobiology, where he has developed original hypotheses on the nature of consciousness.

Francis Harry Compton Crick was born on June 8, 1916, near Northampton, England, a town in the English Midlands, the elder son of Harry and Anne Elizabeth Wilkins Crick. His father, who ran a boot and shoe manufacture when Francis was born, fell upon hard times after 1929 and moved his family to London. There he managed shoe stores during the Depression and sent his two sons to Mill Hill, a British public school.

As a child Francis Crick was fascinated by science, though in retrospect he detected in himself no special genius—apart from a great curiosity about nature and the universe. The codiscoverer of DNA lost his religious faith when he was about twelve years old, and that loss helped determine his choice of career. As he wrote in his brief intellectual autobiography *What Mad Pursuit*, "A knowledge of the true age of the earth and of the fossil record makes it impossible for any balanced intellect to believe in the literal truth of every part of the Bible in the way that fundamentalists do. And if some part of the Bible is manifestly wrong, why should any of the rest of it be accepted automatically?...What could be more foolish than to base one's entire view of life on ideas that, however plausible at the time, now appear to be quite erroneous?" Crick's atheism was one of his motivating forces in choosing his scientific life's work.

In 1934 Crick began studies in physics at University College, London, and he graduated in 1937 with second honors. At this juncture, he was taught only a little quantum mechanics, a subject he learned mainly by himself later. He remained at University College for graduate work, which he had almost completed at the outbreak of World War II. Crick then joined the Admiralty, where he helped design "noncontact" magnetic and acoustic mines, and remained there for a time after the war, assigned to scientific intelligence.

Certain that he wanted to undertake fundamental research, and prompted by his atheism, Crick narrowed his choices to two: the basis of life and the brain. He finally decided upon the "living-nonliving borderline"—the physical and chemical basis of life. He was influenced by *What Is Life?* by ERWIN SCHRÖDINGER [18], and was inspired by LINUS PAULING [16], who spoke in 1946 about the prospects of structural chemistry. In 1947 Crick began working at Strangeways Laboratory, Cambridge; two years later he transferred to Cavendish Laboratory. There a team headed by Max Perutz was applying the technique of X-ray crystallography in attempts to discover the three-dimensional structure of proteins. Crick made the X-ray diffraction of proteins the topic of his Ph.D. thesis.

By the 1940s, the prevailing view held that the genetic material in a cell was a protein. However, knowledge about deoxyribonucleic acid, a large molecule ubiquitous in cells, was growing. DNA had been discovered in 1869 and named in 1899. By 1949, Erwin Chargaff determined the relative composition of its four bases for a variety of species. And Oswald Avery, at Rockefeller University, had brought forth evidence, though tentative, that pure DNA could be the "transforming factor" in a certain kind of bacterial replication.

In general, the discovery of the structure of DNA was an extension of physics into biology, by way of chemistry. To be more specific, in 1948 the chemist Linus Pauling recognized the *helical* shape of the polypeptide chains which form proteins. This suggested a basic model in the microworld; other helical structures might be discovered. By the early 1950s, "Helices were in the air," Crick wrote, "and you would have to be either obtuse or very obstinate not to think along helical lines."

In 1951 James Watson arrived at Cavendish Laboratories and befriended Crick; the two began to share an office and work together. "Jim and I hit it off immediately," Crick wrote later, "partly because our interests were astonishingly similar and partly, I suspect, because a certain youthful arrogance, a ruthlessness, and an impatience with sloppy thinking came naturally to both of us." In addition, Watson's familiarity with the work of MAX DELBRÜCK [68] and his phage group was complemented by Crick's knowledge of X-ray diffraction.

Crick and Watson did not themselves do experimental work on DNA, but relied on several keys, including X-ray photographs of DNA taken by crystallographer Rosalind Franklin. Following the lead of Linus Pauling, they took to building models of the molecule using wire, beads, metal, and cardboard. The crucial discovery, by Watson, came on February 21, 1953, when he recognized the complementary shape of the base pairs: adenine-thymine and guanine-cytosine. In April 1953 they published in

Nature their "Molecular Structure of Nucleic Acids" and noted, somewhat archly, asserting priority, "It has not escaped our notice that the specific pairing we have postulated immediately suggests a possible copying mechanism for the genetic material."

Over the next twenty years, Crick was a leading figure in molecular biology, and he played a principal role in unraveling the nature of the genetic code. He suggested that a sequence of triplets of nucleic acid bases, in a particular order, lead to the manufacture, within the cell, of a specific protein. This was the "sequence hypothesis," and in 1958 Crick predicted the discovery of transfer-RNA to indicate how this task is accomplished. Crick was also responsible for what he called the "central dogma" in molecular genetics: Information once encoded in a DNA molecule is on a one-way street. Once sequence information has got into a protein, it cannot get out again in detail. The central dogma remains a key organizing principle in molecular biology.

In 1976 Crick moved to the Salk Institute for Biological Studies in La Jolla, California, where he took up a new field of inquiry, the study of consciousness and the brain. His arrival in the field came at a time when behaviorism was in decline, cognitive psychology was beginning, and neurobiology was in "techno-foment." Crick was one of several Nobel laureates— Roger Penrose and Gerald Edelman are two others—responsible for investing the field of brain function with a new allure. Much as he had laid open genetics via biochemistry, Crick hoped to show that all thought was explicable in physical, neurological terms. Focusing on the visual system, he had published by 1994 *The Astonishing Hypothesis*, which gave expression to a materialist, purely electrophysical view of consciousness. In it he writes that "your joys and your sorrows, your memories and your ambitions, your sense of personal identity and free will, are in fact no more than the behavior of a vast assembly of nerve cells and their associated molecules." Crick was one scientist willing to emphasize that his views were in "head-on contradiction to the religious beliefs of billions of human beings alive today."

"It is clear that Crick's chief contribution to biology," writes historian of science Robert Olby, "has been his physical sense and his ability to see through to the essence of the problem." Indeed, Crick himself has pointed out the fundamental conceptual importance of DNA in contrast with the work of its actual discovery. "The discovery of the double helix," he writes in *What Mad*

Pursuit, "...was, scientifically, fairly commonplace. What was important was not the way it was discovered but the object discovered—the structure of DNA itself."

According to Watson, on the day of discovery of the double helix, Crick left the laboratory and went into the Eagle Pub, a block away from Cavendish, where he announced in his loud, booming voice that he and Watson had discovered "the secret of life." Crick remembers it rather differently. He says that he returned home to tell his wife, Odile, that he had made an important discovery. She did not believe it and told him years later, "You were always coming home and saying things like that, so naturally I thought nothing of it."

34

Enrico Fermi
and Atomic Physics

1901–1954

Enrico Fermi has a solid place in twentieth-century history as the man who, beneath a football stadium in Chicago in 1942, created the first sustained man-made nuclear reaction—an initial step toward the development of the atomic bomb. Long before this, however, Fermi had become a central organizing figure in modern physics. In the 1920s he developed a statistical method still used for analyzing subatomic particles. And when beta decay, the emission of electrons from a radioactive nucleus, perplexed physicists, Fermi provided a dramatic explanation by proposing the existence of a new force in nature, the weak force.* During the 1930s Fermi conducted a series of experiments that transmuted various elements into radioactive isotopes. Although his achievements are not comparable to those of JAMES CLERK MAXWELL [12], ALBERT EINSTEIN [2], or NIELS BOHR [3], "With his superb intelligence and all-consuming interest in all branches of physics and his mastery of neutron physics," write Lloyd Motz and Jefferson Weaver, "Fermi became the undisputed leader among nuclear physicists."

Enrico Fermi was born in Rome on September 29, 1901, the youngest of three children of Alberto Fermi, a railroad executive, and Ida de Gattis, an elementary school teacher. Fermi long remained close to his family, which was industrious, middle-class, secular, and severe. He excelled early in math and science, showed strong mechanical talent, a trait which he shares with many other physicists, and was endowed with an exceptional memory. As a child, he and his brother built motors and electrical toys; Enrico also committed to rote memory parts of Dante's *Divine Comedy* and Ariosto's epic satire *Orlando Furioso* (also a favorite of GALILEO GALILEI [7]). Although he began to study mathematical physics in early adolescence, he was propelled toward the subject upon the sudden death of his brother, Giulio, with whom he was exceptionally close. Enrico was fourteen years old.

In 1918 Fermi, with the help of a scholarship, entered the Scuola Normale Superiore at the University of Pisa. He received his Ph.D. in physics in 1922, graduating magna cum laude. He was by this time familiar with atomic physics, just then being developed. In fact, he was more conversant with contemporary physics than his professors. By age twenty-two he was considered an authority of some importance in Italy. He had developed, and would retain all his life, an impressive capacity for sustained work. In 1927, after a year's study of quantum theory with MAX BORN [32] at the University of Göttingen, Fermi returned to Italy as a lecturer at the University of Florence.

Fermi's first great contribution to physics came in the mid-twenties, as an application of quantum mechanics. Fermi sug-

---

*The "weak force" apparent in radioactive decay was the obverse of the "strong force," which binds the nucleus together.

gested that the "exclusion principle," proposed by Wolfgang Pauli in 1925, which limited the options for the position of an electron around the nucleus of an atom, could be applied to explain the behavior of atoms in a gas. What became known as Fermi-Dirac statistics was eventually forged into a major tool of quantum statistics.

In 1926 Fermi became the first professor of theoretical physics at the University of Rome, with lifetime tenure. Fermi's rapid advance to the top of physics represented a veritable revival of the discipline in Italy. In 1928 he published *Introduzione alla fisica atomica*. In 1929 he was appointed to the Royal Academy of Italy by the fascist dictator Benito Mussolini. He became its youngest member.

Perhaps Fermi's most influential achievement came, in late 1933, with the theory of beta decay. In this natural process, occurring in any radioactive particle, the nucleus expels electrons. The mechanics of this were disturbing, because they apparently violated the principle of conservation of energy. Just as with the Bohr-Rutherford model of the atom, where it was not clear why supposedly orbiting electrons did not collapse into the atomic nucleus, so beta decay raised the question of why the nucleus held together at all.

Fermi showed that beta decay involves the creation of both an electron and a *neutrino*—an effectively massless particle he postulated and named in the early 1930s. (It was experimentally discovered in 1956.) Thus, although the nucleus of an atom itself contains no electrons, it nevertheless emits them, together with energy, when it decays. Fermi proposed that a *weak force*, stronger than the gravitational force but much weaker than the electromagnetic force, was responsible for beta decay. Although the British journal *Nature* refused to publish Fermi's article on beta decay, the article quickly made an impact when published in Italy. Because of its great explanatory power, physicists readily accepted the notion of a new fundamental force in nature.

In 1934 experiments by Irène and Jean Frédéric Joliot-Curie showed that radioactive elements could be created by bombarding the nuclei of known elements. This was a seminal discovery, and Fermi was inspired to return to the laboratory. Using neutrons slowed up in paraffin for increased power, he created and investigated the properties of a number of radioactive isotopes.

The "footprint" of Fermilab.

Fascism in Italy was a long-established fact, but Benito Mussolini's 1936 alliance with Nazi Germany could not be ignored, and it had a chilling effect on the academic community. Fermi began to avoid publishing his papers in German, and he developed ties with Americans. In 1938 Italy began its own anti-Semitic campaign, and although Fermi was not especially political, he was concerned because his wife, Laura, was Jewish. When, late the same year, he was awarded the Nobel Prize for his experimental work on artificial radioactivity, he decided to emigrate to the United States. After journeying to Stockholm to accept the award, he did not return to Rome, but arrived in New York City on January 2, 1939. He took a position as professor of physics at Columbia University and settled in Leonia, New Jersey.

In 1939 the discovery of fission—which Fermi had barely missed discovering several years before—revealed to physicists the dramatic possibility of creating a chain reaction with great explosive potential. While he had not recognized fission when experimentally bombarding elements with neutrons during the 1930s, Fermi had developed an intuitive grasp of atomic behavior that bordered on the infallible. Although said not to have wanted to actively participate at first, Fermi began commuting to the University of Chicago in 1942, and he became a central figure in both the experimental and theoretical development of the atomic bomb.

Fermi directed the preliminary effort to build an "atomic pile" (he coined the term) to create a "self-sustaining" nuclear reaction at Stagg Field at the University of Chicago. Using pure uranium and uranium oxide, the pile consisted of 40,000 pounds of graphite bricks to diffuse the nuclear reaction throughout the structure, with interstitial cadmium rods to control it. When the rods were removed on December 2, 1942, the pile went "critical" for twenty-eight minutes. It was the world's first controlled nuclear chain reaction.

Under the assumed name of Henry Farmer, Fermi became general adviser to the Manhattan Project in Los Alamos, New Mexico, in the summer of 1944. He was present at Trinity, the test explosion of the bomb, on July 16, 1945. An oft-repeated anecdote relates that, before detonation, he dropped bits of paper on the ground as a way of measuring the force of the bomb by their displacement from the blast.

Fermi returned to the University of Chicago after World War II and spent the rest of his career as professor at the Institute for Nuclear Studies. A force and eminence in science, Fermi was a magnet for students in physics; several graduate students who worked with him became Nobel laureates, including MURRAY GELL-MANN [45]. Toward the end of his life Fermi became interested in the emerging field of particle physics. Fermi also lived to see the beginning of the McCarthy era. Unlike his friend EDWARD TELLER [88], Fermi testified on behalf of J. ROBERT OPPENHEIMER [87].

Fermi received many honors during his life, including several which live on in the body of experimental physics. The *fermion* is any elementary particle that obeys Fermi-Dirac statistics; both electrons and protons are fermions. The hundredth element on the periodical table, discovered in 1952, was subsequently named *fermium*. The *fermi*, a very small unit of length— 10^{-13} cm—is used in nuclear physics.

Enrico Fermi died from stomach cancer on November 30, 1954. When his colleague and biographer Emilio Segrè visited him in the hospital, Fermi was measuring the flow of liquid from his intravenous tube, counting the drops of fluid, and timing them with a stopwatch.

35

Leonhard Euler

and Eighteenth-Century Mathematics

1707–1783

The work of Leonhard Euler builds upon and enlarges the success of Newtonian physics and represents the flowering of mathematics as a tool of analysis. Astronomy, the geometry of surfaces, optics, electricity and magnetism, artillery and ballistics, and hydrostatics are only some of Euler's fields. He put Newton's laws, calculus, trigonometry, and algebra into a recognizably modern form. He was one of the most prolific mathematicians in history, with over eight hundred fifty articles and books to his credit. His output did not diminish even as he went blind in old age, and after his death, the St. Petersburg Academy continued to publish his articles for the next half century. Reading his popular *Letters to a German Princess* today, one finds a model of logic, clear exposition, and bourgeois morality. "This is indeed the best world possible," wrote Euler, "as every thing in it concurs to promote our eternal salvation."

Leonhard Euler was born in Basel, Switzerland, on April 15, 1707, to Margarete Brucker and her husband, Paul Euler. A Calvinist pastor who had studied mathematics with Jacob Bernoulli, Paul Euler was in a position to appreciate his son's mathematical gifts, but initially appears to have wanted Euler to take up theology. However, Leonhard's abilities, which included a prodigious memory, were soon apparent; he learned algebra before he was an adolescent. At fourteen, in 1720, he entered the University of Basel, where he studied medicine, theology, and the humanities, receiving the equivalent of a bachelor's degree in 1722 and a master's degree in philosophy the following year. Even after joining the university's theology department, he continued to devote much of his time to mathematics and finally took it up unequivocally.

The Eulers were friendly with the Bernoulli family, and Leonhard and the sons of Jean Bernoulli, Daniel and Nicolas, became close friends. Both Bernoulli brothers took up academic positions in Russia at the invitation of Catherine I, and in 1727 asked Euler to join them at the Academy of Sciences. Initially, in consequence of Catherine's death that year, Euler's situation was unclear; but by 1730 he was appointed professor of physics and then professor of mathematics three years later. He subsequently played a part in Russia's reform of weights and measures, supervised the geography department, and even wrote elementary mathematics textbooks.

With the publication of *Principia Mathematica* by ISAAC NEWTON [1] in 1687, the possibilities for mathematics expanded enormously. During the 1730s, partly in conjunction with Bernoulli, Euler overhauled Newton's language and notation, developing some of the familiar algebraic symbols as well as theorems in trigonometry and geometry. His 1736 treatise, *Mechanica*, represented the flourishing state of Newtonian physics under the rubric of mathematics, bringing to mechanics a universality which until then it possessed more in principle than practice.

In 1741 Euler left Russia to become professor of mathematics at the Berlin Academy of Sciences and to take his place at the court of the new king of Prussia, Frederick II (Frederick the

Great). Here Euler became prosperous and well known, the owner of a home in Berlin and a farm on its outskirts. His treatise on the calculus of variations appeared in 1744, and his *Introductio in analysin infinitorum*, printed in 1748, is an introduction to pure mathematics, in which Euler treats algebra, the theory of equations, and trigonometry, as well as providing a treatise on analytical geometry. Euler also published the first two complete treatises on calculus: *Institutiones calculi differentialis*, from 1755, and *Institutiones calculi integralis*, from 1768. The Berlin period was remarkably fertile, with some two hundred seventy-five publications.

Although Frederick the Great made considerable use of Euler's abilities for practical ends in problems of engineering and finance, Euler was not a popular figure at court. Frederick understood nothing of mathematics, and their relations eventually went awry. Euler did publish *Letters to a German Princess*, lessons in natural science for the princess of Anhalt-Dessau. This book was a popular success and was translated and often reprinted during the nineteenth century.

In 1766 Euler took up the offer of the Enlightenment empress Catherine the Great, who had come to power four years previously, to return to Russia. Euler was provided for in grand style. He continued to work, although his eyesight worsened; he employed his sons to help him write down long equations which he was able to keep in memory. Nor did other obstacles stop him from working in old age. Although his house burned down, his manuscripts were saved; and while efforts to restore his sight met with some success, he finally went blind entirely. Euler died of a stroke on September 18, 1783, after a day spent on calculating the orbit of the planet Uranus, recently discovered by WILLIAM HERSCHEL [27]. His last words, while playing with one of his grandchildren, were: "I die."

A strict Calvinist, Euler read a chapter in the Bible to his large family every night—complete with some form of exhortation. He was bourgeois in outlook and cared nothing for the insurgencies of such Enlightenment thinkers as Voltaire. Wrote Sir David Brewster of Euler in 1833, "In all his habits he was sober and temperate, in his temper lively and cheerful. In his moral and religious character there is much to admire." When his first wife, Katharina Gsell, died in 1776 after a long and happy marriage, Euler soon turned around and married her half sister, Salome.

36

Justus Liebig
and Nineteenth-Century Chemistry

1803–1873

Practical chemistry developed at a bewildering pace during the nineteenth century. Justus von Liebig, one of its founding and dominant figures, made crucial discoveries in the emerging field of organic chemistry, discovering a host of compounds such as chloroform and the cyanides, and his famous laboratory performed thousands of analyses. Liebig's work was a major factor in the success of the German chemical and dye industry. In mid-career he turned to agricultural chemistry, shaped a new understanding of fertilizers, and promoted their use. He did not establish basic theory, which in chemistry generally trailed well behind the welter of facts and discoveries, but his work importantly influenced such fields as physiology and medicine. "Liebig is not an operator in chemistry," overstated an American chemist, Eben N. Horsford. "Liebig is chemistry itself."

Born on May 12, 1803, in Darmstadt, the capital city of the Grand Duchy of Hesse, near Frankfurt, Justus Liebig was one of nine children of Johann Georg Liebig and Maria Korline Moserin Liebig. His father was a drysalter—dealing in dried meats and other foodstuffs—and mixed some of his own products. As a result Justus acquired an early familiarity with practical chemistry. Although he read voraciously, he later said, it is not clear that he was an excellent student in his early schooling. When his family was relatively impoverished during a period of economic crisis about 1817, Justus was apprenticed to an apothecary. According to a recent biography, Liebig later invented the tale that unforeseen chemical explosions soon terminated his apprenticeship, whereas the real reason was his father's inability to pay the required fees.

Returning to his father's store, Liebig by chance became acquainted with a well-known chemist, Karl Wilhelm Kastner. As a result, Liebig became Kastner's assistant and, soon thereafter, a student at the universities of Bonn and Erlangen. Here his precocity was recognized and demonstrated while, for his part, Liebig was unimpressed by the "philosophical method" of chemical analysis used in Germany—influenced, as it was, by *Naturphilosophie*, the speculative and romantic theory of nature.

Liebig was provided a grant to study in Paris, at a time when France was still the most advanced country in chemistry. There he learned from Gay-Lussac and others new methods of chemical analysis. He received an honorary Ph.D. *in absentia* from the University of Erlangen in 1822, when he was just nineteen years old. In Paris, he also met the geographer and explorer Alexander von Humboldt, who helped him receive an appointment from the Grand Duke of Hesse to the University of Geissen in 1824. Liebig was to remain at Geissen for twenty-eight years.

During the nineteenth century the vast economic potential of chemistry was recognized as raw materials discovered in the course of imperialist ventures were put to use in the service of rapidly developing industrial capitalism. The earth's crust gave up its riches to geologists as a cornucopia of minerals—today numbering about three thousand—were discovered and classified and mined. And it fell to chemistry, a new and not fully competent science, to analyze their composition.

Upon returning to Germany in 1824, Liebig discovered that a virtual revolution had begun in organic chemistry. He soon became its principal figure. When Friedrich Wöhler found that his chemical analysis of silver cyanate was identical to Liebig's analysis of silver fulminate, the two men initially each thought the other mistaken, for the two substances have much different qualities. But in 1826, when they compared their experiments, they not only found that both analyses had to be correct but also developed a fundamental insight: The great profusion of chemical compounds throughout the world is due to the multitudinous combinations of a few simple elements—namely, oxygen, hydrogen, nitrogen, and carbon.

By 1831 Liebig had developed methods of estimating the various quantities of carbon and hydrogen in any given compound. In addition, in 1834 Liebig laid the basis for the theory of radicals—stable compounds that react like atoms in chemical reaction—a basic and necessary simplification.

By the mid-1830s Liebig had established himself as the major force in German chemistry. He was publishing an important review of chemistry, the *Annalen der Chemie und Pharmacie*, and held an academic post which attracted students from all over Europe. The government, aware of his growing significance, acceded readily to Liebig's demands for more funds. His well-equipped laboratory at Geissen became a mecca for young chemists, who learned Liebig's methods and soon engaged in original research. Liebig offered his students a series of lectures to orient them to his theory and method of analysis and then provided an introduction to laboratory work. Some four hundred fifty chemists and over three hundred pharmacists were trained at Geissen.

After about 1838 Liebig turned increasingly to what today would be called biochemistry and agricultural chemistry. His *Organic Chemistry in Its Applications to Agriculture and Physiology*, published in 1840, soon acquired an international reputation and was widely translated. Liebig strongly objected to the humus theory, in which the soil was viewed not so much as a nutrient but as a stimulant to plants, which absorbed and transformed carbon into minerals found in the soil. The reverse is the case. Liebig's analysis was able to show that plants, through chemical reactions, in fact take up minerals from the soil.

In addition to advising farmers to return animal and human waste to the soil as manure, Liebig went on to develop chemical fertilizers containing potassium and phosphorous. Initially, he had some seriously disappointing results because he used insoluble compounds, and at one point he patented a disastrous fertilizer, which was marketed in Germany and Great Britain. When the nutrients were put in soluble form, however, performance improved greatly, and the German chemical fertilizer industry expanded enormously. "If I can impress the farmer with the principles of plant nutrition, soil fertility, and the causes of soil exhaustion," wrote Liebig, "one of the tasks of my life will have been accomplished."

The influence of Liebig spread well beyond the boundaries of organic and agricultural chemistry. He was a well-known public figure in his time—he eventually received a patent of nobility—and for the growing middle class wrote articles on issues of everyday life, such as how meat should be cooked. More significantly, his work had a beneficial impact on medicine. By offering a new chemical perspective on understanding health it had considerable importance for developments later in the nineteenth century.

Leaving the University of Geissen in 1852, Liebig spent the rest of his career teaching at the University of Munich. His achievements there were many, but they did not match his previous works. Today his laboratory at Geissen is a museum, and in it many of his apparatus have been preserved. At one time there also stood a statue of the great chemist, conceived in the most doubtful of bourgeois taste, but it was destroyed by bombs during World War II.

Combative and highly charismatic, Liebig was greatly admired by his students. In fact, so great was the impression he made that, when he prepared anhydrous acid for the first time, he asked several of his students to put forth their bare arms. They obliged without objection as he applied the corrosive liquid to their flesh. "Such was the esprit de corps he engendered and sustained," wrote J. B. Morrell, who also cites several eulogies. "Like all the great generals of every age," said one of his students, "Liebig was the spirit as well as the leader of his battalions, and if he was followed so heartily it was because much as he was admired, he was loved still more."

Liebig died on April 18, 1873.

37

Arthur Eddington
and Modern Astronomy

1882–1944

The British astronomer Arthur Eddington trained the theories of relativity and the atom upon the heavens. His work led to a new understanding of the structure and content of the universe as well as of the evolution and composition of space and the stars. As early as 1917 Eddington proposed that nuclear processes provide stars their source of light, an idea which was vindicated twenty years later. As a renowned figure in British science, in 1919 Eddington was able to organize the expeditions that photographed the solar eclipse, which gave experimental proof of Einstein's general theory of relativity. During the 1920s, he developed a mathematical formula for the relationship between the intensity of a star's brightness, or luminescence, and its mass. And his support for the existence of interstellar matter was a crucial impetus to its further study. From 1913 until his death, Eddington was Plumian professor of astronomy at Cambridge University, where, writes historian John North, he "acted as an incomparable stimulus to world astrophysics."

Arthur Stanley Eddington was born on December 28, 1882, in Kendal, in Westmoreland, England. His father, Arthur Henry Eddington, was a headmaster who died in 1884, and his mother was Sarah Ann Shout. After her husband's death, Mrs. Eddington returned with her family to her native Somerset, where Arthur received a good education in spite of relatively impoverished circumstances. Like JOSEPH J. THOMSON [31], who discovered the electron, Eddington went on to Owen's College (today the University of Manchester), and he graduated in 1902 with a degree in physics. With the help of a scholarship, Eddington went on to Trinity College, Cambridge, where he distinguished himself in mathematics. One of his teachers at Trinity was Alfred North Whitehead, whose grandiose theory making would figure later in Eddington's career. Eddington was elected a fellow of Trinity in 1907.

In 1906 Eddington was appointed chief assistant at the Royal Observatory in Greenwich. Over the next seven years, he received an exceptional practical education in astronomy. He made two field trips, to Malta in 1906 and to Brazil in 1912 as head of an expedition to observe a solar eclipse. He also studied the motion and distribution of the stars, star clusters, and the nebulae and in 1910 published a catalog of some six thousand stars. In *Stellar Movements and the Structure of the Universe*, a collection of papers published in 1914, Eddington suggested, correctly as it turned out, that the distant spiral nebulae are in fact galaxies outside the Milky Way. By 1913 an important figure in astronomical research, Eddington moved to Cambridge University, and a year later became director of the observatory there.

Most types of stars—the sun is a good example—are balls of gas, giving off light and heat, with a stability by no means self-evident. Why do they not burn up or collapse? By 1917 Eddington was working on a theory about their internal composition, invoking atomic physics and the special theory of relativity. He developed a formula utilizing the notion that star formation is a transformation of energy into matter. Eddington published calculations in 1924 giving a lawful relation between a star's mass and its luminosity, and he suggested the composition of burnt-out, collapsed, white dwarf stars.

In 1926 he published *The Internal Constitution of the Stars*, which put forth the general hypothesis that nuclear energy was the source of stellar energy. More specifically—and what counts as a bold hypothesis, for it was intuitive, supported by theory but not entirely by evidence, and turned out to be right—Eddington insisted that, at the exceptionally hot core of stars, atoms fused, releasing energy. While the star's cooler outer envelope is ready to collapse from the force of gravity, furious atoms at its inner core create a counterpressure, resulting in stability.

Two later developments in astrophysics proved Eddington's idea was essentially correct. In 1928 George Gamow and others computed the "tunneling effect," showing that, by the principles of quantum theory, atoms could behave as Eddington predicted. And a decade later HANS BETHE [58] developed a famous equation for the carbon cycle within the sun that demonstrated how hydrogen and carbon nuclei combine to turn into helium, releasing tremendous energy but recombining in a cyclical way to sustain the reaction over billions of years. Later in the century, still more sophisticated models of stellar formation were constructed.

From the end of the nineteenth century, astronomers had accumulated evidence that space contains dark matter and is in no way empty or void. Streams of darkness and spectral absorption indicating the presence of gases led to the conjecture of interstellar matter—together with a reluctance to actually hypothesize its existence. In 1926 Eddington gave a lecture at the Royal Society in which he discussed "Diffuse Matter in Space." Interpreting photographic and spectroscopic evidence, he stated his conviction that interstellar matter—largely in the form of atomic dust—must indeed be spread throughout space. "Once championed by such an august authority as Eddington," writes Marcia Bartusiak in *Through a Universe Darkly*, "the notion of interstellar matter—gas and dust—became far more acceptable." Its existence was clearly demonstrated a few years later, in 1930.

Coincident with his work in astrophysics, Eddington was the central figure in providing experimental proof for, and Anglo-American acceptance of, Albert Einstein's general theory of relativity. Einstein had announced his theory concerning the nature of gravitation in 1915, during World War I, and verification had to wait until the armistice. Because the theory predicts that light from a star will be measurably deflected when it passes a huge heavenly body such as the sun, an experimental test to verify the theory could be made during a solar eclipse. Then, with the sun's light blocked by the moon, the stars beyond would be visible. In 1918 Eddington wrote a "Report on the Theory of Gravitation," which was the first general account in English of the theory. The following year he himself led an expedition to Principe Island, near the coast of West Africa, while other astronomers observed the eclipse from Sobral, in northern Brazil. Newtonian principles predicted one set of numbers for the deflection of light; the theory of relativity predicted another. Einstein's theory proved correct, and the result was announced at the Royal Astronomical Society in London on November 6, 1919. Several years later, Eddington published the *Mathematical Theory of Relativity*, which Einstein believed to be the best exposition of his theory in English or any language.

Most of Eddington's works after the late 1920s are in some measure popular expositions. His Gifford Lectures, delivered in 1927 at the University of Edinburgh, became *The Nature of the Physical World*, a bestseller at the onset of the Great Depression. His *Expanding Universe*, published in 1933, is one of the first fashionable books on the modern cosmology, newly introduced by Einstein's theory. He also wrote *New Pathways in Science* and *The Philosophy of Physical Science*. A good writer who has been called the "foremost popularizer of his time," Eddington's thought had a mystical element that did not appeal to all of his contemporaries. Though he was an admirer of Eddington, ERNEST RUTHERFORD [19] called his books of the mid-1930s "queer; he is like a religious mystic, and is not all there. I don't pay attention to him."

Indeed, Eddington the philosopher is not averse to commenting on mystical religion. "The idea of a universal Mind or Logos would be, I think, a fairly plausible inference from the present state of scientific theory; at least it is in harmony with it." Still, Eddington—a Quaker—offers nothing but a "colorless pantheism," adding, "Science cannot tell whether the world-spirit is good or evil, and its halting argument for the existence of a God might equally well be turned into an argument for the existence of a Devil."

A lifelong bachelor who lived with his mother and sister,

Eddington had a reputation as being quite shy and reticent. But he was not averse to attending nightclubs with pretty women. The wife of Edwin Hubble, Grace, got him to open up on the subject of detective stories, and he preferred Agatha Christie over Dorothy Sayers. He was witty, and once remarked, after slicing a ball on the golf course, "Space seems to be highly curved in this region." He was the recipient of many honors, including knighthood in 1930 and the Order of Merit in 1938. He died relatively young, at age sixty-one, on November 22, 1944.

38

William Harvey
and Circulation of the Blood

1578–1657

In Roman times the brilliant Greek physician Galen viewed the liver as the body's chief internal organ. He believed that it was the site where food was transformed from "chyle" into blood and sent out to nourish the rest of the body. Galen recognized the importance of the heart and noted the different construction of veins and arteries (the latter are far more muscular). But he thought that, while blood flowed through the veins, arteries contained mostly "vital spirits," produced from inhaled air. Galen's complex conception was one of absorption and irrigation, and was based on the notion of purpose and perfection in nature. This had an excellent fit with the cycles of agriculture and so appealed to medieval thinking, but did not outlast it. To William Harvey it thus fell, as the Renaissance drew to an end, to explain the circulation of the blood. By doing so, he made a crucial first step toward a modern physiology.

William Harvey was born in Folkestone, England, on April 1, 1578, the eldest son of Joan and Thomas Harvey. His father was a prosperous businessman, and five of William's brothers grew up to become affluent merchants. At King's School at Canterbury, William became fluent in Latin and Greek, and at age sixteen, in 1593, he obtained a scholarship to Gonville and Caius College, at Cambridge, where he studied medicine and the arts. Although his medical training here was not exceptional, Harvey probably did observe some dissections of executed criminals. He received his bachelor of arts degree in 1597.

Like other of the Renaissance figures in science, Harvey attended the University of Padua, the great secular seat of learning where ANDREAS VESALIUS [21] had taught a half-century earlier. Significantly, Harvey came under the tutelage of Fabricius ab Aquapendente, a celebrated anatomist. Although Fabricius recognized the existence of valves in the veins, he believed they slowed the flow of blood to the periphery of the body—a Galenic interpretation. Harvey would eventually recognize, to the contrary, that the valves help blood flow back to the heart.

Returning to England in 1602 with his medical degree, Harvey soon married Elizabeth Browne, the daughter of Dr. Lancelot Browne, physician to Queen Elizabeth I and later to James I. Not surprisingly, Harvey soon had an important practice, and he also became associated with St. Bartholomew's Hospital. In 1607 he was elected to the Royal College of Physicians, where in 1615 he was appointed Lumleian Lecturer on Anatomy and Surgery. He gave his first medical lectures in 1616. Many of Harvey's papers have been lost, but some of his notes for these lectures, rediscovered in 1876 after more than two centuries, show that he was already discussing the function of the heart and circulation of the blood.

De motu cordis et sanguinis in animalibus (*On the Movement and Circulation of Blood in Animals*) was published in 1628. It is a brief treatise in two parts, a model of clarity in which Harvey first provides a description of how the heart and arterial system function, followed by his argument for the circulation of the blood. Harvey's method of investigation was more empirical than that of Galen, who was constrained from dissecting humans and had to settle for dead animals such as macaques. Equally important, however, Harvey observed animals that he had cut open while they were still alive. He looked into dogs, pigs, and goats and lower animals as well, including shrimps and unhatched chicks. This enabled him to show that the heart, when it contracted, expelled blood, and that this and nothing else was responsible for the pulse. This was, as he noted, "the exact opposite to the commonly accepted views." He showed that the blood entered the heart from the venae cava and was then pumped into the aorta.

In addition to depending on observation and demonstration, Harvey brought into play quantitative explanations. He calculated the amount of blood the heart pumped into the arterial system, based on an estimated capacity per beat of two fluid ounces and seventy-two beats per minute. But that would be an enormous quantity. In an hour 2 ounces × 72 beats × 60 minutes equals 8,640 ounces, or 540 pounds. The liver, Harvey reasoned, could not possibly manufacture that much blood. Rather, the heart was at the center of a system which circulated the blood; and the blood itself passed from the arterial into the venous system. This must stand as one of the most important early, and valid, inductions of modern science. Without a microscope Harvey could not see what connected the arteries and veins, but he perceived that a connection had to exist and so predicted the discovery of "pores." A generation later, in 1660, MARCELLO MALPIGHI [39] discovered the capillaries.

Although *De motu* was attacked in some quarters, its validity could not easily be ignored. Harvey was fairly soon fully recognized for the importance of his discovery, which was described by a contemporary as "enough to overturn all of medicine, just as the invention of the telescope has turned all astronomy upside down...."

William Harvey became court physician to King James I in 1618, and to Charles I until the latter was beheaded in 1649. A royalist, Harvey lost many of his papers, including those pertaining to a study of insects, when his home was ransacked during the Civil War. Apart from *De motu*, Harvey's only other published work of interest is a study of embryology, important in its day but without the revolutionary significance of his work on the circulation of the blood.

The significance of William Harvey to science and medicine abides after nearly four centuries, though he may have been overvalued at one time as an examplar of British scientific excellence. I. Bernard Cohen suggests that, although it did not lead directly to great new technical advances in medicine, Harvey's work "passes all tests for a revolution in science." In certain respects, it may be added, Harvey was not a modern scientist but belonged to a teleological Aristotelian tradition and was mainly influenced by the Paduan anatomists with whom he studied as a youth. But the advance he represented over earlier conceptions is clear. "I do not profess to learn and teach Anatomy from the axioms of the Philosophers," wrote Harvey in his introduction to *De motu*, "but from Dissections and the Fabrick of Nature."

According to the *Brief Lives* of James Aubrey, William Harvey was short of stature, with a tawny complexion and jet black hair which turned white twenty years before his death. Little is known and reliable concerning his personality, but in his old age, when it came to warming his blood, Harvey had the help of a "pretty young wench." Harvey died on June 3, 1657, of a stroke, and he is buried in Hempstead Church, in Essex.

39

Marcello Malpighi
and Microscopic Anatomy

1628–1694

The Italian physician and anatomist Marcello Malpighi is the founder of microscopic anatomy. His extensive investigations created histology, the study of tissue, and had great impact on many fields, including botany, zoology, and embryology. Most famously, in 1661 he discovered the capillaries. This brought to light the missing element in William Harvey's theory of the circulation of the blood, in showing how the arterial system was linked to the venous. Equipped with a microscope, Malpighi also made some of the first careful studies of the spinal cord, kidneys, spleen, brain, skin, and tongue; and he provided minute and unparalleled descriptions of animals in embryo and insects in their larval stages. Though he spent most of his life as a professor in Bologna, his writings "might have been called 'Voyages with the Microscope,'" writes Daniel Boorstin, "for his work was the miscellaneous journal of a traveler into a world invisible to the naked eye."

Little is known of Malpighi's childhood. He was born in Crevalcore, in northern Italy, on March 10, 1628. His parents were prosperous enough that he could attend school with a view to a university education, and he completed his "grammatical studies" in 1645. While attending the University of Bologna, he belonged to the anatomical society of a well-known anatomist, Bartolemeo Massari, with whom he became close—marrying Massari's sister, in fact—and undertook his first dissections of animals. In 1653 Malpighi received his doctorate of medicine and philosophy.

At the University of Pisa, where Malpighi became professor of theoretical medicine in 1656, he became friends with Giovanni Alfonso Borelli. A mathematician who made early attempts to describe the functions of the body using physical laws—famously, he showed how birds fly—Borelli had a profound influence on Malpighi, and until they quarreled in 1668, the two men were close friends and collaborators. About 1659 Malpighi returned to Bologna, where he lectured in theoretical and practical medicine; between 1622 and 1666 he taught at the University of Messina, thereafter returning to Bologna, where he remained until 1691.

Observations using the newly invented microscope to examine the largely invisible structures of bodies became Malpighi's major life's work. As a student, Malpighi had been impressed by William Harvey's work on the circulation of the blood, which had appeared in the year he was born. In two letters addressed to Borelli, which were published in 1661 as a book, De pulmonibus observationes anatomicae (Anatomical Observations on the Lungs), Malpighi described the existence of "small tubes" on the surface of the lungs and the bladder of the frog and turtle. "I could clearly see that the blood is divided and flows through tortuous vessels," writes Malpighi, "and that it is not poured into spaces, but is always driven through tubules and distributed by the manifold bendings of the vessels...." In extrapolating the results to humans, Malpighi vindicated Harvey's views four years after the latter's death.

With the help of microscopy—both Robert Hooke and ANTON VON LEEUWENHOEK [55] were contemporaries—Malpighi made many discoveries that strongly reflect High Renaissance thinking. These discoveries were indicative of radical changes in the way the human body was viewed and experienced. Malpighi discovered the taste buds on the tongue and the pigmentary layer of the skin; he looked at the spinal column, and in 1665, in his *De cerebro*, described how bundles of nerve fibers led to the spinal cord and were connected to the brain. He lent his name to certain structures in the kidney and the spleen, and the deepest stratum of the skin in mammals became known as the Malpighian layer. He described the symptoms of Hodgkin's disease two centuries before Thomas Hodgkin.

Malpighi was a zoologist and botanist, examining the organization of plants and insects, as well as an embryologist. In 1673, the year Leeuwenhoek began sending letters to the Royal Society in London, Malpighi published *De formatione pulli* (*On the Formation of the Chick in the Egg*). His study of the silkworm moth was the first detailed examination of any insect, and its thoroughness is clear from the evaluation of F. J. Cole, who wrote that Malpighi "anatomized all phases of the species, but, apart from his very remarkable and accurate observations on the genitalia of the moth, the larva claimed the greater part of his attention, and it was on this stage that his most novel and important studies were made."

Although he earned renown for his work, Malpighi was sometimes attacked by ecclesiastics; by 1700, however, his discoveries could no longer be contested. When a fire destroyed Malpighi's microscopes in 1684, he received consolation from the Royal Society, which sent him new lenses. And in 1691 Innocent XII, a reformist pope, asked Malpighi to become his personal physician. It was a task to which Malpighi agreed with some misgivings; he moved to Rome and he spent the last three years of his life there. Malpighi had always told his friends that he expected to die when he least expected it, "with his boots on." On November 29, 1694, his end was brought about by a convulsive stroke. Friends carefully dissected his body, and the remains were returned to Bologna and buried.

40

Christiaan Huygens
and the Wave Theory of Light

1629–1695

Historically situated between ISAAC NEWTON [1] and GALILEO
GALILEI [7] is Christiaan Huygens, the great Dutch mathematician, astronomer, and natural scientist. He is best remembered
today for his wave theory of light which, initially ignored, entered
the scientific mainstream with the discovery by JAMES CLERK
MAXWELL [12], in the late nineteenth century, that light is part of
the electromagnetic spectrum. But in his day Huygens was
known for discoveries in many fields. The pendulum clock that
he invented was a great advance in measuring time, and was
adapted and used by scientists throughout Europe. As an astronomer Huygens built his own telescopes and discovered Titan,

Saturn's largest moon. He also made important inroads into mathematical analysis and published the first book on probability. Huygens's influence appears somewhat limited because he had relatively few followers. But as a youth he was called "the new Archimedes," and at his death he was described by Leibniz as "the Incomparable Huygens."

Christiaan Huygens was born in The Hague on April 14, 1629. His father, Constantijn Huygens, was an eminent diplomat, secretary to the Duke of Orange, and a poet, one of the greatest figures in Dutch literature. He desired for his son the best possible education, and so Christiaan was privately tutored until he entered the University of Leiden in 1645. Huygens studied law and mathematics, moving to the College of Orange in the old town of Breda in 1647. By 1649 he had returned to The Hague, where he made many of his most memorable discoveries.

Although in 1610 Galileo's famous *Starry Messenger* alerted the world to the profusion of heavenly bodies, observational astronomy had not greatly advanced in the succeeding generation. During the 1650s, working with his brother Constantijn— Huygens also worked with the lens-grinding philosopher Baruch Spinoza—he improved the simple telescope, creating a better eyepiece and a lens that gave improved definition. As a consequence, he was able in 1656 to describe what Galileo had seen as "handles" around Saturn as a flattened ring; and, in addition, he detected Saturn's great moon, which he named Titan. His *Systema saturnium* was published in 1659.

As a partial consequence of his research in astronomy, which demanded that times be precisely measured, Huygens looked into clockmaking. A half century earlier, Galileo had recognized the harmonic motion of the pendulum, and Newton had later analyzed it in his *Principia*. Huygens now applied this movement to the gear- and weight-driven clocks of the period. Using a pendulum's regular oscillations to control the escapement mechanism, he found, improved accuracy significantly. In 1657 Huygens presented the first pendulum clock to the States-General, and the following year described it in a book, *Horologium*. The clock—effectively, the grandfather of the grandfather clock—became popular in Europe, and was used by scientists for measurements of all sorts. Huygens, who further improved the clock in 1675 by introducing the balance wheel, became famous.

Huygens's other work about the same time was important and varied. In 1657 he published the first work in modern science to deal with probability, *De ratiociniis in ludo aleae* (*On Reasoning in Games of Chance*). He continued his astronomical researches, describing the surface of Mars for the first time in 1659. A decade later he gave a precise formulation of the laws which govern the collision of eclectic bodies, soon after similar work by the British mathematician John Wallis. In 1661 Huygens visited London and two years later he was elected a member of the Royal Society. By the mid-1660s Huygens was living in France and accepted an offer from Louis XIV to reside at the Bibliothèque du Roi. He became a founding member of the Académie Royale des Sciences in 1666.

Huygens's landmark *Horologium oscillatorium sive de motu pendularium*, from 1673, is a long and fruitful treatise on the pendulum. It includes explanations of centripetal force and centrifugal force—concepts which later became part of Newton's law of gravitation. Huygens "showed that a complete and thorough mathematical analysis of a physical system was possible," writes Joella Yoder, the author of *Unrolling Time*, an intellectual biography of Huygens. She adds: "He did not impose mathematics on nature, as if it were some ideal form into which the untidy real world must be pressed. His mathematics grew along with his physics."

But the most influential and enduring work by Huygens was his theory of light. In 1675 Newton had given his lecture on light and color to the Royal Society, proposing a theory of light as a stream of particles from a source to the eye. Huygens challenged this "corpuscular" theory with a view of light propagated as waves. Written in 1678, his *Traité de la lumière* was published in 1690. Although Newton's corpuscular theory became dominant, largely owing to his eminence, experiments by Thomas Young one hundred years later revitalized Huygens's wave theory. Through the early 1800s support for it grew, and it eventually became part of James Clerk Maxwell's theory of electromagnetic radiation. Maxwell's assumption that light waves are propagated through an invisible "ether" became obsolete with the special theory of relativity advanced by ALBERT EINSTEIN [2] in 1905. But the wave description of light abides today as part of quantum theory, in which light may be described as either wavelike or particulate.

Christiaan Huygens was somewhat remote from his contemporaries, was said to lack the temperament of a revolutionary, and in any event did not travel in circles where he would have cultivated disciples. As a Protestant he encountered hostility in Paris, and he returned to Holland in 1681. A lifelong bachelor, he died on June 8, 1695, at The Hague.

Mention must be made of a posthumous work by Huygens, entitled *Cosmotheoros*, published three years after his death, which includes his speculations on extraterrestrial life. Convinced of the Copernican system, Huygens saw that with Earth no longer at the center of the universe, the question of life on other planets had to be addressed. He argued that living beings much like mankind must exist, or else the universe would be senseless and Providence unreasonable, "that otherwise our Earth would have too much the advantage of them, in being the only part of the Universe that could boast of such a Creature so far above, not only Plants and Trees, but all Animals whatsoever."

41

Carl Gauss
and Mathematical Genius

1777–1855

One of the greatest mathematical scientists, Carl Gauss made fundamental contributions to number theory and geometry, probability and statistics, and major discoveries in astronomy and electromagnetism. He also made practical advances in mapmaking and surveying, and one of his inventions was an early version of the telegraph. His anticipation of non-Euclidean geometry—which became important a century after he conceived it—is one of his notable achievements. His stature, especially in the field of pure mathematics, remains extremely high. "Even today," writes Michio Kaku, "if you ask any mathematician to rank the three most famous mathematicians in history, the names of Archimedes, Isaac Newton, and Carl Gauss will invariably appear."

Carl Friedrich Gauss was born on April 30, 1777, in the duchy of Brunswick, part of Germany, to a poor family. His paternal grandfather was a peasant, and his father, Gerhard Diedrich Gauss, who worked as a gardener, bricklayer, and canal tender, was an honest but uncultivated man who would have preferred to keep his son from being educated. However, Carl's mother, Dorothea, when told that her son would be Europe's greatest mathematician, burst into tears. According to most accounts, Dorothea was a strong-willed woman who encouraged and remained proud of her son until she died, in his personal care, at age ninety-seven.

A true mathematical prodigy, Gauss could do sums by age three, when he began to correct his father's addition. Sent to a provincial school at age seven, he began his arithmetic class two years later. The story is told that the schoolmaster gave the class some make-work: to add the first hundred integers. Gauss immediately grasped the principle of an arithmetical progression, wrote down the answer, and as the instructor finished with the sums, tossed town his slate, saying, *Ligget se* ("There it lies!"). By age twelve, after instruction with a tutor, Gauss already saw the limitations of Euclid's axioms and not long thereafter foresaw the possibility of a non-Euclidean geometry, which he later came to privately accept.

With the financial aid of the Duke of Brunswick, and against the wishes of his father, Gauss attended the local gymnasium, the Collegium Carolinum, beginning in 1792. Here he studied the works of LEONHARD EULER [35], Lagrange, and ISAAC NEWTON [1]. Although he possessed an impressive gift for languages, Gauss decided to continue studying mathematics in 1796. This was soon after he had discovered the constructibility, with compass and straight-edge, of a polygon having seventeen sides. A beautiful theorem accompanied this discovery, the first advance in constructing polygons in two thousand years.

Indeed, on March 30, 1796, Gauss began to keep a diary of a welter of discoveries, the last of which he dated in 1814. The diary, written in Latin and published only in 1901, long after his death, is remarkable for anticipating many of the innovations made during the nineteenth century. "There are enough unpublished ideas in the diary," writes Stuart Hollingdale, "to have made half-a-dozen reputations."

From 1795 to 1798 Gauss attended the University of Göttingen, but he received his doctorate from the University of Helmstädt in 1799. His dissertation gave a rigorous proof of what today would be called the fundamental theorem of algebra—namely, that every equation with one variable has at least one root. While still a student Gauss wrote his *Disquisitiones arithemeticae*, published in 1801, his most extensive work in pure mathematics. It immediately brought him attention if not celebrity.

With the dawn of the nineteenth century, the invention of more powerful telescopes, and the discoveries by such figures as WILLIAM HERSCHEL [27], Gauss began to work in astronomy. In January 1801 an asteroid (later named Ceres) was observed by the Italian monk Guiseppe Piazzi. When it disappeared from view, astronomers were perplexed. Gauss, however, was able to predict its reappearance on October 1, nine months later, by a new form of calculating its orbit. This feat (he did not reveal his method) made him famous. In 1809 Gauss published an exhaustive study of the mathematics of celestial mechanics, *Theoria motus corporum coelestium in sectionibus conicis solem ambientium* (*Theory of the Motion of the Heavenly Bodies Revolving Around the Sun in Conic Sections*). Gauss was named director of the observatory at his alma mater, the University of Göttingen, in 1807, and later became professor of astronomy. He remained at Göttingen until his death forty-two years later, and became well known throughout Europe.

Gauss had long been interested in surveying, and took up its practical and theoretical problems after becoming an adviser to the Hanoverian government, about 1818. He undertook the work himself, surveying during the summer months and computing his data in the winter. This led him not only to utilize a variety of mathematical tools to solve problems of curved surfaces but also to develop conformal mapping. (In conformal mapping, angles and circles are conserved, with fewer distortions.) Among his practical inventions is an instrument known as the heliotrope, for augmenting available light while surveying. The actual task of surveying involved considerable fieldwork in unpleasant conditions, but it led Gauss to several new mathematical formulations.

About 1830 Gauss became a friend and collaborator of the

younger Wilhelm Weber, who had just begun teaching at Göttingen. They began working on problems associated with electromagnetism, which was just then undergoing its new and extraordinary conceptualization by MICHAEL FARADAY [11]. With Weber he studied the magnetism of the earth, building a special observatory for that purpose. They provided new theories for experimental evaluation and developed mathematical instruments and techniques applicable to existing physical theories.* The collaboration between Gauss and Weber ended in 1837 when the latter was fired from the university for political reasons. A reactionary in politics and unwilling to challenge authority, Gauss, characteristically, refused to help his friend.

Conservative, too, in his approach to larger issues in mathematics, Gauss dared not elaborate and publish his discovery of non-Euclidean geometry. It would be credited to Nikolai Lobachevski and János Bolyai. "I am becoming more and more convinced that the [physical] necessity of our [Euclidean] geometry cannot be proved, at least not by human reason nor for human reason," Gauss wrote in a letter, and he suspected that at great distances Euclidean geometry would break down. But he did not publish his insight, partly from a realistic fear of being ridiculed.

More generally, this conservatism led to the limitation of Gauss's influence. The "Prince of Mathematicians," as he was sometimes called, did not make major innovations, and as Kenneth O. May noted some years ago, "One might expect the Gaussian impact to be far smaller than his reputation—and indeed this is the case." Non-Euclidean geometry is implicit in the theory of relativity and effectively forms the basis of contemporary theories of "hyperspace" and superstring theory.

Gauss had a rather difficult personal life. He married Joanne Osthof in 1805, and the couple had two children before she died giving birth a third time. Gauss "closed the angel eyes in which for five years I have found a heaven." He subsequently married Minna Waldeck, with whom he had three more children in spite of her poor health. His relations with his sons, whom he did not want to enter science for fear they would be second-rate,

---

*In 1833 Gauss and Weber developed an operating telegraph which linked the observatory with the physics laboratory. They became aware of the commercial possibilities but could not establish priority for the invention, which was later developed in the United States by Samuel Morse.

were not good, although in later years he got on sufficiently well with one of his daughters. By many who knew him, he was considered uncommunicative and not affectionate. In spite of his conservative and antidemocratic political views, Gauss was not religious. He died on February 23, 1855.

42

Albrecht von Haller
and Eighteenth-Century Medicine
1708–1777

The major figure of eighteenth-century medicine was Albrecht von Haller, the Swiss physician, physiologist, botanist, and man of letters. Strongly influenced by ISAAC NEWTON [1], Haller demonstrated a modern dependence on experiment. As originator of the concept of irritability, Haller is sometimes called the founder of neurology, which, although he interpreted it as a manifestation of God, he also viewed not as dogma but as a principle to be verified. Irritability can even today be considered one of the principal signs of life, together with metabolism, growth, and reproduction; and nerve cells are still sometimes called "irritable tissue." Haller's prolific output is legendary—he was the author of some twelve thousand articles—and he is also known for his philosophical romances and a famous poem, *Die Alpen*, which describes the charm of pastoral life in the Swiss mountains.

Albrecht von Haller was born on October 16, 1707, in Berne, Switzerland. He was the son of Niklaus Emanuel Haller and Anna Maria Engel, both of whom died when he was still quite young. Raised by a stepmother in a household of modest means, Haller was said to be frail as a child, but he was also precocious, especially in languages, writing scholarly articles at age eight and creating a Greek dictionary when he was ten. He began his studies in medicine in 1724, at the age of sixteen, at the University of Tübingen, but a year later he went to the University of Leiden, where he could study under Hermann Boerhaave, the greatest (and perhaps wealthiest) physician of his time. Boerhaave, who received patients from all over Europe, became an important influence on Haller, who received his medical degree in 1727.

Haller's early career reflects the encyclopedic range of his interests in medicine and anatomy, as well as in botany. Anatomy as a course of study had been deficient at the university, and so Haller traveled to England and France, where he was able to watch operations and dissections. In Basel he took mathematics under Johann Bernoulli, but also had time to pursue his botanical interests. He journeyed into the Alps and accumulated an impressive collection of Swiss flora as well as the experience and lore that became the basis of *Die Alpen*.

In Berne, then an important canton of the Swiss Federation, Haller practiced medicine from 1729 to 1736 while also acquiring a reputation for botanical and anatomical research. This enabled him to assume the chair of medicine, anatomy, surgery, and botany at the University of Göttingen in 1736. This university, recently founded, was not burdened by tradition; it gave Haller, over the next seventeen years, the opportunity to perform some of his most significant investigations and to create a medical school of considerable renown. In 1747 he published *Primae lineae physiologiae*, a medical book which supplanted Boerhaave's famous *Institutiones medicae* in light of more contemporary findings. It is sometimes considered the first textbook in physiology and medicine. Haller revised it twice before his death.

Somewhat incongruously, Haller's greatest work took place after 1753, when he left Göttingen and returned to Berne. There he worked for five years in the civil service and then became manager of the Bernese Saltworks. Poor health, overwork, and professional quarrels have all been adduced to explain this sudden change in mid-career. Haller nonetheless retained the presidency of the Göttingen Academy; he had already acquired an international reputation and was a zealous correspondent.

In 1753 there appeared the first volume of Haller's central and culminating work, for which he was most famous, his *Elementa physiologiae corporis humani* (*Elements of Human Physiology*). Seven more volumes appeared over the next quarter century and brought together his work in anatomy and physiology. Most significant of all, Haller provided descriptions of all the known organs of the body in a scholarly context that assessed the work of previous investigators. Haller's work was not merely descriptive but explanatory; it was based on Newtonian ideas, including a dynamic conception of force. "Whoever writes a physiology," wrote Haller, "must explain the inner movements of the animal body, the functions of the organs, the changes of the fluids, and the forces through which life is sustained."

In showing that specific nerve fibers and muscles had particular functions, Haller developed the concept of irritability. While WILLIAM HARVEY [38] had explained the circulation of the blood, Haller showed that the heart was not simply a self-regulating mechanism. Its regular beats occurred, Haller thought, as its muscles were stimulated when its cavities filled with blood. He went on to show that the functioning of all the parts of the body relied on stimulation, and he saw in muscle contraction the work of various mechanical and chemical forces.

Although Haller did not recognize the role played by the nerves, his tendency to seek answers through experimentation is responsible for his reputation as founder of neurophysiology. He would identify the organ of an animal he wished to study and then apply a variety of stimuli. Response through pain and annoyance led Haller to describe the part as sensitive, or "irritable." In a famous phrase, Haller wrote that physiology is "animated anatomy." However, he was not a mechanist in terms of simple cause and effect. Rather, he aimed at understanding what he believed to be the unique operations of "animal mechanics." "Irritability" was a special property of animals and could not be reduced to kinetics.

Indeed, although an Enlightenment thinker, Haller was not a mechanist, and he placed himself at considerable remove from

Boerhaave lecturing students.

many of the more widely known French *philosophes*. Living not far from him, across Lake Geneva, was the philosopher Voltaire, an embodiment of the liberal spirit of an age. But Haller tended toward piety, was "devoid of any sense of humour," writes Henry Sigerist, "and an arch-conservative.... He thought as a rationalist, and he believed as a sincere Christian." Like Newton, Haller thought that the laws of motion were imparted to the world by God. And so, in what must count as one of the great bibliographic jests of all time, the brilliant (and neglected) hedonist philosopher Julian Offray de la Mettrie dedicated to Haller his subversive *Man a Machine*—the better to rankle him.

Haller could not be expected to remain silent on an issue as important to the eighteenth century as embryology. He conducted a complex debate with Caspar Friedrich Wolff, who held an epigenetic theory of development, while Haller believed in preformationism. Epigeneticists argued that the chick, for example, developed from a fertilized egg; preformationists held that a sperm stimulated an ovum which already contained the chick in miniature. The debate has been the subject of an interesting recent study by Shirley Roe, who shows that each man was influenced by fundamentally extrascientific notions. Wolff's Cartesian, rationalist approach was distrusted by Haller who, for his part, could not accept a theory which might threaten his strongly held religious beliefs. The debate was not resolved. However, after he adopted preformationism, Haller's prepotent influence was such that embryology was impeded for many years. It was consonant, observes Roe, with Haller's more general view of science, "as leading toward a deeper appreciation of and reverence for God and away from the dangers of atheism and materialism." The debate remains resonant today in light of the contemporary controversies concerning abortion and the human fetus.

Although he was married—three times, in fact, leaving eight children—Haller, like Newton, possessed a difficult personality and attained prominence in spite of a number of eccentricities. He was a devoted Zwinglian (after Huldreich Zwingli, the Swiss counterpart to Martin Luther) and was tormented by doubts about his religious belief after God took his first wife. He suffered from bad eyesight, bladder problems, melancholia, and insomnia. (To cure the latter he became an opium addict.) In his old age he grew obese and suffered from gout and could no longer go collecting specimens. Yet a year before his death, in 1776, Haller published a vast bibliography listing some fifty-two thousand works on medicine, which was yet incomplete. He was stilled for good on December 12, 1777.

43

August Kekulé
and Chemical Structure

1829–1896

A theory of the underlying structure of chemical compounds emerged with difficulty in the nineteenth century, even as a welter of substances were discovered and characterized. A theory of "types" and radicals emerged to explain how chemical reactions might take place, but for a time it was unclear if even the most basic compounds could be thoroughly analyzed. This was especially true of the "organic" compounds which, unlike metals, are dissipated through burning. The situation was clarified, however, beginning in 1858, by the German scientist August Kekulé.

Kekulé is often said to have fathered organic chemistry

because, by explaining the central role of the carbon molecule in organic reactions, he showed how it combines with other elements to form a prodigious number of substances. In addition, Kekulé's resolution of the structure of benzene in 1865 ushered in a new era in the history of chemistry. Chemists could henceforth visualize, and to some extent explain and predict, chemical reactions. From this ability to provide structural formulas which indicate stepwise molecular changes arises modern synthetic organic chemistry. Kekulé's contribution was, according to Frederick Japp, a "most brilliant piece of scientific production" which laid the foundation for the entire field.

Friedrich August Kekulé was born on September 7, 1829, in Darmstadt, in Hesse. Descended from a noble Bohemian family, he was the son of the Grand-ducal Hessian Head Councillor, Ludwig Carl Emil Kekulé; his father had replaced *e* with *é* in the family surname during Napoleonic rule. Following his father's wishes, August first studied architecture at the University of Giessen in 1847, where he excelled as a draftsman. But he was also intrigued by mathematics and became fascinated by the lectures of JUSTUS LIEBIG [36]. Kekulé began his scientific studies in 1849, and, with financial help from a friendly stepbrother, took courses in chemistry in Paris during 1851, returning to Germany to receive his doctorate in 1852.

With Liebig's support, Kekulé worked in Switzerland and London before becoming privatdozent at the University of Heidelberg in 1856 and a professor at Ghent two years later. It is from this period, soon following this long apprenticeship, that Kekulé's most significant accomplishments date. Not particularly interested in laboratory study, Kekulé was drawn most of all to the considerable conceptual problems that plagued chemistry in the 1850s.

By the middle of the nineteenth century, it was known that some atoms, such as oxygen and carbon, combine readily with other elements, and in definite ratios. The central concept of *valency* arose because each sort of atom seemed to have a different number of "hooks" for combining with other atoms. One part oxygen combined with two parts hydrogen to make water, for example; and carbon atoms, it was known, were particularly versatile. In addition, chemists had developed the idea of the *radical*, or a stable group of atoms which react as a functional group with other elements. These potent and suggestive notions were weakened, however, by theories of "types," which restricted the number of possible chemical combinations and, most of all, precluded detailed knowledge of their actual structures.

Kekulé's own account of his major discoveries is interesting and amusing, if not perhaps the whole story. His sudden insight into the central importance of carbon atoms came on a summer's night about 1855, he later said, as he was riding on the top deck of a London omnibus "through the deserted streets of the metropolis." Drowsing, he saw carbon atoms whirling—"gamboling"—and then forming chains in his mind's eye. All this before being awakened by the conductor, crying, "Clapham Road!" as he reached his destination. It was now apparent to him that carbon atoms could combine both with each other and with various other atoms to form long and complex chains.

Not the ratio but the structure of the combination of elements was responsible for all their various qualities and potencies. Briefly, this became the foundation for organic chemistry, and although Kekulé developed a sausage-like notation, chemists eventually adopted a system proposed by Archibald Scott Couper about the same time. Nevertheless, over the next several years Kekulé transformed his vision into a trenchant investigation of the different properties of the carbon compounds. He held as a postulate the four-pronged nature of the carbon atom—that, as he put it, "in general the sum of the chemical units of the elements united with one atom of carbon is four." Although cautious in generalizing, he had, in fact, brought a structural theory to bear on chemical composition.

Indeed, the notion of chains worked exceptionally well to describe all the carbon compounds save those known as the aromatics. Benzene, composed of hydrogen and carbon and found in those days in coal tar, was the parent compound of the aromatics.* But it would not conform to Kekulé's chain theory without violating the valency rules. Yet another dream, according to Kekulé, was to account for his discovery of its structure. About 1862, while working on the problem, he fell half-asleep by the fire. "Again the atoms gamboled before my eyes. Smaller groups

---

*A colorless liquid with a low boiling point, which burns with a smoky, yellow flame, benzene is an excellent solvent. It had been discovered by Michael Faraday in 1825, and about the time Kekulé's work with it began, its importance to industry was expanding. It was used in the dye industry, was also a fuel and solvent, and is found in all sorts of products, from detergents to insecticides.

this time kept modestly in the background....Long rows, in many ways more densely joined; everything in movement, winding and turning like snakes. And look, what was that? One snake grabbed its own tail, and mockingly the shape whirled before my eyes."

Kekulé had discovered benzene's ringlike structure—in its modern form, a hexagon of six carbon atoms with alternating double bonds surrounded by hydrogen atoms. This satisfies the requirements of both atoms. Each carbon atom had four bonds, each hydrogen atom, one. The structure, as well as many of the properties that can be predicted from it, was confirmed within a short time.

Whether the story of snakes in a circle—which was also an alchemical symbol known as *Ouroboros*—is accurate or was fabricated to insure priority has been debated recently, but the importance of the benzene structure to the subsequent development of chemistry cannot be doubted. With benzene, as with other compounds, the structural formula enabled chemists to visualize compounds and predict their formulas and variations. "Just as Picasso later transformed art by allowing the viewer to see within and behind things," writes William H. Brock in a recent history, "so Kekulé had transformed chemistry....The future of chemistry, as well as industry, after 1865 was, indeed, to lie in structural chemistry at the sign of this hexagon." In the twentieth century, it should be added, LINUS PAULING [16] deepened Kekulé's insight with the help of quantum mechanics.

Sometimes said not to have been an overly competent experimenter, Kekulé found it useful and convenient to build three-dimensional atomic models with wooden spheres of various colors representing the different atoms connected by brass rods. This proved a fine heuristic tool and was an idea taken up in the twentieth century by Linus Pauling and then used by JAMES WATSON [49] and FRANCIS CRICK [33] to model the structure of DNA.

Kekulé's influence was spread in great measure by his textbook on organic chemistry, the first volume of which was issued in 1859; it eventually came to three volumes over two thousand pages long but was never completed. In addition, Kekulé wanted chemistry to develop a "systematic and rational nomenclature," and he was instrumental in organizing the First International Chemical Congress at Karlsruhe in 1860. It was here that Stanislao Cannizzaro convincingly showed the importance of atomic masses of elements, reviving the molecular theory and leading chemistry a step closer to the periodic table, which would be unveiled by DMITRI MENDELEEV [47] several years later.

From 1865 Kekulé taught at the University of Bonn, but his later years were not entirely happy. After his first wife died in childbirth, his second marriage to his young housekeeper was not a success. Nor did he entirely recover from an attack of measles in 1876, which he contracted from his infant son. He was highly esteemed, however. It was in 1890, when he was honored on the twenty-fifth anniversary of his discovery of the benzene ring, that Kekulé recalled the story of his sleep-induced inspirations. When in 1895 he received the title of nobility, as not a few Germans did in those days, he dropped the Napoleonic *é* for *e*; and thus his name in its royal form is Kekule von Stradonitz. He died on July 13, 1896.

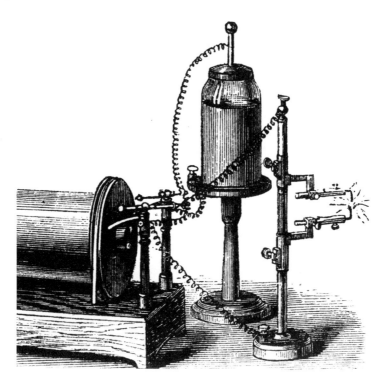

44

Robert Koch
and Bacteriology

1843–1910

The enormous number and variety of microorganisms—the human body contains literally billions of them—makes it difficult to prove that a particular bacterium or virus causes a specific disease. How this might be done was systematized in the final two decades of the nineteenth century by Robert Koch. His isolation of the microbes which cause anthrax and tuberculosis were major discoveries, and they had powerful repercussions on the practice of medicine. Equally instrumental for research were his principles of microbacterial investigation known as Koch's postulates. He is often described, with Louis Pasteur [5], with whom he had an adversarial relationship, as the cofounder of the germ theory of disease. In the imaginative bestseller *The Microbe Hunters*, Koch is the "Death Fighter," and Paul de Kruif writes, "I beg leave to remove my hat and make bows of respect to Koch—the man who really *proved* that microbes are our most deadly enemies, who brought microbe hunting near to being a science, the man who is now the partly forgotten captain of an obscure heroic age."

One of thirteen children, Robert Koch was born to Hermann and Mathilde Koch on December 11, 1843, in Clausthal-Zellerfeld, a city in the Harz Mountains, an important mining region of Germany. His father was a mining engineer, and his grandfather and uncle were both amateur geologists, and young Koch became a collector of minerals as well as insects, mosses, and lichen. When he entered the University of Göttingen in 1862, he initially studied the natural sciences. He later resolved to study medicine, however, and came under the influence of Jacob Henle, an anatomist who, about twenty years before Pasteur, had adumbrated the idea of contagion by microbes. After graduating from medical school in 1866, Koch interned at Hamburg, served in the Franco-Prussian War, and settled down as a district medical officer in a small village in Silesia in what is today part of Poland.

Koch received a microscope from his wife for his birthday in 1871 and began to study microorganisms during his spare time. He developed great technical skill, using new staining techniques as well as photography. By the mid-1870s he was investigating anthrax, a disease common in his region of Silesia. The disease, which mainly afflicted cattle and sheep, caused ulcerating sores, lesions in the lung, and death, and could be transmitted to humans. In 1876, by infecting mice, Koch succeeded in showing that the cause of anthrax was what became known as the *Bacillus anthracis*, a specific microorganism with definite actions in the blood. Identification of the anthrax microbe was the first unequivocal proof that a microorganism caused a particular disease, and it opened the way, in 1881, for the development of a vaccine by Louis Pasteur. Koch's papers on anthrax in 1876 to 1877 brought him his first great acclaim. In 1881, he developed a method of using gelatin as a medium for culture; this became a staple of research for many years. He also published *Methods for the Study of Pathogenic Organisms*.

Koch's discovery of the tuberculosis bacterium is a tale of exceptional accomplishment and egregious error. Appointed adviser to the Imperial Department of Health in Berlin in 1880, Koch began seeking a microbial agent responsible for tuberculosis. The dread and often fatal disease of the lungs had been widely but unsuccessfully studied in the early nineteenth century—indeed, a number of researchers died from it—and it was untreatable except, in mild cases, by rest at sanitoriums. On March 24, 1882, in a brief lecture to the Physiological Society of Berlin, Koch reported that he had succeeded in isolating the bacterium which causes tuberculosis. The potential importance for diagnosis and a possible vaccine was immediately clear.

With this discovery Koch laid the groundwork for all modern bacteriology, for he put forth a set of principles, known ever since as Koch's postulates, that provide medical research with a basic structure. The postulates, as given today, are four in number: (1) The organism that causes the disease must be present in every case. (2) A pure culture of the organism must be obtainable. (3) The culture must produce the disease when healthy, susceptible animals are inoculated. (4) The organism must be found in the sick animals. These constituted a new formulation of principles put forth earlier by Koch's teacher Henle. Koch's postulates are sound governing generalizations and are still frequently cited and highly influential.

Driven to conquer an infectious disease much as Pasteur had done with anthrax and rabies, Koch eventually believed that he had developed a cure for tuberculosis from killed tubercle bacilli. He announced as much suddenly, almost impulsively, on August 4, 1890, before sufficient trials had been carried out. In fact, the treatment, tuberculin, turned out to be worse than the disease itself.

"Koch's announcement that he had discovered a remedy for tuberculosis," writes Victor Robinson, "warmed the breast of Mother Earth with a strange hope and everywhere her afflicted children stretched their hands for the health-bringing vial." As a consequence, thousands of tubercular patients swarmed to Berlin clamoring for tuberculin which killed many of them. Koch's subsequent report on his cure was hobbled by vague and misleading statements. Although he remained a superstar of his time in medical research, he soon left Berlin on an extended vacation.*

Koch's later career reflected his great stature and wide influence. In 1891 he was named director of the Berlin Institute for Infectious Disorders, where he remained until his retirement in 1904. He was awarded the Nobel Prize for his work on tuberculosis in 1905. Apart from his own studies, Koch was the prime force behind research into the numerous infectious diseases that constituted a major cause of premature death in the late nineteenth century. Koch directed studies of cholera, malaria, dysentery, trachoma, typhus, bubonic plague, and a number of cattle diseases, including rinderpest and Texas fever. In addition, his work, along with that of Louis Pasteur and Joseph Lister, gave important impetus to the evolving sanitary movement; Koch himself once called the cholera bacteria "our best ally" in fighting for improved sanitation.

It is instructive to note that Koch's work is a strong example of the relationship between medicine and economic and political life. Koch came of age with the formation of Germany and its emergence as a world power in the context of European imperialism. Newly discovered and exotic diseases formed the basis of much of his research, and he journeyed widely, traveling to Egypt, Africa, and India to seek the microbes responsible. Many of these diseases would have remained local phenomena, little understood but not widespread, were it not for European expansionism. Interregional contact today, augmented by rapid air travel and the destruction of the tropical rain forests, is likely at the root of the worldwide AIDS epidemic.

Like Pasteur—indeed, like many contemporary medical researchers—Koch was an aggressive polemicist and capable of arrogance. Although widely admired, he created a scandal when he left his first wife, Emmy Fratz, for a young actress named Hedwig Freiberg. That made his employer, the German government, unhappy, and some of his close relations stopped talking to him. Townspeople in his natal Clausthal tore down the tablet they had erected outside his birthplace. But as Claude E. Dolman said

---

*Some good came of this medical disaster when it was recognized that Koch's "cure" could serve as a diagnostic test for the disease. His attenuated bacteria became the basis for the so-called patch test which schoolchildren in the United States still take. A vaccine for tuberculosis, discovered in 1924, some years after Koch's death, is today used in many countries.

in an elegant eulogy, "The Faustian weaknesses and perplexities do not diminish the lasting benefits that his aspirations bestowed on mankind." Koch remained at work until April 7, 1910, when he fell ill and was taken to a spa at Baden-Baden. There he died on May 27, 1910.

Murray Gell-Mann
and the Eightfold Way

1929–

A preeminent physicist in the second half of the twentieth century, Murray Gell-Mann possesses some of the breadth of vision of ALBERT EINSTEIN [2], NIELS BOHR [3], and other founders of modern physics. To Gell-Mann, an originator of the theory of "quarks," is owed the development of quantum chromodynamics (QCD), the powerful theory that describes the basic building blocks and interactions of subatomic particles. In general, Gell-Mann's quark model, which evolved from his classification scheme known as the Eightfold Way, has put an end to the confusion that reigned in physics after hundreds of subatomic particles were discovered by experimental physicists following World War II. In addition, Gell-Mann has been one of the major theorists behind the evolving "standard model," which would merge the strong and electroweak forces in a single unified theory. In recent years, at the Santa Fe Institute in New Mexico, he has also broached questions of cosmology, in which particle physicists have played an increasingly important role, as well as other of the broadest problems of science.

Murray Gell-Mann was born on September 15, 1929, in New York City, the son of Arthur Gell-Mann and Pauline Reichstein. An immigrant from Austria-Hungary who had been compelled to abandon his studies to help his parents in the United States, Arthur Gell-Mann learned to speak perfect English and operated a language school which failed with the advent of the Great Depression. Of wide learning himself, he encouraged his son's interest in natural science, but Gell-Mann has said that his most important mentor was his elder brother, Ben, who taught him to read at age three and nurtured a wide variety of cultural and scientific interests. Growing up in New York, Ben and Murray took extensive walks in Van Cortlandt Park in the Bronx, frequented the city museums, learned foreign grammars, and read poetry and fiction together. "Ben and I wanted to understand the world and enjoy it," Gell-Mann wrote later, "not to slice it up in some arbitrary way. We didn't differentiate sharply among such categories as the natural sciences, the social and behavioral sciences, the humanities, and the arts. In fact, I have never believed in the primacy of such distinctions."

Attending a school for the gifted, Gell-Mann found much of the curriculum dull. He did not like physics in high school, and when he began Yale University at age fifteen, he agreed to take courses in the subject only to humor his father. But he soon was captivated by the elegance and aesthetic appeal of theoretical physics. After graduating in 1948, he obtained a fellowship to the Massachusetts Institute of Technology. He received his Ph.D. three years later.

The trajectory of Gell-Mann's career is related to two major developments in physics following World War II. One was the theoretical flowering of quantum electrodynamics (QED), which brought remarkable accuracy to the physics of the electron and other charged particles. The other was experimental. During the 1950s and 1960s, from analysis of cosmic rays, and using increasingly powerful accelerators, physicists observed an ever-growing number of subatomic particles. But although atoms were smashed, photographed, and analyzed over and over again, their underlying unity remained less than clear—indeed, the term "particle zoo" was coined to describe the plethora of subatomic components.

Gell-Mann undertook his first important work at age twenty-three at the University of Chicago's Institute for Nuclear Studies. In 1953 he recognized that the persistence of certain subatomic particles, which would normally be expected to undergo rapid decay, was due to properties of what he concluded was a new class of matter.* Gell-Mann described the properties of these "strange particles" and was able to classify them, assign "strange" numbers to each, and provide equations that could predict their interactions. The theory's profile was enhanced by the discovery, six years later, of the xi zero particle, which Gell-Mann had predicted.

Introducing order into chaos is generally a significant accomplishment in science, and SHELDON GLASHOW [48] has written that "Gell-Mann provided the dominant thrust in theoretical particle physics during much of the 1950s and 60s." In 1955 Gell-Mann moved to the California Institute of Technology. In 1961 he began publishing a series of crucial papers establishing what he called the Eightfold Way. A means of classifying the hadrons, or relatively heavy subatomic particles, the Eightfold Way proved the most successful of a number of schemes proposed about the same time. The term referred to the manner in which particles could be grouped and was taken from Buddha's notion of the eight virtues which lead to nirvana. Gell-Mann was later annoyed when the Eightfold Way was taken to mean that contemporary physics bore some arcane relationship to Eastern religion.

Just as the periodic table had first been proposed by DMITRI MENDELEEV [47] to provide order in the expectation that some underlying explanation would not be long in coming, so it was with the Eightfold Way. In 1964 Gell-Mann was able to suggest that the hadrons, or particles which "feel the strangeness," were themselves composed of constituent particles he called "quarks." Initially, he described three quarks of different fractional charges which combined to create any of the known elementary particles, and he gave them several flavors: "up," "down," and "strange." A fourth quark, "charm," was later predicted, as were the "top" and "bottom" quarks. In addition to coming in "flavors," quarks were not all the same "color."

---

*A relatively long life for a "strange" particle is still quite short, ranging up to ten nanoseconds. A nanosecond is one billionth of a second.

From the beginning Gell-Mann believed that although quarks were real, they were permanently confined to the various particles they comprise; thus, neither the flavor nor the color of quarks is expressed in the world. However, when experimenters eventually used a beam of high-energy electrons to illuminate (in a manner of speaking) the interior of a proton, the quark structure was revealed. By 1995 all six quarks, including the most elusive, "top" quark were experimentally supported.

At a conference in 1972 at Fermilab, Gell-Mann brought forth the theory of quantum chromodynamics (QCD), which gave an account of the interaction of quarks and antiquarks through the mediating particles known as "gluons." Analogous in certain respects to quantum electrodynamics, QCD eventually provided a virtually complete account of the operation of the "strong force" that holds atomic particles together. By 1994 Gell-Mann could write that the nuclear particle collisions observed since the 1940s "have all now been explained as composites of quarks, antiquarks, and gluons. The quark scheme, embodied in the explicit theory of quantum chromodynamics, has thus exposed the simplicity underlying an apparently very complicated pattern of states."

Recipient of the Nobel Prize in physics in 1969 for his work on elementary particle theory, Gell-Mann remained at Caltech until his retirement in 1993. In 1984 he became one of the founders of the Santa Fe Institute, a multidisciplinary think tank located in New Mexico, where he continues to serve as professor and cochairman of the science board. There, much in consonance with his aims as a youth, Gell-Mann was able to expand the base of his interest in physics to such widely diverse fields as cosmology, ecology, and conservation, the evolution of language, and the global economy. The broad focus in this later stage of his career has been an effort to understand what he calls "complex adaptive systems"—the interrelatedness between the basic simplicity of physical laws and the intricate schemes of the natural world. He has sketched the nature of such systems in some detail in his *The Quark and the Jaguar*, published in 1994.

Gell-Mann married a British student of archaeology, J. Margaret Dow, in 1955, and they had two children, Elizabeth Sarah and Nicolas Webster. Margaret's death in 1981 left him a widower. In 1992 Gell-Mann married Marcia Southwick, a poet and professor of English.

46

Emil Fischer
and Organic Chemistry

1852–1919

Instead of entering the lumber business in 1869, Emil Fischer became a chemist and issued from his laboratory a wealth of basic research. Many of his discoveries were passed on to industry and, in addition, helped to found the science of biochemistry. Fischer's extensive studies of the properties of the various sugars, for example, not only led to their manufacture but also formed the basis for the entire range of carbohydrate chemistry. And his investigations of both the molecules known as purines and the amino acids known as polypeptides proved precocious starting points for molecular biology. In 1902 Fischer—an austere scientist who ended his life by suicide—would regret that his father "did not live to see his impractical son receive the Nobel Prize in chemistry." Fischer was, ventures Trevor I. Williams, "perhaps the greatest of organic chemists."

Emil Hermann Fischer was born on October 9, 1852, at Euskirchen, a small city in Rhenish Prussia. He was the son of Laurenz Fischer, a prosperous merchant, and Julie Poensgen Fischer. Fischer was an exceptional student and graduated from Bonn gymnasium with honors in 1869. But he did not want to become a businessman as his father had hoped. After a brief time with the family firm, he went on to the University of Bonn. There he attended lectures by AUGUST KEKULÉ [43], but was discouraged by the great chemist's lack of interest in experimental work. In 1872 Fischer transferred to the University of Strasbourg. His interest in chemistry was rekindled at the bench of another important figure, Adolf Baeyer. Fischer received his doctorate in 1874, and his dissertation concerned the chemistry of dyestuffs. When the dissertation was completed, Fischer remained at Strasbourg as Baeyer's assistant.

Beginning while he was a student and continuing through the 1880s, Fischer was an active young participant in the great expansion of chemical investigations in Germany. This research fueled a booming industry in a rapidly expanding economy. Working with the organic chemicals that could be made from hydrazine, one of the harsher compounds that nitrogen forms with hydrogen (it eats through rubber and even glass), Fischer developed derivatives with various industrial applications. Most important was his discovery of phenylhydrazine, which brought him a reputation before he achieved his doctorate. He later found it a useful agent in distinguishing sugars with the same chemical formula but different structures.

Fischer took an appointment at the University of Munich in 1879, and three years later he moved to Erlangen University, where he began an important, long-term study of uric acid and compounds related to it. The wide distribution of uric acid in nature suggested an undiscovered significance, and in 1882 Fischer made a preliminary effort to formulate a family of such compounds. At first his work only confused matters. But in 1897 he recognized how a single molecular base was the underlying component of uric acid and several other chemicals. This base Fischer called *purine*, coining the name from the Latin *purum* and *uricum*, because it was the pure base of uric acid, a compound of nitrogen. Among the purines are guanine and adenine, the nitrogen bases of the nucleic acids. Wrapped in a sugar phosphate backbone, these molecules form two of the four bases of DNA.

The importance of some of the substances which Fischer synthesized did not go unnoticed by the German pharmaceutical industry. Caffeine is a vegetable base found in coffee, tea, and cocoa; it was first synthesized in Fischer's laboratory and was subsequently manufactured in bulk. Still more important for the nascent modern pharmaceutical industry were Fischer's syntheses of the barbiturates. They were quickly marketed to doctors and psychiatrists, who put them to use drugging anxious patients since they were more effective than chloral hydrate or the compounds of bromide. The barbiturates were also used in animal research as anesthetics. And from phenyl, which Fischer discovered in 1912, came phenobarbital, a drug of considerable value in treating heart attacks and still used against epilepsy. Not surprisingly, Fischer was often courted by industry but refused all offers to join it.

In the 1890s Fischer undertook a long-term study of enzymes, types of proteins that act as catalysts in biochemical reactions. In recognizing that specific enzymes have specialized functions, he suggested, essentially correctly, that they were asymmetric molecules which reacted only upon certain substances. This lock-and-key approach laid the groundwork for a whole branch of enzyme chemistry.

As one consequence of his work with enzymes, Fischer was led to study carbohydrates. He had his greatest success with their breakdown products, the sugars. Although the composition of several sugars had been known for some time, the various forms were mysterious and could not be separated from their syrupy substrate. Fischer rightly surmised that the difference between glucose, fructose, and mannose—structurally the same, but with different properties—was an instance of asymmetrical carbon atoms. By 1897 he had managed to synthesize all three of these sugars in the laboratory. "By the end of the nineteenth century," writes historian of science Alexander Findlay, "the genius of Fischer seemed to have solved the riddle of the sugars." For both his work with sugars and purines, Fischer was awarded the Nobel Prize in chemistry in 1902.

While not principally a theoretician, Fischer had a firm grasp of biochemistry's potential reach. "The veil behind which

Nature has so carefully concealed her secrets is being lifted where the carbohydrates are concerned," he said in his Nobel address, and he prophesied: "Nevertheless, the chemical enigma of Life will not be solved until organic chemistry has mastered another, even more difficult subject, the proteins."

Indeed, Fischer's work on protein chemistry formed his final clutch of discoveries, begun in 1899, which are of equal significance to his earlier work. It was already known that the proteins are formed of amino acids and that they may be broken down through hydrolysis. Fischer could not hope to synthesize something as complex as a protein, but he succeeded in building groups of amino acids called peptides. In 1914 he brought about the first synthetic nucleotide; and his summary of peptide chemistry two years later provided a perspective on the complexity of the whole field. This work eventually led to the recognition that proteins owe their various functions to their shapes, and their shapes to their sequences of amino acids. Indeed, protein synthesis through the assembly of amino acids is the main work of DNA. The great anticipatory character of Fischer's work is evident from the fact that it was not until 1953 that FREDERICK SANGER [72], for the first time, determined the full amino acid sequence of a protein, the hormone known as insulin.

The eldest of Fischer's sons, Hermann Fischer, became himself a well-known organic chemist who eventually emigrated to the United States. Fischer's wife, Agnes Gerlach, had given him two other sons before she died in 1895; both these young men were killed in World War I. Fischer had been active in the war effort—the invention of ester margarine as a butter substitute followed from his work—but at the end he was left despondent. Ill from skin disease and gastrointestinal disorders contracted from years of exposure to mercury and the harsh chemical phenylhydrazine, Emil Fischer killed himself on July 15, 1919.

Dmitri Mendeleev
and the Periodic Table of Elements
1834–1907

A relatively small number of distinct elements, made up of atoms of different weights, combine in different ways to become the multitude of molecules that make up the whole of the physical world. During the nineteenth century, as many new elements were isolated and characterized, chemists made sporadic efforts to classify them. Although the various metals, nonmetals, and gases seemed to possess some underlying relationship, its character long remained a mystery. By the 1860s, however, with almost seventy elements discovered and their properties better understood, chemistry was ready for a forceful new generalization. And Dmitri Mendeleev, the memorable and imposing Russian, took that step in 1869 when he introduced the periodic table.

Dmitri Ivanovich Mendeleev was born in the Siberian city of Tobolsk—a frequent destination for political prisoners in Czarist Russia—on January 27, 1834. He was the youngest of about sixteen children of Ivan Pavlovich Mendeleev and Marya Kornileva. A teacher of philosophy, politics, and fine arts, Ivan Mendeleev unfortunately became blind as a result of cataracts and was forced to give up his post at the gymnasium shortly after Dmitri's birth. His pension was inadequate and thereafter the family was headed by his dominating and capable wife. From a well-known Siberian family, Marya managed to revive and run an abandoned family glass factory after her husband's death.

Mendeleev's childhood is a story of intellect and driving ambition in nineteenth-century Russia. At the Tobolsk gymnasium, young Mendeleev disliked reading Latin and the classics but quickly took to physics and mathematics. When Dmitri's mother was told of his exceptional intellect, she journeyed with him to St. Petersburg, where he gained a place at the Chief Pedagogical Institute. She died soon thereafter. Mendeleev himself had a brush with death when he contracted tuberculosis and a famous doctor told him that he didn't have long to live. Mendeleev sought a second opinion from Nikolai Pirogov, a still more celebrated physician, who told him that, on the contrary, he would outlive all his doctors. His health improved dramatically in 1856, the same year that he received his master's degree in chemistry.

After teaching for several years at the University of St. Petersburg, Mendeleev studied at Heidelberg, where he effectively discovered the phenomenon today called critical temperature—the point at which a gas can no longer be condensed into a liquid. In 1860 he attended the pathbreaking Chemical Congress at Karlsruhe where Stanislao Cannizzaro revived Avogadro's hypothesis and the relationship between atoms and molecules was finally clarified.* After receiving his doctorate in 1865, Mendeleev was appointed professor of general chemistry at the University of St. Petersburg in 1867.

During the 1860s Mendeleev undertook to write *Principles of Chemistry*, recognizing the need in Russia for a textbook of inorganic chemistry. As he did so, however, he developed the

---

*Amedeo Avagadro had suggested that equal volumes of gases, at the same temperature and pressure, contain equal numbers of molecules. This equivalence enabled the elements that composed molecules to be weighed.

larger purpose—though he was by no means alone—of bringing order to a confused field. Like other chemists, he believed that the various elements had to have some underlying unity. "But nothing, from mushrooms to a scientific law, can be discovered without looking and trying," he wrote. "So I began to look about and write down the elements with their atomic weights and typical properties, analogous elements and like atomic weights on separate cards, and this soon convinced me that the properties of elements are in periodic dependence upon their atomic weights."

Indeed, one of Mendeleev's strategies was to prepare individual cards, and in laying them out, he eventually noticed the repetition of properties—the regular, or periodic character of the elements. Ranging them in rows by atomic weight, he saw that *the size of the atomic weight determines the nature of the elements.* Chemicals which have similar properties have weights close together; manganese (55) and iron (56) are examples. In addition, certain elements have distinct similarities over a uniform increase in their atomic weights. Thus lithium, weighted at 7, is similar to sodium, weighted at 23, and both are related to potassium at 39.* All three are soft and silvery in appearance, and today are classified (with rubidium, caesium, and francium) as the alkali metals, or group 1 of the periodic table.

It should be emphasized that, in developing the table, Mendeleev employed his vast knowledge of chemistry and his highly developed intuition. Atomic weights were relative, in some instances were approximations, and arrived at through experiment. The periodic table was thus itself an organizing force, and Mendeleev had the temerity to predict the existence of elements that had not yet been discovered. "Among the ordinary elements," he wrote, "the lack of a number of analogues of boron and aluminum is very striking." Consequently, Mendeleev predicted the existence and forecast the properties of three elements which he called eka-aluminum, eka-boron, and eka-silicon. These turned out to be gallium, discovered in 1875, and scandium and germanium, found in 1879 and 1885, respectively. Some of his other predictions were less successful.

Mendeleev's periodic table was one of several efforts to classify the elements during the 1860s, and it was the most successful. Lothar Meyer, who arrived at a classification similar to

---

*These are the relative atomic weights from Mendeleev's 1869 table.

Mendeleev's about the same time, is sometimes given a share of the credit, and so is Alexandre-Émile Beguyer de Chancourtois. But Mendeleev's clarity of explanation, and his willingness to predict the properties of as-yet-undiscovered elements made his table the standard, and he became one of the most famous scientists of his time. His *Principles of Chemistry*, a unique text, clearly written yet with many long footnotes and anecdotes, was translated into a number of languages.

In Russia Mendeleev is remembered today for these achievements and for his pioneering work in developing the petroleum industry in the region of the Black Sea. To this end, he visited the United States in 1876, then in the throes of its centennial celebration. Echoing the views of other Europeans at the time, Mendeleev thoroughly disliked the United States, which he found primitive and basically uninterested in science.

Viewing pictures of the hypnotic Mendeleev is enough to convince one that his personal life must have been fascinating. In 1863, when he was thirty-one, his sister cajoled him into marrying Feozva Nikitichna Leshcheva; it was an extremely unhappy union. After producing two children, the couple separated, each unable to tolerate the presence of the other in the same house. In 1876, before leaving for his trip to the United States, Mendeleev met a beautiful seventeen-year-old, Anna Ivanova Popov, whom he resolved to marry or else jump into the ocean and drown. Though he was unable to receive an immediate divorce through the Orthodox Church, Mendeleev nevertheless found a priest willing to marry him and Anna. In this way, he became for a time a bigamist. He avoided prosecution by appealing to the czar. According to one story, a nobleman desirous of the same dispensation later also appealed to Alexander, alluding to the chemist. "Mendeleev has two wives, yes," replied the czar, "but I have only one Mendeleev."

His second marriage was exceptionally happy, and the couple had four children. Anna introduced Mendeleev to the world of art, and he became a collector and critic and was eventually elected to the Russian Academy of Art. At the end of his life he suffered, as had his father, from cataracts. He died on January 20, 1907.

48

Sheldon Glashow
and the Discovery of Charm

1932–

By the late twentieth century physicists had developed a powerful "standard theory" of elementary particles and the forces which combine them. Initiated by the work of MURRAY GELL-MANN [45], who proposed the theory of quarks, which evolved into quantum chromodynamics, the standard theory has emerged robust from thousands of experiments over the past twenty years. Although many questions remain, the theory describes an array of fundamental force and matter particles which can be shown to make up the physical universe and even be employed to help account for its genesis. The standard theory unites the strong, weak, and electromagnetic forces under one conceptual roof and holds out the possibility of a grand unified theory, or GUT. Although it was the work of numerous physicists, the pivotal figure, and the most influential among them, is arguably Sheldon Glashow. "The theory we now have is an integral work of art," he has asserted. "The patchwork quilt has become a tapestry."

Sheldon Lee Glashow was born in New York City on December 5, 1932, the son of Lewis Glashow, a Russian immigrant and proprietor of a plumbing business, and Bella Rubin Glashow. Encouraged to pursue science by his parents and an older brother, Sam, Glashow dates his interest in physics to World War II, when he became curious as to why bombs, when dropped from airplanes, have forward momentum as they fall. After attending the Bronx High School of Science—one of his classmates was Steven Weinberg, with whom he would later share the Nobel Prize—he went on to Cornell University in 1950 and received his B.A. degree in 1954. Although he was not challenged as an undergraduate, in graduate school at Harvard University, Glashow encountered the 1950s enthusiasm for quantum theory from his work with Julian Schwinger, one of the architects of quantum electrodynamics. From this period dates Glashow's initiation into the most challenging problems of theoretical physics.

Physicists by the 1950s had identified four basic forces in nature: gravity, electromagnetic, and strong and weak interactions. The "strong force" accounted for the binding together of atoms, while the "weak force" was seen in radioactive decay. However, although exquisitely precise predictions could be obtained for electromagnetic interactions using quantum electrodynamics (QED), efforts to apply similar methods to the other forces led to impossible, meaningless results. To ameliorate the situation, Julian Schwinger had suggested, tentatively, that the weak and electromagnetic forces might be described by a single, coherent theory. He did not develop the idea, however, but suggested that Glashow take the topic for his doctoral dissertation. "He asked me to think about it," Glashow said later. "And that's what I did for two years—think about it."

In his dissertation, "The Vector Meson in Elementary Particle Decays," which brought him his doctorate in 1958, Glashow discussed the possibility of a theory of the weak force which, like QED, would be a "renormalizable" gauge theory—that is, one that allowed adjustments in calculations to avoid incomprehensible results. He suggested that because such a theory would depend on QED, "a fully acceptable theory of these interactions may *only* be achieved if they are treated together."

The electroweak theory was difficult to formulate and did not win easy acceptance. Recipient of a National Science Foundation Fellowship, Glashow undertook postdoctoral work at the Institute of Theoretical Physics in Copenhagen, Denmark, from 1958 to 1960, as well as at the European Center for Nuclear Research (CERN) in Geneva, Switzerland. In late 1958, he was correct in predicting the possibility of an electroweak theory, but his actual formulation was faulty. Delivering a lecture on the topic in London the spring of 1959, his work was roundly criticized and for some time afterward largely ignored. However, in late 1961 he published a landmark paper, entitled "Partial Symmetries of Weak Interactions." In Glashow's formulation, wrote Robert P. Crease and Charles C. Mann, "The weak and electromagnetic forces within the atom are like two children with an elaborate [toy] train set, each at a separate control panel: they frantically throw the switches, toot the whistle, and turn the throttle without consulting each other." The actual movement of the train results from a combination of the actions of both—and so with atomic particles. Evaluating it years later, Glashow conceded, "It was a brilliant paper, but almost nobody ever read it."

However, at the invitation of Gell-Mann, who was already a dominant figure in theoretical physics, Glashow took a research fellowship at the California Institute of Technology in 1960 and remained on the West Coast to teach for several years at Stanford University and the University of California at Berkeley. Gell-Mann's Eightfold Way and his theory of quarks bore directly on Glashow's own work, and in 1964 he published a prescient paper on quark theory, written with James D. Bjorken.

In Gell-Mann's initial theory, he hypothesized that three subatomic quarks identified as "up," "down," and "strange," were the building blocks of the "hadrons," or heavy subatomic particles. Glashow and Bjorken soon suggested a fourth quark, "charm," which could, they reasoned, give the theory a broader unity. This idea, however, like Glashow's earlier paper on electroweak theory, was initially ignored, largely for a lack of experimental evidence. In 1966, Glashow accepted a full professorship at Harvard University, and returned to the East Coast, but for the next few years he found physics in a period of doldrums.

Two crucial developments set the stage for a revolution that would culminate in the new standard model. One was the completion of a working electroweak theory, which Glashow had begun years before, by Steve Weinberg and, independently in England, Abdus Salam. The other was a problem in the decay scheme of the "strange" particles, which Glashow called "strange-ness-changing neutral currents" (SCNC). Glashow and his colleagues, John Iliopoulos and Luciano Maiana, now realized that the problem could be rectified by including in calculations the fourth quark—"charm"—which he had proposed years earlier. "Charm, we found, not only restores the lost symmetry between leptons and quarks," wrote Glashow later, "but it also provides a natural and elegant mechanism for the suppression of strange-ness-changing neutral currents. As the dictionary says, charm averts evil."

At a conference of mass spectroscopists at Northeastern University in 1974, Glashow suggested that experimenters soon should be able to find charm. In "Charm: An Invention That Awaits Discovery," Glashow proposed a wager: "One, charm is not found, and I eat my hat. Two, charm is found by spectrosco-pists, and we celebrate. Three, charm is found by outlanders, and you eat *your* hats." In fact, the charmed particles were soon discovered—though not by spectroscopy but in high energy accelerators. Indeed, the particle which experimentalists called "J/psi" confirmed at one blow the existence of quarks and of charm. Glashow's key theoretical paper, "Is Bound Charm Found?" written in collaboration with Alvaro De Rújula, in 1975, reprised the importance of these discoveries and made a variety of predictions, most of which proved correct, including the prediction of particles with "naked charm"—a quark with all the predicted qualities of charm. At a meeting in 1976 mass spectros-copists were provided candy hats to eat.

A determinant event in twentieth-century physics, the discovery of charm led to a broader theory which incorporated the discoveries of Glashow, Gell-Mann, Weinberg, and many other theoretical and experimental physicists. What became known as the "standard model" laid to rest the "bootstrap model," which had for years competed with the developing theory of quarks.*

---

*The "bootstrap" model ("nuclear democracy") suggested that the familiar subatomic particles—electrons, neutrons, and protons—were no more fundamental than other less well-known particles, basic building blocks of matter.

Comprised of the electroweak theory and quantum chromodynamics, the standard model explains the strong, weak, and electromagnetic interactions of all the elementary particles. (Gravitation is not included in the theory.) The theory, writes Glashow, "appears to offer, in terms of seventeen arbitrary parameters, a complete and correct description of particle phenomenology. There are no loose ends, no observed phenomena that are incompatible with the theory."

The great success of the standard theory in explaining physical interactions still leaves a variety of questions unanswered, and Glashow has become one of the major physicists seeking a grand unified theory that would provide an overall theory of QCD, together with the electroweak force. Beginning in 1974 Glashow developed the first GUT, which became known as SU(5), in a short paper which brought together the basic discoveries in physics since the 1950s. The term SU(5) stands for *Special Unitary group in *five* dimensions*, and includes the provocative notion that even the presumably stable proton is also subject to decay—over extremely long periods of time. SU(5) has not been experimentally verified. Today it is one of a number of competing GUT theories available to physicists.

Considered "courteous, responsible, cooperative and mature" when he won the Westinghouse Talent Search in 1950, Glashow was a popular as well as renowned figure in the physics community nearly half a century later. In 1979 Glashow was awarded the Nobel Prize for his work in developing the electroweak theory, which he shared with Steven Weinberg and Abdus Salam. He is a member of the National Academy of Sciences, and, among many honors, was awarded the J. R. Oppenheimer Award in 1976. Since 1987 he has been Mellon Professor of the Sciences at Harvard University. In 1972 Glashow married Joan Shirley Alexander (who happens to be a sister of LYNN MARGULIS [80]), and they have raised four children. Glashow's *Interactions*, published in 1988, is an entertaining mixture of autobiography and theoretical physics.

49

James Watson
and the Structure of DNA

1928–

To discover the structure of deoxyribonucleic acid (DNA), James Watson embarked on a quest which embodies the international character of twentieth-century science. In Chicago, Illinois, reading *What Is Life?* by ERWIN SCHRÖDINGER [18], he was moved to discover the biological secrets of living systems. Under the tutelage of immigrant scientists who had fled Nazi Germany, he became interested in work on bacteriophages, viral particles that are nothing but strands of DNA wrapped in a protein sheath. To learn more about them he went to Copenhagen, and at a meeting in Italy discovered how their crystal structure might be divined using X-ray diffraction photography. Moving on to England he collaborated with FRANCIS CRICK [33], in a fervent competition with other scientists to unravel the structure of DNA. Together they came to recognize that it has a ladderlike, double-helical structure, ideal for replicating genetic information. Not surprisingly, Watson, as an American, contended somewhat less easily with fame than Crick. He was moved to write an arch memoir that annoyed his colleagues, and within a decade he ended his career in original research. But he has remained a potent force in biology, highly regarded for his integrity; and for the discovery of DNA, Sir Lawrence Bragg, director of the Cavendish Laboratory, once said, "I don't think Crick would ever have done it, apart from Watson, for a moment."

Born in Chicago, Illinois, on April 6, 1928, James Dewey Watson was raised in a financially impoverished but intellectually rich environment. His father, James Watson Sr., made a modest living as a debt collector but was also a devoted bird watcher who instilled in his son an interest in ornithology. His mother, Jean Mitchell Watson, worked as an admissions officer at the University of Chicago, was active in Democratic politics, and engaged James in debates on the relative influence of heredity and environment. Endowed with a photographic memory, Watson appeared on the *Quiz Kids*, a popular radio show featuring youngsters with exceptional talents.

In 1943 Watson entered the University of Chicago on a scholarship, receiving a bachelor's degree in 1947 after majoring in zoology. While a senior, he had become interested in genetics and, like Francis Crick, was strongly impressed by Erwin Schrödinger's *What Is Life?*, which was published in 1945. "I became polarized toward finding out the secret of the gene," Watson later said, even to the extent of overcoming his resistance to learning organic chemistry.

Watson's subsequent education brought him into contact with a virtually ideal group of scientists. "I was trained to find the structure of DNA," he once said, "as Prince Charles is trained to be a king." At Indiana University, Watson studied with Hermann Joseph Müller, the Nobel laureate who had fled both Germany and the Soviet Union and discovered that X rays can cause genetic mutations. Watson's thesis adviser was biologist Salvador Luria, one of the founders of the group of scientists studying the genetics of simple organisms known as bacteriophages—a form of virus which multiplies inside bacteria. In addition, during his graduate studies Watson journeyed to Cold Spring Harbor on Long Island and to the California Institute of Technology, where he met MAX DELBRÜCK [68], the initiator of phage studies.

Receiving his doctorate from Indiana in 1950, Watson traveled to Copenhagen on a National Research Council fellowship for postdoctoral research. At a meeting in Naples, Italy, in 1951, he attended a lecture by Maurice Wilkins, a nuclear physicist who had turned to biology and was beginning to use X-ray crystallography to study the complex molecule deoxyribonucleic acid (DNA). "Suddenly I was excited about chemistry," Watson wrote in *The Double Helix*. "Before Maurice's talk I had been worried about the possibility that the gene might be fantastically irregular. Now, however, I knew that genes could crystallize; hence they must have a regular structure that could be solved in a straightforward fashion." This insight united Watson's knowledge of phage theory with a technique originating in atomic physics. Interest in the studies by Wilkins took Watson to Cavendish Laboratory, Cambridge, where he met and began his collaboration with the British physicist and doctoral candidate Francis Crick.

The story of the Watson-Crick collaboration and how it led to the discovery of the structure of DNA has been told often, and Watson himself provided a personal account in *The Double Helix*, published in 1968. Their backgrounds were complementary, and they soon began to share an office. Over the next two years they worked out the structure of DNA. "Mr. Crick was thirty-five, Dr. Watson twenty-three," writes Horace Freeland Judson in *The Eighth Day of Creation*. "As Watson had done before with Luria and Delbrück, he was able once more to create almost instantly a mutual intellectual trust with an older scientist of brilliance, which was free of the scathing competitiveness most colleagues of his own age have felt."

Following the lead of the great chemist LINUS PAULING [16], with whom they were effectively in competition, Watson and Crick undertook to build cardboard and metal models of the DNA molecule as they conceived it hypothetically. DNA, known to exist in every cell, and thought to control the production of enzymes, consisted of four bases, a sugar molecule, and a phosphate molecule. Although its structure was crucial, it could only be guessed at from the X-ray diffraction studies. The configuration of the bases relative to the molecule's backbone, the number of chains forming the backbone, and the types of bonds remained to be determined.

After initial efforts failed in 1951, Watson and Crick returned to the problem. Then, in February 1953, while working with a cardboard model, Watson had what can be characterized as the key insight. "Suddenly I became aware," he wrote, "that an adenine-thymine pair held together by two hydrogen bonds was identical in shape to a guanine-cytosine pair held together by at least two hydrogen bonds." There were, in effect, *two* chains of molecules, linked by hydrogen bonds and wound round a sugar and phosphate base. Within about a month, Crick and Watson had developed a model in accord with what was experimentally known. It promised a complementary structure that could enable replication. They followed their publication of a brief paper in *Nature*, on April 25, 1953, with a longer explanatory article on May 30.

While Crick remained for many years at Cambridge and became the prime force behind many of the key developments in molecular biology, Watson returned to the United States, where he joined Delbrück and others at the California Institute of Technology. In 1955 he moved to Harvard University. Although he published little research after receiving the Nobel Prize, which he shared with Crick and Maurice Wilkins in 1962, he remained a figure of potent influence in molecular biology. He wrote *The Molecular Biology of the Gene*, a comprehensive and standard work first published in 1965, and in 1983 published *The Molecular Biology of the Cell*.

By the 1960s Watson's influence was felt throughout the field of molecular biology. In 1968 he accepted a position as director of Cold Spring Harbor Laboratory. For the next eight years he commuted between the laboratory and Harvard, leaving the university in 1976 to direct Cold Spring Harbor full-time. Under his administration the research focus became the genetics of cancer, and in 1981 scientists at the laboratory were the first to isolate *ras*, the cancer-causing "oncogene." Research on the biochemistry and genetics of tumor formation, as well as other topics, made Cold Spring Harbor one of the country's leading research facilities.

When the Human Genome Project got under way, in 1987, Watson became the natural choice to lead it, lending it prestige and raising its profile. An effort to characterize the entire human genome by charting all its fifty to one hundred thousand genes, the project was driven by new technological advances. A complete map of the genome promised new ways to prevent, detect, and treat diseases as well as a variety of industrial applications. It was a joint effort of the National Institutes of Health and the U.S. Department of Energy, and the program's complexity demanded someone with Watson's stature and intellectual credentials. Watson served as the head of the Office of Human Genome Research from October 1988 until he resigned in April 1992. Known for forthrightness, Watson had a controversial tenure as a bureaucrat.

James Watson remained director of Cold Spring Harbor until the end of 1993, when he stepped down to become the organization's president. In 1968 Watson married Elizabeth Lewis, his laboratory assistant, twenty years his junior. They raised two sons, Rufus and Duncan. In 1993, celebrating the fortieth anniversary of the discovery of the structure of DNA, Watson brought 130 colleagues, including Francis Crick, to Cold Spring Harbor. He recalled his first visit to the laboratory as a graduate student, which "sort of completed my total liberation because there were all these wonderful people here, whose sole ambition was not to make money but...[to answer] only one question: What was the gene?...It was *paradise!*"

50

John Bardeen
and Superconductivity
1908–1991

John Bardeen was a key participant in two fundamental discoveries in recent physics having immense promise and practical consequence. Working at the Bell Laboratories after World War II, Bardeen was one of three central figures in the development of the transistor, which within a few years became a crucial component everywhere in electronics technology. During the 1950s Bardeen also discovered a theoretical solution to the problem of superconductivity—the property of certain metals at low temperatures to lose all resistance to electrical conduction. The BCS theory (named for Bardeen, Leon Cooper, and John R. Schrieffer) became the basis for research that continues today, promising new technologies with enormous and global economic impact. Highly efficient superconducting motors, generators, and other machines hold the potential, in the twenty-first century, of revolutionary advances in electronics.

John Bardeen was born on May 23, 1908, in Madison, Wisconsin. His father, Charles Russell Bardeen, was a professor of anatomy who became dean of the University of Wisconsin Medical School. His mother, Althea Harmer Bardeen, was a teacher and an artist who died when John was an adolescent. Encouraged academically by his parents, Bardeen excelled in school, taking algebra at age ten, and he was skipped ahead in grade several times. He attended the University of Wisconsin beginning in 1923, at age fifteen, where he became interested in mathematical physics under the influence of the visiting PAUL DIRAC [20]. However, he received his bachelor's degree in engineering in 1928 and his master's degree in 1929.

For several years during the Great Depression, Bardeen worked as a geophysicist with the Gulf Research and Development Corporation in Pittsburgh, specializing in problems of electromagnetic prospecting for petroleum deposits. In the mid-1930s he was able to follow his inclination to study pure science and attended the Institute for Advanced Study at Princeton University. He received his doctorate in mathematical physics in 1936. His adviser at the Institute was Eugene Wigner, one of the great Hungarian physicists, known for his work in solid-state physics. Bardeen went on to do postdoctoral research at Harvard University, taught at the University of Minnesota, and during World War II worked with the U.S. Naval Ordnance Laboratory, which took advantage of his earlier work as a geophysicist to develop countermeasures against torpedoes.

After World War II, U.S. industrial hegemony created the future that belonged to electronics in which innovation and new product development were to play determining roles. This was the context for the development of solid-state physics, the study of the way certain metalloid materials, such as silicon and germanium, conduct electricity. Scientists at Bell Laboratories were hoping to use these "semiconductors" to supplant electron tube technology. Electron or vacuum tubes are circuits in which the electricity can be easily and instantaneously controlled. They were widely used in radio and the emergent computer technologies. But they are big and bulky and have strict limits of practicability. By contrast, semiconductors are many times smaller, more reliable, and cheaper; silicon, for example, is the earth's second most abundant element.

Although he had considered turning to nuclear physics, Bardeen was recruited in 1945 to solid-state research by Bell. He became, with W. H. Brattain, part of a famous team led by William Shockley. Using crystals of germanium, Bardeen and Brattain in 1948 invented a "point-contact" device which could amplify an audio signal. They showed how it was possible to obtain the same fine control of an electrical current through semiconductors as with vacuum tubes. Resistance could be carefully controlled through "doping" the semiconductor, and a whole range of effects could be demonstrated, including sensitivity to light. These early transistors—as they were named— were fragile, however, and not practical until Shockley developed a more stable version in 1952. The subsequent development of integrated circuits and silicon chips, with all their massive consequences for technology, was based upon this work. It is not surprising that, in 1956, Bardeen shared the Nobel Prize with Shockley and Brattain.

One of the great twentieth-century puzzles in physics had been set in 1911, when the Dutch physicist HEIKE KAMERLINGH ONNES [61] found that at a very low temperature mercury suddenly loses resistance to an electrical current. This was eventually shown to be true of many metals and metallic compounds, although nothing in the laws of physics explained why. Kamerlingh Onnes correctly surmised that the answer would be found through an application of quantum theory. Forty years passed without progress, however. "John passionately aspired to lead the effort to decipher the mystery of superconductivity," wrote Bardeen's colleague, Conyers Herring. To that end Bardeen took a position as professor of physics and engineering at the University of Illinois in 1951. He also may have been motivated to leave Bell Labs because of conflicts with Shockley, who was considered exceptionally difficult to work with.

The BCS theory evolved beginning about 1950, when Bardeen learned that isotopes, or different forms, of certain elements become superconducting at different temperatures. This suggested to Bardeen a unique interaction between electrons and the vibrations in the atomic lattice through which they move. After publishing an early, incomplete version of a theory, Bardeen continued to work on it with Leon N. Cooper, a New York scientist—whom Bardeen called "my quantum mechanic from the East"—and a graduate student, John R. Schrieffer. In 1957 they announced a general theory to explain superconductivity.

An elegant theoretical edifice, which NIELS BOHR [3] considered beautiful in its simplicity, the BCS theory shows how superconductivity is a consequence of the relationship between electrons and "phonons," which are quantums of vibrational energy. Phonons help disrupt the movement of electrons and thereby cause resistance to electrical conduction through a metal. At low temperatures, however, these vibrations are reduced. This affects the relationship between electrons: They form "pairs" in which two electrons of opposite spin and momentum are united. (The mathematical analysis of these "Cooper pairs" was worked out by Schrieffer.) When a current is applied, the paired electrons will move through the supercold solid, all with the same momentum and without resistance.

The BCS theory, as it came to be called, was quickly accepted and brought Bardeen, Cooper, and Schrieffer the Nobel Prize for physics in 1972. (Bardeen thus became the first scientist ever to receive two Nobel awards in the same field.) Superconductivity did not find immediate applicability because of the low temperatures required for it to take place. But finding materials which superconducted at higher temperatures had become a practical goal. In 1986 came the announcement of a ceramic material that became superconductive at 35°K—still cold but getting warmer. Within a short time other substances had been found which superconduct at about 100°K. This enabled technologists to develop small devices known as SQUIDS (*S*uperconducting *Q*uantum *I*nterference *D*evices) for applications in medicine, geology, and other fields. The prospect of a usable material at near-room temperature remains a plausible goal. It could lead to profound changes in everyday life.

John Bardeen taught at the Center for Advanced Study at the University of Illinois from 1959 until his retirement in 1975. He was quiet and amiable, occasionally lighthearted though capable of considerable anger. He was married to Jane Maxwell, with whom he had two daughters and a son, William, who became an elementary particle theorist. John Bardeen died of heart failure on January 30, 1991.

51

John von Neumann
and the Modern Computer

1903–1957

One of the major architects of the modern computer, John von Neumann is also remembered for his development of game theory, an aspect of statistics that has been adopted in economics and military strategy and other fields. Von Neumann was widely considered a genius. Eugene Wigner called his mind "a true miracle" and HANS BETHE [58] wondered whether his brain "did not indicate a species superior to that of man." Following World War II, his role as consultant to the U.S. military establishment made him a major figure in the cold war arms race. Von Neumann, according to physicist Herbert York, had a "credibility with military officers, engineers, industrialists and scientists that

240

nobody could match." His exceptional influence in the corridors of power has made von Neumann a controversial figure in recent years and a source for reflecting on the aims and achievements of science in the contemporary world.

Perhaps the most significant of several great scientists to come out of Hungary in the early twentieth century, John von Neumann was born Margittai Neumann János on December 28, 1903, in Budapest. His mother, Margaret, was from the prosperous Jewish middle class, and his father, Max, was a banker who carefully nurtured his son's intellect, turning family dinners into virtual classrooms leavened with wit. A genuine child prodigy, Neumann could divide eight-digit numbers in his head by age six and learned calculus by the time he was eight. He also developed an interest in history, and he could recite minutiae from the trial of Joan of Arc and the battles of the American Civil War. Although mathematics became his major interest as a child, his father succeeded in convincing him that he ought to study chemistry, which he did, at the University of Berlin, from 1921 to 1923, and at Zurich from 1923 to 1925. In 1925 he received a degree in chemical engineering from Zurich, and the following year took a Ph.D. in mathematics from Budapest.

In the mid-1920s Neumann made an effort to advance mathematical logic. An attempt to derive a fully self-consistent mathematical system by Bertrand Russell and Alfred North Whitehead in *Principia Mathematica* had entailed much discussion of its underlying foundations. Working with David Hilbert, who had developed a non-Euclidean geometry some years earlier, von Neumann made a variety of contributions toward discovering self-consistent mathematics. In 1931, however, Kurt Gödel's powerful proof that any consistent system using numbers will generate formulas that cannot be proved without recourse to axioms from without put an end to such efforts. More successful was von Neumann's analysis of quantum theory; his *Mathematical Foundation of Quantum Mechanics* became a principal textbook in the field for many years.

Von Neumann's interest in game theory also dates from the late 1920s, when he established a mathematical analysis of various games of chance together with strategic rules for playing them. In his "Theory of Parlor Games," published in 1928, von Neumann distinguished "strictly determined" games, such as chess, in which an opponent's potential strategy has no effect on finding the best move, from others in which strategies are interrelated, such as poker or matching pennies. For the latter, von Neumann showed, there is an optimum "mixed strategy" in which a player changes strategy at random. In the early 1940s von Neumann collaborated with an economist, Oskar Morgenstern, to apply "minimax theory" to problems such as exchange, monopoly, and free trade; and they published *The Theory of Games and Economic Behavior* in 1944. The concept of the *non-zero-sum game*, in which players may find it useful to form coalitions, belongs to von Neumann. Over time, game theory has been adapted, with varying degrees of success, to economics and evolutionary biology, the social sciences, epidemiology, military strategy, business organization, philosophy, and politics. In general, it was characteristic of von Neumann to translate terms of ordinary language into nuanced mathematical analysis. When he was asked how American congressional seats might be fairly apportioned, he replied that there were no less than five mathematical measures of what was "fair."

In 1930 von Neumann was invited to teach at Princeton University, where he was named a professor the following year. He joined the university's Institute for Advanced Study in 1933, to which he remained attached for the rest of his career. He became a full-fledged émigré with the rise of Nazism in Europe. In 1937, with war approaching, he was named consultant to the U.S. Army's Ballistics Research Laboratory. Von Neumann expanded his work for the military with the onset of war, and joined the atomic bomb project as a consultant at Los Alamos in 1943. He and EDWARD TELLER [88] recommended that implosion be used to set off the atomic bomb, and worked on calculations to clarify how to make such a device. For maximum impact, von Neumann also advocated dropping the bomb on Kyoto, a city having great historic and religious significance that had been preserved untouched during the war. But this choice of target was rejected by the secretary of war, Henry Stimson.

John von Neumann's contribution to the development of the computer was perhaps his most notable and far-reaching accomplishment. In his wartime work, von Neumann began investigating the prospects of developing an electronic machine to perform the work of mechanical calculators. He found the relatively simple punch-card computers in use at the time unimpressive, but his interest—he called it his "obscene interest"—was aroused and led to a meeting, in 1944, with John William Mauchly and J. Presper Eckert. They had developed an "Electrical Numerical Integrator and Calculator," a huge and unwieldy machine which occupied 1,800 square feet of floor space, used punch cards for input and output, and had a complex and fairly awkward means of programming instructions for calculations. It was primitive by later standards but crunched numbers a thousand times faster than earlier computers. According to Norman Macrae, when von Neumann saw the primitive ENIAC, "The visionary part of his mind soared to imitating the brain with the 17,000 radio tubes."

In the complex and sometimes bitter history that followed, which included patent rights battles, von Neumann is generally credited with the concept of the stored-program device and, thus, the programmed computer we use today. Joel Shurkin states in *Engines of the Mind*: "von Neumann's genius clarified and described the paths better than anyone else.... While others were using crude digital instructions for their machines, von Neumann and his team were developing instructions that would last, with modification, through most of the computer age." He recognized in computers the potential for making statistical predictions based on calculations that were fundamentally too complex for humans, and he also was possessed of a variety of creative notions concerning their potential applications.

Gaining interest and funding from the military, and working at the Institute for Advanced Study (IAS) after the war ended, von Neumann set out to create a digital computer unlike anything seen before. The IAS machine was a highly influential model whose "von Neumann" architecture was borrowed by other researchers while it was still in the development stage. By 1952, von Neumann's computer was operating, as were a number of important machines based on his design, including the MANNIAC at Los Alamos, the JOHNNIAC at Argonne National Laboratory, and the IBM 701, which would eventually lead that company to dominate the market for some years. Von Neumann's first project for the computer was meteorological forecasting, which had important implications for military strategy and represented a particular use of the nonlinear mathematics at which computers excel.

The last phase of von Neumann's career was spent largely as a consultant to the government and the military. He joined the advisory committee of the Atomic Energy Commission following the resignation of J. ROBERT OPPENHEIMER [87], accepted a consultancy at Edward Teller's Lawrence Livermore Laboratory, and took an advisory role with the air force. A major scientific figure in cold war politics, he viewed the Soviet Union's atomic bomb as a threat to peace and the United States' hydrogen bomb as the best way to maintain it. He was a partisan of the feisty president Harry Truman and, in 1952, voted for Dwight D. Eisenhower, both of whom regarded him as an ally in science. In 1954 he headed what became known as the "von Neumann committee" of the U.S. Air Force's Scientific Advisory Board, which played a major role in shaping arms policy. He remained a valued member of this board even after he fell ill two years later.

In recognizing von Neumann's great contribution to the architecture of computers, it is customary to praise his foresight and his genius in producing the great technological advances of the computer age. But such an evaluation is too simplistic. "The view of von Neumann as a paragon of science and as a technologist par excellence," writes Steve Heims, "raises fundamental issues concerning the scientific community, technology, and our advancing but simultaneously deteriorating civilization." Not only von Neumann's genius but his character determined his influence. His thought was fruitful, but as historian of technology David F. Noble has pointed out, von Neumann's "mathematical axiomatic approach reflected his affinity for military authority and power." Indeed, von Neumann had overweening respect for the military and all its trappings, and as a representative of science his aims were scarcely "value neutral." Moreover, his computer designs were carried from the military into industry, where they led to particular forms of automation that show a striking lack of concern for the needs of human beings. It is von Neumann's vision of an electronic world, and not Norbert Wiener's notion of the "human use of human beings," that has been largely adopted by industry as it has incorporated the computer into the workplace and into the everyday lives of millions of people. Von Neumann's legacy is very great, but also complex and controversial.

John von Neumann was highly personable in superficial relationships, and the psychoanalytic powerbroker Lawrence Kubie found him "very friendly and accessible." He enjoyed living in relative luxury, was imperious with servants, treasured dirty limericks, and was reckless behind the wheel, frequently destroying the cars he drove. According to physicist Eugene Wigner, one of von Neumann's oldest friends, he enjoyed the pleasure of sexual relationships but did not like emotional attachments and "mostly saw women in terms of their bodies." He was married to Klari Dan, who drowned herself several years after von Neumann's death. Their daughter, Marina, became a well-known economist.

In 1956 von Neumann was diagnosed with pancreatic cancer. He suffered considerably before his death. Of Jewish origin, von Neumann's family had converted in the 1930s to Christianity to avoid anti-Semitism. Although von Neumann himself was an agnostic most of his life, he converted to Catholicism on his deathbed. There he was also visited frequently by friends and military personnel, and toward the end a soldier was posted at his bedside in case he became delirious and gave away classified information. He did become delirious, but whether he revealed atomic secrets is not known, because the language he spoke was Hungarian. He died on February 8, 1957.

52

Richard Feynman
and Quantum Electrodynamics

1918–1988

Soon after it was shown that quantum mechanics could predict the properties of atoms, mathematical tools were created to understand all the various phenomena of electromagnetism. The result, quantum electrodynamics, originated about 1930 with the work of PAUL DIRAC [20], WERNER HEISENBERG [15], and others. However, for nearly two decades its results were often imprecise and so only approximately satisfactory. The reformulation of QED, which lent it tremendous precision, is associated with several important figures, the most prominent being Richard Feynman.

This self-described "one-sided guy" shared with Ludwig

Wittgenstein, the philosopher, the intriguing ability to compensate for a limited formal knowledge of contemporary developments in his field with profound intuition and a unique capacity to work through problems on his own. As remarkable a mathematical physicist as Dirac, with whom he is sometimes compared, Feynman developed a reputation "that transcended any raw sum of his actual contributions," writes his biographer James Gleick. He became a unique, iconoclastic presence in physics and eventually gained a wide lay audience through his humorous, autobiographical *Surely You're Joking, Mr. Feynman.*

Richard Phillips Feynman was born in New York City on May 11, 1918, to Lucille Phillips Feynman and Melville Arthur Feynman. A salesman by profession, Melville Feynman transmitted to his son a considerable curiosity about nature. Growing up in Far Rockaway, Feynman became adept at repairing radios, fixing typewriters, and solving thought puzzles of all sorts. "Every puzzle that was known to man must have come to me," he wrote later. "Every damn, crazy conundrum that people had invented, I knew." Exceptional in mathematics and science, Feynman resented academic pressure to achieve in other areas of learning; he did not become as widely read or highly cultured as many physicists.*

At the Massachusetts Institute of Technology, which he entered in 1935, Feynman's preternatural talents as a mathematician became apparent. He built up a considerable stock of procedures for solving a wide variety of problems in theoretical physics, and his senior thesis, entitled "Forces and Stresses in Molecules," was an impressive harbinger. After graduating from MIT in 1939, Feynman went on to Princeton, overcoming the institutional prejudices against Jews common at that time. He worked with John Wheeler, a leader in the development of nuclear physics, who quickly recognized Feynman's abilities. He received his Ph.D. in 1942 for a dissertation on "The Principle of Least Action in Quantum Mechanics." By his early twenties Feynman was already regarded as one of the leading American theoretical physicists.

Feynman was recruited to work on the atomic bomb and joined the Manhattan Project while he was still at Princeton. In

---

*His IQ was a modest 125, which, given his later accomplishments, makes him a one-man testament to a strong cultural component in measuring intelligence.

1943 he moved to Los Alamos, New Mexico, where the bomb was being constructed. He impressed HANS BETHE [58]—Feynman "combined brilliance with greatness"—who assigned him to a post as group leader. Feynman performed impressively at Los Alamos, bringing a variety of unique techniques to bear on complex calculations concerning the diffusion of neutrons through a critical mass. He was assigned to estimate how much radioactive material could be stored in one place without danger and gave lectures on theoretical aspects of the developing bomb. He was present at the test of the first nuclear device, in July 1945. The great explosion produced in him "a kind of elation, because during all this time we'd been working very hard to make this thing go, and we weren't sure exactly how it went. I've always had some distrust of theoretical calculations, although that's my business, and I'm never really sure that nature does what you calculate she ought to do. Here she was, doing what we'd calculated."

At Cornell University from 1945, where he joined Bethe as an assistant professor, Feynman turned his attention to quantum electrodynamics; his revision of QED was one of the pivotal events in postwar physics. Although the existing theory was not wrong, as Feynman once explained, "When you went to calculate answers, you ran into complicated equations that were very hard to solve. You could get a good first-order approximation, but when you tried to refine it with corrections, these infinite quantities started to crop up." Although it was clear that an electron, for example, acted in a predictable way in an electromagnetic field, its explanation in quantum mechanical terms involved a basically infinite number of emissions and absorptions of photons—known as "virtual" particles because they cannot be perceived by the senses. Although numerous efforts had been made by such figures as Wolfgang Pauli and Werner Heisenberg to refine the calculations, they continued to give impossible results even though the theory on which they were based remained unassailable.

Feynman's unique approach employed a series of representations (later called Feynman diagrams) which make it possible to keep track of electrons and photons as well as the absorption or emission of photons by electrons. These are the basic actions which quantum electrodynamics describes. The diagrams concretize the abstract calculations so that the numbers can be "renormalized" and unwanted infinities can be eliminated. As a consequence of this "path integral" approach, quantum electrodynamics was thoroughly revitalized and today enables calculations to reach a remarkable accuracy of 10^9. In 1965 Feynman was awarded the Nobel Prize in physics, which he shared with Julian Schwinger and Sin-Ituro Tomonaga, who had also reformulated QED about the same time. Feynman's method was the simplest and most intuitive; the diagrams became widely used to solve problems involving elementary particles.

In 1951 Feynman moved to California Institute of Technology, where he became one of the most productive theoretical physicists in the world. Among his accomplishments was an atomic account of the strange properties of liquid helium, which at very low temperatures defies gravity. In explaining "superfluidity" Feynman came close to understanding the related phenomena of superconductivity, which was clarified in 1957 by JOHN BARDEEN [50], Leon Cooper, and Robert Schrieffer. Feynman also furthered the theory of beta decay—the behavior of the "weak force" exemplified by the gradual disintegration of radioactive elements.

Feynman's discovery that the law of conservation of parity was breached in the weak interaction—hinted at by experiments during the 1950s—led him to a moment that he described as "the first time, and the only time, in my career, that I knew a law of nature that nobody else knew." MURRAY GELL-MANN [45], Feynman's friend and colleague at Caltech, was angered by this conceit, but together he and Feynman went on to develop a general theory of the weak interaction, first published in 1958 as "Theory of the Fermi Interaction." Feynman also contributed to the development of Gell-Mann's theory of quantum chromodynamics (QCD), which provides an account of the internal structure of subatomic particles.

Feynman was a colorful teacher who sometimes lectured while playing bongo drums; his style was vivid and humorous, and he seldom lost sight of physics' broader themes. In 1963 he taught an introductory physics course at Caltech, later published as *The Feynman Lectures on Physics;* although intended as college-level texts, their originality was such that they became standard works of basic physics. A series of six talks for a lay audience, first published in 1965 as *The Character of Physical Law*, gives the flavor of Feynman's lecture style and is a basic introduction to gravitation, the relationship between science and mathematics, and the problems of conservation of energy, the laws of symmetry, and the concept of entropy. During the 1980s Feynman also gave lectures to laid-back but self-actualizing audiences at the Esalen Institute in Big Sur, California. He became known to a wider public through an autobiographical memoir that became a best-seller: *Surely You're Joking, Mr. Feynman*, in 1985.

In 1986 Feynman joined the Rogers Commission, a government panel appointed to investigate the explosion during launch of the U.S. space shuttle *Challenger*. Seven crew members had been killed. Feynman made national headlines when he recognized that the principal cause of the crash lay with rubber seals which became stiff in cold weather. In a dramatic moment at the hearings, he dropped a piece of the material into a glass of ice water, demonstrating how at a cold temperature it momentarily lost its resiliency. In a separate appendix to the final report, Feynman was strongly critical of the bureaucratic pressure which had operated on NASA scientists and engineers in the *Challenger* disaster. Feynman's account of his work on the Rogers Commission is detailed in his *"What Do You Care What Other People Think?"* published in 1988.

Feynman, like many twentieth-century physicists, was an atheist, as his father had been. He was upset when a rabbi insisted on reading kaddish at his father's funeral; later in life, some of his remarks on religion were censored by a television station in California. "It doesn't seem to me that this fantastically marvelous universe," said Feynman, "this tremendous range of time and space and different kinds of animals, and all the different planets, and all these atoms with all their motions, and so on, all this complicated thing can merely be a stage so that God can watch human beings struggle for good and evil—which is the view that religion has. The stage is too big for the drama."

Feynman married three times. His first wife, Arlene Greenbaum, died of tuberculosis in 1945. After a brief second union, Feynman married Gweneth Howarth in 1960, and they had two children. In 1978 Feynman was first diagnosed with a rare type of cancerous tumor, which was removed by surgery. Another form of cancer, macroglobulinemia, which affects the lymphocytes, appeared in 1986, and doctors discovered an abdominal tumor not long after. Feynman would not consider the possibility that his neoplasms were related in any way to exposure to radiation while working on the atomic bomb. Richard Feynman died on February 15, 1988.

In Feynman's last years he sought to visit Tannu Tuva, a land his father had told him about as a child. During the 1980s, with his friend Ralph Leighton, Feynman conducted a lengthy, amusing correspondence in an effort to gain permission to visit the country, which lies in Russia (then the Soviet Union), near Mongolia. Two weeks before his death, he received permission to travel there. Ralph Leighton made the visit to Tannu Tuva for him in July. And that is why a memorial plaque to Richard Feynman can be found at the Center of Asia monument in Kyzyl.

53

Alfred Wegener
and Continental Drift

1880–1930

As geology evolved into a science, one of its untested assumptions was that the continents upon the earth were stable. Geologists offered chemical explanations of common features such as mountain ranges and rock strata, and one popular theory held that they were results of the earth's contraction from an initially molten state. Land bridges such as Beringia, which was supposed to have connected North America and Asia, were thought to explain similarities in the fossil record. In the early twentieth century, however, Alfred Lothar Wegener developed a theory of "continental drift," suggesting that the earth's land masses had been united in the distant past. Largely rejected at first, derided, and sometimes described as a "fairy tale" and the "dream of a great poet," new evidence accumulating by the 1960s brought the theory back to robust life. Plate tectonics, successor to Wegener's conjectures, is today the principal theory behind the genesis, structure, and dynamics of Earth's continents.

Alfred Lothar Wegener was born on November 1, 1880, in Berlin, the son of a pastor, Richard Wegener, and Anna Schwarz Wegener. He attended the University of Berlin, where he studied mathematics and natural science, with his greatest interest in astronomy. He passed his doctoral examination magna cum laude in 1904, and for his dissertation he recalculated the old Alfonsine Tables of Ptolemaic astronomy.

Wegener's career from the beginning mingled academic interests with exploration and adventure. Rather than make a career of astronomy, he began to work for the Aeronautic Observatory in Lindenberg, where he participated in atmospheric research with his brother, Kurt, using balloons and weather kites. The Wegener brothers' fifty-two hour journey in a balloon in 1906 broke the world's record. That same year Wegener undertook his first of four expeditions to Greenland. Returning to Germany, he qualified in 1909 as a professor at Marburg University, where he taught meteorology and astronomy until 1919. Following World War I he taught at the University of Hamburg, headed the German Marine Observatory, and made several more expeditions to Greenland. Meteorology became the focus of much of Wegener's scientific work, and he became a noted authority, writing a textbook, *Thermodynamics of the Atmosphere*, when he was just thirty years old.

Although the genesis of Wegener's thinking is not entirely clear, he planned to examine the idea of continental drift as early as 1910, when he wrote his fiancée: "Doesn't the east coast of South America fit exactly against the west coast of Africa, as if they had once been joined?" The general congruence of continents had been noted by Francis Bacon as early as the seventeenth century, and other scientists had questioned the stability of the continents. But as geology had developed in the early nineteenth century, the assumption of gradualism became successful and dominant. Wegener was the first to frame an alternative hypothesis as a serious theory and to support it with geological evidence.

Announcing the theory of continental drift in a lecture in

1912, he subsequently wrote a book, *The Origin of Continents and Oceans*, first published in 1915. Some two hundred million years ago, Wegener proposed, the earth contained a single continent, or protocontinent, which he called Pangaea, from the Greek for "the whole land." During the last of the age of reptiles, the Cretaceous period, about one hundred million years ago, this mass split up. America separated from Eurasia and Africa, leaving the Atlantic Ocean between; and India drifted off from Africa before colliding with Asia.

Although these ideas sound speculative, they were based on geological evidence as well as on the fossil record. Wegener pointed not only to the jigsawlike fit of the continents but also to similarities between plant and animal fossils found in South America and Africa. Mountain ranges were plausibly created during movement, which would explain why they frequently appear near the edge of continents. Deposits of coal and other minerals in both Europe and North America were also suggestive. Furthermore, Wegener argued that the older assumption of a "land bridge" between continents was not supported by evidence. Wegener was aware that the theory as he advanced it would need to be modified and wrote that "The Newton of the drift theory has not yet appeared."

Continental drift became a controversial theory and was much disputed in the years after World War I. The debate raged until 1928, when at a colloquium of geologists, a majority declared themselves against the theory. This remained the dominant viewpoint until after World War II. In classrooms, the theory was often held up to ridicule, and Ursula Marvin has described how one Harvard professor would jocularly tell students that "two halves of the same pelecypod" had been found—one in Newfoundland, the other in Ireland. GEORGE GAYLORD SIMPSON [78] was a particularly famous and vocal opponent of Wegener.

It should be added that Wegener never lacked eminent supporters, including Arthur Holmes, a British authority. The South African geologist Alexander du Toit believed that continental drift occasioned so much resistance because geology, historically, was pervasively conservative. When one considers that although the geologist CHARLES LYELL [28] was a crucial inspiration to his friend CHARLES DARWIN [4], yet Lyell himself could not embrace the theory of the descent of man, this seems plausible. In addition, a theory which proposed the continents were broken fragments of a former whole, coming on the heels of the Great War, suggests more than irony; the historical climate may have favored forever separate continents.

The reevaluation of continental drift came about after World War II. Exploration of the ocean floor by sonar led to the discovery of ridges in midocean. It gradually became clear that huge portions of the earth's crust could move as units. About the same time there arose the field of paleomagnetism—the study of magnetism in rocks dating from their molten state—and here evidence suggested that the continents had indeed been joined together. Based on new explorations, the modern theory of "sea floor spreading," together with the discovery of "subduction zones," led to the notion of plates of crust and mantle moving relative to each other across the earth. Plate tectonics recognizes six major plates at present as well as some smaller ones. The theory of stabilism has been interred.

Sometimes described as a lesser NICOLAUS COPERNICUS [10], Wegener is all the more admired for his recognition of the complexity of the problem and for his "comprehensive vision." Writes Mott T. Greene: "Wegener, working in astronomy, geology, paleontology, meteorology, oceanography, and geophysics, was one of the first modern *earth* scientists, and saw not only the fundamental problem to be solved but the range of the evidence which must be amassed for its solution."

Wegener did not live to see the vindication of his theory. In 1930 he made a third expedition to Greenland to collect geophysical and climatological data. He realized as early as May that the mission he envisioned was in trouble, and in September he made a perilous journey from West Station to bring supplies to the outpost at "Mid-Ice." On November 1, his birthday, Wegener began the return trip, by dogsled, but neither he nor his companion was seen alive again. His body was not found until May of the following year, zipped into his sleeping bag, a peaceful expression on his face. Wegener had died not from the cold, in all probability, but from a heart attack due to exertion. He was buried where he was found, and an iron cross some eighteen feet high was erected to mark his grave. It has long since been covered by ice and snow.

54

Stephen Hawking
and Quantum Cosmology

1942–

At the forefront of efforts to unite cosmology with the quantum theory of elementary matter is Stephen Hawking. A theoretical physicist by training—he has no interest in observational astronomy—Hawking's work remains to be verified, but he has steered many of the important recent discussions about the origin and nature of the universe. In the 1960s Hawking developed a proof that the universe must have had a beginning, and he attempted to describe the nature of hypothetical collapsed stars known as "black holes" deep in space. Most significantly, perhaps, Hawking helped ignite renewed interest in the big bang theory of the universe and recently elaborated a "no boundary

boundary" concept of its origin. Like ALBERT EINSTEIN [2], Stephen Hawking has been often lauded in the popular press, and a wide public has been taught to regard him with awe. His great celebrity is due in part to an affliction. Since his early twenties, Hawking has suffered from a physically disabling, degenerative disease, amyotrophic lateral sclerosis.

Stephen William Hawking was born on January 8, 1942, in Oxford, England, the son of Frank Hawking, a physician and research biologist who specialized in tropical diseases, and Isobel Hawking. Both Hawking's parents were from middle-class families, and both had attended Oxford. After World War II, Frank Hawking was named head of the Division of Parasitology at the National Institute of Medical Research. From the age of thirteen, Stephen attended St. Alban's School, where he was a good but not outstanding student, ranked about the middle of his class, and not prone to work hard. But while a teenager, Hawking became convinced he wanted to read in mathematics or physics. "I knew I wanted to research in physics," he wrote later, "because it was the most fundamental science." In 1959, at age seventeen, he received a scholarship to Oxford, where he studied for two years before going on to Cambridge. Although ready to specialize in astronomy, Hawking was "not impressed" with its observational side, and he undertook a minimum of such work as an undergraduate.

By early 1963 Hawking had been diagnosed with amyotrophic lateral sclerosis (ALS), which involves an irreversible deterioration of the spinal cord, medulla, and cortex, resulting in atrophy of the body. The sole consolation of the disease is that it is painless and does not affect intelligence. Hawking was initially devastated by the diagnosis, but once his physical deterioration stabilized and it not longer appeared that an early death was imminent, he overcame his depression. He determined to continue his studies, even though he was soon confined to a wheelchair and was losing control over his speech. In 1966, after receiving his doctorate with a thesis on "Properties of the Expanding Universe," he remained on the faculty of Gonville and Caius College, a member of the department of applied mathematics and the Institute of Theoretical Astronomy.

From the beginning of his career, Hawking contended with issues basic to cosmology. During the mid-1960s he was influenced by Roger Penrose, the celebrated mathematician and theoretical physicist who was examining the concept of "singularities." Predicted by Einstein's general theory of relativity, the singularity evokes the notion of an expanding universe originally concentrated as a single point—where, in fact, the laws of physics break down. Although Einstein had known that singularities were consequences of relativity, he assumed them to be purely theoretical entities. However, collaborating with Penrose in developing methods to model singularities, Hawking made his first important theoretical discovery by showing their implications for the concept of time. "The big question was, Was there a beginning or not?" Hawking later wrote. "Roger Penrose and I discovered that, if general relativity is correct, there did have to be a beginning." Hawking's early arguments to this effect appeared in his doctoral thesis and were later refined with Penrose. The singularity theorem of Hawking and Penrose was published in 1970.

In general, theoretical probings of the universe generated considerable interest within observational astronomy, which, working with ever more powerful instruments, was accumulating a great deal of inexplicable data. Thus, if singularities existed, a logical place to find them would be in the vortex of burned-out and collapsed stars—"black holes" was the term suggested by John Wheeler in 1967. Black holes might help explain pointlike "quasars," which had been discovered in 1961, and the detection of "pulsars" several years later. (So bewildering were pulsars that at first they were given the initials LGM—for "Little Green Men.") And in 1970 satellite-based telescopes detected X-ray sources in the heavens, including such unusual centers of gravitational attraction as *Cygnus X-1*. While it could not be proved to anybody's satisfaction that this was a black hole, the evidence of unusual activity surrounding it was captivating.

Hawking's work on black holes intensified in the mid-1970s. Recognizing that the surface of a black hole can never decrease led him to propose a relationship with entropy, which describes the disorder of a system, a concept drawn from thermodynamics. Although Hawking initially intended this only as an analogy, the idea was further developed by Jacob Bekenstein, who suggested that the relationship might be real and measurable. Hawking first disagreed, but later changed his mind, and in 1974 described black holes as having temperature and emitting radiation. This idea, which he described mathematically, became known (to Bekenstein's dismay) as Hawking radiation, a discovery, wrote John Gribbin, which "is regarded as one of the great achievements not just of Hawking's career but of the past fifty years of physics." Initially so startling that it was firmly rejected, Hawking's use of quantm theory and thermodynamic relationships to characterize gravitational sinks such as black holes was nevertheless intriguing and, to some extent, convincing. "With all these fascinating theoretical developments," writes Heinz Pagels, "black holes moved from 'mathematical curiosities' to the center of speculative astronomy."

In 1979 Hawking was named Lucasian Professor of Mathematics at Cambridge University. In his inaugural lecture, entitled, "Is the End in Sight for Theoretical Physics?" he suggested that a unified theory might be achieved before the end of the century, and he thought that the life of theoretical physics might be limited by exponential advances in computer technology. Although these predictions will probably not be fulfilled, it was at this point in his career that Hawking was dubbed "the new Einstein" and accorded tremendous adulation and renown. He won numerous awards, was profiled on the BBC, and eventually wrote *A Brief History of Time*, which became a bestselling book that was turned into a documentary film starring Hawking himself.

During the mid-1980s Hawking became interested in applying quantum theory to the initial conditions of the universe, prior to the big bang. With James Hartle he wrote an important paper, "The Wave Function of the Universe," which has given impetus to what has come to be known as quantum cosmology. Drawing on concepts from quantum mechanics, Hawking and Hartle developed the "no boundary boundary proposal" to describe the initial condition of the universe.* Quantum laws which apply to elementary matter, and which may apply to the universe as a whole, might also be said to have operated at the beginning of the universe. This pure quantum state remains to be fully described, but Hawking's probabilistic, no boundary theory is currently one of several under scrutiny in contemporary theoretical physics and cosmology.

Stephen Hawking married Jane Wilde several years after the onset of ALS, and they had three children. Although for years Jane was portrayed in the press as his eternal helpmeet, the two grew estranged, and in 1985 Hawking began living with Elaine

---

*With this theory Hawking gave up his earlier notion of a "singularity." And he calls the idea that the contraction of the universe would be symmetrical with its expansion his greatest blunder.

Mason, one of his nurses. A principal cause of the Hawkings' separation was religion. Hawking had grown increasingly atheistic over the years, while his wife retained strong religious beliefs. In his *A Brief History of Time*, Hawking attempted to comprehend "the mind of God." "And this makes all the more unexpected the conclusion so far..." writes Carl Sagan, for Hawking has discovered "a universe with no edge in space, no beginning or end in time, and nothing for a Creator to do."

55

Anton van Leeuwenhoek
and the Simple Microscope
1632–1723

Traditionally, Leeuwenhoek is regarded as one of the great technical facilitators in science. Although he did not invent the microscope, he was the first to use it with great observational and descriptive skills. Of undistinguished background and little education—his communications to the British Royal Society had to be translated from his vernacular Dutch—his achievements in retrospect are both unique and varied. Generally considered a founder of microbiology, he also made contributions to other sciences, such as embryology, crystallography, and chemistry; and some of his observations were so precise that they could be newly interpreted two centuries later. "It would be hard to find any serious challenger to Leeuwenhoek," writes Brian J. Ford, "in terms of the variety and depth of his interests." Using a simple microscope, he achieved spectacular results, and the complexity of the natural world, viewed through his eyes, took on new dimensions.

Anton van Leeuwenhoek was born in Delft, in the United Netherlands, on October 24, 1632, the son of Philips Antonyszoon van Leeuwenhoek and his wife, Margaretha Bel van den Berch. His father was a basketmaker who died when Leeuwenhoek was about six years old, and his mother subsequently remarried a painter, Jacob Molijn. Receiving a basic education, Leeuwenhoek at age sixteen began an apprenticeship to a linen-draper and, at its completion, set up business for himself in his native town. In addition to his commercial activities, while still in his twenties he received a sinecure as caretaker for the Sheriff of Delft, and in later years became the town's inspector of weights and measures. He knew the great painter Jan Vermeer and was named executor of Vermeer's estate. Leeuwenhoek was not highly educated, but his scientific career begins at age forty and spans fifty years.

The microscope was probably invented somewhat earlier than the telescope, perhaps as early as 1590. Unlike the telescope, it did not immediately yield important information. But in 1660, MARCELLO MALPIGHI [39] discovered capillaries in the lungs of a frog, consolidating the achievement of WILLIAM HARVEY [38] in discovering the circulation of the blood. And in 1665 Robert Hooke published his *Micrographia*. Using a compound microscope of his own design, Hooke provided detailed presentations of the structures of insects and plants and, noting the tiny compartments in a sliver of cork, coined the word *cell*. These discoveries explain the warm reception accorded Leeuwenhoek, whose fame rested upon the quality and extent of his observations, his technical excellence, and his intuitive grasp of scientific method.

In 1673 Leeuwenhoek sent the first of many letters to the Royal Society in England, in which he offered descriptions of a mold, a bee's sting, and a louse. The letter was soon published in the *Philosophical Transactions* and was followed by many more— 165 in all—over the next half century. Writing in his native language, Leeuwenhoek possessed a straightforward yet comprehensive style. He wrote of a great diversity of specimens. In

1676, he described protozoa found in rainwater, describing the "little animalcules" as "the most wretched creatures that I have ever seen; for when…they did but hit on any particles or little filaments (of which there are many in water, especially if it hath stood for some days), they stuck intangled in them; and then pulled their body out into an oval, and did struggle, by strongly stretching themselves, to get their tail loose; whereby their whole body then sprang back toward the pellet of the tail, and their tails then coiled up serpentwise, after the fashion of a copper or iron wire that, having been wound close about a round stick, and then taken off, kept all its windings."

Leeuwenhoek's "animalcules"—his generic term for living organisms seen through his microscope—he found also in his neighbor's teeth as well as his own feces, which he carefully examined when they were "looser than ordinary."

In 1683 Leeuwenhoek made his first drawing of bacteria, but he had no idea of their function. Indeed, many of Leeuwenhoek's discoveries awaited further advances in order to be better understood. He observed globules of yeast but could not explain fermentation, and his comparative studies of sperm led him to an "animalcule" theory of reproduction which did not, however, contribute much to embryology. Generally, Leeuwenhoek's unwillingness to go beyond his evidence was one of his important assets; his observations were valuable in themselves and not burdened with elaborate theories. Historically, it is implausible to suppose that he might have suggested the bacterial origin of disease, or that the ovum did more than nourish a fetus.* But he did show that weevils did not originate in grains but are hatched from eggs laid down by flying insects. And he was opposed to the old idea of spontaneous generation through putrefaction—a view which would only be finally proved correct two centuries later.

Leeuwenhoek did not use a compound microscope with a

---

*In a genuine example of what historians of science deride as a "Whiggish" approach to history ("Why couldn't they have known then what we know now?") Paul de Kruif in his famous *Microbe Hunters* suggested that Leeuwenhoek "had too little imagination to predict the role of assassin for his wretched creatures…." One cannot argue with nonsense, but still, what is the best reply? One possibility is to point out that, in a sense, we are infected all our lives—that Leeuwenhoek had no reason to suspect that microbes such as found in his neighbor's teeth could cause disease, because his neighbor was healthy. But perhaps a better answer is that the germ theory of disease required a chemistry which was not coherently formulated for another century and a half.

system of lenses but rather, a simple microscope with a single lens, which he ground himself. His most elementary apparatus was a flat brass plate, in which the lens was fitted, together with a pointed screw for holding and focusing the specimens. Leeuwenhoek's remarkable results were effectively reproduced in the twentieth century by Brian J. Ford in his fascinating *Single Lens: The Story of the Simple Microscope*. Examining Leeuwenhoek's original specimens, many of which were carefully preserved, Ford found both instrument and scientist to have been extraordinary.

If Leeuwenhoek had a scientific fault, it was the secrecy with which he guarded his methods from others. As his fame spread, learned men and nobility came to see him, but he was sometimes impatient with them, and suspicious that they would steal his instruments. Leeuwenhoek was friendly when visited by Czar Peter the Great of Russia, however, and in 1698 showed him the circulation in the tail of an eel. This "so delighted the Prince," writes Leeuwenhoek's friend and early biographer, Gerard von Loon, "that in these and other contemplations he spent no less than two hours, and on taking his leave shook Leeuwenhoek by the hand, and assured him of his special gratitude for letting him see such extreme small objects."

In 1680 Leeuwenhoek was unanimously elected to the Royal Society of England, which pleased him a great deal, and he also became a member of the French Academy of Sciences. He was married and widowed twice. He lived to the advanced age of ninety, dying on August 26, 1723.

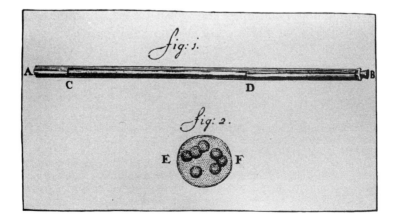

56

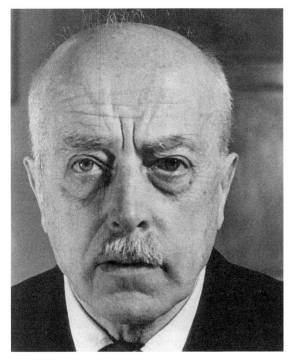

Max von Laue
and X-ray Crystallography
1879–1960

The story is told that Max von Laue went to see his colleague Arnold Sommerfeld one day in 1912 and found him discussing with P. P. Ewald the nature of some experiments the latter was performing with molecules. Laue was surprised to learn that the structure of crystals—because of their arrangements of atoms— was like a three-dimensional grating or lattice. From this information he performed an epochal experiment and devised the theory of X-ray diffraction. He was quickly awarded the Nobel Prize.

X-ray diffraction illuminated the atomic structure of molecules as could no other method, and became a crucial tool in twentieth-century physics. It is the basis for the science of X-ray crystallography, which has rivaled the microscope and spectroscopy in providing clues to the structure of all kinds of matter. In addition, its discovery also entailed proof that X rays belong to the electromagnetic spectrum. For ALBERT EINSTEIN [2], Laue's discovery was "one of the most beautiful in physics." It should be no surprise that in this volume, Laue finds a place near ANTON VON LEEUWENHOEK [55] and GUSTAV KIRCHHOFF [57].

Max Theodor Felix von Laue was born on October 9, 1879, in Pfaffendorf, near the city of Koblenz, Germany, the son of Julius Laue, an army official, and Minna Zerrenner. (The family was joined to the hereditary nobility in 1913, and so the surname became von Laue.) During his childhood, his parents moved often because of his father's work. Said to be an intense and serious child, Max had an early interest in physics and frequently visited exhibits at the Urania, a scientific society in Berlin. Most of his secondary education took place at the Protestant Gymnasium in Strasbourg, from which he graduated in 1898. He first attended the University of Strasbourg for a year, where he studied physics, chemistry, and mathematics. He then went on to the universities of Göttingen, Munich, and Berlin, where his adviser was MAX PLANCK [25], and he received his Ph.D. magna cum laude in 1903. His doctoral dissertation was in optics and concerned the interaction of light waves.

In 1905 Laue returned to the Institute for Theoretical Physics in Berlin, where he became Max Planck's assistant. Laue was one of the first young physicists to realize the great significance of Albert Einstein's 1905 paper on special relativity, and he began to apply it to optics. Indeed, he offered an important, early experimental proof of relativity, based in optics, in 1907. His work helped gain acceptance of the theory, and in 1911 Laue published a comprehensive textbook on the still controversial work, entitled *Das Relativitätsprinzip*. Meanwhile, in 1909 Laue began teaching optics and thermodynamics at the University of Munich, where he became friends with Arnold Sommerfeld.

Following the discovery of X rays in 1895, much speculation and experimentation was aimed at clarifying their nature. Experiments by Charles Barkla strongly suggested that X rays belonged to the electromagnetic spectrum but were waves of much shorter length than light; this, however, could not be proved. In 1912 Sommerfeld suggested a numerical value for this wavelength, which led Laue to hypothesize that if X-ray waves were, in fact, shorter than visible light, they might be revealed through some form of diffraction grating. And it was now that, by chance, he came upon the notion that crystals had just such a latticelike structure.

Laue immediately advised his colleagues to conduct an experiment in which a beam of X rays was directed through pinholes onto a crystal of zinc sulphite. Behind the crystal was a photographic plate. The result was a beautifully symmetric pattern. Later that evening—it was April 21, 1912—as he walked home, Laue realized the vast possibilities for calculations used in measuring optical gratings. In principle, similar and quite individual patterns could be produced for the whole multitude of chemical molecules in nature. Not only did X-ray diffraction reveal the basic structure of atoms, it also provided a means of measuring the wavelength of X rays.

The importance of Laue's work was recognized almost immediately—indeed, he caused a sensation—and it was rapidly adopted and vastly extended by others. William Lawrence Bragg and his father, William Henry Bragg, soon founded X-ray crystallography, used to examine the structures of crystals and molecules. In addition, Maurice de Broglie developed X-ray spectroscopy, which Henry Mosely immediately employed to revise the periodic table of elements. Laue won the Nobel Prize in 1914; the Braggs, the following year. Mosely was killed in World War I in the bloody battle of Gallipoli.

In 1919, after several years of teaching in Zurich and Würzburg, Laue returned to work with an aging Max Planck at the University of Berlin. Although Laue's later research on superconductivity was productive, he remained in many ways a classical physicist, and so did not participate much in the development of quantum theory.

Laue is the most admirable of figures in the sorry history of German science during the period of Nazi rule. Joined by only two of his colleagues of the Prussian Academy of Sciences, he strongly protested when Albert Einstein resigned under pressure from the Kaiser Wilhelm Institute in 1933. Laue ridiculed the Nazi idea that the theory of relativity was a "world-wide Jewish trick" and compared such rhetoric to the church's sanctioning of GALILEO GALILEI [7] in the seventeenth century. He attacked the anti-Semitic position of Johannes Stark, another Nobel laureate, and tried with little success to save German physics from a disastrous brain drain. He was outspokenly anti-Nazi, but he remained in Germany and retired from teaching during World War II. The fact that he had no part in Adolf Hitler's uranium project did not prevent Laue, like the younger and more compliant WERNER HEISENBERG [15], from being interned in England by the Allies at war's end.

In the last phase of his career, Laue helped to rebuild German science and was named director of the Fritz Haber Institute of Physical Chemistry in 1950, a post he held until 1959. Laue married Magdalene Degen in 1910, and the couple had two children. Laue was a sensation seeker, fond of mountain climbing and sailing and, like JOHN VON NEUMANN [51], enjoyed driving at high speed. On April 8, 1960, Laue was injured in a collision with a motorcycle. At his death two weeks later, on April 23, 1960, he was much mourned by scientists both in Germany and abroad.

57

Gustav Kirchhoff
and Spectroscopy

1824–1887

Although he is frequently neglected in history books, Gustav Kirchhoff made contributions which lie at the root of twentieth-century physics. In 1859 Kirchhoff stated the general principle that each chemical element emits a characteristic spectrum of light. Together with Robert Bunsen, he established spectroscopy as a powerful analytic tool.* It provided a means of characterizing all the elements in nature. Kirchhoff immediately recognized an even broader implication: a new basis for discerning the

---

*In its simplest form, a spectroscope comprises a light source, a tube leading to a prism, and a small telescope.

chemistry of the heavens. Kirchhoff soon presented to physics the vexing but crucial problem of "blackbody radiation," which ultimately led to the development of quantum theory—forty years later. An influential teacher, Kirchhoff "strove for clarity and rigor in the quantitative statement of experience," writes Léon Rosenfeld, "using a direct and straightforward approach and simple ideas."

Gustav Robert Kirchhoff was born on March 12, 1824, in Königsberg, then Prussia, and today, as Kaliningrad, in Russia. The son of a lawyer and state functionary, Kirchhoff evinced an early interest in mathematics. At the University of Königsberg he studied under Franz Neumann, a mineralogist who had become interested in the new mathematical physics and the theory of electromagnetism. Graduating in 1847, Kirchhoff received a scholarship to study in Paris, but the revolutions of 1848 intervened. Instead, he moved first to Berlin, when he began to teach, and in 1850 became an adjunct professor at the University of Breslau. During this period he met and formed a close friendship with Robert Bunsen, the inorganic chemist and physicist who popularized use of the "Bunsen burner." Thirteen years his senior, Bunsen was instrumental in bringing Kirchhoff to the University of Heidelberg in 1854, and the two began a long and productive collaboration.

Kirchhoff's early contributions in the domain of electricity had both practical and theoretical importance, and include an important miss. While still a student, Kirchhoff in 1845 formulated two laws that bear his name, and which are still used today in electronics applications. Discovering the source of a defect in Ohm's Law, which states the relationship between the resistance and flow of current, Kirchhoff's Laws give the proper formulas for measuring the potentials and current in any part of a network of electrical conductors. In 1857 he made another significant contribution to electromagnetism when he offered a general theory of how electricity is conducted. He based his calculations on experimental results which determine a constant for the speed of the propagation of electric current. Kirchhoff noted that this constant is approximately the equivalent of the measured speed of light—but the greater implications of this fact escaped him. He dismissed it as a coincidence. It remained for JAMES CLERK MAXWELL [12] to propose that light belongs to the electromagnetic spectrum.

Kirchhoff's most significant work, dating from 1859 to 1862, involves the birth of spectroscopy as an instrument of analysis. The story is told that Kirchhoff visited Bunsen in his laboratory, where the latter was analyzing various salts that impart specific colors to a flame when burned. Bunsen was using colored glasses to view the flame. Kirchhoff suggested that a better analysis might be achieved by passing the light from the flame through a prism. This they did. The value of spectroscopy was immediately clear. Spectroscopy, which had its origins in the demonstration by Isaac Newton of the composite nature of light, had suddenly a vast new field of application. Each element showed a definite spectrum which could be viewed, recorded, and measured.

"Their results," Abraham Pais notes, "were of the greatest importance." Each element and compound had a spectrum as distinct as any fingerprint. Spectral analysis, Kirchhoff and Bunsen wrote not long afterward, promises "the chemical exploration of a domain which up till now has been completely closed." They not only analyzed known elements; they discovered new ones. Analyzing salts from evaporated mineral water, Kirchhoff and Bunsen detected a blue spectral line; it belonged to an element they christened *caesium*. Studying lepidolite, in 1862 Bunsen found an alkali metal he called *rubidium*, an element used today in atomic clocks. Using spectroscopy, some ten more new elements were discovered before the end of the century, and the field had expanded enormously. Between 1900 and 1912, H. G. J. Kayser published the *Handbuch der Spectroscopie* in six volumes comprising five thousand pages.

One result of their spectral analysis was particularly significant. Kirchhoff noticed that certain dark lines in the spectrum of sunlight—called Fraunhofer's lines—coincided with yellow lines in the spectrum of burning sodium. Viewing the solar spectrum with the light from a sodium flame, these dark lines grew darker still. Kirchhoff, recognizing he was close to a fundamental discovery, drew the correct conclusion: The darkening of the spectral lines indicates their absorption, because the sun's atmosphere contains sodium. Spectra of other chemical elements in the sun would likewise show distinctive dark bands.

Through the comparison of spectra, Kirchhoff and Bunsen were immediately aware of the significance of their technique to the study of the composition of the sun and the chemistry of the heavens. "It is plausible," Kirchhoff wrote, "that spectroscopy is

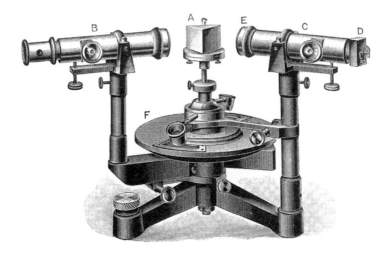

The spectroscope: Key tool for chemical analysis.

also applicable to the solar atmosphere and the brighter fixed stars." Indeed this was the case, and the notion was later extended to the universe as a whole. In 1861 Kirchhoff and Bunsen further compared the spectral lines of the elements with those of the sun, which led to the discovery of helium. In the twentieth century, application of spectroscopy was a basic technical facilitator both to developing atomic theory and to astrophysics.

As a consequence of his work with Fraunhofer's lines, Kirchhoff developed a general theory of emission and radiation in terms of thermodynamics, known as Kirchhoff's law. It has a quantitative form, but, simply put, states that a substance's capacity to emit light is equivalent to its ability to absorb it at the same temperature.

One of the results of Kirchhoff's law of radiation was the "blackbody problem," which was to plague physics for forty years. This peculiar but fundamental quandary arose because heating a black body—an iron bar, for example—causes it to give off heat and light. Its radiation may be at first invisible, or infrared; it subsequently becomes visible and red-hot. Eventually it turns white hot, which indicates that it is emitting all the colors of the spectrum. The spectral radiation, which depends only on the temperature to which the body is heated and not on the material of which it is made, could not be predicted by classical physics. Kirchhoff recognized that "it is a highly important task to find this universal function." Because of its general importance to understanding energy, the blackbody problem eventually found a solution. In 1900 MAX PLANCK [25] discovered the quanta, with enormous implications for twentieth-century science.

In a hagiographic memoir by Robert von Helmholtz, published in 1890, Kirchhoff is called "a perfect example of the true German investigator. To search after truth in its purest shape and to give utterance with almost an abstract self-forgetfulness, was the religion and purpose of his life." Indeed, although his major accomplishments have not been overlooked and he appears in standard histories of physics in English, he is rarely profiled. This may be because he was not a devoted atomist and his direct influence ends with classical physics. But as Lloyd Motz and Jefferson Weaver point out, the spectroscope, "despite its simplicity, is probably the single most important scientific instrument ever devised. Since its invention, it has led to more great scientific discoveries, ranging from the nuclear to the cosmological domain in physics and astronomy, and incorporating all branches of geology, chemistry, and medicine, than any other instrument or combination of instruments." And it remains that Kirchhoff, with Bunsen, was the first to generalize the concept from which its power derives.

A highly regarded professor, but not necessarily an excellent lecturer, Kirchhoff suffered from an accident-related disability that forced him to use crutches or a wheelchair. This apparently did not detract from his good humor and wit, and he continued experimental work until 1875, when he reduced his workload to become professor of theoretical physics at the University of Berlin. Here he remained until 1886, retiring a short while before his death, on October 17, 1887.

Hans Bethe

and the Energy of the Sun

1906–

In the nuclear reaction known as fusion, the collision and binding together of two atomic nuclei leads to a release of energy. The discovery of how fusion might take place in stellar bodies such as the sun, and so provide a constant release of enormous amounts of light and energy, is one of the principal achievements of Hans Bethe. Historically, this work constituted, as SHELDON GLASHOW [48] has put it, the point at which "macroverse and microverse began to converge" in modern physics.

One of the most admired scientists of the twentieth century, Bethe became an emigré to the United States during the 1930s when he fled Nazi Germany. During World War II, he played a major role in the construction of the atomic bomb, and subsequently, like some other physicists, he became active in opposing its wider use. In 1991, following the collapse of the Soviet Union, Bethe was one of many influential figures who urged a sharp bilateral reduction in nuclear warheads.

Hans Bethe (his name is pronounced like the Greek letter, beta) was born in Strasbourg, Germany, on July 2, 1906, the son of Albrecht Theodore Julius Bethe and Anna Kuhn, who was from a Jewish family. His father was trained in physiology and worked as a privatdozent at the University of Strasbourg. Through much of his youth, Bethe had few friends of his own age. He has said: "My life was spent almost entirely with grown-ups—with my parents and close relatives.... My father did talk to me about scientific things." Advanced in mathematics, he taught himself some calculus at age fourteen. During these years after World War I, Bethe's mildly left-wing attitudes were formed, in part under the influence of his father, who was a political liberal and activist.

Attending the University of Frankfurt beginning in 1924, Bethe soon moved to the University of Munich, where he came under the influence of Arnold Sommerfeld, a prominent professor of theoretical physics. Bethe received his Ph.D. in 1928 and taught at the universities of Frankfurt and Stuttgart. His dissertation and first papers emerge from the fertile ground of early quantum mechanics. In 1930 Bethe spent some time in England as well as in Italy, where he worked with ENRICO FERMI [34], and also at the Copenhagen institute of NIELS BOHR [3]. One of his first papers provided a useful and elegant way to calculate how charged particles are slowed down when they pass through matter.

Like many other scientists from a Jewish background, Bethe was compelled to leave Germany with the Nazis' rise to power. In 1931 he returned to teach at the University of Tübingen. But by 1932 young fascists were coming to his class wearing swastika armbands, and the following year, when Hitler became chancellor, Bethe lost his university position. He migrated to England, and worked at the universities of Manchester and Bristol. In 1935 he arrived in the United States and took a position as assistant professor of theoretical physics at Cornell University; he became a full professor two years later.

Recognizing the deficits in the American physics community's grasp of nuclear physics, Bethe wrote a series of three summary articles for the *Review of Modern Physics* in 1936 and 1937. These constituted a comprehensive review of virtually all the knowledge of nuclear physics up to that time. Widely circulated, "Bethe's Bible," as the papers were called, rapidly established his reputation in American physics.

Bethe's most significant accomplishment in theoretical physics was his theory of stellar energy. In 1938 he attended an astrophysics conference in Washington, D.C., organized by George Gamow and EDWARD TELLER [88]. The topic was the energy production of stars, a question just then coming into the purview of particle physics. The actual source of the energy of a star like the sun was not known; neither gravitation nor ordinary chemical reactions could explain the tremendous output of heat. To simplify a complex question: How can the sun continue to shine and radiate light and heat without soon burning up? As more became known about collisions among atomic particles, it became plausible to suppose that the fusion of atoms played a determining role. This had been suggested by ARTHUR EDDINGTON [37] as early as 1930, and seemed plausible, though he could not say how or what subatomic particles were involved.

Bethe's 1938 discovery, which emerged soon after the Washington conference, showed that a star's energy was continually created through a cyclical thermonuclear reaction. It was known that the sun contained mostly hydrogen and helium, the lightest elements, as well as small amounts of heavier elements. Bethe searched for an element that could serve as a catalyst in stellar fusion. "I went systematically through the periodic table," he recounted years later, "but everything gave nonsense because whatever atom I used, lithium, beryllium, etc., would be destroyed in the reaction, and there was very little of these substances anyway, as we know from abundances both on Earth and in the stars. So these elements could not possibly give the energy production for the length of time that the universe has been functioning. Finally I got to carbon, and...in the case of carbon the reaction works out beautifully. One goes through six reactions, and at the end one comes back to carbon."

In six weeks following the Washington conference, Bethe worked out the calculations. Hydrogen protons smashing into carbon nuclei, he discovered, would create an unstable isotope of nitrogen. This soon is transformed into a form of carbon, then into stable nitrogen, with a release of gamma rays as energy. When the nitrogen is again struck by protons, an isotope of oxygen is created, and it turns into another stable nitrogen isotope. When this nucleus splits, it results in two nuclei—one of helium, the other of carbon. And the chain begins all over again. Bethe showed that this six-step cycle basically agreed with available data on the temperature and energy emitted by stars. Calculations were subsequently refined as these variables were revised and as fusion and its role in the generation of stellar energy came to be understood in greater detail.

During World War II Bethe overcame his initial skepticism and agreed to work on developing the atomic bomb. At the invitation of ROBERT OPPENHEIMER [87] he joined the Manhattan Project and was appointed chief of the Theoretical Division at Los Alamos. One of Bethe's challenges was to discover how to ignite the chain reaction which would detonate the bomb. The leader of five subgroups, each with specialized tasks, at Los Alamos, Bethe, according to one observer, "resembled a battle-ship surrounded by an escort of smaller vessels, the younger theorists, moving majestically forward through the ocean of the unknown."

Although his work was crucial to the effort to create the atomic bomb, nuclear disarmament became an important theme throughout the rest of Bethe's career. Famously, at Los Alamos, Bethe's relationship with his close friend Edward Teller deteriorated. The disruption of their relationship had historic resonance. After the war, Teller became a strong advocate of developing the hydrogen bomb and was an architect of cold war weapons policy. Bethe, by contrast, made consistent efforts to educate the public about the dangers of nuclear warfare. He was initially opposed to building the hydrogen "superbomb" which Teller advocated during and after World War II. He eventually changed his mind when he became convinced that the Soviet Union would be capable of producing the H-bomb, and he participated in its design.

Bethe also continued his work in theoretical and applied physics after World War II, returning to Cornell in 1946. He worked on a variety of problems, including shock wave theory and the theory of elementary particles known as mesons. In 1947 he developed—while traveling from Shelter Island to Schenectady, New York—a theory to account for the "Lamb shift," an infinitesimal change in a hydrogen atom's energy level. This was one of several critical contributions Bethe made to the development of quantum electrodynamics. In 1967 he was awarded the Nobel Prize for his contributions to nuclear physics, most particularly his work on stellar energy.

Bethe became a major figure in the effort to halt the proliferation of nuclear weapons. In 1958 he was a delegate to the Geneva Conference which worked out the first nuclear test ban treaty. During the Nixon administration he was a leader in opposing the deployment of the Safeguard missile system. He supported the antiballistic missile treaty of 1972. The Bethe-Teller debates continued into the 1980s as Bethe loudly opposed Edward Teller's costly Star Wars program, and by the 1990s he was promoting further reductions in the world's nuclear arsenals. "I feel the most intense relief," Bethe wrote late in life, "that these weapons have not been used since World War II, mixed with the horror that tens of thousands of such weapons have been built since that time..."

Highly regarded as a teacher, Bethe has continued to publish widely well after his retirement from Cornell in 1975. "There is nothing as interesting as science," he has said. "So long as the brain lasts, that's what I'm going to do." In 1939 Bethe married Rose Ewald, the daughter of Paul Ewald, a well-known physicist, and they have two children.

59

Euclid
and the Foundations of Mathematics

ca. 295 B.C.

For centuries Euclid's geometry has been the first and fundamental mathematical tool for understanding the physical world. It is taught to schoolchildren, but the simple character of many of his axioms can be misleading. Early in his career, ISAAC NEWTON [1] skimmed Euclid's propositions and, according to one of his disciples, "wondered how any body would amuse themselves to write any demonstrations of them." But Newton soon realized his mistake, returned to the *Elements* with greater attention, and eventually emerged with his theory of fluxions, or calculus. Euclid's geometry, wrote the neo-Platonist philosopher Proclus, "bears the same relationship to the rest of mathematics as do the letters of the alphabet to the language." In the everyday world on a human scale, this statement, which dates from the fifth century A.D., needs only slight revision today.

Virtually nothing is known of Euclid's life, save that he lived toward the end of the Hellenistic Age, a generation younger than Aristotle, at about the same time as ARCHIMEDES [100]. In all likelihood, he attended Plato's Academy, which had been founded a century earlier and had become the most important school of mathematics extant. In Alexandria, during the enlightened reign of Ptolemy I, who had come to power in Egypt following the death of Alexander the Great, Euclid subsequently established a school himself. The story is told that Ptolemy asked Euclid if there were not an easier way to understand geometry then by studying the *Elements*. Euclid replied, "There is no royal road to geometry."

The *Elements*, consisting of thirteen books, comprises a synthesis of works previously compiled by others, drawing especially upon the theorems of Pythagoras and Eudoxus. In an admirably concise style, the first six books set forth the theorems of plane geometry. (Book I includes the crucial Pythagorean theorem, which may be said to form the underlying principle of geometrical explanations of nature.) The next three books are concerned with number theory and include Euclid's discussions of perfect numbers and prime numbers.* The tenth book is concerned with irrational numbers, which had been discussed by Eudoxus, and the last three books reprise solid geometry.

It is not difficult to see why Euclid's work endured. He gives clear and timeless definitions of his terms—a point, for example, is "that which has no parts, or which has no magnitude"—and he develops from postulates, or axioms, the series of propositions, problems, and theorems that constitute the bulk of the books. Altogether, the *Elements* contains 467 theorems. Historically, Euclid's most significant postulate is the problematical fifth: that given a line A and a point, only one line B may be drawn which is *parallel* to line A. Although many mathematicians later attempted proofs, it was finally established in the nineteenth century that this postulate could not, in fact, be proven. Non-Euclidean

---

*Perfect numbers are numbers whose factors add up to the number itself. The number 6 is perfect because it is the sum of 1, 2, and 3. Perfect numbers are scarce: e.g., 1, 2, 498, and 8128. Prime numbers are numbers with only 1 and the number as their factors. To Euclid is owed the proof that the number of primes is infinite.

geometries were thereupon developed, putting a necessary end to Euclidean hegemony. Today, in addition to Euclid's plane geometry, there are hyperbolic and elliptical geometries of curved space.

The significance of Euclid's geometry for the physical world, as it evolved in Western culture, is as extraordinary as it is incalculable. It is the clear foundation of Occidental engineering and design—consider all the monumental construction until the present day. And it is the basis for fundamental assumptions in physics: for example, that a straight line is the shortest distance between two points. Euclidean geometry only begins to yield a false impression of the world at extreme magnitudes and distances. It is the mathematics of common-sense space, whose limitations have become apparent only over the past two centuries. ALBERT EINSTEIN [2] begins his popular exposition, *Relativity*, with a discussion of Euclidean concepts.

Euclid died about 270 B.C., according to intelligent conjecture. An assessment of his character which comes down through the ages describes him as a fair, modest, and exact scholar. Some of the untold legions of schoolchildren, however, who have wrestled with Euclid's theorems, have seen in him something different, and a few have taken revenge. Among them is Wilbur D. Birdwood, the pseudonymous author, in 1922, of *Euclid's Outline of Sex*. In this text, Freud was enlisted to describe Euclid as a man with "an aggravated case of the Grandmother complex." A straight line is the shortest distance between two points:

A————————————————————————————B

At least, writes Birdwood, where "A is Euclid and B is Grandmother."

60

Gregor Mendel
and the Laws of Inheritance

1822–1884

The story of how Gregor Mendel, a retiring monk, discovered three laws of heredity, offered them to the world in 1865 but was rejected, and died neglected only to be resurrected after death as a scientific genius is a twentieth-century parable. It is true that Mendel's basic insight—that specific traits are transmitted to offspring according to definite, quantifiable rules—helped to shape biological thought in highly significant ways. But in recent years, as historians of science have looked carefully at Mendel's work and at the scientific community at the end of the nineteenth century, his aspirations and his findings are not what they seemed. The "priest who held the key to evolution," as science writer Loren Eiseley described him a generation ago, has undergone considerable scrutiny. But although Mendel's aims and results were not as grand as has sometimes been claimed, his posthumous influence on biology is undeniable.

Born on July 22, 1822, Mendel's name at birth was Johann. His parents were prosperous peasants from Heizendorf, in Silesia, a part of the Austro-Hungarian empire which later became part of Czechoslovakia and today lies within the borders of the Czech Republic. When his intellectual gifts were recognized, he was sent to the gymnasium at Troppau. Later he attended the University of Olmütz. As a youth he was frequently ill, with maladies that were perhaps psychosomatic. At age twenty-one, he entered the Augustinian monastery at Brünn (now Brno), a career decision that probably had little religious significance. After studies in theology as well as agriculture and botany between 1844 and 1848, Mendel was ordained and took the monastic name Gregor. From 1851 to 1853 Mendel studied mathematics and the physical sciences at the University of Vienna. Returning to his monastery, he taught there for fourteen years beginning in 1854.

In 1856 Mendel began his long series of experiments with culinary peas. Over a period of about two years he bred peas to develop "pure" lines with seven distinct traits, focusing on visible characteristics such as size, color, shape, and texture. He then bred pedigrees with alternative traits, crossing short with tall plants, smooth with wrinkled, and so on. Expecting a blend to result—medium tall or partially smooth, for example—Mendel was instead able to show that the alternative traits themselves were inherited. Some plants grew tall, others short; some peas smooth, others wrinkled. The *law of independent segregation* became the first of the three Mendelian laws of inheritance.

Mendel also discovered that individual traits, not the entire complement of characteristics, were passed on in reproduction. Each pair of the seven traits which Mendel studied operated independently of the others. The various aspects of this theory would eventually be nuanced when the physical basis of genetics was established; but Mendel, for his part, had the good fortune to deal with peas, whose external traits are sorted independently of each other. This became the second of Mendel's laws: the *law of independent assortment*. When THOMAS HUNT MORGAN [62] discovered that some traits were linked, this law was modified.

The third of Mendel's laws, the *law of dominance*, states that of the paired factors in inherited traits one is always dominant and the other recessive. This law operates in definite proportions and today is known to have only limited applicability.

Carefully conceived experimental design was an important aspect of Mendel's research. He bred some 28,000 plants, fertilized them by hand (bees usually do the work), and used a number of varieties as control groups. Mendel was not oblivious to the tedious nature of his experiments. He wrote, "It requires indeed some courage to undertake a labor of such far-reaching extent; this appears, however, to be the only right way by which we can finally reach the solution of a question the importance of which cannot be overestimated in connection with the history of the evolution of organic forms."

In a paper presented to the Brünn Natural History Society in 1865, and published the following year, Mendel put forth the results of his experiments. The paper was ignored. He subsequently conducted a correspondence with a well-known Swiss botanist, K. W. von Nägeli, which was discouraging. After Nägeli advised him to experiment with milkweeds, which reproduce in an unusual way, Mendel could not confirm his earlier results with peas. He soon abandoned further research. He continued in later life to work with apples and pears and became known among pomologists (people who study apples). In 1868 Mendel was appointed abbot of his monastery, a position which occupied him with administrative duties for the rest of his life. In 1878 Mendel conducted C. W. Eichling, a visiting horticulturalist, through his garden and showed off peas "which he said he had reshaped in height as well as in type of fruit....I asked him how he did it and he replied, 'It is just a little trick, but there is a long story connected with it which it would take too long to tell.'"

In 1900, sixteen years after his death, Mendel's papers were rediscovered by three botanists: Hugo De Vries, Carl Correns, and Erich Tschermak von Seysenegg. The importance they attached to the work, which came through a search of the literature, is now believed to have been a means by which they avoided an unpleasant dispute of priority over the laws of dominance and segregation. It was also a way for them to understand and organize the results of their own experiments. Subsequently, William Bateson, the Cambridge scientist who coined the term *genetics*, fitted Mendelian laws into the context of his own research into heredity. Bateson rejected Darwin's hypothesis of gradual speciation, and Mendel's experiments could be used to help explain his scheme of mutations. Only in the 1930s, with the work of a new generation of geneticists, did the confusion over Mendel's contribution seem to clear. When it did, Mendel was viewed as having explained the basic mechanism of inherited traits, which now became part of a larger theory of natural selection supported by the discovery of chromosomal inheritance.

So it is that today, under the scrutiny of recent scholars, this picture has been corrected and the work of Gregor Mendel has been reevaluated. His own main interest is now seen to have centered on the development of new plant hybrids, which were not understood, although he had read Darwin and was aware of the larger issues involved in heredity. And while his experiments are impressive, his results are too good to be true; they cannot be easily replicated. Historically, however, his work represented a new emphasis on quantification in biology, and Mendel was responsible for what Peter J. Bowler calls a "conceptual revolution." Mendelism "was a stepping stone toward the exciting—and perhaps frightening—world of late twentieth century biology. If we wish to understand the role played by science in the complex world we live in, Mendelism's origins certainly repay serious investigation."

At the end of his life Mendel, the gentle monk, became embroiled in a bitter tax dispute with the government. He seems to have contracted heart disease and a kidney condition, and he began smoking twenty cigars a day. Suffering from dropsy, he spent his last days sitting on a couch with his feet in bandages. That is how his caretaker found him, on January 6, 1884, dead.

Heike Kamerlingh Onnes
and Superconductivity

1853–1926

Low-temperature physics, or cryogenics, has brought about refrigeration, new fertilizers, blow torches, and rocket engines, among many other commercial developments. But in addition, studying the behavior of certain substances at temperatures below −100°C illuminates fundamental properties of matter and electromagnetism. *Superconductivity,* the disappearance of electrical resistance at very low temperature, has both technological and theoretical implications. It was the culminating discovery, in 1911, of the Dutch scientist Heike Kamerlingh Onnes. A masterful experimenter, Nobel laureate, and director of an influential

286

laboratory in Leiden, Kamerlingh Onnes was known as the "gentleman of absolute zero."

Heike Kamerlingh Onnes was born on September 21, 1853, in the moderately large city of Groningen, in northeastern Netherlands, into a strict household and a family of means. His mother was Anna Gerdina Coers, daughter of an architect, and his father, Harm Kamerlingh Onnes, was a tile manufacturer. Beginning in 1870 he studied physics and mathematics at the University of Groningen, where he won prizes for his research and received a candidate's degree in 1871. Traveling to Germany, he had the distinction of studying with GUSTAV KIRCHHOFF [57] and Robert Bunsen at the University of Heidelberg before returning to Groningen to complete academic work for his doctoral degree, which he received magna cum laude. Kamerlingh Onnes's dissertation, entitled "New Proofs for the Axial Rotation of the Earth," was inspired by his work with Kirchhoff and brought him his doctorate in 1879, a year after he began teaching at the Polytechnic School in Delft.

Early in the nineteenth century experimentalists had discovered that gases respond in unforeseen ways to changes in temperature and pressure. MICHAEL FARADAY [11], for example, found that he could liquefy chlorine and carbon dioxide. As experimental methods improved, scientists were able to produce small quantities of liquid oxygen. Historically, this new research in low-temperature physics merged with the modern theories of thermodynamics and the chemistry of atoms and molecules in the late nineteenth century. Not surprisingly—for centuries human beings had struggled to keep perishables cool—it also coincided with attempts to develop new forms of refrigeration.

By the late 1870s Kamerlingh Onnes had become interested in the theories of gases and critical temperature which had been developed by Johannes van der Waals, his senior colleague at Polytechnic. Van der Waals had suggested a "law of corresponding states," which Kamerlingh Onnes set out to verify. This was based on the guess that all gases share some general properties and will behave alike when pressure, temperature, and volume are adjusted with respect to the size of the specific molecule. Kamerlingh Onnes was strongly impressed by this idea for its importance to basic research. In addition to finding practical applications, he hoped, as he later said, to "lift the veil which thermal motions at normal temperatures spread over the inner world of atoms and electrons." For studies of this kind, however, gases would need to be brought down to the lowest possible temperatures—indeed, the point at which they would liquefy. Kamerlingh Onnes dedicated his laboratory to this project when he moved from Delft to become professor of physics at the University of Leiden, in 1882.

Two techniques in the 1870s had been developed to cool gases, and Kamerlingh Onnes employed both in his early research. One method, the work of Carl Linde, involved subjecting gas to pressure and forcing it through a coil, entailing a heat exchange, with the gas becoming increasingly cooler. The other entailed compressing the gas and allowing it to expand suddenly. By 1892 Kamerlingh Onnes had developed an apparatus that used a "cascade method" for progressive cooling. His first gases were oxygen and air, and his apparatus was finally able to produce about fourteen liters per hour of liquid air—a pale blue fluid. The apparatus required for these experiments was complex, difficult to build, and tedious to operate. In 1901 he established a school to train glassblowers to fashion the special flasks he needed, as well as instrument makers to manufacture the various coils and pumps. Over a period of more than two decades, Kamerlingh Onnes "introduced sound engineering practice and a truly scientific approach to all low-temperature physics," writes Emilio Segrè.

As cryogenics developed, it became clear that for any gas there was a temperature at which it liquefied. One holdout, hydrogen, was turned to liquid in 1898, by the Scottish scientist James Dewar, but was not produced in quantity until eight years later in the Leiden laboratory. By 1907, Kamerlingh Onnes and others had succeeded in liquefying all the known gases except the lightest, helium. A rare gas, helium becomes liquid at the very, very cold temperature of four degrees above absolute zero.* Its liquefaction became an important goal, which Kamerlingh Onnes achieved in 1908. Helium as a liquid is perfectly clear, and when the meniscus—the telltale crescent of a liquid in a container—formed in the apparatus, Kamerlingh Onnes initially did not see it. A visitor to his laboratory pointed out that he had succeeded. "With this liquefaction," states J. van den Handel, "a

---

*Absolute zero indicates the absence of heat. Jacques Charles had discovered by the late eighteenth century that a gas contracts by 1/273 of its volume when cooled from 1° to 0°C. Absolute zero on the Kelvin scale is thus −273°C.

vast new temperature region was opened for research—a field in which, until his retirement in 1923, Kamerlingh Onnes remained absolute monarch." His results were regularly published abroad. It was by no means a surprise when, in 1913, he received the Nobel Prize for physics for his cryogenic research.

However, the discovery which constitutes Kamerlingh Onnes's best-known legacy dates from 1911. Experimenting with mercury, he found that resistance to an electrical current at temperatures of 4.2 Kelvin (about −269°C) suddenly drops to nothing. He showed similar results with tin, lead, and other metals. Although he could not explain the phenomenon, he was fully aware of its significance. He described this lack of resistance as a new state of matter, and called it *supraconductivity;* today it is known as superconductivity. It cannot be interpreted by classical mechanics, and its expected explanation in quantum electrodynamics did not come about until 1957, with the theory of JOHN BARDEEN [50], Leon Cooper, and John Schrieffer. The prospect of developing superconductivity in materials at higher than the coldest temperatures has caused a good deal of excitement in recent years. Such materials would have applications in medicine and nuclear energy, and promise such fine things as levitating trains. For some years, small devices known as SQUIDS (*s*uperconducting *qu*antum *i*nterference *d*evices) have been used on a modest scale in medical diagnosis and other applications.

By no means an uninvolved scientist, Kamerlingh Onnes took steps to find applications for cryogenics in food storage, ice production, and other industries. During World War I he took part in famine relief. He was married to Elizabeth Bijleveld, and they had one child, a son. He was an active and energetic man through much of his life despite chronically poor health. Kamerlingh Onnes died on February 21, 1926 in Leiden.

When Kamerlingh Onnes took up his duties at Leiden in 1882, his inaugural address was entitled "The Significance of Quantitative Research in Physics." If it were up to him, he said, he would have a motto at the entrance to every physics laboratory. It would read, *Door meten tot weten:* Knowledge through measurement.

62

Thomas Hunt Morgan
and the Chromosomal Theory of Heredity

1866–1945

A revolution in biology began in the late nineteenth century when, in the generation after CHARLES DARWIN [4], a search began to discover the physical basis of heredity. Advances in chemistry and microscopy had clarified the notion of the cell, which came to be understood as the basic unit of living things. When cells divide, it was discovered, small threadlike bodies can be observed within, which double in number and then migrate to each daughter cell. These *chromosomes* were discovered and named about 1880, but their function remained unknown until, about twenty years later, it was hypothesized that they carried genetic information. That this was indeed the case, and that the genes were located upon them, was shown at the end of the first decade of the twentieth century by Thomas Hunt Morgan. Morgan is the principal founder of what became known as the chromosomal theory of heredity.

A Kentuckian of distinguished lineage, Thomas Hunt Morgan was born on September 25, 1866, at Lexington. His father, Charlton Hunt Morgan, who had once served as U.S. consul to Sicily, ran a hemp manufactory and counted among his relatives J. Pierpont Morgan, the financier. His mother, Ellen Key Morgan, was the granddaughter of Francis Scott Key, composer of "The Star Spangled Banner." As a child, Thomas evinced a collector's interest in natural history, amassing birds' eggs and fossils. At sixteen he matriculated at Kentucky State College (today the University of Kentucky), majoring in zoology, and received his bachelor's degree in 1866. He went on to study morphology—the structure of animals and plants—at Johns Hopkins University, and received his doctorate in 1890, with a dissertation on sea spiders—pycnogonids, which inhabit the ocean floor. After a year's postgraduate study in Naples, Italy, he went on to teach at Bryn Mawr, in 1891. In 1904, having gained a considerable reputation for experimental research, he moved to Columbia University, where he did his most important work. The cramped "fly room" at Columbia, with Morgan at its center, examining specimens with a jeweler's magnifying glass, has a place in scientific lore.

At the time Morgan began his studies of hereditary mechanisms, various domains of biology were undergoing rapid change. Evolutionary theory was coming to exercise great attraction for biometricians and cytologists, while confusion reigned in the old science of morphology, where efforts to classify animals according to physical structure entailed considerable speculation. Under the influence of the biogenetic law of ERNST HAECKEL [90], for example, fish were thought to be ancestral to humans. Morgan was skeptical of the usefulness of this approach, which was influential in such fields as comparative anatomy and paleontology. Its broad but not really testable hypotheses annoyed him, and he wrote that "It is notorious that the human mind without control has a bad habit of wandering." Morgan was also initially critical of the theory of inheritance expressed by GREGOR MENDEL [60], which was rediscovered in 1900, and he doubted that the slow accumulation of variations could account for evolution.

Rather, visiting Hugo de Vries in the Netherlands, Morgan was impressed by the possibility that mutation was the motor of evolutionary change. As a consequence, in 1907 he began to experiment upon the common fruit fly, *Drosophila melanogaster*, looking for evidence of sudden change over generations. Given a piece of banana or other food, the fruit fly can replicate quickly and efficiently, and within a couple of years can produce as many descendants as men and women have done, in their relations together, over two millennia. In addition to being prolific, fruit flies have just four chromosomes, which are unusually large, making them relatively easy to study.

Morgan worked with his flies without positive results for two years before noting, in 1910, that one specimen possessed eyes which were white instead of red. Over the next several months, as he carefully bred the fly and awaited results, his excitement was considerable. According to one story, visiting his wife just after she gave birth to a baby girl, Morgan regaled her with information about the white-eyed fly before stopping to ask, "And how is the baby?"

Breeding the mutant, Morgan found that the first generation was normal, that is, red-eyed. But in the following generation white eyes reappeared in a proportion which—against his expectations—confirmed Mendel's third law of inheritance, giving a ratio of 3:1 for the dominant and recessive traits. Moreover, and of equal importance, all the white-eyed flies were male. Morgan correctly hypothesized that the characteristic for white eyes was a sex-linked trait; he had discovered what became known as *gene linkage*. Now an adherent of the laws of inheritance, no longer skeptical, Morgan published *The Mechanism of Mendelian Heredity* in 1915. In what have been called "some of the most beautiful experimental results in the history of science," Morgan showed that genes were physical entities, located along chromosomes.

In his work published after World War I, Morgan developed what became known as the chromosomal theory of inheritance and created the basic language of genetics. He authored several key texts in genetics, including *The Physical Basis of Heredity*, published in 1919, and *Evolution and Genetics* in 1925. In 1926 *The Theory of the Gene* appeared, and *Embryology and Genetics* in 1933. In experiments, Morgan mapped the genetic structure of the fruit fly, elucidating a variety of mechanisms, including *recombina-*

tion, assortment, and *segregation.* He revised the meaning of *mutation,* applying it to specific traits instead of the appearance of new beasts. In Morgan's view, which became predominant, small variations enter the population as alternative characteristics (called alleles), with the environment exerting selective pressure on their adaptability. Thus do species acquire a wide range of individual variation while remaining unitary. In 1933, for his work on genetics, Morgan received the Nobel Prize in physiology or medicine.

In 1928, although just a few years from retirement at Columbia, Morgan moved to the California Institute of Technology, where he was invited to thoroughly reorganize the biology department. Although his own days as an original scientist were largely past, he had great influence on the department, promoting interaction between biologists and physicists and chemists and bringing MAX DELBRÜCK [68] and many other scientists to Caltech. He died on December 4, 1945.

Possessing a complex character, Morgan is recalled as promoting a highly creative atmosphere of open discussion in his laboratory. One of his devoted students described Morgan's approach as "compounded with enthusiasm combined with a strong critical sense, generosity, open-mindedness, and a remarkable sense of humor." To this it should be added that Morgan was not himself interested much in the genes as physical entities, and he did not foresee the significance of DNA. In addition, he was not at home in mathematics, although he appreciated quantitative work and could follow its major outlines. However, "In his strong commitment to materialism and experimentalism," writes Garland E. Allen, "Morgan helped create a wave of the future that today has entered into every area of modern biology."

63

Hermann von Helmholtz
and the Rise of German Science

1821–1894

Known affectionately as the Reichchancellor of Physics by colleagues, Hermann von Helmholtz is a preeminent figure in the nineteenth-century scientific renaissance in Germany. He made fundamental contributions to physiology and to physics, and also made basic and vital innovations in optics as well as in acoustics. One of the last great scientists to do original research in many fields, Helmholtz worked on thermodynamics, electrodynamics, and hydrodynamics. A strong influence on other scientists, notably Heinrich Hertz and MAX PLANCK [25], Helmholtz dominated science at the University of Berlin during the incubation of the twentieth-century revolution in physics. "As the confidant of emperors and industrialists, artists and social philosophers, men of science and government officials," wrote Richard I. Kremer recently, "Helmholtz also reigned as the political and even spiritual leader of the powerful German scientific community."

Hermann von Ludwig Ferdinand von Helmholtz, as he became known when he joined the nobility in later life, was born on August 31, 1821, in Potsdam, near Berlin. His mother, Caroline Penn, was a descendant of William Penn. Frail as a youth, he had a strong and profound relationship with his father, who taught philosophy and literature at the University of Potsdam. Ferdinand Helmholtz was a sensitive man of considerable learning, and taught his son ancient Latin and Greek as well as Hebrew, French, English, Arabic, and Italian. He also introduced Hermann to the transcendental philosophy of Hegel and to the writings of Kant.

Although Helmholtz was attracted to physics from an early age, his family was not financially able to provide him with a university education. Instead, he attended the Friedrich Wilhelm Medical Institute, beginning in 1838, where he received free medical training in exchange for a term in the military as an army physician. In 1842 Helmholtz received his degree, after studying under the well-known physiologist and anatomist Johannes Müller. His thesis, on the structure of the nervous system of invertebrate animals, nicely summarizes the range of his interest in physiology, physics, and electricity. Helmholtz thereafter served five years in the army. Posted to his hometown, he was able to continue his research, even setting up a working laboratory while on duty, and he kept informed of contemporary developments in science. In 1848, he was permitted to leave the military to take up a teaching post at the University of Königsberg.

One of Helmholtz's major efforts was to join the challenge to vitalism, the doctrine that living things required a "vital force" which could never be explained by chemistry and physics. In 1842 Julius Robert von Mayer had concluded that chemical energy and heat could be expressed as quantitatively equivalent, basing his conclusions on metabolism in the human body; and in 1845 he extended this idea to electromagnetic and chemical phenomena. Helmholtz was unaware of this work when he read his "On the Conservation of Energy" to the Physical Society of

Berlin in 1847. But he similarly hypothesized an underlying unity of matter which did not respect vitalist ideas: Heat and muscle contraction in animals were the results of physical and chemical reactions. Like Mayer's paper, "On the Conservation of Energy" helped to establish what became known as the first law of thermodynamics, which defines heat as a form of energy. Mayer's presentation was not readily accepted—which contributed to his subsequent insanity—but similar conclusions by Helmholtz were far more mathematically sophisticated. Although its importance was not recognized overnight, this paper alone would serve to commend Helmholtz to the twentieth century.

In 1851, while investigating the luminosity of the eye, Helmholtz invented the ophthalmoscope, an elegant accomplishment. As he explained years later, it occurred to him that when the eyes were examined, red rays were reflected back. Earlier, Ernst von Brücke had noticed that the pupil reflexively widens and narrows, but "had not asked himself to what optical image the rays reflected from the illuminated eye belong." In fact, the source of reflection is the light-sensitive retina within the eye. Helmholtz constructed a simple handheld instrument—a concave mirror with a hole in the middle. The apparatus did not work at first, and "had it not been for my firm theoretical conviction that it would be possible to see the [retinal] fundus, I might not have persevered. But after about a week, I was the first who ever succeeded in getting a clear view of the living human retina."

Helmholtz also developed the ophthalmometer for measuring the curvature of the eye, making it possible to diagnose the degree of astigmatism. An invention which a leading ophthalmologist, von Grafe, called "the most influential of all inventions," it brought Helmholtz considerable renown. Helmholtz made other contributions to the study of vision and in 1856 published the first volume of his *Handbuch der Physiologischen Optik,* translated in 1924 as *Treatise on Physiological Optics.*

A catalog of Helmholtz's achievements beginning in the 1850s is daunting. He invented the myograph in 1852, and used this measurement device to make the first estimate of the velocity of a nerve impulse. He rectified the theory of color vision proposed by Thomas Young so that it became a comprehensive and influential explanation. Most notably, he studied the ear, developing a new understanding of its structure. This led him to celebrated research in acoustics, and to produce the resonance theory of hearing. In 1863, his *On the Sensation of Tone as a Physiological Basis for the Theory of Music* offered a mechanistic explanation of the aesthetics of music, which, in its broad outlines, would still be valid today.

In 1855 Helmholtz moved to the University of Bonn, and three years later, to the University of Heidelberg, where a new institute of physiology was established at his request. However, toward the end of the 1860s Helmholtz began to think that the rapidly expanding field of physiology could no longer be investigated in its totality. He therefore turned to physics. In 1871, he accepted the prestigious position of professor of physics at the University of Berlin. He soon was contributing to the theories of mechanics, fluid dynamics, and electromagnetism.

Historically, the major contribution of Helmholtz to physics in Germany was to reorient it toward an appreciation of the work of MICHAEL FARADAY [11] and JAMES CLERK MAXWELL [12]. While Maxwell's theory of electromagnetism was a field theory which would soon help give birth to the new theory of matter, the idea dominant in German physics at the time was that electricity involved "action at a distance." Helmholtz gradually moved toward accepting Maxwell's view, recognizing that the implication was a particle theory of electrical phenomena. "If we accept the hypothesis that the elementary substances [elements] are composed of atoms," stated Helmholtz in 1881, "we cannot avoid concluding that electricity, also, positive as well as negative, is divided into elementary portions which behave like atoms of electricity."

At Helmholtz's instigation, his student Heinrich Hertz experimentally confirmed Maxwell's equations in 1886. Announcing Hertz's results to the Physical Society of Berlin, Helmholtz was not diffident. "Gentlemen!" he exclaimed. "I am about to share with you today the most important physics discovery of the century." Helmholtz himself made an interesting effort to reduce electrodynamics to a set of mathematical ideas, which was unsuccessful broadly because classical physics had reached its limits. Further major advances awaited the solution to the blackbody problem by MAX PLANCK [25] and the discovery of X rays near the turn of the century.

An impressive personality, Helmholtz was by 1885 the undisputed leader of German science. He served to mentor a number of students who later became important physicists. What he lacked in personal warmth and a sense of humor, he made up for with personal integrity, a genuine interest in his students, and some measure of charisma. Max Planck, who developed the basis of quantum theory, described his own case of full-fledged paternal awe: "When during a conversation [Helmholtz] would look at me with those calm, searching, penetrating, and yet so benign eyes, I would be overwhelmed by a feeling of boundless filial trust and devotion...." And this though Helmholtz was a poor lecturer. Planck also described how "it was obvious that Helmholtz never prepared his lectures properly. He spoke haltingly, and would interrupt his discourse...and we had the unmistakable impression that the class bored him as much as it did us."

Helmholtz's first wife was Olga von Velten, and they had two children before her death in 1859. Two years later he married Anna von Mohl, a woman many years his junior, with whom he had three more children. In 1883 Helmholtz was joined to the hereditary nobility. Toward the end of his life he suffered from migraine headaches and bouts of depression. Helmholtz died following a stroke on September 8, 1894, "the last scholar," wrote R. Stevens Turner, "whose work, in the tradition of Leibniz, embraced all the sciences, as well as philosophy and the fine arts."

64

Paul Ehrlich
and Chemotherapy
1854–1915

While Louis Pasteur [5] and Robert Koch [44] developed the germ theory of disease, Paul Ehrlich is responsible for the generalization that illness is essentially chemical. To him, in consequence, is owed the advent of chemotherapy, a term which he coined. For thousands of years the sick had been treated with herbs and all manner of concoction; now the industrial revolution led to new methods of examining all the products of nature. Ehrlich benefited from the advanced chemical and dye industries in Germany at the end of the nineteenth century. His early work in staining techniques brought about new ways of looking at cells and the actions of microbes inside them. He suggested and searched for "magic bullets"—compounds which might be designed to treat specific diseases. In 1910 Ehrlich's announcement of a cure for syphilis by an arsenic substance, Salvarsan, was the culmination, albeit controversial, of a brilliant career.

The son of Ismar Ehrlich, a well-to-do innkeeper, and Rosa Weigert, Paul Ehrlich was born on March 14, 1854, in Strehlen, Upper Silesia, then a part of Germany but now in Poland. Both his parents came from families with some connection to science, and Ehrlich was influenced early in life by his cousin, Carl Weigert, a chemist who discovered new staining techniques for microscopy. In 1872 Ehrlich entered the University of Breslau, but he attended several institutions before receiving his medical degree from Leipzig University in 1878. His university career was exceptional, and his doctoral thesis, on staining tissue, was a strong harbinger of his future. Upon graduation, Ehrlich was appointed to Charité Hospital in Berlin, where he immediately was named head physician, spared from clinical rounds, and allowed to undertake his own research.

Possessed of a detailed knowledge of chemistry, Ehrlich combined a singular capacity for sketching the larger outlines of theory with an exceptional ability to conceive and mentally manipulate the three-dimensional composition of molecular structure. In his early years as a researcher, Ehrlich laid the groundwork for modern hematology and the study of leukemia by developing staining techniques to distinguish the various types of white blood cells.* He also applied methods of tissue staining to bacteria. In 1882 Ehrlich introduced a method of diagnosing typhoid fever and, after hearing Robert Koch announce isolation of the tuberculosis bacterium, provided a staining method for its diagnosis. In 1885 he discovered the blood-brain barrier, the filtration system which maintains the chemistry of the brain in equilibrium; this had great consequences in later pharmacology research.

Ehrlich's *Das Sauerstoffbedürfnis des Organismus (The Organism's Need for Oxygen)*, published in 1885, provided a general theory of cell function. He assumed that a cell's nucleus was responsible for its specific function in the organism and therefore was bathed in molecular complexes which served its purposes. Although this

---

*White blood cells, or leukocytes, had been discovered eating bacteria in 1884 by the Russian Ilya Mechnikov, with whom, in 1908, Ehrlich shared the Nobel Prize for medicine.

formulation, called a "side-chain theory," would later be much modified, it enabled Ehrlich to hypothesize that the operation of the cell was essentially chemical. Ehrlich continued to develop this theory, and by the turn of the century he had applied it to immunology. Antibodies are produced in the presence of toxins, he theorized, as a natural chemical reaction. They bind and disable toxins in the bloodstream according to ordinary rules of chemical composition. This theoretical yield enabled Ehrlich to begin the culminating phase of his work, the development of specific compounds to treat particular diseases.

An interregnum in Ehrlich's career occurred in 1888 when he contracted tuberculosis himself and moved to the hot, dry climate of Egypt for a cure. Returning to Berlin eighteen months later, he joined Robert Koch at the latter's newly opened Institute for Infectious Diseases. With Koch and Emil von Behring, who had the year before identified a potential cure for diphtheria, Ehrlich discovered a means for deriving the antitoxin from horses' blood and making it effective in human veins. Essentially the same method is used today.

In 1906 a wealthy widow, intrigued by his work, provided Ehrlich with funds for the construction of a laboratory, and he became head of the George Speyer-Haus for Chemotherapy. There he remained for the rest of his working life, directing a research effort aimed at finding what he called "charmed bullets which strike only those objects for whose destruction they have been produced." Early work on a cure for trypanosomiasis, or African sleeping sickness, led Ehrlich to combine a dye substance, benzopurpurin, with a sulphuric acid derivative. The result, trypan red, he could show was effective in mice. Although it failed to work in other animals—there is still no cure for the disease—Ehrlich was encouraged, and tested the chemotherapeutic potential of a large number of compounds.

After testing over six hundred compounds, Ehrlich announced the discovery of Salvarsan in 1910. Or, as Dr. Galdston put it years ago, "Here he crowned his labors with the discovery of Salvarsan. Here the dream of youth was realized, and chemotherapy was established as a fruitful reality." An arsenic derivative which attacked the syphilis spirochete, it was not free of side effects. Still, Salvarsan was a great advance over mercury, which was still more poisonous. It remained the only serious treatment for the disease until the advent of penicillin in the 1940s.

Incidentally, Ehrlich endured personal attacks for developing a cure for syphilis; many people thought victims of a sexually transmitted disease ought to suffer the wrath of God for their immorality.

Known as kind and modest, forgetful and absentminded, Ehrlich smoked twenty-five thick cigars a day, frequently neglected to eat, and was venerated by younger colleagues. A visitor in 1914 reported in *Nature* that Ehrlich was found in his laboratory, where "the chairs and tables were covered with books, reprints, memoranda, flasks and tubes of every possible form, and cigar boxes in which were either imported cigars or tubes full of chemical preparations." As cheerful and congenial as a man could be, if one is to believe the hagiographic memoirs, Ehrlich made a happy marriage to Hedwig Pinkus in 1883, and they had two daughters, Stephanie and Marianne.

In addition to receiving the Nobel Prize, Ehrlich was much honored during his lifetime. He was awarded the Great Golden Medal of Prussia and received the title of Excellence from the German government in 1911, and the street in front of his institute was named Paul Ehrlichstrasse. The last honor was suppressed during the Nazi era, when Ehrlich's widow and children were forced to flee Germany. Today it has been restored, and Frankfurt is home to the Paul Ehrlich Institute.

Distressed by the beginning of World War I, and still attacked in the press, which accused him of testing Salvarsan on prostitutes against their will, Ehrlich suffered a mild stroke in December 1914. "He was loath to die," writes Dr. Galdston, "since, as he put it, there was so much in his head that might prove useful to man." Nevertheless, on August 20, 1915, a second cerebral event put an end to his life while he was on vacation at Bad Homburg.

65

Ernst Mayr
and Evolutionary Theory

1904–

Soon after CHARLES DARWIN [4] published *The Origin of Species,* in 1859, his notion of evolution was widely admired for its explanatory power. However, his allied notion of *natural selection* as the mechanism for speciation was much debated, as was the idea of common descent. Did species change slowly over time, accumulating small variations, or was evolution more sudden? In brief, Darwinism lacked sufficient data to provide an adequate theory of how species develop. By the turn of the twentieth century, in fact, Darwinism underwent an historical partial eclipse from which it did not completely emerge for several decades. A major figure in its renaissance, one of the architects of what is often called the modern synthesis, is Ernst Mayr.

Ornithologist, taxonomist, biologist, Mayr combines, as did Darwin himself, an unparalleled grasp of detail with a theoretically fertile mind. Mayr is, writes John C. Greene, "one of the founders of modern neo-Darwinism and has restored natural selection to a central place in the theory of evolution." In 1984, when his career had already spanned more than half a century, he was described by Stephen Jay Gould as "our greatest living evolutionary biologist."

Born in Kempten, Germany, on July 5, 1904, Ernst Walter Mayr—"very careful in the selection of my ancestors," he once said—was the son of Otto Mayr, a judge, and Helene Pusinelli Mayr. Receiving a broad classical education, he early developed a consuming interest in ornithology. One day in 1923, he spotted the red-crested pochard, a species of diving duck whose presence had not been noted in Europe for over seventy-five years. This discovery brought him into contact with the great German ornithologist Erwin Stresemann, who encouraged Mayr's aviary pursuits. Indeed, while Mayr attended the University of Greifswald, Stresemann encouraged him to come to work at the Zoological Museum of the University of Berlin. Mayr eventually abandoned plans for a medical career in favor of zoology. He received his doctorate summa cum laude in zoology from the University of Berlin in 1926.

From 1926 until 1932 Mayr served as curator at the University of Berlin Zoological Museum. In 1927 Lord Walter Rothschild asked him to lead an ornithological expedition to Dutch New Guinea. This represented the fulfillment of a long-held ambition, and over the next several years Mayr made three trips to New Guinea and the Solomon Islands, gathering a wealth of material on the bird fauna in the Arfak, Wandammen, and Cyclopop Mountains. Mayr's third expedition was sponsored by the American Museum of Natural History in New York, where he became assistant curator in 1932. During the 1930s Mayr devoted himself to taxonomy, in particular to classifying the birds he had observed and collected in the South Seas.

Mayr developed considerable evidence from which to formulate a new definition of species that would eventually be based on genetic makeup. At the time Mayr began his career, a "nominalist" school believed that "species" was basically a convenient classification of animals based on shape or form. But the reality of the concept of species was forcefully brought home to Mayr while still in New Guinea. As he explained later, "I collected 137 species of birds. The natives had 136 names for these birds—they confused only two of them."

In a 1940 paper Mayr proposed that species be defined as "groups of actually or potentially interbreeding natural populations which are reproductively isolated from other such groups." Although the idea of geographic speciation had been formulated during the nineteenth century, it languished before being revived by Mayr. His carefully compiled descriptions, together with his species hypothesis, were published in 1941 as *List of New Guinea Birds* and *Systematics and the Origin of Species* appeared in 1942.

Amassing abundant evidence to support the species concept, Mayr also provided a basic scenario of how new species are formed. New species, Mayr argued, are generated when some small subpopulation becomes, for some reason, physically isolated from its parent population. This "founder population" has a limited gene pool which over time will acquire characteristic breeding habits and structures. A new species is the result. With Mayr's concept, it was no longer necessary to entertain the possibility that chance mutations created "hopeful monsters."

Subsequently Mayr distinguished geographic or "allopatric" speciation, in which the founder population is separated physically from the main group, from "peripatric speciation," in which a small population (even a single female) wanders by chance beyond the natural boundaries. Mayr described peripatric speciation, which he considered his most successful theory, in his *Animal Species and Evolution,* published in 1963.

In the three decades immediately after World War II, Mayr's contribution to the emergent modern synthesis of evolutionary biology became widely accepted, and is reflected in his ascension to academic seats of power. From 1944 Mayr served as curator of the Whitney-Rothschild Collection at the American Museum of Natural History; he moved to Harvard University in 1953, where he became Alexander Agassiz professor of zoology, a chair he held until his retirement in 1975. In 1961, he also took over as director of Harvard's Museum of Comparative Zoology, a position he held until 1970.

An aggressive polemicist, Mayr became a contentious figure

in American biology whose role has been compared to Thomas Huxley, the nineteenth-century supporter of evolution often called "Darwin's bulldog." Mayr has carefully and at length argued the multiple aspects of evolution; and its historical development became important to Mayr later in his career, as exemplified in his massive and comprehensive *Growth of Biological Thought*, published in 1982. Together with THEODOSIUS DOBZHANSKY [67] and GEORGE GAYLORD SIMPSON [78], he also became spokesperson for the "modern synthesis" in contemporary biology, writing such works as *One Long Argument*. Mayr insists on the integrity of biology and respect for the scientific consensus concerning the basic evidence of evolution—that, in spite of disagreements, the various legitimate competing viewpoints "do not question any of the basic theses of the synthetic theory; they merely have different answers for some of the pathways of evolution."

Primarily interested in concepts, Mayr views biology as an autonomous science with a unique outlook and stresses its concern with the natural history and development of species. He is not impressed by the mathematical arguments of population genetics. And while he accepts the "strictly physicochemical nature of all processes at the so-called cellular and molecular level," he rejects the reductionism implied in much of molecular biology. Mayr's iconoclastic attitude toward physics deserves to be recorded. Once reminded of Francis Crick's hypothesis that life may have arrived on Earth from outer space, he scoffed, "Ah, Francis Crick is a physicist and thinks like a physicist. He knows next to nothing about the biology of higher organisms. Forget about it!...It's always some physicist who comes up with these totally nonsensical theories about biology."

Mayr is pessimistic in his outlook when broadened to examine social and political life, and his reflections are in part those of a transplanted and cultivated European. He confesses to being astonished by what he discovered in American culture: "The majority of people are incredibly ignorant," Mayr has said. "I have lived in New York City suburbs, where, in most of my neighbor's houses, not a single book was to be found. It's shocking, but there is nothing that can be done except to try to improve our schools." He has characterized American elementary education as "absolutely horrible."

The prolific author of over six hundred fifty papers and

twenty major books, Ernst Mayr has received many honors, including the Sarton medal, given in the history of science, and the National Medal of Science. His wife of fifty-five years, Margarete Simon, died in 1990, but John Rennie, visiting Mayr in his ninetieth year, found a "neatly-dressed, gray-haired figure walking without benefit of a cane. His vitality strips at least a decade off his appearance." Indeed, he told Rennie, a couple of days earlier he had noticed that his kitchen floor was dirty. "So I got a bucket," said Ernst Mayr, "and I washed it."

66

Charles Sherrington
and Neurophysiology
1857–1952

At the end of the nineteenth century, Charles Sherrington explained the basic operation of the neuromuscular system. During the Renaissance, Leonardo da Vinci had observed the movements of frogs with their heads cut off, and over one hundred years later René Descartes offered a mechanistic definition of the reflex action in animals. ALBRECHT VON HALLER [42] showed that nerve fibers in the body lead to the spinal cord and the brain. But throughout most of the nineteenth century, even after anatomists had mapped parts of it, the nervous system was viewed as a diffuse "protoplasmic network." Sherrington's explanation of how a system of nerve cells can control thousands of ordinary acts and events in the human body was a prepotent achievement—and the culmination of four hundred years of observation.

Charles Scott Sherrington was born on November 27, 1857, in Islington, a suburb of London. His father, James Norton Sherrington, was a physician who died while Charles was still young. His mother, Anne Brookes Sherrington, remarried, to Caleb Rose, who was not only a physician but a cultivated gentleman, classically educated, and interested in geology and archeology. Rose had a strong influence on Sherrington, both in his decision to study medicine and in his broad intellectual reach. Although interested in art and philosophy, Sherrington attended the Royal College of Surgeons and received his medical degree from Gonville and Caius College, Cambridge, in 1884. Sherrington was still a student when his first paper was read to the Royal Society: an anatomical study of a dog whose forebrain had been removed, with little apparent consequence, by F. L. Goltz several years before.

In his early career, however, Sherrington was not committed to neurology. In 1885 he and other physicians traveled to Spain to investigate a cholera epidemic, where at considerable danger to themselves they performed numerous autopsies on victims. Subsequently, he met RUDOLF VIRCHOW [17] in Berlin and took a six-week course with ROBERT KOCH [44]. For a time he intended to enter bacteriology, but when he returned to England, Sherrington began to turn away from pathology. He came under the sway of the noted physiologist W. H. Gaskell and opted to work on the problems of the spinal cord and reflex action. In 1887 he was appointed lecturer in systematic physiology at St. Thomas's Hospital and elected a fellow at Cambridge.

When Sherrington began his work, relatively little was known of the nervous system, and the theory of the cell as the basic unit of life, established by Virchow, was scarcely a generation old. The nerves were known to have electrical properties, and some of the spinal cord had been sectioned and mapped. Initially, Sherrington continued research in this vein, and in 1891 published his "Note on the Knee Jerk." By 1894 he recognized a fundamental difference between motor nerves, which deliver instructions to muscles, and the proprioceptors (a term he coined), which transmit information in the opposite direction. As a consequence, a picture began to emerge in which the central nervous system performs an integrative role in coordinating and operating the muscular apparatus.

Blinking, walking, breathing, and a myriad of other actions share a general explanation, which Sherrington provided. When the knee is tapped sharply, for example, the leg extends involuntarily and immediately falls back. Certain muscles contract to force the leg to straighten while others relax. Sherrington developed the concepts of innervation and inhibition to describe this process, which involves a reciprocal connection between the two sets of muscles. Many other relationships of the same order were discovered throughout the nervous system, and Sherrington formulated his generalization in the following way: "The whole quantitative grading of the operations of the spinal cord and brain appears to rest upon mutual interaction between the two central processes, excitation and inhibition, the one no less important than the other."

The thorough explanation of what is sometimes called the "vegetative system" of involuntary neuromuscular control is by no means Sherrington's alone, but it was he who integrated into the growing body of neurological knowledge major concepts and discoveries made by others. Most notably, he incorporated the insight that the nervous system is not made up of fibers but of cells, which belongs to the Spanish neuroanatomist Santiago Ramón y Cajal. Recognizing the interface between Cajal's notion of nerve cell and his own work on reflexes, Sherrington in 1897 suggested the term *synapse* to describe the transmission of impulse from one of these neurons to the next, creating an evanescent but reliable pathway. The notion of the synapse put an end to the "reticular" theory that nerve fibers formed a diffuse protoplasmic network throughout the body.

When *The Integrative Action of the Nervous System* was published in 1906, Sherrington was compared to SIR ISAAC NEWTON [1] and to WILLIAM HARVEY [38]. The book immediately became a standard and remains the classic text in neurophysiology. In 1913, Sherrington was named Wayneflete professor of physiology at Oxford, but World War I soon interrupted his research. During the war Sherrington, then in his fifties, took unskilled jobs in factories in order to study the problem of fatigue for the British War Office. After the war he continued his neurological work and served as president of the Royal Society from 1920 to

1925. At Oxford, Sherrington acquired an international reputation, and his influence was spread worldwide by his students. His *Reflex Activity of the Spinal Cord* was published in 1932, the year in which he was awarded the Nobel Prize for medicine or physiology, shared with Edgar D. Adrian.

Sherrington's work on the central nervous system extended to the brain. He published a mapping of the motor cortex in the primate brain, which encouraged further research. In addition, he brought evolutionary concepts to bear on neurophysiology and neurology, showing that the higher centers of the central nervous system have an inhibitory effect on the lower centers. However, in *The Brain and Its Mechanisms* in 1933, he declared, "We have to regard the relation of mind to brain as not merely unsolved but still devoid of a basis for its very beginning." For his acceptance of and reflections on mind/body dualism, Sherrington was sometimes called "the philosopher of the nervous system." But it should be pointed out that, although advances have been made and a variety of theories proposed, a satisfactory explanation of brain function is still lacking today.

Sherrington also wrote for a general audience. He published the expansive, widely read *Man on His Nature* in 1940, espousing what has been called a sort of "evolutionary pantheism." He also wrote a biography of the French physiologist Jean Ferel, a book on Goethe, and a volume of poetry, *The Assaying of Brabantius*.

In addition to his literary pursuits, Sherrington was a bibliophile (he collected incunabula), and an art aficionado; he loved music and drama. He had a special affection for the French language and culture, and he and his wife frequently visited France. Sherrington had married Ethel Mary Wright in 1891, and their only child, Carr E. R. Sherrington, became a well-known economist. Sherrington's sensitive side caused his biographer, Ragnar Granit, to comment, "The wide emotional register of a Sherrington, a Ramón y Cajal, a Pascal is one of the traits most difficult to reconcile with what is known about their work as great experimenters or accurate thinkers in wholly unemotional terms."

Charles Sherrington died at the age of ninety-five following a heart attack on March 4, 1952, at Eastbourne, Sussex.

67

Theodosius Dobzhansky
and the Modern Synthesis
1900–1975

In 1937 Theodosius Dobzhansky published his exceptionally influential *Genetics and the Origin of Species,* a tour de force in which both the chromosomal theory of inheritance and population genetics are integrated into the theory of natural selection of CHARLES DARWIN [4]. This was the first statement of the "modern synthesis," and together with the work of ERNST MAYR [65] and GEORGE GAYLORD SIMPSON [78], led to the robust neo-Darwinism we know today. A naturalist, geneticist, and evolutionary biologist, Dobzhansky over a long career wrote extensively on the broader issues of biological thought. "The most important contributions to the modern biological theory of

312

evolution," states Ernest Boesiger flatly, "have been accomplished by Dobzhansky."

Born on January 25, 1900, in Nemirov, Russia, Theodosius Dobzhansky was the son of Grigory Karlovich Doberzhansky, a mathematics instructor of Polish ancestry, and Sophia Vasilievna Voinarsky, whose family included both Russian Orthodox priests and the novelist Fyodor Dostoyevsky. Moving to Kiev after his father suffered an accident, Dobzhansky began attending the gymnasium in 1910. As a youth he became an avid collector, first of butterflies, then beetles, and finally ladybugs. With the outbreak of World War I, Dobzhansky barely escaped the draft. During the Russian Revolution he instead attended the University of Kiev, and passed his time at the local entomological society, collecting tens of thousands of insects. While civil war raged, he weathered a confusing succession of White Russian and Soviet governments, which brought hardship and uncertainty but also professional opportunities. After graduating from the University of Kiev in 1921, Dobzhansky became a lecturer in biology and engaged in practical work for the revolutionary soviets, investigating diseases of the sugar beet plant in 1922.

In the early 1920s Dobzhansky learned with enthusiasm of the confirmation by THOMAS HUNT MORGAN [62] of Mendelian inheritance in the common fruit fly, *Drosophila*. He soon moved from Kiev to the University of Petrograd (shortly after renamed Leningrad), where he began performing his own experiments with these insects. His first studies, however, were not in genetics per se, but efforts to understand mutations via the morphology, or physical construction, of the *Drosophila*. An assistant in the Laboratory of Genetics and Experimental Zoology, Dobzhansky worked under Iuril Filipchenko, one of the most influential Russian zoologists. Interested in Mendelian genetics, Filipchenko by the mid-1920s had formulated the distinction between *microevolution*, which appears at the level of the individual, and *macroevolution*, which operates on whole populations. These hierarchical concepts became important to Dobzhansky in his later work.

Dobzhansky's career took a turn in 1927, when, with Filipchenko's support, he traveled on a fellowship to the United States to work at Morgan's laboratory at Columbia University. Filipchenko, who soon fell from grace in the Russian Thermidor, died in 1930, and the political situation soon precluded

Dobzhansky's return. Before his death Filipchenko wrote Dobzhansky, encouraging him to remain with Morgan as long as he could, the better to become a "splendid morganoid." In fact, in the grimy fly room at Columbia, Dobzhansky gained Morgan's confidence and was invited to move with him to the California Institute of Technology in 1928. Dobzhansky was to remain based in the United States for the rest of his career.

While Dobzhansky learned the techniques of chromosomal analysis which Morgan had pioneered, as a trained naturalist he retained his interests in the larger issues of evolutionary theory. "My interest in genetics came from my interest in evolution [which] was philosophical," Dobzhansky later said, although this ran counter to the focus of Morgan and his associates. Dobzhansky made signal contributions to *Drosophila* research with work on chromosomal maps and analysis of the fine variations between different populations of insects. By 1935 he had formulated how species develop "isolating mechanisms" to ensure their integrity. More generally, he had constructed an intellectual bridge from Morgan's laboratory to the world of the naturalist. In 1936 Dobzhansky began publishing a series of major papers, "Genetics of Natural Populations"—which continued for the next forty years. Much of his influential research was performed on a particular species of fruit fly, the *Drosophila pseudoobscura*.

Dobzhansky's philosophical and experimental interests were combined during this period as he monitored an important movement toward quantified analysis. In 1918 Ronald Fischer had suggested that statistics could provide a way of understanding how genes behave in whole populations, and in 1930 he published his *Genetical Theory of Natural Selection*. Two years later J. B. S. Haldane published *Causes of Evolution,* which showed not only that natural selection could direct evolution over many generations but that dependence on widespread and frequent mutations was unnecessary. These basically mathematical analyses became for Dobzhansky the instruments of a new synthesis. They supported the notion that small changes on the level of the individual can, if favored by natural selection, generate tremendous changes in the species as a whole over a relatively short time.

In 1936 Dobzhansky delivered a series of lectures, published the following year as *Genetics and the Origin of Species,* in which he was able to present "a connected story" of the basic assumptions of the theory of evolution. Dobzhansky provides a hierarchical structure with a statistical basis. He views mutations and chromosomal change as a "first stage, or level, of the evolutionary process, governed entirely by the laws of the physiology of the individuals." Genetic mutations at this level may flourish or be lost by chance. On a second level, however, "The influence of selection, migration, and geographical isolation then mold the genetic structure of populations into new shapes, in conformity with the secular environment and the ecology, especially the breeding habits of the species." Thus, natural selection operates on whole species as the environment produces "historical changes in the living population." Finally, Dobzhansky points to a third level, which is the development of mechanisms to preserve the species as distinct—whether through geographic isolation, sexual isolation, or hybrid sterility.*

As one of the most significant results of this theoretical formulation, Dobzhansky could now describe how experiments on whole populations might be conducted in nature, based on mathematical predictions. *Genetics and the Origin of Species* "signalizes very clearly something which can only be called the Back-to-Nature movement." wrote Leslie C. Dunn at the time. "The methods learned in the laboratory are good enough now to be put to the test in the open and applied in that ultimate laboratory of biology, free nature itself." Now that the relationship between genetics and natural selection was understood, Dobzhansky could make his classic formulation, "Nothing in biology makes sense except in the light of evolution."

When Dobzhansky's work was combined with that of Ernst Mayr from ornithology and George Gaylord Simpson from paleontology, the resulting neo-Darwinism laid down what is sometimes called "one long argument" for understanding biological phenomena from the macroscopic to the molecular level. The modern synthesis remains essentially valid to the present. It has had the highly practical effect of reconciling the world of naturalists and taxonomists with that of geneticists. "For the first time," writes EDWARD O. WILSON [83], "new data from the field and laboratory defined the differences among species and races with precision, illuminating the nature of variation within popu-

---

*The mule is a well-known example of hybrid sterility. A male mule, born of a male donkey and female horse, is generally sterile. Like many hybrids, the mule is more durable than either parent, and will work for you for twenty years, as William Faulkner once said, for the pleasure of kicking you once.

lations in chromosomes and genes, and the steps of microevolution."

In 1940 Dobzhansky moved from Caltech to Columbia University, and from 1962 until 1970 he was associated with Rockefeller University. He continued his work in technical genetics until the end of his career. Dobzhansky enjoyed field work, and during the 1940s undertook extensive visits to the Amazon Valley, Brazil, Peru, Argentina, Ecuador, and Columbia. He also translated (and thereby exposed) TROFIM LYSENKO [93] for bewildered Western biologists. But some of Dobzhansky's most significant contributions, after *Genetics and the Origin of Species* brought him considerable prestige, were his examinations, for a general audience, of the larger issues of evolutionary biology and its impact on society. This was a distinct shift in emphasis, which dates from the end of World War II.

In 1946 Dobzhansky's *Heredity, Race and Society,* written with Leslie C. Dunn, debunked racism and was a bestseller. His *Mankind Evolving* (1962) surveyed various aspects of human evolution, and investigated the influence of genetics on culture. Dobzhansky's world view, expressed in that book, finds a place for biological thought to interweave with psychoanalysis, art, aesthetics, and language. In 1973 his *Genetic Diversity and Human Equality* was also meant for a wide audience. Dobzhansky's thought encompassed both hereditarian and culturalist perspectives. At the time he wrote, prior to the more recent and bitter nature vs. nurture debates, he represented a basically environmentalist view from the most advanced outposts of biology. Politically a proud liberal, Dobzhansky valued the individual; he was both convinced of the significance of genetic endowment and believed in the determining influences of environment and culture.

Unlike Mayr or Simpson, the other major architects of the modern synthesis, Dobzhansky had a lifelong belief in God. He belonged to the Eastern Orthodox Church, and at the end of his life, when he suffered from cancer, he prayed every day. He believed religion should adapt to scientific progress, and, according to Costas B. Krimbas, "saw himself as aiding the evolution of religious thinking in a scientifically evolving world." His belief that the universe is anthropocentric, at odds with most scientific thought in the twentieth century, is the subject of *The Biology of Ultimate Concern,* published in 1967. "Man, this mysterious product of the world's evolution," he writes, "may also be its protagonist, and eventually its pilot."

Theodosius Dobzhansky was covered with honors in his later years. Among many others, he won the Darwin Medal in 1959 and was awarded the National Medal of Science in 1964. In 1924 he married Natalia Petrovna Sivertseva, also a biologist, and they had one daughter, Sophia Dobzhansky Coe, who became an anthropologist. After leaving Rockefeller University in 1970, Dobzhansky was associated with the University of California at Davis. At the end of his life Dobzhansky suffered from leukemia, and he died on December 18, 1975. He is buried in Mather, California, the site of a botanical field station where he often worked, rode horseback, and collected *Drosophila*.

68

Max Delbrück
and the Bacteriophage
1906–1981

A key figure in determining the importance of the DNA molecule, which encodes genetic information in the cell, Max Delbrück helped to export the twentieth-century revolution in physics to biology. No fundamental discovery belongs to Delbrück, but his influence was decisive, according to William Hayes, as "the pioneer of a new approach to an understanding of fundamental biological processes." Developing a model of genetic transmission through the simplest of organisms, the bacteriophage, Delbrück founded bacterial genetics and laid open one of the principal paths to the discovery of the structure of deoxyribonucleic acid. An influence upon ERWIN SCHRÖDINGER

[18], whose *What Is Life?* led both FRANCIS CRICK [33] and JAMES WATSON [49] to molecular biology, Delbrück was the "fastidious aesthetician of science," writes Horace Freeland Judson, "…in this drama a messenger."

Max Delbrück was born on September 4, 1906, in suburban Berlin, the youngest child of Hans and Lina Delbrück. His father was a professor of history at the University of Berlin, a liberal member of the intelligentsia, and editor of a magazine devoted to politics. Lina Delbrück descended from a medical family, and her grandfather was the world-famous chemist JUSTUS VON LIEBIG [36]. Max grew up in a highly intellectual environment, emerging from this distinguished background both ambitious and sensitive. He had complex feelings toward his parents. His hardworking father was about sixty years old when he was born, and Max experienced considerable ambivalence as an adolescent, according to his biographer Ernst Fischer, "manifesting subconscious hatred and jealousy mixed with admiration and respect." In later life, Delbrück attributed his own tendency for tireless work to his love for his mother, as a strategy, he said, "to outshine his father."

Finishing secondary school as valedictorian, Max Delbrück was first taken up with astronomy, which he studied at the University of Tübingen beginning in 1924. At the University of Göttingen, to which he transferred in 1926, he shifted the focus of his interest to quantum theory, then taking its definitive form. Delbrück arranged to make up for the physics he had missed as an undergraduate and received his doctorate in 1930 under the guidance of MAX BORN [32]. The following year Delbrück studied in Copenhagen at the institute headed by NIELS BOHR [3], undertaking research with George Gamow, and in 1932 he became an assistant to Lise Meitner, the famed German physicist. He published fundamental papers on the scattering of light and thermodynamics as understood via statistical mechanics and quantum theory; but these were only a prelude to his work in biology, to which he began to migrate as early as 1932.

Quantum theory had put an end to strict causality in physics, and Delbrück found some of its philosophical implications highly appealing. In a famous lecture on "Light and Life" on August 15, 1932, Neils Bohr described the dilemma of quantum mechanics by which, for example, light cannot be measured with infinite precision, and so a statistical analysis must be adopted. Human perception set limits on the description of nature, and Bohr wondered if life processes, too, might be governed by a similar kind of uncertainty. Bohr's lecture had a singular influence upon Delbrück. Obtaining a copy of the speech, Delbrück studied it in fine detail and soon began investigating such phenomena as photosynthesis, population genetics, and natural selection.

Rather to his surprise, Delbrück initially discovered that it did appear possible to provide an atomic model that fully accounted for the results of genetic mutations. Whatever the genetic material consisted of, ordinary chemistry could explain its fundamental constancy, as well as its instability via mutations. Bohr's idea was fruitful, but not correct. It *was* plausible to hypothesize that life processes can be fully understood. Genes behaved like molecules, and it was logical to suppose that they were molecules.

With the Nazis in power Delbrück recognized that it would be impossible for him to continue to work in Germany, and in 1937 he emigrated to the United States, where he remained until the end of his life. From 1937 to 1939 he was on the faculty at the California Institute of Technology. He then moved to Vanderbilt University, where he spent the years of World War II as a physics instructor. But he also continued his research, and, seeking a reliable and simple form of life on which to conduct experiments, Delbrück soon began to study the viruses known as bacteriophages. From this work derives his most direct influence on molecular biology.

Bacteriophages are a type of virus that invades bacteria and uses the host's cells to reproduce. The "phages" had been discovered early in the twentieth century and were initially considered a curiosity. With the development of dark-field microscopy, they were seen to be made up of a nucleic acid, known as DNA, with a protein covering. Without divining the significance of DNA, Delbrück recognized that bacteriophages—on the border between the living and nonliving—could be used to study the reproduction and transmission of genetic information. "This seemed to me," Delbrück later said, "just beyond my wildest dreams of doing simple experiments on something like atoms in biology."

Indeed, Delbrück's accomplishment was to devise experimental and statistical techniques of great precision for the study of these elementary forms of life. How the tadpole-shaped phage transmitted genetic information to the bacteria remained unknown, but clearly it was accomplished either through its DNA molecule or its protein sheath. It turned out, moreover, that the intact phage never physically entered the bacteria from which its offspring somehow emerged. A series of important papers by Delbrück, in collaboration with Salvador Luria, attracted widespread attention when they were published in 1943. Delbrück and Luria soon established what became known as the "phage group" of researchers. Delbrück's "phage treaty" of 1944 brought an essential order to the inquiry, ensuring that only certain strains of bacteriophage were used.

Delbrück, now of considerable renown, in 1945 began a summer course on phages at the laboratory at Cold Spring Harbor, Long Island. It attracted a number of physicists, biochemists, and biologists, and Delbrück began holding annual phage meetings two years later. At Caltech, where Delbrück returned to teach in 1947, his laboratory became "the phage group's Vatican," according to one of his colleagues, "where most of the disciples of what was later to be called the 'informational school of molecular biology' took their orders." Modeled on the Copenhagen Institute of Niels Bohr, Delbrück's phage group was, as Horace Freeland Judson wrote in *The Eighth Day of Creation*, "one of the rare refuges of the twentieth century, a republic of the mind, a glimpse of the commonwealth of intellect held together by the subtlest bonds, by the excitement of understanding, the promise of the subject, the authentic freedom of the style."

The yield of the phage studies became clear toward the end of World War II. Careful experiments by Oswald Avery, at the Rockefeller Institute (now Rockefeller University), indicated that DNA, rather than protein, might contain the genetic information. Phages, which are little more than lumps of DNA wrapped in protein, provided an excellent means of verifying such an idea. They "make themselves known," wrote Delbrück, "by the bacteria they destroy, as a small boy announces his presence when a piece of cake disappears." In 1946 it was discovered that phages could mutate, and in 1952 Alfred Chase and Martha Hershey performed a famous experiment in which chemically tagged phages and bacteria were mixed in a Waring blender. They showed that the phage's modus operandi was to attach itself to a bacterial cell membrane, then inject its DNA into its host.

All these results were highly suggestive. Then, in 1952, the mechanism for genetic transmission was elucidated, when James Watson and Francis Crick discovered the double-stranded, helical structure of DNA. Receiving a letter from Watson—who had been writing him monthly reports on the progress of their research—Delbrück was immediately convinced. He was soon comparing the Watson-Crick discovery to the elucidation by ERNEST RUTHERFORD [19] of the structure of the atom at the beginning of the century. And he wrote to Watson, "I have the feeling that if your structure is true, and if its suggestions concerning the nature of replication have any validity at all, then all hell will break loose, and theoretically biology will enter into a most tumultuous phase."

In the last phase of his career, Delbrück studied problems of sensory perception and reflex in organisms such as fungi, hoping that he could again make major contributions to physiology. This work was not so productive as his work with phages. Delbrück also played a role in establishing the Institute of Genetics in Cologne, which he continued to visit and work at on a regular basis until 1963. In 1969, for his work in genetics Max Delbrück was awarded the Nobel Prize with Alfred Hershey and Salvador Luria. He retired from Caltech in 1977.

Meeting Delbrück in 1972, Horace Freeland Judson described him as "quick, courteous, accessible, subtle, aware, contemptuous of pretense." At once charming and critical, Delbrück enjoyed practical jokes. He married Mary Adeline Bruce in 1941, and they had two sons and two daughters. At the end of his life he fell ill from heart disease, eye problems, and multiple myeloma. Max Delbrück died on March 10, 1981.

69

Jean Baptiste Lamarck
and the Foundations of Biology

1744–1829

Jean Baptiste Lamarck has long been associated with the theory that acquired traits can be inherited, that a violinist, for example, can pass on to his or her children the manual dexterity learned by years of practicing scales. This theory has long since been discredited, and Lamarck's reputation has suffered, especially in the United States and England. Only recently have his contributions been properly evaluated in biology texts.

Lamarck, who died blind and impoverished, is in fact one of the great historical figures in biology. He remains a founder of the science in spite of the antipathy of CHARLES DARWIN [4] and the association of his name with the ideological aims of TROFIM LYSENKO [93]. In breaking with the notion of fixed and immutable

323

species, Lamarck's positive influence on evolutionary thought is quite strong, and he was an important authority for the geologist CHARLES LYELL [28]. "One wishes," wrote Loren Eiseley, redressing the balance in *Darwin's Century*, "that Darwin and Huxley...might have been just a little kinder to that old man whose bones are lost among the forgotten millions of the Paris poor."

Jean Baptiste Pierre Antoine de Monet Lamarck was born on August 1, 1744, in Byzantine-le-Petit, a manor in the Somme of which his father was the lord. About 1755, at age eleven, he was sent to a school run by Jesuits in the expectation that he would become a priest. He preferred adventure. At age sixteen he joined the army at Bergen-op-Zoom, fought in the Seven Years' War, apparently acquitting himself well, and won a commission for bravery. He remained in the army after the war's end in 1763, leaving only in 1768.

Beginning about 1769 Lamarck studied medicine in Paris while working in a bank. He was also interested in the new discoveries in chemistry and meteorology, but his most important early work proved to be a classification of plants, published as *Flore française* in 1778. Lamarck developed a particularly useful, dichotomous key to the classification that allowed for the quick identification of plants. The book was an immediate success, and soon Lamarck was elected to the academy of sciences, at the young age of thirty-five.

With the help of COMTE DE BUFFON [23], the aging but still active eminence in natural history, Lamarck became a botanist to King Louis XVI and, subsequently, in 1781, the conservator of the herbarium of the Royal Gardens. This institution reopened as the Museum of Natural History after the French Revolution, and Lamarck was named its professor of zoology. He was charged with organizing the collections of the orders which the classifier CARL LINNAEUS [76] had named *Insecta* and *Vermes*. For these animals Lamarck created the distinction still used today, calling them invertebrates. At the turn of the century he published several books based on his researches, including his *Système des animaux sans vertèbres* in 1801, and *Philosophie zoölogique* in 1809. His colossal *Histoire naturelle des animaux sans vertèbres* was published between 1815 and 1822 and represents the culmination of his labors.

In classifying the invertebrates, Lamarck described and named numerous species with great precision. The philosophical implications of taxonomy did not escape him. He became acutely aware of the variability of species together with the basic unity of living things, and Lamarck may be credited with insisting on the radical distinction between organic and inorganic. These basic distinctions enabled Lamarck to view the complex world of plants and animals as one of growing diversity. Adumbrating Darwin, Lamarck recognized that a vast amount of time was involved in the evolutionary process, and that the notion of stability derived from the slow rate of change. Lamarck proposed, finally, four laws governing the organization of development of animals. They embodied his eighteenth-century notion that species would tend toward perfection, that there was a relationship between the importance of an organ and its actual use (or disuse), and, most memorably, that animals would transmit to their offspring what-ever had changed structurally within. In addition, Lamarck viewed desire as an active principle in evolution.

Lamarck's laws proved not to be tenable. But it should be noted that some such hypothesis as Lamarck's theory of inheri-tance of acquired characteristics was virtually inevitable. Once the idea of immutable species was abandoned, the obvious adaptation of organisms to their environment required an expla-nation. To take a famous example, how *do* giraffes get their long necks? Only gradually did Lamarckian ideas come to be at odds with the Darwinian hypothesis of evolution through natural selection and with the later theory of speciation through muta-tion. Moreover, Lamarck's theory could be and was tested. A whole body of evidence accumulated to falsify it. Scientists exchanged ovaries in black and white fowl, examined the wings of moths over many generations, studied spotted salamanders and the cabbage butterfly, and persecuted rats. Nothing they did ever vindicated the idea that acquired characteristics are transmissible.

Lamarck continued to work until the end of his life, though he fell from favor with the scientific establishment and was strongly criticized by Baron Cuvier, who rejected the idea of transmutation of species and held to the idea of catastrophism rather than evolution. Though he was blind in old age, "He continued his work," writes Charles Bocquet, "with unyielding courage, until the end of his life. He died in Paris, misun-derstood by some, forgotten by others." When the end came, on December 18, 1829, many of his papers were sold to pay the cost of his funeral.

70

William Bayliss
and Modern Physiology

1860–1924

The discovery of hormones, at the turn of the twentieth century, set the stage for broad advances throughout medicine. Chemical regulators of a host of functions in animals and plants, most hormones in humans are manufactured in the endocrine glands and distributed to various sites in the body through the blood-stream. In this way they regulate growth, metabolism, reproduction, and the work of the various organs. They are potent in tiny amounts, and the hormonal system represents a basic form of organization and control necessary for the integrated function of complex organisms. It is not surprising that manipulation of hormones has become a major avenue of medical treatment, and their synthesis, through genetic recombination, is a highly profitable business with a shining future in therapeutics.

William Bayliss discovered how hormones work a century ago, and his biography reads like a life of one of the saints. In addition to unraveling the mystery of the hormone, secretin, Bayliss also performed electrocardiograms before they were invented, investigated how the blood vessels constrict and dilate, and found out much about enzymes. He was one of the founders of modern physiology and biochemistry, honored and esteemed by his colleagues, but he was slandered by the antivivisectionists, who accused him of being hateful toward experimental dogs. He was forced to sue and win a judgment against them. Wealthy through his family, he was liberal, even socialist, and cared deeply for the well-being of others. During World War I, when soldiers were dying from the physical shock caused by their wounds, Bayliss found a way to stanch the bleeding, and he saved thousands of lives. It is not surprising that his brilliantly written *Principles of Physiology*, one of the first basic summaries, is a literary ancestor of the huge textbooks medical students read today.

William Maddock Bayliss was born on May 2, 1860, in Wednesbury, a town in Staffordshire, an industrial region in the English Midlands. His mother was Jan Maddock, who died when he was young, and his father, Moses Bayliss, was originally a blacksmith who became a prosperous manufacturer. After attending a private school, William spent a short time working in his father's firm of Bayliss, Jones, and Bayliss, but he preferred science. As a result, as was still sometimes done, he was apprenticed to a medical practitioner and worked in a local hospital. But in 1880, when his father retired and the family moved to Hampstead, outside London, William was able to attend University College. He received his bachelor of science degree in 1882 and began medical studies. After failing the anatomy examination, however, he decided to abandon medicine and concentrate on physiology. He moved to Oxford in 1885, received his doctorate in 1888, then returned for good to University College, initially as a teaching assistant.

In 1890 Bayliss formed a pivotal friendship with Ernest Henry Starling, who had trained as a physician. "Bayliss was the more fundamental and erudite, but of a retiring disposition," wrote Charles L. Evans, "Starling was a pragmatic and forceful extrovert, with an essentially medical outlook." Their collaboration was a great success, and over the next decade the pair undertook a series of researches which applied some of the new discoveries in electricity to physiology. Using the recently invented capillary electrometer, they were able to study the electrical activity of the heart. They showed that the heartbeats of frogs and tortoises were electrically triphasic and went on to find the same was true of humans, using themselves as subjects. They also sought to describe the working of the vasomotor system—how the blood vessels are controlled by the nerves. But Bayliss and Starling made their most enduring contribution in 1902: they discovered the hormone function.

Sir Charles Martin, who was present in the laboratory, recorded the crucial experiment for posterity. Bayliss and Starling cut open an anesthetized dog and injected some hydrochloric acid into the duodenum. They were not surprised when the pancreas started to work. Indeed, some years before, Ivan Pavlov had discovered that stimulating certain nerves led to the secretion of digestive juices. But then Bayliss and Starling tied off a loop of the intestine and severed those nerves so that the intestine was connected only by blood vessels to the rest of the body. When this cut-off part of the intestine received hydrochloric acid, Bayliss and Starling had the *same* result: The pancreas started to function. "It was a great afternoon," wrote Sir Charles. The pathway to excitation, Bayliss and Starling had discovered, was chemical as well as nervous and could take place through the bloodstream. They went on to isolate the substance, which is manufactured in the membrane of the small intestine and exported to the pancreas, where it signals the need for digestive juice. It came to be known as *secretin,* one of a whole class of substances known as *hormones.* (Starling coined both terms in 1905.)

Bayliss's career was interrupted in 1903 when he was accused in the London newspapers of having failed to anesthetize a dog during a public lecture on secretin. Known ever since as the "Brown Dog" libel action—and giving a new twist to Pavlov's saying that "Appetite spells gastric juice"—Bayliss fought back in the courts. The accusation, based on reports from two Swedish antivivisectionists, was false, and Bayliss had the financial means to pursue the matter. He also had a kindly personality that bore up well in the courtroom. The trial, an international sensation, was widely reported in the newspapers. At its center was "a small brown mongrel allied to a terrier with short roughish hair." In the end Bayliss was awarded two thousand pounds in damages, which he used to create a research fund at the university. He also received a good deal of blasphemous and obscene hate mail.

During World War I, Bayliss made an important contribution to treating the wounded. All too commonly, hospitalized soldiers would appear to be recovering when, suddenly, they would experience "secondary shock." Their blood pressure would plummet, and they would die. Bayliss discovered that extensive wounding of the tissue led to the release of toxic substances into the blood. These toxins acted to dilate the small blood vessels and slowed the circulation. He found that injecting a solution of gum acacia into the veins could raise the blood pressure—which, in an era before blood transfusion, saved thousands of lives.

In 1914 Bayliss published *Principles of General Physiology*. It was described by Starling as a "revelation of the personality of the writer. It might almost be called an autobiography, and is indeed the history of a mind and its achievements." This is not hyperbole. In the *Principles* Bayliss not only treats all aspects of human physiology but evinces grace of style, recommends Kropotkin's *Mutual Aid,* and quotes Saint Paul. It has been called an "extension into the twentieth century" of the work of CLAUDE BERNARD [13]. In fact, in another tribute to Bayliss, his son has written, "One of the fascinations of the book is that it gives so well the feeling of historical continuity." At universities in the United States, the book was so much admired that Bayliss Clubs were formed to discuss it.

At the comfortable house where Bayliss lived in Hampstead, there were not only the regular "at homes"—required of university professors in those days—but also garden parties, tennis parties, and dinner parties. Bayliss supported women's suffrage, advocated birth control, and moved toward socialism in his later years. Students adored him. Bayliss had the good fortune to marry the sister of his collaborator Starling, and the couple's extremely happy life together was blessed with four children, one of whom became a well-known physiologist. Bayliss died after a short illness on August 27, 1924.

71

Noam Chomsky
and Twentieth-Century Linguistics

1928–

Linguistics can be traced historically to Sanskrit grammarians
of the fifth century B.C. as well as to Hellenic civilization. And
there evolved a long tradition of European scholars dedicated to
studying the rhetoric, grammar, etymology, and written texts of
early languages. In the twentieth century language became a
major topic in philosophy and a central concern in much anthropological research. But the field of linguistics itself was long
constrained, by empiricist and behaviorist disposition, from
moving beyond schemes of classification and taxonomy. This
changed, beginning in the 1950s, with a revolutionary departure
initiated by Noam Chomsky.

In a seminal analysis suggesting that all human language depends on innate mental structures, Chomsky founded what became known as transformational-generative linguistics. With his work, linguistics found a scientific footing consonant with other tools developed to probe human cognition and psychological development. The aim of Chomsky and the school of transformational grammar was "higher than that explicitly set by any previous group of linguists," writes R. H. Robins. "It amounts to nothing less than presenting in a description of a language everything that is implied by the linguistic competence of a native speaker." Today, after four decades of academic battle over a constantly evolving theory, Chomsky remains a major figure in contemporary linguistics.

The background of Avram Noam Chomsky is at once left-wing and scholarly. He was born on December 7, 1928, in Philadelphia, the son of William Chomsky, an educator and philologist, and Elsie Simonofsky, a teacher and author. Noam read his father's book on Hebrew grammar in proof at about the age of twelve. He attended the Oak Lane Country Day School, an experimental elementary school run by Temple University, and before reaching adolescence was writing editorials on the Spanish Civil War for his school newspaper. He later attended the prestigious Central High School in Philadelphia, graduating in 1945, and remained in the city to attend the University of Pennsylvania. There he began studying language and came under the determining influence of Zellig Harris, a linguist and political activist. Chomsky has said that he first learned about contemporary issues in linguistics from reading, in proof, Harris's *Methods in Structural Linguistics*.

While still an undergraduate, at the suggestion of Harris, Chomsky undertook a study of Hebrew. An ancient language undergoing a renaissance and transformation, by the 1940s it was "a spoken language of a rather normal type." Although he initially attempted to use ordinary methods, which called for the use of native speakers as informants, he found that he was mainly receiving information he already knew. "I therefore dropped the official procedures and just worked on the language as one would deal with any problem of science, using native informants for the counterpart of experiments (checking the consequences of hypotheses, etc.) when I didn't already know the facts." This led to a goal which was broader than that allowed by cataloging methods then in vogue. Chomsky attempted, as he later said, "to find a system of rules for generating the phonetic forms of sentences, that is, what is now called a generative grammar."

Working largely on his own, Chomsky turned his study of Hebrew into his undergraduate honors thesis. He received his bachelor's degree from the University of Pennsylvania in 1949, and his master's degree in linguistics two years later. In 1951 Chomsky was named a junior fellow by the Harvard Society of Fellows. He received his doctorate from the University of Pennsylvania in 1955, and began teaching linguistics and modern languages at the Massachusetts Institute of Technology.

Chomsky's connection to MIT, which he has maintained throughout his career, was noteworthy, not least because it put him close to the center of the development of information theory. "One could have thought—in fact, some people did think—that computers were going to permit the automation of discovery procedures in linguistics..." Chomsky later said. "But when I began to study these topics, I was quickly convinced that the prevailing assumptions were false and the popular models inadequate...." Retrospectively, it can also be seen that while mathematicians were successfully developing new computer languages, it was unlikely that linguistics could remain for long in a largely descriptive and taxonomic mode.

In 1956, at a meeting of the Institute of Radio Engineers, Chomsky delivered a paper on the prospect of a generative grammar that could be stated in more-or-less mathematical terms. In 1957 he published *Syntactic Structures*. A monograph of ten chapters, this seminal work changed the course of linguistics in the twentieth century. It contains several crucial, interrelated arguments.

Chomsky contended that a purely taxonomic approach to language construction would not yield basic principles without recourse to vague intuition and that structuralist linguistics had unnecessary, inherent deficits. He postulated that the syntax of any language—broadly, its grammatical structure—possesses some underlying lawfulness. With analysis of syntax a central issue, he suggested a quasi-mathematical formalism, from which could emerge the rules which govern the production of sentences. He showed in *Syntactic Structures* how this might be possible and set out a basic agenda "for a more general theory of language concerned with syntax and semantics and their points of connection."

When it was proposed, transformational grammar was much discussed, but it encountered considerable resistance from behaviorism, a psychological theory then championed by B. F. SKINNER [98]. Skinner's *Verbal Behavior*, also published in 1957, sought to account for language in simple terms of stimulus-response and reinforcement. Adopting elementary operationalist concepts while ignoring aspects of language which were not easy to describe or explain, Skinner was vulnerable to a variety of charges, including oversimplification. In a now-famous review of *Verbal Behavior* in 1959, Chomsky made a devastating critique of the behaviorist project, to which Skinner never replied. Behaviorism's "blank slate" approach could not account for children's exceptional capacity to rapidly learn something as complex as language. Rather, Chomsky argued, human beings are somehow specially designed to do this, with complex data-handling or "hypothesis-formulating" abilities. He explicitly allied himself with rationalist, Cartesian precepts which invoked the innateness of what he came to call a Language Acquisition Device.

Chomsky elaborated his project during the 1960s. His renown had become international with publication of "The Logical Basis of Linguistics Theory," in which he explained the basic difference between structural linguistics and his generative grammar. In the highly influential *Aspects of the Theory of Syntax*, published in 1965, Chomsky made some notable theoretical innovations and, together with others working along the same lines, proposed what he called the "standard theory." He introduced the notion of "linguistic competence" and suggested a fundamental cognitive ability to construct sentences while providing sets of rules to chart their generation. With a broad and increasingly explicit theory, by the mid-1960s there was already considerable discussion of a Chomskian revolution, as well as reaction to it, and a large number of graduate students entered the field.

Over the next twenty years, and continuing to the present, linguistics was reshaped by Chomsky's work, which spawned considerable research, much debate, and eventually what is sometimes described, with too much hyperbole, as the "language wars." A good deal of Chomsky's significance resided in the adaptability of his theory to psycholinguistics, one of the developing pillars of an emerging new science of cognitive psychology. The study of language acquisition, speech pathology, and sign language for the deaf have been areas of particular importance for Chomskian linguistics.

Generative grammar was also subject to numerous theoretical mutations and sundry quarrels, all as developments in such fields as molecular biology discredited earlier empiricist notions and lent broad support to Chomsky's idea of innate mental functioning. In 1994 Neil Smith could write in *Nature*: "After a decade of academic savagery in which the discipline was severely factionalized, it was Chomsky rather than the young Turks who emerged victorious." Chomsky's most recent work—sometimes characterized as a "second revolution"—has emphasized an effort to discover the "initial state" of a genetically driven ability to use language.

Another major area of Chomsky's thought lay partially outside the realm of language, in politics. Like RUDOLPH VIRCHOW [17] and several other great scientists, Chomsky acquired a left-wing political commitment when he was young, and it was later shaped by current issues. As a libertarian socialist, Chomsky became a strong critic of the United States, its pretensions to democracy, and its foreign policy. If "international law and elementary morality were operative," he wrote, "thousands of U.S. politicians and military planners would be regarded as candidates for Nuremburg-type trials." The selective morality by which the intellectual and political establishment operates is a source of much of Chomsky's outrage.

Chomsky wrote extensively on political issues beginning with the Vietnam War and was widely regarded as an effective rhetorician and dedicated activist. For his controversial views, he is sometimes compared to Thoreau. Chomsky's limitation as an antiestablishment voice is a seeming lack of the depth of human compassion and breadth of historical vision that drove Karl Marx in *Das Kapital* and has appeared in more recent thinkers such as Herbert Marcuse. Chomsky's works on government and politics include *American Power and the New Mandarins*, published in 1969, *Peace in the Middle East*, 1974, *Human Rights and American Foreign Policy*, published in 1978, and *Necessary Illusions*, 1989. He has collaborated with Edward Herman on several works, including

The Political Economy of Human Rights in 1979, and *Manufacturing Dissent: The Political Economy of the Mass Media* in 1988.

Noam Chomsky was made a full professor at the Massachusetts Institute of Technology in 1961; in 1966 he was named Ferrari P. Ward professor of foreign languages and linguistics; and a decade later he became Institute professor. He has also been a resident fellow at the Institute for Advanced Study at Princeton, the University of California at Berkeley, and the Harvard Center for Cognitive Studies. He married Carol Doris Schatz in 1949, and they have had three children.

72

Frederick Sanger
and the Genetic Code

1918–

At the foundation of genetics research, which today includes a gigantic effort to map the entire human genome—100,000 genes and 3 billion base pairs—is the work of Frederick Sanger, the British biochemist. An experimentalist rather than theoretician, his importance derives from two discoveries which were absolutely essential for progress in molecular biology. In 1954 Sanger was the first to fully analyze the arrangement of amino acids in a protein, insulin. Then, turning to the study of DNA itself, Sanger developed methods for deciphering long sequences of its nucleotides, in which is embedded the genetic code. These methods were the key to a series of technical breakthroughs having

336

enormous potential consequence for medical and biological research. "Thus, perhaps more than anyone else," writes Christopher Wills, "Sanger made the Human Genome Project and the
current ferment in human genetics possible." As a measure of
recognition, Sanger was twice awarded the Nobel Prize, and over
the past two decades his central role in the complex development
of molecular biology has become apparent.

Frederick Sanger was born on August 13, 1918, at Rend-
comb, Gloucestershire. He was the namesake of his father, a
physician, and Cicely Crewdson Sanger. Raised in reasonably
prosperous circumstances, although only an average student at
Bryanston School, in 1936 he was able to enter St. John's College,
Cambridge, which his father had attended. There he originally
planned to study medicine, but he developed an interest in
biochemistry, then a relatively new discipline. As was true for
others who began research in the same period, "The idea that
biology could be explained in terms of chemistry," Sanger later
said, "seemed an exciting one." He received a first-class bachelor's
degree in 1939 and was therefore able to continue his studies,
taking a Ph.D. in 1943, with a dissertation on the metabolism of
lysine, one of the amino acids. As a Quaker, he was exempt from
military service during World War II. From 1944 until 1951
Sanger worked at Cambridge on a fellowship for medical
research.

When Sanger entered the field of biochemistry, the confusions which had plagued it for a half-century were beginning to
clear up. The multitude of compounds in the cell were beginning
to be classified and understood, and the "lock and key" relationship between enzyme and substrate formulated by EMIL FISCHER
[46], was vindicated. Enzymes were finally understood to be
proteins, made up of amino acids having specific functions.
Indeed, the amino-acid composition of all proteins was becoming
apparent. One of the least complex, insulin, was undergoing
intensive study at the Cambridge laboratory of A. C. Chibnall,
where Sanger worked. Sanger continued this research.

Insulin is a hormone produced in pancreatic cells. It has the
crucial function of converting carbohydrates to the simple sugar
glucose and regulating its level in the blood. Without enough
insulin, humans develop diabetes and die. One of the most
famous discoveries in medicine dates from 1922, when Frederick
Banting and Charles Best used purified insulin to treat a young

man suffering from diabetes. Over the next two decades insulin was produced in crystalline form, and its various amino acids were identified. It was at this juncture that Sanger began his work.

In a lengthy and vitally important analysis, Sanger determined the specific order of insulin's two linked chains of amino acids. To label the ends of the chains, he employed a solution, since called Sanger's reagent. But the order of the amino acids themselves remained invisible until he discovered how to nest and analyze them (as peptide groups of amino acids) by the telltale stains they left as he filtered them through paper. By 1955, after nearly a dozen years' work, Sanger had a complete analysis of insulin—the significance of which was recognized immediately. In 1958 he was awarded the Nobel Prize for chemistry.

Discovering insulin's structure held out long-term promises for medicine; it also had immediate repercussions in the rapidly expanding field of molecular biology. It proved—for the first time beyond doubt—that combinations of amino acids alone constitute proteins. Not long afterward, FRANCIS CRICK [33] articulated the notion that the major task of the genetic material, DNA, is to manufacture the great variety of proteins, each with its specialized function. Understanding exactly how DNA contained and disseminated protein-building instructions then became a major challenge.

A preliminary step before Sanger's research in nucleic acids could begin was deciphering the genetic code. About 1961 experiments showed that various triplets, or groups of three nucleotides located along the DNA strand, constituted *codons*. These codons stand for the various amino acids.* They thus constitute a set of instructions for assembling amino acids in a specific order. When complete, they naturally fold themselves into proteins. A specific length of DNA, copied onto a template of ribonucleic acid (RNA) generates this assembly according to a principle which is sometimes stated: *DNA makes RNA makes protein*. There is no gainsaying the significance of this finding. Humans by dry body weight are 50 percent protein.

---

*Each of the various codons is a combination of the four bases of RNA: Uracil [U], Cytosine [C], Adenine [A], Guanine [G]. Thus, for example, the amino acid Cysteine has two codons, *UGU* and *UGC*. (DNA bears the same code but Thymine [T] takes the place of Uracil.) Together, the codons comprise the genetic code.

A nucleotide is one of the bases together with a sugar and phosphate, which together constitute a "rung" on the helical "ladder."

In 1962 Sanger joined the Medical Research Council Laboratory of Molecular Biology at Cambridge University. He was ready, after several "lean years" in which he had made few original contributions, to begin to study DNA and RNA. He and his laboratory colleagues undertook to find ways to analyze, or sequence, the order of the nucleotides which embed genetic information. Sanger's research, which would take years, involved adapting, adopting, and developing procedures for reading out the long succession of bases on a length of RNA or a single strand of DNA.

As some of the complex molecular processes of DNA chemistry were identified, new strategies for sequencing the nucleotides became possible. Thus, at first, Sanger had only methods similar to those he employed with insulin. By 1968 he had managed to decode a length of RNA having 120 nucleotides, then a record. But much faster and less cumbersome techniques were necessary. By the early 1970s, rather than break down DNA into fragments, Sanger began attempting to build up a copy of a strand of DNA using radioactively labeled nucleotides.

Sanger employed several methods with this building-up approach. Applying DNA polymerase, a newly discovered catalyst, to a strand of DNA, and supplying the various radioactively labeled nucleotides, Sanger was able to synthesize and identify ever longer fragments. When he found that he could control the operation of the DNA polymerase if certain bases were left out, Sanger invented what he called a "plus-minus" method of sequencing, which was "the best idea I have ever had, being original and ultimately successful." And he found that the sequencing could be further governed by using chemically altered bases as terminal links in the chain. The result, an ordered, labeled group of fragments of DNA, could then be forced through a gel using a method that electrically separates them by length. In each fragment the nucleotides are clearly visible as small bands, segregated in four rows, each corresponding to one of the bases. In 1974 Sanger began using these and other methods to sequence the relatively simple Phi X174 virus; four years later he published its full sequence of 5,386 bases. This, the longest strand sequenced up to that time, was a high point of Sanger's career. Subsequent progress was rapid, then exponential.

In 1980 Sanger received a second Nobel Prize for chemistry, shared with Walter Gilbert and Paul Berg, in recognition of what promised to become, in the next decade, a biological revolution. The ability to decode DNA implied new techniques for manipulating genetic material in all sorts of ways, including the manufacture of specific genes to produce certain proteins. In 1982 the human insulin gene, inserted into bacteria, became the first of many products of recombinant DNA technology.

The prospect of sequencing the entire human genome—a five-foot strand of DNA, 50 billionths of an inch wide, containing 3 billion base pairs—came under discussion in the mid-1980s, and the possibility advanced rapidly with the help of still faster, more sophisticated, and automated methods of sequencing. In the United States it became a broad, government-sponsored project led for a time by JAMES WATSON [49]. By the mid-1990s it was drawing frequent headlines as the "code of codes."

Frederick Sanger stopped doing original research in 1983, and five years later, at age seventy, retired from the laboratory to his home in nearby Swaffam Bulbeck. Although he had not expected to retire so young, "The possibility seemed surprisingly attractive, especially as our work had reached a climax with the DNA sequencing method and I rather felt that to continue would be something of an anticlimax." He tends to his garden, sails, and lives with his wife, Margaret Joan Howe, whom he married in 1940, and with whom he fathered three children.

73

Lucretius
and Scientific Thinking

c. 98–55 B.C.

The single surviving work of Lucretius, a great Roman poet of antiquity, is a long didactic poem that resonates with scientific thinking as we understand it today. The skeptical and inquiring sensibility of Lucretius was lost to Christian dogma during the Middle Ages, but when a single ravaged copy of *De rerum natura* was found in Italy in 1417, he reentered history with considerable force. Lucretius was responsible for bringing to Renaissance Europe an infusion of Epicurean thought and the atomism of Democritus. He was an influence upon the mechanical philosophers as well as upon ISAAC NEWTON [1] and many figures of the Enlightenment.

Nothing of substance is known of the life of Titus Lucretius Carus. He came of age during the cruel and dangerous reign of Sulla and lived to see the rise, though not the assassination, of Julius Caesar. A general view of this period in Roman history, borne out in the work of Lucretius, is that the ruling class had lost much of its former integrity and become known for its selfish and arrogant character. In addition, a significant and oppressed urban population had emerged, and brigandage was rife. Lucretius was about twenty years old when Spartacus, the gladiator and rebel, staged his uprising of fugitive slaves. The Roman senator Cicero, who had been forced into exile and was devoting himself to literature, wrote in a letter to a brother, around 55 B.C., that the poems of Lucretius "show many glimpses of genius, yet also of art."

De rerum natura is addressed to a politician, Memmius, praetor and later governor of Bithynia, who was reputed to be unsavory and unworthy of Lucretius's poetry. It is in great part a reprise of the philosophy of Epicurus (341–271 B.C.), the Greek thinker who had been influenced by Democritus (c. 470–360 B.C.), the founder of atomism.* In six books Lucretius deals with atomic theory, offers a psychology, and provides a theory of the cosmos and of natural phenomena. Although it is impossible to give the whole range of Lucretius' thought, among his propositions are the following:

1. The world is comprised of atoms which are in constant motion.

2. Objects which can be seen and touched are composed of compounds of different sorts of atoms; and only certain compounds can exist.

3. The universe has a beginning and will end at some time in the future.

4. The mind and the body are not separate things, but there is a single corporeal substance.

5. The mind is born and will die; there is no afterlife; imagining hell is a projection of suffering experienced on earth.

---

*Epicurus is said to have been the author of some three hundred works, but only fragments of them remain. Democritus was also prolific, but little remains of his seventy-two books. This is to underscore that the potent influence one may ascribe to Lucretius—indeed, his inclusion here—is due not to his originality but to the beauty of his verse and its publication in Renaissance Europe.

6. Plants and animals grew up on earth, though not all species survived.

7. Superstition derives from ignorance.

Lucretius appears exceptionally modern because his thinking is nonteleological, that is, he does not endow things or events with a higher aim or an ideal purpose. "You must not imagine," Lucretius writes, "that the bright orbs of our eyes were created purposely [or that] our arms were fitted to stout shoulders, and helpful hands attached at either side, in order that we might do what is needful to sustain life." Rather, he emphasizes, "the thing born creates the use. There was no seeing before the eyes were born, no talking before the tongue was created." Nonteleological thinking, a refusal to ascribe an underlying design to things, is basic and necessary to scientific thinking, which otherwise becomes dogma and can advance no further. Teleological thinking, by contrast, is a primary feature of all prescientific thought in Europe, and continues to distinguish so-called creation science.

In biology Lucretius adumbrates the theory of the origin of the species, of natural selection, and the inheritance of specific traits. "It may also happen at times that children take after their grandparents, or recall the features of great-grandparents," Lucretius writes. "This is because the parents' bodies often preserve a quantity of latent seeds, grouped in many combinations, which derive from an ancestral stock handed down from generation to generation." Lucretius did not have the notion of the evolution of species, however; it would be surprising if he did, without being exposed, as was Darwin, to a broader world teeming with plants and animals as well as the people who breed them.

De rerum natura is a book that one may say has surely changed the history of the world. It was effectively lost to European thought until an Italian humanist, Gian Francesco Poggio, discovered a single deteriorating copy in a German monastery in the early fifteenth century. Lucretius was published and studied during the Renaissance, and although he was attacked for being irreligious, *De rerum natura* was never formally banned by the Catholic Church. His admirers grew throughout the sixteenth century and he was an important figure for Enlightenment thinkers. His importance to scientific thought only increased with the recovery of atomic theory in the nineteenth century via JOHN DALTON [74].

Lucretius has many admirers in literature, from Virgil in the first century A.D. to Voltaire in the eighteenth. In 1924 ALBERT EINSTEIN [2] praised the genius of his inquiring mind in an introduction to a German edition of his work. "Though not a scientist in the modern sense of the term," wrote George Hadzsits more recently, "his search for the laws that govern the universe and his faith in them established [for Lucretius] a great position.... He was...a great adventurer who sought the objective of all scientific inquiry, freedom from nature's control, freedom from a fearful control of ignorance, superstition and fear." It is not too much to say—at the risk of sounding Whiggish, didactic, and hagiographic—that if Lucretius were read and discussed by every schoolchild today, the world would be a better place.

74

John Dalton

and the Theory of the Atom

1766–1844

B_y the end of the eighteenth century, ANTOINE LAURENT
LAVOISIER [8] had clarified the concept of an element, and
chemistry entirely left behind its alchemical past. Experiments
showed clearly that the various known elements—oxygen, carbon, hydrogen, fewer than a dozen in all—combined in definite
and constant proportions. But the physical model behind this
phenomenon was not understood until, in 1803, John Dalton
proposed that the elements themselves are made up of atoms—
"solid, massy, hard, impenetrable, moveable particles." Although
described as a self-taught genius by nineteenth-century biographers, John Dalton is not considered to have been a formidable

experimenter; his theoretical cast of mind was rigid, and his theory not in every way fruitful. But he was a beloved English scientist, and his work represented an important advance for chemistry and a harbinger for modern physics, "a bridge," writes historian of science William H. Brock, "between experimental data and hypothetical atoms."

John Dalton was born on September 5 or 6, 1766, in Eaglesfield, a small village near Cockermouth in Cumberland County, England. His father, Joseph Dalton, was a weaver by trade, and a Quaker; his mother came from a prosperous family. He attended the local school, and at age twelve, when the schoolmaster retired, young Dalton began teaching in his place. Elihu Robinson, a local, well-educated, wealthy Quaker and distant relative, encouraged Dalton and tutored him in science.

In 1781, at age fifteen, Dalton moved to Kendall, where he taught at a boarding school for some twelve years. During this period he studied mathematics and the natural sciences with John Gough, a blind but lively and eloquent philosopher described by William Wordsworth in the poem "Excursion" ("Methinks I see him now, his eyeballs roll'd beneath his ample brow"). Encouraged by Gough and the capricious climate of the English countryside, Dalton kept a record of the weather from 1787 almost until his death; his first work, published in 1793, was *Meteorological Observations and Essays*. Dalton's observations of changing weather may have been unrelated to his later atomic theory; he could imagine, for example, how water vapor did not blend with air but dispersed as particles in the atmosphere, to condense as clouds and return to the earth's surface as precipitation.

In 1793 Dalton accepted a position at New College in Manchester, the rapidly expanding city that was becoming the hub of the industrial revolution. He joined the Manchester Literary and Philosophical Society, a fairly important scientific circle which offered an appropriate milieu for Dalton's continuing studies. In 1794 he published the first serious study of color blindness—for a long time afterward called *Daltonism*—a condition from which both he and his brother suffered. By 1799 Dalton gave up his formal teaching duties at New College and began supporting himself through private tutoring of the sons and daughters of Manchester's expanding middle class. He seems to have been a committed teacher; he published *Elements of*

English Grammar in 1801, just before his scientific career began in earnest.

Dalton first presented his theory of atoms in some detail in an 1803 lecture. It depended upon his study of the properties of gases, which had much occupied scientists during the previous century. The elements which combine to form the various gases, Dalton suggested, are made up of small, indestructible atomic particles of definite weights, surrounded by a variable amount of heat. Each kind of atom had a distinctive weight and represented a different element; under certain conditions the elements combine to create what he called "compound atoms." Thus, water, as Lavoisier helped to discover, was a compound atom of about twelve parts hydrogen and eighty-seven parts oxygen—a ratio of about seven to one. Dalton suggested that this constant proportion was due to their relative weight. Hydrogen being the lightest of the known gases, Dalton made it the unitary atom in his system, assigning it a weight of 1; thus, oxygen is 7.

Dalton went on to provide relative atomic weights for all the known elements. In doing so, he helped clarify much of the experimental literature in chemistry. Although atomic theory formed only a brief chapter in Dalton's *New System of Chemical Philosophy*, published in 1808, it was soon recognized as a seminal work.

Historians of science have long been reticent about the ultimate value of John Dalton's theory. Although his influence was felt throughout chemistry, atoms met with a certain skepticism through most of the nineteenth century. Partly, this was because Dalton's "compound atom" was not the same as the later concept of the molecule. Dalton's assumption was that bonds were formed only between different kinds of atoms. This was influential and wrong. Atoms of the same element may combine to create simple molecules; and simple molecules combine to create complex molecules. As early as 1811 Amedeo Avogardo proposed such a theory, and suggested that equal volumes of gases must contain the same number of molecules at the same pressure and temperature. This would show that the water molecule, for example, is comprised of two atoms of hydrogen, and one of oxygen. Avogardo's law was not recognized, however, until about 1860; only thereafter did the concept of the molecule gain prominence.

After 1810 Dalton produced no great work but continued to

perform experiments, to write, and to revise his work. While continuing to teach, he became an important figure of the scientific world. He became president of the Literary and Philosophical Society of Manchester in 1817, a post he retained until he died. He was elected to the Royal Society in 1822 and in the same year took a voyage to France, where he met the major scientists of that country. In 1826 he received a Royal Medal "for promoting the objects and progress of science, by awakening honourable competition among philosophers."

In his later years, Dalton did not keep up with advances in chemistry, and by the 1830s his mental powers were declining. He had created his own pictographic system of chemical symbols and was never reconciled to the simpler and more informative system introduced by Jacob Berzelius. Indeed, in the wake of an angry discussion about the system put forth in 1837 by Berzelius, Dalton suffered the first of two enfeebling strokes. On July 27, 1844, a servant found him fallen across the bed, with his head on the floor. Dalton was a hero of England and of British science, and some forty thousand persons paid their respects as he lay in Manchester Town Hall. He had never married, perhaps less from lack of desire than because he was not financially secure until middle age.

The importance of the atomic theory does not today need to be vaunted, as Dalton's biographer Frank Greenaway wrote, for with it "we have made new materials, utilized new sources of energy, defeated one disease after another, and come within sight of the mechanism of life." He adds that John Dalton "was not entirely the maker of this gift to mankind, but he was the bearer of the gift which had come a long way to reach him," from the ancient Greek philosophy, transformed into the atom of nineteenth-century science.

75

Louis Victor de Broglie
and Wave/Particle Duality

1892–1987

In showing that matter on an atomic scale has the properties of both waves and particles, Prince Louis Victor de Broglie in the mid-1920s poured the foundation for the mature theory of quantum mechanics. His equations, which were confirmed by experiment soon after they were proposed, opened the way to formulation of the theory of the atom much as we know it today. However, like ALBERT EINSTEIN [2], from whom he drew his major inspiration, de Broglie himself did not much care for the final form of quantum wave mechanics, with its statistical interpretation of the microworld. He became, in his later career, a venerable but old-fangled presence. "Today, in the autumn of my life," he wrote, two decades before his death in fact, "... I do not believe that the enigma has really been resolved." For most physicists, there is no enigma, and de Broglie's work itself is one of the reasons why.

From a Piedmontese family of hereditary nobles, Louis Victor Pierre Raymond de Broglie was born on August 15, 1892, in Dieppe, in the north of France. The youngest of five children, he counted among his ancestors Madame de Staël, the great writer, and her father, Jacques Necker, the famous financier and statesman under Louis XVI. His mother was Pauline d'Armaille and his father, Duc Victor de Broglie, was a member of the French parliament. His early education took place at home, followed by the Lycée Janson de Sailly in Paris. At only age eighteen de Broglie received his *licence*, the approximate equivalent of an American bachelor's degree, in history, from the Sorbonne. He continued at the university, planning to study law, but was soon influenced by Henri Poincaré to turn to science and mathematics. Through his elder brother, Maurice, a well-known physicist, de Broglie became aware of relativity and the new quantum theory. "I was nineteen," he wrote later, "when I felt born inside me a vocation for theoretical physics." He was soon reading and discovering the theories of MAX PLANCK [25] and ALBERT EINSTEIN [2] and giving considerable thought to the major new theoretical advances in physics. He received a second *licence*, in science, in 1913.

During World War I de Broglie served a long stint in the military. He was assigned to a radiotelegraphy unit which had its quarters at the Eiffel Tower, and for nearly six years he studied no physics. He became familiar with the wireless, however, during the period in which it evolved into the shortwave radio. After the war de Broglie returned to his brother's laboratory and over the next several years, from about 1920 to 1924, undertook his most important work. His research in Maurice's laboratory, which essentially involved an investigation of X rays and the photoelectric effect, put him in touch with recent experimental results of atomic theory; his first papers date from these years. But he also had considerable time to reflect on the theoretical implications of quantum theory.

The problem which de Broglie addressed was the ultimate nature of matter, at a time when the new theory of the atom, developed by NIELS BOHR [3] and ERNEST RUTHERFORD [19], was both promising and frustrating to physicists. Bohr had developed an ingenious view of the atom in which electrons occupy—and jump from—definite orbits around a nucleus, but it did not square with various experimental results. This seemed unfortunate because Bohr's model represented clear progress in atomic theory. The Bohr-Rutherford atom, for example, promised the first substantial explanation of the periodic table of the elements, while, at the same time, experimental measurements showed that it must be wrong in important ways.

De Broglie's doctoral dissertation, "Investigations into the Quantum Theory," contains the basic statement of his theory of wave mechanics. It is based on two articles he wrote in 1923. De Broglie's inspiration was due in part to mathematical work done in the nineteenth century by William Rowan Hamilton on refraction, but also to Einstein's insight, which dates from 1905, that light waves, under certain circumstances, behave like particles. If that is so, de Broglie wondered, might not particles also behave like waves? As he put it later, "After long reflection in solitude and meditation, I suddenly had the idea, during the year 1923, that the discovery made by Einstein in 1905 should be generalized by extending it to all material particles and notably to electrons."

This idea was undergirded, furthermore, by Einstein's yet more basic proposal that mass and light are both forms of energy. All elementary matter, de Broglie hypothesized, may be seen to behave as both particles and waves. He embodied this notion in a mathematical formula, and when his examiner, Paul Langevin, forwarded a copy of de Broglie's dissertation to Einstein, the latter immediately understood its significance. "Read it," Einstein told MAX BORN [32]. "Even though it might look crazy it is absolutely solid."

Theoretically, de Broglie's equations form the cornerstone of wave mechanics, developed by ERWIN SCHRÖDINGER [18] two years later, in 1926. Experimentally, in spite of Einstein's imprimatur, de Broglie's notion seemed so bizarre that initially it caused some confusion. However, American physicists Clinton Davisson and Lester Germer managed to read through Schrödinger's papers on wave mechanics. Their experiments at Bell Telephone Laboratories in 1927, in which they examined what happens when light beams strike a target made of nickel, confirmed de Broglie's work. They showed that electrons possessed two properties of waves, diffraction and interference; and the amplitude of the wavelengths was precisely related to the particles' energy.

De Broglie did not share the majority view of quantum physicists in the philosophical debate that evolved in the late 1920s. Admitting the mathematical beauty and rigor of what is called the "Copenhagen interpretation" of quantum mechanics, de Broglie remained a "little perplexed" inasmuch as, like Einstein, he remained attached to causal principles. He spent a good deal of time attempting to show that the particle was, in effect, the wave localized. He never succeeded at this, however, and admitted that his effort was flawed.

In 1929 de Broglie received the Nobel Prize for physics. He had begun teaching physics shortly before this at the University of Paris, and the award was an excellent stimulus to his career. He became professor of physics in 1932 and joined the Henri Poincaré Institute a year later. He remained there until his retirement in 1962. He was interested in applied physics, and many of his later works dealt with practical problems concerning atomic energy and particle accelerators, optics, and cybernetics.

While becoming a durable and influential figure in French science—part of a small pantheon of great physicists in that country—de Broglie wrote a score of books for both scientific and lay audiences. Some have been translated into English: *Matter and Light*, which he wrote in 1937; *Revolution in Physics* in 1953; *Current Interpretation of Wave Mechanics*, in 1964, and, at the end of his life, *Quantum, Space, and Time*. De Broglie died on March 19, 1987.

76

Carl Linnaeus
and the Binomial Nomenclature

1707–1778

In the midst of the Enlightenment, Carolus Linnaeus, a Swedish physician and botanist, spearheaded a movement which led to a rational taxonomy of the natural world. Animals and plants are still named according to the binomial system created by Linnaeus and promulgated by his students, some of whom traveled across the world to collect and name new specimens. Although the "prince of botanists" had limited scientific capacities, and did not possess the great brilliance of Comte de Buffon, he combined with his classificatory zeal a sensual, poetic imagination and considerable lucidity. "Anyone who knows anything about taxonomy before Linnaeus," writes his biographer Heinz Goerke, "will acknowledge without hesitation the great importance of his systematic writings for the development of the natural sciences in the eighteenth century." His work "marks an epoch in the history of science."

Carolus Linné, as he was named in Swedish, was born on May 23, 1707, in Raschult, a town in southern Sweden. His mother was Christiana Brodersonia; his father, originally Nils Ingemarsson, had taken the name Linné during his theological studies. Nils Linné was a pastor with an interest in gardening, and Carl soon became known as the Little Botanist. Not surprisingly, as a child Carl read *Historia animalium* by Aristotle, but he was not an especially good student after entering a Latin school in 1717. One of his teachers even suggested that he might best be apprenticed to a cobbler. However, after coming under the influence of his physics teacher, and putting aside his father's hopes that he would become a minister, Linné entered medical school. In 1727 he began to study at the University of Lund, transferring the following year to the University of Uppsala. Here he was befriended by Olaf Celsius, a botanist (as well as uncle to the astronomer who invented the centigrade thermometer) who encouraged Linnaeus—although nominally a medical student—to study the natural world.

In 1732 Linnaeus made an expedition to Lapland, above the Arctic Circle. He had already recognized the need for a system of classifying the natural world, and for five months he collected plants and described in detail the birds, insects, and other animals he found there. His studies of Lapland's minerals enabled him to lecture on the subject the following year. His *Flora lapponica* was published in 1737.

Linnaeus's fame dates from the years he spent abroad, in Holland. He went there to obtain his medical degree, a requirement of the parents of Sara Lisa Moraea, the woman he wished to marry. Linnaeus took the opportunity to visit the important Dutch scientists. They were impressed by his botanical knowledge. As a consequence, in 1735 he published the first, very brief edition of *Systema naturae*. Over the next quarter century it underwent constant revision, growing from fifteen pages to thirteen hundred by 1758. Thus, in a brief pamphlet Linnaeus laid out, as a young man, Daniel J. Boorstin writes, "a prospectus for his lifework and for all modern systematic biology."

Although highly poetic in style and not free of religious

thinking, Linnaeus's underlying argument belongs to Enlightenment thought and the age of discovery. Clarity is its salient
quality. In *Systema naturae*, Linnaeus distinguishes minerals,
which have bodies but not life or sensation, from plants and
animals. Plants have bodies, and are living, but lack sensation.
Animals have sensation as well, together with the power of
locomotion. Mankind, endowed with intellect, can come to know
all these bodies and can distinguish them by name. Linnaeus
provides the nomenclature that assigns an animal or plant to a
particular *class, order, genus, species,* and *variety*. The six classes of
animals, for example, are mammals, birds, amphibians, fishes,
insects, and worms.

It is easy to see why such eminent figures as Johann
Friedrich Gronovius and Isaac Lawson were impressed by Linnaeus, for his system's intelligibility was exceptional and his data
extensive. Over the next several years, with help of patrons,
Linnaeus published writings on the fundamentals of botany, the
various plant genera, and other books. In 1739 Linnaeus received
the imprimatur of Antoine Jussieu, the French physician, botanist and director of the Jardin des Plantes.

Associated with the Linnaean system is the binomial nomenclature, which names animals and plants according to genus and
species. Thus, the cougar is the *Felis concolor*, the house cat a *Felis
domesticus*, and the lion the *Felis leo*. The species name was
sometimes descriptive, although Linnaeus was hard-pressed to
find Latin names, and when he received novel specimens from
amateur naturalists, he often honored the finder. It became a
considerable compliment for a gentlemen or professional botanist or zoologist to have a species named after him by Linnaeus.

Perhaps the most intriguing aspect of Linnaeus's thought is
its root in sexual metaphor. It dates from the earliest years of his
career when he presented, and quite impressed, his mentor
Celsius with a paper entitled, "Preliminaries on the Marriage of
Plants," in which he likened the stamen of a flower to the
bridegroom and the pistil to the bride. In general, Linnaeus
made the reproductive system the hallmark of his classification
system. Some of the terms drawn from Greek or Latin had sexual
connotations, which applied in some poetic or morphological way
to the plant's reproductive equipment. Plants with two groups of
stamens, for example, constitute the class *Diadelphia*, which derives from the Latin for "brotherhood of husbands." In discuss-

ing the outer covering of a flower, he wrote that the calyx "might be regarded as the *labia majora* or the foreskin" while the corolla was the *labia minora.* Although his sexual imagination did not detract from his reputation, botanist Rev. Samuel Goodenough alluded to the "gross prurience of Linnaeus' mind" and Goethe was concerned that women and schoolchildren should not be exposed to this aspect of his thought. The barrier against female knowledge has fallen, but even today when Linnaeus is taught in school, the sexual nature of his nomenclature is passed over. He is also censored a fortiori by ignorance, for few children are taught Latin anymore.

Linnaeus became exceptionally famous through his system of classification. He was married to a domineering woman and did not have a tranquil domestic life, but at the university "his lectures were attended by hundreds," writes Grant G. Cannon, "and his field trips were gay parades complete with drums and horns. At the end of the day, his students were accustomed to gather around his home to shout a final, '*Vivat scientie! Vivat Linnaeus!*'" He was made a noble in 1761. In 1774 he suffered the first of several strokes, which he described as the "message of death," and a second stroke, four years later, was disabling. He died on January 10, 1778, and is buried in the cathedral in Uppsala.

Frontispiece of *Systema Naturæ*, Second Edition

77

Jean Piaget
and Child Development

1896–1980

The study of the cognitive development of children begins in the twentieth century, with Jean Piaget, the Swiss psychologist. Through observation and experiment, over a long and prolific career, Piaget provided a useful "stage" theory that shows how, from infancy through adolescence, children acquire operations of thought that gradually enable them to manipulate abstract concepts and concrete ideas. Long associated with the Institut Jean-Jacques Rousseau in Geneva, Piaget was a moderately charismatic figure whose reputation survived and flourished after his death. He has had considerable influence on education and some salutary influence on psychoanalytic theory; but, most impor-

357

tant, Piaget's work has been a decisive component in the birth of the new cognitive psychology, beginning in the 1960s. There is a consensus, writes Morton Hunt, that Piaget "was the greatest child psychologist of the twentieth century....What made his work so influential was in part the beauty and explanatory power of his theory, and in part the many remarkable discoveries, made through painstaking research, on which he based it."

Jean Piaget was born August 9, 1896, in Neuchâtel, a French-speaking canton in Switzerland. His mother was from a strongly religious, Calvinist background while his father, Arthur Piaget, was a skeptical professor and medievalist. As a child Jean was serious and possessed of a precocious interest in nature. At about age eleven, he sent to a local nature journal a three-paragraph report, which was published, on an albino sparrow he had observed in a park. Befriended by the curator of the local museum, he developed an interest in molluscs, and at age sixteen published the first of many articles on these invertebrates in the *Journal de la Conchycologie*. Meanwhile, Piaget had done well at the progressive lycée he attended. In 1914 he went on to the University of Neuchâtel, from which he received a doctorate in 1918 with a dissertation on the distribution of molluscs in the Swiss Alps. Biological thought—specifically as concerns embryology and evolutionary theory at the turn of the century—became an enduring aspect of Piaget's style of investigation.

In Zurich after World War I, Piaget studied experimental psychology. He attended lectures by psychiatrists Eugen Bleuler and Carl Jung and was influenced by their use of the clinical interview to elicit material from patients. Piaget soon moved to Paris, where he began to work with Théodore Simon, the former collaborator of the late Alfred Binet, who had devised the intelligence test. Asked by Simon to do some work standardizing items from a test which Cyril Burt, the British psychologist, was administering to children in England, Piaget noted patterns in certain wrong responses. "It was at this point," notes David Cohen, "that Piaget showed extraordinary flair." To discover how and when children came to believe such simple ideas as, say, the equivalence of such operations as 3 + 2 and 2 + 3, Piaget decided to undertake experiments.

Early in his career, Piaget had some interest in the theories of SIGMUND FREUD [6]—though subsequently he had little taste for discussing the emotions—and published some articles on psychoanalysis and other topics in the *Archives de Psychologie*, published in Switzerland. This led to an invitation in 1921 to head the pedagogical Institut Jean-Jacques Rousseau in Zurich. Here Piaget began his research in the institute's kindergarten, observing and interviewing young children, from age four to six, and analyzing their responses to his questions. His first book on child psychology was published in 1924 and translated two years later into English as *Language and Thought of the Child*. An entire series of books appeared during the 1920s, including *Judgment and Reasoning in the Child, The Child's Conception of the World*, and *The Child's Conception of Physical Causality*. Famous before he was thirty, Piaget addressed the British Psychological Society in 1927.

Piaget's essential finding is that children do not reason in the same way as adults, and only gradually abandon their age-specific, "primitive" belief systems. At different ages children believe that anything that is moving is alive, for example; that dreams come from the outside; and that all things have a purpose. The gradual abandonment of these views is a stagewise process, and involves several cognitive patterns, which Piaget identified as "functional invariants." *Accommodation* is one of these invariants, and represents the tendency of a person to adapt to the impositions of reality. Piaget proposed *assimilation* as another general term and referred to his theory as an "assimilation-accommodation model."

Assimilation, after a term Piaget borrowed from physiology, is the process by which a child incorporates aspects of the outside world into the developing intellectual structure. Piaget in turn named several forms or methods of assimilation. Through repetitive actions, discrimination by recognition, generalizing thought processes, and "reciprocal" mental operations—vision and touch, for example—infants and children gradually build up a mental picture of the world, together with an overall theory of how it operates.

The relation of children's thinking to philosophical discourse was not lost on Piaget, who greatly admired Kant's theory of knowledge, and he referred to his own studies as "genetic epistemology." A meeting in 1928 with ALBERT EINSTEIN [2], who made a variety of suggestions for further research, led Piaget to his 1946 work, *The Child's Conception of Time*.

Piaget's theories were elaborated and changed over many years. He ultimately distinguished four basic stages of cognitive development, from birth through adolescence. In the *sensorimotor stage*, from birth to about two years of age, infants gradually acquire the capacity to perceive and develop behaviors by which they can manipulate perception. Piaget calls the stage from about two to seven the *preoperational* stage, during which children acquire language and a basic representation of the world. They remain egocentric, however, and are unable to take the part of someone else. In the stage of *concrete operations*, from about seven until adolescence, children can learn to count, put things in order, and think about concepts. Their limitations are related to abstract thinking. The stage of *formal operations* begins at twelve or thereabouts and represents the basically mature form of thought.

Although Piaget initially expected that his studies of children would take him four or five years, they came to dominate a career that spanned several decades. In addition to his studies of children at the Institut Rousseau, Piaget made painstaking longitudinal observations of his own children—Jacqueline, Lucienne, and Laurent—which are recorded in several classic books: *The Origins of Intelligence in Children,* published in 1936, *The Construction of Reality in the Child,* in 1937, and *Play Dreams and Imitations in Childhood,* in 1946. In the 1940s, Piaget entered yet another phase of his career when he began to investigate adolescence—the stage of formal operations—to discover how the child contends with change and abstract thought. His *Growth of Logical Thinking From Childhood to Adolescence,* published in English in 1958, was a study of some fifteen hundred Swiss children; it was written in collaboration with Barbel Inhelder.

From 1929 until 1954, Piaget was professor of psychology at the University of Geneva, where from 1956 he directed the Center for Genetic Epistemology. During these years his work was frequently ignored by behaviorist-oriented psychologists. But Piaget was much admired by students and colleagues in Geneva and by a growing number of academics in the United States. By the 1960s his work had become widely known and was much debated. Charismatic and friendly, Piaget engendered intellectual disagreements, but they generated neither the bitter rivalry frequent in American psychology nor the factional strife that has so demeaned psychoanalysis.

In spite of his importance, a reformulation of Piaget's thought was probably inevitable, given his subject and the idiosyncratic aspects of his thought. "Piaget's grandiose claims have proved less robust than his specific experimental demonstrations," writes Howard Gardner. "The logical formalisms underlying specific stages are invalid, the stages themselves are under attack, and his description of the biological processes of stage transformation have eluded even sympathetic scholars." But, Gardner adds, Piaget "launched an entire field of psychology— that concerned with human cognitive development—and provided the research agenda that keeps it occupied until this day. Even disproofs of his specific claims are a tribute to his general influence."

Jean Piaget died on September 17, 1980.

78

George Gaylord Simpson
and the Tempo of Evolution

1902–1984

A vertebrate paleontologist, George Gaylord Simpson made expeditions to Patagonia and traveled up the Amazon River, discovered the Dawn Horses, fifteen inches high, and dug up the bones of human ancestors in sub-Saharan Africa. He studied fossils around the world and penguins in Antarctica; to him we owe the bon mot "Penguins are habit forming." But more important, in the course of this fieldwork Simpson became a philosopher of organismic biology. He is one of the architects of what is known as the "modern synthesis" of evolution, which unites paleontology and genetics. By introducing quantitative methods, Simpson brought new rigor to the study of the fossil record. His work, writes Niles Eldredge, "brought paleontology back into the mainstream of evolutionary biology—all the while insisting that paleontological phenomena had much to tell genetics about the true nature of the evolutionary process."

The last of three children, George Gaylord Simpson was born in Chicago, Illinois, on June 16, 1902. His father, Joseph Alexander Simpson, was an attorney whose involvement in land speculation and mining soon led him to relocate the family to Denver, Colorado. His mother, Helen Julia Kinney, had been raised by her grandparents, who were missionaries in Hawaii. The Simpson household was strict and Presbyterian, but although George lost his religious faith as a teenager, he remained close to his parents throughout their lives. George excelled in school, was skipped ahead, and graduated high school just as he turned sixteen. In 1918 he began studies at the University of Colorado but dropped out for a time due to financial difficulties; he then transferred to Yale as the best means of pursuing his interest in geology and paleontology. He received his bachelor's degree in 1923, his doctorate in 1926, and undertook postgraduate research in London at the British Museum of Natural History. His major work at this early stage already was focused on the vertebrate fossils, particularly of mammals. But his larger motivation, as he noted toward the end of his life, was "an uncontrollable drive to know and understand the world in which I live."

Simpson began a long association with the American Museum of Natural History in New York City in 1927, when he was appointed assistant curator of vertebrate fossils. To raise money for two expeditions to Patagonia, where CHARLES DARWIN [4] had discovered fossils in the 1830s, Simpson sought out a wealthy patron of the museum. He was compelled to spend so much time imbibing with him that he later said, "I only regret that I have but one liver to lose for my museum." *Attending Marvels*, an account of this first expedition, in 1930–31, brought Simpson considerable celebrity; he returned to Patagonia in 1933. These trips established him as a leading paleontologist. They also convinced him, he later wrote, that South American mammals were "of greatest value as a basis for the study of evolution in general."

Although Simpson was not alone in recognizing the need for a new synthesis in evolutionary theory—THEODOSIUS DOBZHANSKY [67] had first proposed it in 1937—he became the leading American paleontologist in support of it. Darwin's theory of evolution was proposed long before genes were established as the units of heredity. Paleontologists of the early twentieth century, studying the fossil record, thus developed taxonomies and natural histories of various species using a framework that was evolutionary—but not genetic. On the other hand, geneticists such as THOMAS HUNT MORGAN [62] were studying generations of fruit flies to establish the rules of Mendelian transmission, but they were not primarily interested in the problems of evolution— and most assuredly they were not interested in fossils. By the 1930s the need to join these complementary disciplines had become evident.

Simpson's first effort at developing a modern evolutionary synthesis of paleontology and genetics dates from *Tempo and Mode in Evolution*, which he began writing in 1938, finished four years later, and published in 1944. Although "fossil animals cannot be brought into the laboratory for the experimental determination of their genetic constitutions," Simpson pointed out that neither could the geneticist "reproduce the vast and complex horizontal extent of the natural environment and, particularly, the immense span of time in which population changes really occur." Simpson developed a theory of three modes of evolution. *Speciation* is differentiation of new species by a reorganization of a group from a larger population. *Phyletic* evolution is the gradual change in a whole species or population. Finally, *quantum* evolution—the most hypothetical—is the relatively sudden evolution of species. Quantum evolution conceptualized processes at work in otherwise unaccountable jumps in the fossil record. It would no longer be assumed that discontinuities were "gaps" that new fossil discoveries would one day fill. Quantum evolution is an ancestral component of the theory, developed years later by Niles Eldredge and Stephen Jay Gould, known as "punctuated equilibrium."

One of Simpson's important innovations was the use of statistical methods to assess the fossil record and quantify evolutionary hypotheses. There was irony in this, for Simpson, though scientifically educated, had no statistical training. But his second wife, Anne Roe, whom he married in 1938, had trained in psychology at a time when that discipline was using statistics to distance itself from philosophy. Thus, quantitative methods came to zoology through what Simpson called a "figurative marriage of minds." Jointly he and Roe authored *Quantitative Zoology*, published in 1939.

During World War II, Simpson served in military intelligence. He subsequently began fieldwork in the southwestern United States, and he eventually built a second home in New Mexico. But he retained his ties with the American Museum of Natural History and accepted a professorship at Columbia University. His *Principles of Classification of Mammals* was published in 1945, *Horses* in 1951, and *Major Features of Evolution* (an updated version of *Tempo and Mode*) in 1954. For a popular audience, Simpson wrote *The Meaning of Evolution* in 1949; it became a durable bestseller. He also wrote a college text, titled simply *Life*.

In 1959 Simpson ended his relationship with the American Museum of Natural History to become Agassiz Professor at the Museum of Comparative Zoology as well as professor of vertebrate paleontology at Harvard University. He achieved a high professional profile as founder and president of the Society for the Study of Evolution and the Society of Vertebrate Paleontology. His *Principles of Animal Taxonomy* was published in 1961, and a wide-ranging collection of essays entitled *This View of Life* appeared three years later.

In 1965 Simpson made the mistake of publishing *The Geography of Evolution*, which restated his support for continental stability just when evidence was mounting in favor of plate tectonics. Simpson believed that the hypothesis of continental drift advanced by ALFRED WEGENER [53] was not supported by the fossil record. This was a signal error in his career.

In the last phase of his life, Simpson and his wife—she had also become a professor at Harvard—were frequently ill. In 1964 they seem to have suffered simultaneous "his and her" heart attacks; they occupied twin hospital beds in Albuquerque, New Mexico. Simpson subsequently curtailed his teaching at Harvard, eventually leaving the university in 1970. He retired to Arizona but continued to travel and write. His ventures to Antarctica brought forth *Penguins: Past and Present, Here and There*, and he returned to his South American fossils for *Splendid Isolation*, published in 1980, and *Discoverers of the Lost World*, published in the last year of his life. Simpson's memoirs, *Concession to the Improbable*, appeared in 1978.

Fully retired in 1982, Simpson developed pneumonia while on a cruise in the South Seas. It did not kill him but brought on complications that laid him low for months. He wrote his friend Léo Laporte in July, "I am slowly getting better but it looks like a long haul. I can't write more." This was a significant concession from a man who in many ways preferred writing to speaking—"I do not value the spoken word as a means of serious communication," he once wrote. George Gaylord Simpson died on the evening of October 6, 1984.

A decade after his death, Joan Simpson Burns discovered among her father's papers the manuscript of a science fiction novel. The story of a scientist from the future who is returned to the prehistoric Jurassic era, *The Dechronization of Sam Magruder*, published in 1996, is a brief but effective tale which reveals a good deal about Simpson himself. The "themes of loneliness and fear of intellectual impotence (not being heard, remembered, believed, or honored)," wrote Stephen Jay Gould in an afterword, "pervade the text and story line of *Sam Magruder* and elevate the work from an instructive fable about the earth's past to a profound work about the sense and meaning of human life."

79

Claude Lévi-Strauss

and Structural Anthropology

1908–

From the middle of the nineteenth century, as imperialism flourished and European nations carved up much of the rest of the world, early anthropologists examined the features of a large number of indigenous cultures. As anthropology emerged as a science, it employed various intellectual tools to understand the dynamics of these cultures, but with limited success. The customs of preliterate tribes, for example, could be described, but how were they to be interpreted? The difficulty of finding general laws of culture was known to FRANZ BOAS [14], who rejected "evolutionist" anthropology but at his death could leave only a mass of raw data on Indians he had studied for four decades.

Serious steps were taken toward improving the larger propositions of anthropology after World War II. Structural anthropology, which involves a thorough rejection of ethnocentrism
together with an effort to understand how culture develops from
basic constellations of human thought, is the substantial achievement of Claude Lévi-Strauss.

Claude Lévi-Strauss was born in Brussels, Belgium on
November 28, 1908, but his family soon returned to France. His
mother was originally from Verdun and his father, a Parisian, was
a portrait painter. Claude grew up in the sixteenth arrondisse-
ment in Paris, in an intellectually sophisticated, highly cultivated,
though not wealthy environment. After attending the Lycée
Janson-de-Sailly, he began law studies, which bored him, and so
also took courses in philosophy. He passed his *agrégation* in 1931.
After military service and some time spent teaching in a lycée,
Lévi-Strauss's interest in anthropology—a relatively undefined
discipline in France at the time—became crystallized as ambition.

In 1935 Lévi-Strauss journeyed to Brazil, where he taught at
the University of São Paulo until 1939 and also undertook a
certain amount of field work. Back in France, he was drafted at
the outbreak of World War II. After the French defeat he
managed to leave the country, spending most of the war's dura-
tion in New York, where he absorbed a good deal of American
anthropology. He met leading academicians and undertook an
extensive review of the anthropological literature. He also became a companion of André Breton and the surrealists and
worked for a period at the New School for Social Research. In
1950, three years after returning to Paris, Lévi-Strauss became
director of the École Pratiques des Hautes Études. He was elected
a professor of the Collége de France in 1959.

The initial impact of Lévi-Strauss on anthropology came
through the study of kinship patterns, a staple of anthropology
since its origins in the nineteenth century. Conceived as a
universal phenomenon, kinship represents basic relationships
among individuals having many practical consequences—both
for the cultural group and for those who study that group.
Kinship embraces such formal aspects as the rules of marriage,
the inheritance of property, and the structure of family relations.
Thus, when in 1949 Lévi-Strauss published *Elementary Structures of
Kinship*, which he had presented as his doctoral dissertation, it
was a synthetic work which, bringing together a century of

research, received considerable attention. It also defined his relationship to scientific thought. Dedicated to Lewis Morgan, the American pioneer anthropologist, the book made use of Roman Jakobson's linguistic analysis.* Lévi-Strauss specifically hoped that just as physics looked toward a convergence with biology and psychology, the social sciences now had a similar potential. Finally, the first part of the book concluded with a mathematical appendix by André Weil which gave an algebraic analysis of marriage patterns.

An important consequence of Lévi-Strauss's work was the emergence of common themes among cultures at fine levels of analysis. Not only were basic elements such as language, family, and music common to all cultures; so do fundamental structures, he argued, illuminate basic similarities in the construction of the human mind. This was the yield of Lévi-Strauss's collection *Structural Anthropology*, published in 1958. In his continuing effort to utilize precepts of structuralist linguistics, it should be cautioned that "structuralism" subsequently became a diffuse catchword. "The vogue for structuralism unleashed all manner of unfortunate results," Lévi-Strauss said later. "The term was besmirched; illegitimate, sometimes ridiculous applications were made of it. There was nothing I could do."

Four years later, in *Totemism*, Lévi-Strauss offered a new interpretation of a well-known phenomenon, as well as a strong rejection of ethnocentrism. Totemism is a perplexing phenomenon found in many cultures, in which an animal, plant, or other object becomes identified with a group or clan. Emile Durkheim viewed totemism as a primitive religion, and SIGMUND FREUD [6] examined it in relation to the incest taboo. But Lévi-Strauss viewed it as a system of signs and a means by which preliterate peoples could organize their experience in relation to nature. And he viewed the concept of totemism as itself defective, an anthropological artifact of Western thought, a "projection outside our universe, as if by an exorcism, of mental attitudes incompatible with the claim of a discontinuity between man and nature which Christian thought has held to be essential."

Lévi-Strauss had begun investigating myth as early as 1950, and it became a major focus of his career. "For twenty years," he

---

*Linguistics, of all the social sciences, Lévi-Strauss believed was "probably the only one which lays claim to the name of science and which has succeeded both in formulating a positive method and in understanding the nature of the facts submitted to its analysis."

has said, "I would get up at dawn, drunk with myths—truly I lived in another world." During the 1960s, he published a four-volume investigation: *The Raw and the Cooked, From Honey to Ashes, The Origin of Table Manners,* and *The Naked Man.* He examined, in all, some 813 basic stories as well as 1,000 variants. Using materials gathered by others, Lévi-Strauss managed to derive a common framework for their data and yield meaningful generalizations. He avoided, however, what he called a "comparativist mania" based on superficial resemblances. Rather, he broke down stories into their various elements. An analysis of several myths at once can reveal their internal logic and significance for the culture.

Several aspects of the work of Lévi-Strauss require clarification. His interest in American anthropology, first of all, is highly significant, and he examined great amounts of its data. The influence of Franz Boas, whose cultural relativism he shares, is quite strong. Like Boas, Lévi-Strauss is committed to anthropology as a scientific enterprise while recognizing its limitations as a science. At the same time he has always been a French *homme de lettres,* influenced moderately by Kantian philosophy and mildly by Freud and Marx. (In politics he has moved, generally speaking, from left to right over the years.) It is in this context that Lévi-Strauss became the object of much academic attention. Cultural historian David Pace writes, "By the late 1960s it was difficult to contradict the claim that Lévi-Strauss was the most prestigious anthropologist of his generation and one of the greats of twentieth century anthropological theory."

With the broad hypothesis that human myths and cultural customs emerge from a variety of common mental structures, Lévi-Strauss has had an important impact on the emerging cognitive sciences. Wondering whether he is "a pivotal contributor...or just an isolated, humanistically-oriented savant," Howard Gardner predicts: "Lévi-Strauss will endure because he posed questions that are central to both anthropology and cognition; outlined methods of analysis that might be applicable; and proposed the kinds of systematic relations which *may* obtain in such diverse fields as kinship, social organization, classification, and mythology."

The influence of Lévi-Strauss has been felt outside anthropology, and he has become a cultural icon, particularly in France and the United States. He has also made a signal contribution to a broad feature of scientific endeavor over the past four hundred years: the dethronement of human beings from a privileged place in the universe. The heliocentric theory of NICOLAUS COPERNICUS [10] displaced the earth from the center of the universe; the evolutionary theory of CHARLES DARWIN [4] removed man from a privileged place in relation to animals. The theory of unconscious motivation of SIGMUND FREUD [6] toppled mankind's gratifying self-image, and quantum theory destroyed the universality of human concepts such as cause and effect. Claude Lévi-Strauss exposed Eurocentrism in anthropological discourse. In its place he has offered words of caution: "By setting mankind apart from the rest of creation, Western humanism has deprived it of a safeguard. The moment man knows no limit to his power, he sets about destroying himself."

The author of complex anthropological texts, Lévi-Strauss has also written several more accessible works. *Tristes Tropiques* is a travelogue and meditation written in the 1950s, which Clifford Geertz once called "the best book ever written by an anthropologist." A collection of essays, *The View From Afar*, and a book of interviews with Didier Eribon, *Conversations with Claude Lévi-Strauss*, both provide insight into his way of thinking, and reveal his range and originality.

80

Lynn Margulis
and Symbiosis Theory

1938–

The symbiotic theory of the origin of the cell is one of the most impressive developments in recent biology and owes much to Lynn Margulis. Controversial when she first proposed it in 1967, and still without final formulation, in technical terms, its main lines are clear. Bacteria, which have inhabited Earth for three billion years, were crucial partners in evolution of the stable, self-replicating structure known as the eukaryotic cell.* Evolutionary remnants of these origins can be found in ordinary plant and

---

*"Eukaryotes" are cells with a nucleus, bounded by membranes, possessing DNA in chromosomal form. Plants, animals, protoctists, and fungi, from yeast to mammals, are eukaryotes. By contrast, bacterial cells are "prokaryotes" and possess no nucleus.

animal cells and in DNA itself. To gain acceptance for sym-biogenesis, Margulis had to overcome considerable resistance on the part of many biologists, which has shaped her provocative and sometimes antagonistic stance toward contemporary evolutionary theory. But the significance of her work, its grander implications, and promise for future research should not be in doubt. "The evolution of the eukaryotic cell was the single most important event in the history of the organic world," according to ERNST MAYR [65]. "And Margulis's contribution to our understanding the symbiotic factors was of enormous importance."

The eldest of four daughters, Margulis was born Lynn Alexander on March 5, 1938, in Chicago, Illinois. Her father was Morris Alexander, of Polish Jewish heritage, a lawyer and businessman who owned the Permaline Corporation, which manufactured thermoplastic markings for streets and highways. Her mother, Leone Wise, worked as a travel agent. As a child Lynn began to read widely and precociously, as well as to write journals, essays, and plays, which she sometimes staged with the help of her friends. She attended Hyde Park High School, and, at age fourteen, she entered the University of Chicago as part of its early entrant program; she gained her twelfth grade certificate in 1955, and continued her studies there at a college level. She was inspired by the university's science curriculum, which required that students read classic scientific works, and she was intrigued by the basic, still unsolved questions concerning reproduction and heredity.

Margulis received her A.B. degree in 1957 and the same year began a six-year marriage to Carl Sagan, a physics student later to become a well-known astronomer. She moved on to attend the University of Wisconsin, receiving a master's degree in genetics and zoology in 1960. In 1963, a mother of two, she completed graduate work at the University of California, Berkeley, receiving her Ph.D. two years later. In 1965, two years after her divorce from Sagan, she married Thomas Margulis, a chemist. That union, which also produced two children, ended in 1978.

Margulis commenced her critique of evolutionary theory while she was a graduate student, when she was not impressed by population genetics, and, in particular, became suspicious of dogma surrounding the generally accepted gene frequency theory of evolution. She doubted the view, best articulated by THOMAS HUNT MORGAN [62] two decades before the discovery of

DNA, that geneticists could study the cell's nucleus and essentially ignore the surrounding cytoplasm. Margulis was aware of the hypothesis of symbiosis as an evolutionary mechanism. It had been proposed just after the turn of the twentieth century by Konstantin Mereschkovsky and others. But by the 1960s, partly because of the success of the chromosomal theory of heredity, symbiosis was summarily dismissed and held up to ridicule. However, about 1963 Hans Ris, a professor of cell biology under whom Margulis studied at the University of Wisconsin, published photographs showing DNA in chloroplasts, green structures in the cytoplasm of plant cells, used in photosynthesis. The chloroplasts themselves closely resembled a form of bacteria, leading Ris to wonder whether their presence in the cell represented a form of evolutionary incorporation.

For her doctoral dissertation in 1965, Margulis essentially developed a new symbiotic hypothesis with global implications for biology: Nucleated cells evolved from symbiotic relationships among different kinds of bacteria. She predicted that certain cell structures, sites of photosynthesis or respiration, such as chloroplasts and mitochondria, provide evolutionary evidence for symbiosis. The theory did not meet with easy acceptance. Her paper "Origins of Mitosing Cells" was rejected over ten times before it was published in the *Journal of Theoretical Biology* in 1967. However, Margulis did receive the support of J. D. Bernal, the eminent crystallographer, who had included the origin of the nucleated cell on a list of unsolved biological mysteries. When Margulis sent Bernal a short paper, he agreed that she had solved the problem. "We and all beings made of nucleated cells," Margulis wrote later, "are probably composites, mergers of once different creatures."

Support for Margulis's theory of symbiogenesis soon also came from other scientists. Research zoologist Kwang W. Jeon, at the University of Tennessee, found amoebas that he was studying had been invaded by a form of bacteria. Though most of the amoebas then died, a few survived and, in an entirely unanticipated result, subsequently flourished while becoming dependent upon the bacteria living inside them. In addition, the composition of DNA found in chloroplasts of cells was shown, as Margulis had supposed it would be, to be nearly identical to DNA from blue-green, oxygen-producing photosynthetic bacteria known as cyanobacteria. Evidence from protein, DNA, and RNA sequencing also bore out Margulis's contentions.

Margulis's early work on symbiosis was published in 1970 as *Origin of Eukaryotic Cells*. Over the next decade, the theory was developed in a variety of directions by a number of researchers, and the book was revised and expanded in 1981 as *Symbiosis in Cell Evolution*. Recognition of the influence of her work came in 1983, when Margulis was elected to the National Academy of Sciences. The theory meanwhile evolved as "Serial Endosymbiosis Theory" (SET), as it was named by F. J. R. Taylor, who made his own, unsuccessful efforts to falsify it. In her more recent, radical version of the theory, Margulis suggests that certain hairlike structures found in cells, collectively the "undulipodia"—such as cilia and the tails of sperm—are also of symbiotic origin. Once again, she has encountered resistance from cell biologists.

In the late 1980s an intriguing confirmation of SET theory came with the discovery of single-cell plankton deep in the ocean. The existence of "prochlorophytes," as these photosynthetic bacteria are called, lend weight to SET because they so closely resemble the chloroplasts of green algae and plants.

Although SET in some form has won wide acceptance, Margulis has become a provocative presence in biology, in part because she draws conclusions from symbiogenesis which are at odds with basic dogmas of population genetics–based evolutionary theory. Margulis does not believe that the basic unit of evolution called the "individual" is fixed and rigid. In her view, individuals—all organisms larger than bacteria (animals, plants, fungi, etc.)—are recognized by her to be symbiotic systems. Rather, individuals larger than bacteria are all symbiotic systems; individuals are tightly integrated microbial communities. And she casts doubt on the idea that species evolve only through the buildup of chance mutations—rather, she thinks, most come from ancestors that have accumulated bacterial symbionts. She suggests that "the major source of evolutionary novelty is the acquisition of symbionts, the whole thing then edited by natural selection. It is never just the accumulation of mutations."

In recent years Margulis has also been a strong supporter of the Gaia hypothesis, originated by James E. Lovelock, which holds that Earth as a whole is a living system. Margulis has contributed to the development of this controversial theory, which has not won wide acceptance. However, she points out that it represents a further dethronement of human beings as privileged characters in the universe, in consonance with the overarching scientific theories of the last four hundred years. "*Homo sapiens* is not wise by virtue of his self-appointed name," Lynn Margulis writes; "to me the species reeks of arrogance fraught with ignorance."

In spite of her doubts about the completeness of the theory of natural selection, Margulis has not proposed any accompaniment of spiritual themes. Indeed, she has written passionately that her "rejection of Judeo-Christian nonsense is complete—I know less about Islam but I've seen that the Koran advocates the death of the infidel. The passivity of Buddhism reminds me of stagnant resignation. I confess to my own beliefs: all organized religion is institutionalized delusion, shared muddle, and derisive savage tribalism."

Lynn Margulis is Distinguished University Professor of Biology at the University of Massachusetts at Amherst. She is the author of over 130 articles and a dozen books, including several for a nontechnical audience. Her *Five Kingdoms: An Illustrated Guide to the Phyla of Life on Earth*, written with Karlene V. Schwartz, was based on a taxonomy originally proposed by ERNST HAECKEL [90], which debunked the plant–animal dichotomy; it was recently refined by Robert H. Whittaker. Margulis has also collaborated with her eldest son, Dorion Sagan, on several books: *Origins of Sex: Three Billion Years of Genetic Recombination; Garden of Microbial Delights; Microcosmos; Mystery Dance: On the Evolution of Human Sexuality;* and *What Is Life?*

81

Karl Landsteiner
and the Blood Groups

1868–1943

At the turn of the twentieth century, Karl Landsteiner developed a method of typing human blood which had far-reaching consequences for medicine and surgery as well as the field of forensics. In addition, Landsteiner subsequently contributed key discoveries to the emerging field of immunology. He helped to isolate the virus which causes polio and showed how syphilis might be studied in experimental animals. He also played a role in understanding the antigen-antibody response and allergic reactions. At the end of his life he discovered the Rh factor in blood, which led to a life-saving test for affected infants. Considered in conjunction with more recent innovations, such as the polio vaccine and organ transplantation, Landsteiner's achievements become archetypical of advances in physiology and medicine. They are not the result of global conceptual insights, but nodal points from which evolve new paths and, sometimes, create new needs.

Karl Landsteiner was born on June 14, 1868, in Baden bei Wien, a suburb of Vienna, the son of Leopold Landsteiner, a well-known Austrian journalist and editor, and Fanny Hess. He entered the University of Vienna in 1885 and received his medical degree in 1891. Landsteiner's pursuit of medicine was strongly shaped by his interest in the greatly expanding field of chemistry, and he had an extensive postgraduate education. Following studies at the University of Würzburg with the celebrated chemist EMIL FISCHER [46], Landsteiner went on to learn benzene chemistry in Germany and to further his knowledge of organic chemistry in Switzerland. He returned to Austria and after some experience in clinical medicine, worked in the department of hygiene at the University of Vienna. In 1897 he became assistant to the director of the University's Pathological-Anatomical Institute. Over the next decade he developed a considerable knowledge of disease, death, and human anatomy. He performed 3,639 postmortem examinations.

With his dual background in medicine and chemistry, Landsteiner developed a focal interest in the composition of blood. In 1895 Jules Bordet had discovered the tendency of blood from different species to form clumps when mixed together. Landsteiner noted the same "agglutination" when blood from different human beings was combined. This information was carried in a footnote in an article which appeared in 1900, but its importance was not lost on Landsteiner. In the following year he discovered that human blood could be divided into three groups, each containing a specific agglutinin, which he named A, B, and C. (C was subsequently renamed O, and a fourth group, AB, was discovered later.) The blood of every human being belonged to one of the types, and the groups could be shown to occur in definite proportions in various populations, showing that agglutination was not due to some disease process but was an ordinary chemical reaction.

The significance of Landsteiner's discovery was recognized within a few years. By 1907 the first transfusions were performed, and together with new advances in anaesthesia, all kinds of new operations became possible. It should be added that the relationship between the specificity of human blood and invasive procedures remains strong. Jean Dausset's discovery of the "histocompatibility complex" in the middle of the twentieth century sharpened both blood-typing procedures and surgeon's scalpels: it opened the way to organ transplantation.

When Landsteiner first discovered blood groups, he was unaware that they represented heritable factors. But the laws of Mendelian inheritance, which were rediscovered at the turn of the century, were soon seen to apply to blood groups. This ultimately led to serological genetics, which gave the courts—as well as unwed mothers and suspected fathers—a scientifically credible method to establish paternity. Recognizing the individuality of human blood, Landsteiner also conceived the idea of a serological "fingerprint" and as early as 1902 lectured before the Institute of Forensic Medicine in Vienna.

Landsteiner's subsequent career was impressively productive. About 1905 he established a means of infecting monkeys with syphilis, and that made possible experimental work against the disease. Landsteiner soon discovered the mechanism of the just-invented Wassermann test, which was used to detect syphilis. By showing how an extract from the hearts of animals could be substituted for the antigen previously obtained from humans, the test achieved much wider use.

Between 1908, when he became chief pathologist at the University of Vienna, and the end of World War I, Landsteiner conducted a number of investigations into poliomyelitis. Injecting various animals with a substance derived from the brain and spinal cord of a young victim of the disease, he showed that monkeys would develop signs of the disease. In 1912 Landsteiner drew the correct conclusion when he was unable to find any unusual bacteria in the substance: the causative agent was a virus. However, an effective vaccine would not be developed for another four decades.

Landsteiner's interests shifted further toward immunology in the 1920s. During the postwar economic hardship in Vienna, he moved for three years to the Netherlands and worked on the antigen-antibody response. He performed impressive experiments in allergy, applying to animals the agents which cause contact dermatitis in human beings, with the same irritating result—showing, as he believed, an antibody reaction at work.

Still more important, in 1921 he and his colleagues demonstrated the existence of small molecules that came to be called "haptens"—important components for the body's synthesis of antibodies. This was a major early step in a long process of understanding the human immune system.

In 1922, at the invitation of the Rockefeller Institute, Landsteiner moved to the United States, where he remained. He published *The Specificity of Serological Reactions*, a classic medical text originally issued in German in 1936, three years before he officially retired. He continued to work, however, and in 1940 demonstrated the existence of an Rh factor in blood, linking it to brain damage and death in newborns. Antibodies appear in the blood of an Rh-negative mother in response to an Rh-positive fetus. *In utero* the mother's antibodies destroy the blood cells of the fetus, frequently with catastrophic consequences. Transfusions can treat Rh incompatibility.

Landsteiner was awarded the Nobel Prize in 1930 for his discovery of the blood groups. He did not appreciate his growing fame and never became used to living in New York City. He had married Helene Wlasto in 1916, and they had one child, Ernst Karl. Said to possess a rather timid personality, Landsteiner nevertheless served as president of the American Association of Immunologists in 1929. A Jew who was converted to Catholicism as a child, he became obsessed toward the end of his life with fear of Nazi Germany. With his wife and son, who had become a physician, Landsteiner celebrated his seventy-fifth birthday on June 14, 1943. He died shortly thereafter, on June 26, two days after suffering a heart attack while at his laboratory bench.

82

Konrad Lorenz
and Ethology
1903–1989

Konrad Lorenz is widely known as the author of such popular books as *On Aggression, Man Meets Dog*, and *King Solomon's Ring*. But he is also one of the founders of ethology, which is the study of animal behavior, primarily in natural surroundings, from an evolutionary perspective. Behind the popular image of Konrad Lorenz—a widely published photograph shows him followed single file by a gaggle of geese—is the scientist who demonstrated that an unsuspected variety of behaviors may be regarded as genetically programmed and environmentally induced. His powerful and original generalizations have stimulated research in genetics, evolutionary biology, and psychology. At one and the same time, Lorenz underscored both the complex interplay between organism and environment—and its underlying simplicity.

Konrad Zacharias Lorenz was born in Vienna on November 7, 1903, the son of Emma Lecher and Adolf Lorenz, a famous orthopedic surgeon who discovered a simple way of treating a common kind of congenital hip deformation. Adolf Lorenz, who nearly won the Nobel Prize himself, became a celebrity and millionaire after treating the daughter of a Chicago meatpacker. At Altenburg, a summer home overlooking the Danube River, Konrad, an outgoing and mischievous child, acquired his passion for animals and became a young naturalist. Growing up in Vienna, he received a broad liberal education at the Schottengymnasium.

Although Konrad was interested in zoology (he is said to have read CHARLES DARWIN [4] at age ten), his father expected him to become a physician. After a semester at Columbia University—where he saw his first chromosomes in the laboratory of THOMAS HUNT MORGAN [62]—Lorenz returned to Europe to study medicine at the University of Vienna. But his greater enthusiasm for animals, especially birds, abided throughout. His father later wrote that "Konrad...preferred ornithology to medical practice. I was not over-enthusiastic about his choice and had deeply aroused my boy's anger when I said that it was of no great importance to know whether herons were more or less stupid than they were thought to be."

After receiving his medical degree in 1928, Lorenz declined to practice. Rather, he took a position as lecturer at the anatomy department of the University of Vienna, and in 1933 received a Ph.D. in zoology. At the university's Anatomical Institute he became a protégé of a well-known anatomist, Ferdinand Hochstetter. Lorenz was intrigued by the possibility of distinguishing evolutionary descent via physical structure, as Hochstetter was attempting to do through comparative anatomy. This method, Lorenz began to believe, "was as applicable to behavior patterns as it was to anatomical structure." This insight was the starting point of his work.

Lorenz's "goose years," from about 1934 to 1938, included both an original approach to experiment and an emerging theoretical framework. Studying the greylag goose in a natural habitat, at the family estate at Altenburg, Lorenz mothered the birds himself. His motivation was close-range observation, and he was able to follow patterns of growth, courtship ritual, mating, and nesting. When goslings hatched from incubated eggs were exposed first to him—or any moving object, he later found— they thereafter treated him as their mother. As it turned out, the greylag goose was well-suited to this kind of study because some other birds not only would become attached to the maternal substitute, but eventually would court and approach it sexually. Lorenz coined the term "imprinting" to generalize this neonatal behavior.

In 1936 Lorenz met Nikolaas Tinbergen, an animal behaviorist whose views turned out to be remarkably like his own, and the two began a fruitful and friendly collaboration. The yield of their work was to further conceptualize the basic strategies which animals employ to negotiate their environment in a multitude of ways. Animals were shown to have not only complex preprogrammed learning patterns such as imprinting, but also genetically driven motor programs for acquiring skills. Birds will sing, for example, but must first be exposed to birdsongs. In addition, "innate releasers" or "sign stimuli" are cues which, once perceived, invoke fixed patterns of response. Sign stimuli are usually related to hunting, avoiding predators, or communicating. A robin, for example, recognizing red as the sign of a male intruder, will attack a lifeless tuft of red feathers. And, as EDWARD O. WILSON [83] discovered, an ant, following food, will lay down a path which can be scented by others. The description and elucidation of these strategies, which can be found in a wide array of animals as well as insects, took place over many years and eventually extended the influence of ethology worldwide.

A number of biological thinkers in the twentieth century have found it difficult to separate scientific thought from the influence of politics, and the case of Konrad Lorenz is one of the most striking. In 1940 he published a paper comparing the domestication of animals to human beings, in both of which he saw dangers of genetic "degradation." In a style which may be described as pro-Nazi, Lorenz talked about "decadent art" and called for "selection for toughness, heroism, social utility." He wrote, "The racial idea as the basis of our [German] state has accomplished much in this respect." Lorenz was subsequently strongly criticized for this paper, and he later admitted that it had been written to please Nazi authorities. Although he recanted his enthusiasm, Lorenz continued to think that "domestication threatens humanity."

At the University of Vienna Lorenz was a lecturer in comparative anatomy and animal psychology from 1937 until 1940. Briefly he became head of general psychology at Albertus University. During World War II he was put to work as a neurologist and worked in a psychiatric hospital before being posted to the Eastern Front, where he was captured by the Russians. Although his conditions as a prisoner of war were not bad, and he worked as a prison doctor, his detention lasted well after the war ended; he was not released until early 1948.

When Lorenz returned to Germany, he soon recommenced his research at Altenburg. After several years of financial scraping, Lorenz received funds from the Max Planck Institute to establish a center for the study of behavioral physiology. In 1955 construction of the Max Planck Institute for Behavioral Physiology began in a bucolic setting in the German Lake District. Lorenz worked there from 1958 to 1973, when he returned to Austria, where he was welcomed by the Institute for Research in Comparative Behavior. His reputation continued to spread as ethology became well regarded in Europe and made inroads into the United States, where its influence was initially limited by behaviorism. In 1973 Lorenz, together with Tinbergen and Karl von Frisch, won the Nobel Prize in physiology or medicine for "their discoveries concerning organization of individual and social behavior patterns." This was the first Nobel Prize ever awarded to a behavioral scientist.

In the 1950s Lorenz wrote *Man Meets Dog*, the first of several books which were to make him a popular author. His *King Solomon's Ring* was a bestseller. Perhaps his most widely read book was *On Aggression*, published in 1966. Drawing on his animal studies, Lorenz delineated aggression in animals and went on to extrapolate its role in humans. He viewed aggressivity as a "fighting instinct" which is genetically useful to a species in terms of territory and survival. In humans, Lorenz viewed aggression as serving similar functions, and he suggested that "the invention of artificial weapons upset the equilibrium of killing potential and social inhibitions." The speculative nature of the book, with its view that aggressive behavior is innate and natural, made *On Aggression* controversial.

An assertive and complex personality—as a reading of his popular books makes clear—Lorenz enjoyed the fame that came to him late in life. But his biographer, Alec Nisbett, wrote that Lorenz also "claims humility and proclaims that a sense of humor is one of man's greatest assets since no one with a true sense of humor can be a megalomaniac, or can fail to be humble." As a young man he became romantically involved with a childhood friend, Margarethe Gebhart, whom he eventually married. Lorenz expected to live to be ninety-two, the age at which his father had died. But he was to live and work at Altenburg only until February 27, 1989, when his death came from kidney failure; he was eighty-three.

Placing Lorenz in any pantheon of scientific achievement is difficult. He stimulated a great deal of research and offered a fruitful challenge to behaviorism, although advances in evolutionary theory do not stem from him in any direct way. His influence upon the development of sociobiology is clear, while his theory of instinct has not won acceptance. "He studied animals for their own sake," wrote Nikolaas Tinbergen, "rather than as convenient subjects for controlled testing in severely restricted laboratory conditions. He restored the status of observation of complex events as a valid, respectable, in fact highly sophisticated part of scientific procedure." Most important, Lorenz's fundamental generalizations about the interrelations of genetic endowment and environment remain part of the frontier of ethology, just as their influence has been felt well beyond its boundaries.

83

Edward O. Wilson
and Sociobiology

1929–

Edward O. Wilson, originally an entomologist widely known for his studies of ants, is also the primary author of the controversial theory of sociobiology. Suggesting a genetic explanation for a variety of behaviors viewed as traits, such as altruism, aggression, and mate selection, sociobiology has been both hailed as a major new scientific paradigm and treated to strong criticism as a form of genetic determinism. A committed reductionist, Wilson has stated his belief that "human nature can be laid open as an object of fully empirical research, biology can be put to the service of liberal education, and our self-conception can be enormously and truthfully enriched." The fin-de-siècle debate

386

inspired by Wilson is an impressive demonstration of the persistence of politically charged arguments in biological thought.

Edward Osborne Wilson was born on June 10, 1929, in Birmingham, Alabama. He has described his childhood as "blessed," writing that "I grew up in the Old South, in a beautiful environment, mostly insulated from its social problems." Nevertheless, when a little boy, he lost the sight of his right eye in a fishing accident. "The attention of my surviving eye turned to the ground. I would thereafter celebrate the little things of the world, the animals that can be picked up between thumb and forefinger and brought close for inspection." When he was seven years old, his father, Edward Wilson, and his mother, Inez Freeman, separated and divorced, following which he spent a year at a military academy. In 1943 at age fourteen, he was baptized, but subsequently he abandoned religious faith as he developed an interest in science, engendering contradictory emotions which he has never fully resolved to his own satisfaction. Wilson graduated from high school in Decatur, Alabama, in 1946.

At the University of Alabama Wilson studied biology, receiving his bachelor's degree in 1949 and his master's the following year. He had already begun studying ants in his native South and published an article in 1950 on the dacetine species, which he has described as "under the microscope the most aesthetically pleasing of all insects." It was not surprising that, in 1951, Wilson continued his studies at Harvard University, which, he wrote, "was my destiny. The largest collection of ants in the world was there, and the tradition of the study of these insects built around the collection was long and deep." A junior fellow of the Society of Fellows at Harvard from 1953 to 1956, Wilson received his doctorate in 1955, remaining at the school initially as an assistant professor.

While still a graduate student, Wilson had become interested in how ants communicate, and he was intrigued by the work of the ethologist KONRAD LORENZ [82], who had shown that animals respond to environmental stimuli with fixed, inherited patterns of behavior. Although little was known at the time about the chemistry of smell, Wilson performed an impressive experiment with fire ants, which he observed touching their abdomens with their stings which they then trailed along the ground. Wilson cut open individual ants and crushed each of their internal organs, searching for a substance which exuded an attractive odor. He found that the tiny Dufour's gland, then of unknown function, contained a chemical communicator which came to be known as a "pheromone." Other pheromones were subsequently discovered and linked to various signals, opening a new field of biochemistry, contributing importantly to further research not only with insects but also with other animals and microorganisms.

Wilson's other investigations during the mid-1950s formed the basis of a series of influential discoveries in entomology. In 1954, he journeyed to New Guinea to collect ants and did extensive taxonomic work in their classification. At the same time, with William L. Brown, he developed a controversial critique of the notion of "subspecies." And he undertook seminal research on "character displacement," which occurs when two similar species, occupying the same geographic area, diverge genetically—presumably to avoid either competition for resources or combination as hybrids. Wilson also outlined an important principle of biogeography that he called the taxon cycle: the tendency of a species or group of species to adapt in a lawful relationship to the marginal habitats.

The rise of molecular biology, following the 1953 discovery of the structure of DNA, had by 1960 led to new academic divisions. Wilson was, as he later recalled, "physically trapped in Harvard's Biological Laboratories among the molecular and cellular biologists." He was neither a friend of JAMES WATSON [49]—whom he has described as the "Caligula of biology"—nor of ERNST MAYR [65], who was then personally cool toward him. In 1964 Wilson moved to Harvard's Museum for Comparative Zoology, where he became curator in entomology while continuing to teach as a full professor of zoology. By the mid-1960s Wilson's research on ants had brought him considerable recognition in the rapidly expanding, multidisciplinary field of evolutionary biology.

During the early 1960s, in one of his most original contributions, Wilson developed and then tested the hypothesis that species exist in chosen environments in a state of dynamic equilibrium. He went with Daniel Simberloff to the Florida keys, where, first, they identified the whole range of fauna on a pair of tiny islets. Then they systematically wiped it out, employing a professional exterminator who used methyl bromide to penetrate and kill off all forms of life. Following the extermination, they carefully charted the recolonization of the islets. They showed that the repopulation reestablished, as predicted, the basic equilibrium. The Florida keys experiment and the theory of species equilibrium became an important basis of further research in ecology and conservation. Wilson collaborated with Robert MacArthur on *The Theory of Island Biogeography* in 1967, and with William Bossert on *A Primer of Population Biology* in 1971.

Early in his career, while observing macaques, Wilson had wondered about new ways to understand diversity in the social animals, but no new theory was possible at the time. "A congenital synthesizer," Wilson wrote in his autobiography, "I held on to the dream of a unifying theory. By the early 1960s I began to see the promise in population biology of a possible foundation discipline for sociobiology." Wilson developed a theory of the evolution of caste, as well as of aggression, and soon became aware of a new thesis of kin selection—and that led to the hypothesis of a genetic basis for "altruistic" behavior, when one animal will sacrifice itself, for example, to insure the survival of its kin. After publishing *The Insect Societies* in 1971, which incorporated some of these notions, Wilson was "roused by the amphetamine of ambition" to write *Sociobiology: The New Synthesis*, which appeared in 1975. "I covered all the organisms that could even remotely be called social," he wrote, "from colonial bacteria and amoebae to troops of monkeys and other primates."

Sociobiology was widely hailed as laying the basis for a new means of understanding various social behaviors as evolved from genetic structures. But the book also ignited great controversy because of a single chapter, "Man—From Sociobiology to Biology." Here Wilson put forth, with all the evidence previously accumulated for insects and animals at his back, the generalization that an evolutionary basis exists for a genetic component in a wide range of human behaviors. Religiosity, conformity, sexual preference, xenophobia, aggression, self-sacrifice, and numerous other propensities which might be classified as traits—Wilson suggested all may have an adaptive genetic basis. "It may not be too much to say that sociology and the other social sciences," wrote Wilson in *Sociobiology*, "are the last branches of biology waiting to be included in the Modern Synthesis."

Wilson was not prepared for the furor which was unleashed by his suggesting that genes play an important role in determining human behavior on individual and cultural levels. At Harvard some of Wilson's colleagues, including Stephen Jay Gould and Richard C. Lewontin, formed the Sociobiology Study Group and eventually published a widely publicized letter in the *New York Review of Books*. Sociobiology, they argued, was the sort of theory which "tends to provide a genetic justification of the status quo and of existing privileges for certain groups according to class, race, or sex." Considerable debate followed over the next two years, both in the academic and lay press, with vestiges of the New Left taking to the classroom and to Harvard Square, where a protester with a bullhorn called for Wilson's dismissal. Anger came to a head in 1978, at a meeting of the American Association for the Advancement of Science, when demonstrators, chanting, "Wilson, you're all wet," poured a pitcher of water over him. Wilson, who was quite angry, "withstood these assaults upon his integrity," understated Ashley Montagu, "with civility and the appropriate sense of humor."

Wilson participated in the debates that followed upon the publication of *Sociobiology*, beginning with a long article for popular consumption in the *New York Times* in 1975. His *On Human Nature* was awarded the Pulitzer Prize, and in 1981 he wrote, with Charles Lumsden, *Genes, Mind, and Culture*. Although these books succeeded in evoking the important issues and stoking a long-standing nature-nurture conflict, they by no means resolved it. Following the appearance of *Promethean Fire*, also written with Charles Lumsden, and aimed at a broad public, Wilson effectively retired from the debate, having given what he called his final word on the subject.

The implications of sociobiology for human behavior are manifold, continue to be widely discussed, and have inspired a good deal of research, which has solidified the convictions of its proponents and scarcely convinced its foes. "A society that chooses to ignore the existence of the innate epigenetic rules will nevertheless continue to navigate by them and at each moment of decision yield to their dictates by default," Wilson warned at the end of *Promethean Fire*. "Economic policy, moral tenets, the practices of child-rearing, and almost every other social activity will be guided by inner feelings whose origins are beyond comprehension."

At the same time, it was possible to argue that sociobiology can be dangerous because it impedes a grasp of the subtler expressions of human intelligence, emotion, and behavior. "When sociobiology is injudicious and trades in speculative genetic arguments about specific human behaviors," Stephen Jay Gould writes, "it speaks nonsense. When it is judicious and implicates genetics openly in setting the capacity for broad spectra of culturally conditioned behaviors, then it is not very enlightening." The aggravating character of human sociobiology was enhanced by its being at once highly reductionist *and* speculative, and by resolving complex behaviors—such as homosexuality—by resorting to genetic platitudes.

With the debate not at an end, one can marvel at the extent to which genes are the conduit in biology for the expression of strong emotion. Most recently, however, Michael Lind has suggested, "Both radical environmentalism and the crude kind of sociobiology that tried to directly connect specific behavioral traits with genes appear to be giving away in the scholarly community to a nuanced consensus view that human potential is flexible but constrained at the margins by heredity." Whatever its faults, Wilson's work should not be confused with cruder forms of genetic determinism which remain present at the social margins, with a strongly nativist political bias.

In recent years Wilson has been an environmental activist, concerned with the loss of biodiversity occasioned by the pitiless destruction of rain forests and other natural habitats. He has also developed a speculative theory he calls "biophilia" to account for the affinity which humans have for other living things. *The Ants*, published in 1991, brought him a second Pulitzer Prize, and *The Diversity of Life*, in 1992, was also widely praised.

In 1955 Edward Wilson married Irene Kelly, and they have one daughter, Catherine. Wilson's *Naturalist*, published in 1994, is an appealing and elegantly written mixture of intellectual and personal autobiography. Among Wilson's many awards in science are the National Medal of Science for 1977, the Crafoord Prize of the Royal Swedish Academy of Sciences in 1990, and the Japanese government's International Prize for Biology in 1993.

84

Frederick Gowland Hopkins

and Vitamins

1861–1947

For centuries the major ideas about diet and nutrition derived from such figures as Hippocrates and Galen, who were taken as authorities by medieval scholastics. Food was recognized as a component of health and disease, and part of a larger concept of a *diatia*, or "way of life," and the various foodstuffs were classified in accordance with the prevailing "humoral" theory. And in Enlightenment thought, digestion was believed to be a mechanical process of grinding and mashing in the service of machine maintenance. With the advent of experimental medicine and such figures as CLAUDE BERNARD [13], more subtlety was possible. Finally, nineteenth-century advances in chemistry laid the groundwork for a fuller grasp of nutrition. New concepts were applied to its study, most successfully, by one of the founders of biochemistry, the British medical researcher Frederick Gowland Hopkins.

Hopkins was born in Eastbourne, Sussex, on June 20, 1861. His father, Frederick Hopkins, died soon after his birth, and his widowed mother, Elizabeth Gowland Hopkins, rejoined her family in London. There young Frederick found an uncharitable father figure in an uncle, and he received an undistinguished education. Solitary and often lonely as a boy, he became a voracious reader and a fan of Charles Dickens. The Hopkins family held literary stock, for the poet Gerard Manley Hopkins was Frederick's second cousin. Though he was not exceptional in school, at home, Frederick was entranced by his dead father's microscope. "I felt in my bones," he later wrote, "that the powers of the microscope thus revealed to me were something very important." He was interested in bugs, and his first scientific writing, published when he was seventeen years old, concerned the defensive purple cloud emitted by the bombardier beetle.

Gowland's higher education followed a long and tortuous path. When he was seventeen and not destined for the university, his uncle found him a job with an insurance business. He remained there only six months. He then had three years of training in statistical methods before taking part-time courses in chemistry at the University of London. When a small inheritance enabled him to continue his education, he began studying medicine. He received his degree in 1894. Until 1898 he worked as an assistant to a forensic expert at Guy's Hospital and was involved in some notable murder trials. Among his cases was that of Florence Maybrick, who purchased a great deal of flypaper before her husband was found dead of arsenic poisoning, and of the lovely Adelaide Bartlett, whose paramour bought her a bottle of chloroform not long before her husband experienced an excess of it.

While working at Guy's Hospital, Hopkins developed a test for the presence of uric acid in bodily fluids. This test soon became widely employed in medicine and research. But his most important work, on proteins, amino acids, and the chemistry of enzymes, awaited his move to Cambridge University. He went there in 1898 at the invitation of Michael Foster, who had also recognized the talents of CHARLES SHERRINGTON [66]. It was here, finally, at nearly forty years of age, that Hopkins began the most important work of his career.

Hopkin's discovery of the vitamin concept came at the turn of the century. In 1900 he discovered the amino acid tryptophan and the tryptophane reaction, isolating this substance from proteins and showing its importance in diet. Effectively, Hopkins reached a historic juncture, for the belief had arisen that proteins alone were responsible for nutrition. Hopkins found that tryptophan was an essential nutrient and, in addition, that the amino acids determine the quality of the various proteins they compose. During the first decade of the century, Hopkins conducted experiments which showed that animals cannot properly grow, as he declared in 1909, "when fed upon so-called 'synthetic' dietaries consisting of mixtures of pure protein, fats, carbohydrates, and salts." And, at the same time, other substances found in various ordinary foods, "can, when added to the dietary in astonishingly small amount, secure the utilization for growth of the protein and energy contained in such artificial mixtures." What Hopkins called, in 1906, "accessory food factors" were the substances known now as vitamins.

Today about fourteen substances qualify as the major vitamins, those defined as necessary for normal growth and maintenance of health. The first of these had already been discovered in 1897, as was realized years later. Christiaan Eijkman had recognized that his experimental hens would develop beriberi, a neurologically based degenerative disease, if he fed them only polished rice. The vital substance lost from the natural grain turned out to be thiamine, or Vitamin B_1. The isolation of the various vitamins proceeded over several decades. Vitamin E, for example, was first noticed in 1922, purified in 1936, and chemically analyzed two years later. But the underlying principle for all the vitamins remains Hopkins's concept of a necessary "accessory" nutrient. "It was only through Hopkins's work," writes Ernest Baldwin, "that the existence of vitamins became firmly and finally established." It was for this work that in 1929 Hopkins was awarded the Nobel Prize in physiology or medicine, which he shared with Eijkman.

Hopkins's work on the vitamin concept is representative of his more general significance for the development of biochemistry. Although an experimentalist, he brought to this developing science considerable conceptual ability. He recognized the importance of utilizing such physical concepts as the laws of thermodynamics in understanding the tremendous intricacy of the cell. And at the same time, he realized that experiments had to be designed for living organisms. The chemistry of the cell could not be understood in its full complexity when studied as a form of chemical mechanics in test tubes. In his "The Dynamic Side of Biochemistry," a lecture given in 1913, he provided what Neil Morgan calls "a classic statement formulating biochemistry as a unitary science based on the study of dynamic metabolism mediated through enzymes."

Named to the first chair of biochemistry at Cambridge University in 1914, during World War I Hopkins recognized that margarine—the new substitute for rationed butter—lacked essential nutrients; this led to the first fortified food. He continued his research after the war, and discovered glutathione, an important antioxidant with crucial biochemical functions in the cell. Research on glutathione continued to occupy him for some years. Hopkins also undertook studies of the chemistry of lactic acid, the breakdown product of glucose in muscle tissue.

No single individual may be said to have founded biochemistry, but Hopkins was a key figure not only in stating its fundamental principles but also in his work as a teacher. From 1921 until 1943 Hopkins was the Sir Frederick William Dunn Professor of Biochemistry at Cambridge. In 1924 his laboratory facilities improved greatly with the opening of the Dunn Institute of Biochemistry. Hopkins developed an international reputation, training numerous students who furthered his work and disseminated his ideas abroad.

Curiously, Hopkins was said not to be emotionally so solid as his achievements. He seems to have suffered a brief nervous breakdown in 1910 and entertained doubts about his intellectual abilities throughout his life. This was presumably true even after he was elected a Fellow of the Royal Society in 1905. He served as the society's president in 1931, was knighted in 1925, and received the prestigious Copley Medal in 1926. He was married to Jessie Ann Stevens, and the father of three children. Hopkins died on May 16, 1947.

85

Gertrude Belle Elion
and Pharmacology

1918–

In the last half of the twentieth century, broad advances in biochemistry and medical technology created a climate favorable to developing new drug treatments for a wide variety of diseases. There is no shortage of figures who made key discoveries in pharmacology, but perhaps none is more outstanding than Gertrude Belle Elion. In collaboration with George Hitchings at Burroughs Wellcome, Elion made a broad advance in developing one of the first effective drugs to combat leukemia. A derivative of this same basic medicine was later used to facilitate organ transplants. During the 1970s Elion went on to develop the first safe and potent antiviral medication, acyclovir, to combat herpes infections. Undergirding these drug discoveries were new insights about the way in which various microbes and viruses metabolize nucleic acids, their basic building blocks. In 1988 Elion, together with Hitchings and James Black, received the Nobel Prize in physiology or medicine.

The daughter of eastern European Jewish immigrants, Gertrude Belle Elion was born in New York City on January 23, 1918. Her father, Robert Elion, was originally from Lithuania, and her mother, Bertha Cohen, from a scholarly family of Russian Jews, had emigrated to the United States in 1914. Although Robert Elion was a successful dentist, the Depression brought an end to family prosperity. The death of Gertrude's grandfather when she was fifteen provided her with an enduring motivation, she has said, to help people through medicine, which was intensified when her fiancé died of a bacterial infection. Elion attended Walton High School, graduating in 1933 at age fifteen. At Hunter College, then a free New York City women's college with a competitive entrance system, Elion immediately chose to major in chemistry. She graduated summa cum laude in 1937.

As a woman during the Great Depression, it was difficult for Elion to find employment in medical research. After several jobs as a laboratory assistant, she taught high school physics and chemistry while working for a master's degree, which she received from New York University in 1941. Soon after the United States entered World War II, Elion worked as a food analyst for Quaker Maid—she verified the color of mayonnaise, among other tasks—and she worked briefly for Johnson & Johnson in a new but short-lived pharmaceutical laboratory. In the early years of her career, Elion experienced a fair amount of discrimination; she was not hired for one job, for example, on the pretext that her physical attractiveness would distract other workers. "War changed everything," she once said. "Whatever reservations there were about employing women in laboratories simply evaporated." In 1944—acting on a suggestion of her father's—she found a position as biochemist with Wellcome Research Laboratories, where she would remain for the rest of her career.

At Burroughs Wellcome, a British firm which encouraged research to discover drugs to treat serious diseases, Elion came under the influence of George Hitchings, head of the biochemistry department. Hitchings possessed, and transmitted to Elion, his commitment to a rational program of drug research, in place of older, fairly haphazard searches for new drugs through screening of large numbers of chemicals. Powerful sulfa drugs had been recently developed, and Hitchings and others suspected that other substances which interfere with the metabolism of microbes could serve as powerful drugs.* This led him to study the nucleic acids, which were not then understood as DNA and RNA, bearers of the genetic code, but as molecular structures necessary to growth and reproduction. Hitchings assigned Elion to the study of the purines—molecules that comprise two of the building blocks of nucleic acids, adenine and guanine.

Although the process of making and testing various compounds was slow, by 1948 Elion and Hitchings had found a purine substance called diaminopurine. When tested in patients at Sloan-Kettering Institute, it was found to inhibit the course of leukemia. Initially the toxic side effects of diaminopurine were too severe, but several years later a more appropriate compound was introduced after Elion synthesized a substance called 6-mercaptopurine. 6-MP was launched on the market during the 1950s with the help of the radio broadcaster and newspaper columnist Walter Winchell, at a time when the dramatic remissions lasted only about a year or less before the disease returned. Later improvements in therapy, however, made childhood leukemia a largely curable disease, and 6-MP is still a staple of treatment.

Following their success with 6-MP, Elion and Hitchings developed other drugs on the same basis. A chemical relative, 6-thioguanine, was effective in treating another form of leukemia. These drugs worked by interfering with the multiplication of white blood cells, and later were also found to suppress the immune system. This was a desirable reaction in the case of organ transplants, it was soon realized, and in the late 1950s a form of 6-MP was devised which, by disabling the body's host-vs.-graft response, permitted the first successful kidney transplants. It is still part of treatment. One of the drugs developed by Elion and Hitchings, allopurinol, did not work against cancer but was successful in treating gout and preventing kidney stones.

The achievements of Elion and Hitchings were impressive

---

*The first sulfa drug, prontosil, was synthesized in 1932 by Gerhard Domagk to combat streptococcal infections. It worked, as was understood several years later, by interrupting the bacteria's metabolism. Penicillin, discovered by ALEXANDER FLEMING [97] and others, worked more efficiently on a wider range of bacteria and was much less toxic.

accomplishments in organic chemistry. Their success, writes Bruce Chabner, "stresses the importance of patience, persistence, innovative chemistry, and astute clinical collaboration in drug discovery." Upon Hitchings' promotion to research director in 1967, Elion was named head of the Burroughs Wellcome's Department of Experimental Therapy.

Antibacterials had been widely developed by the 1960s, and vaccination was able to prevent smallpox. But apart from rabies and polio, little progress had been made in treating any of the known viral diseases, which range from the common cold to measles, influenza, and hepatitis. One family of viruses, the herpes virus, causes several diseases, from the fairly harmless cold sore to genital herpes, which can lead to birth defects. Herpes virus is also on rare occasions responsible for a form of encephalitis that can be fatal. Beginning in the late 1960s, Elion began investigating the properties of compounds related to one of her early anticancer substances. The result was acyclovir.

An antiviral compound based on a poison-pill strategy, Elion showed that acyclovir—the generic name for a particular acyclic purine nucleoside—will interfere with the normal replication cycle of the herpes virus. The virus, having invaded a cell, produces an enzyme it uses for reproduction and takes up acyclovir in an effort to manufacture a nucleotide—a building block of DNA—which, however, is fatal to the whole operation. Initially kept a secret for proprietary reasons until clinical trials began, Burroughs Wellcome announced the drug in 1978 with a fanfare that proved justified by its potency. Elion has described the discovery of acyclovir, which she has credited to the entire team at Burroughs Wellcome, as her "final jewel" of discovery.

Acyclovir also represented a further vindication of the basic antimetabolite strategy. "We had finally shown that antiviral drugs could be selective," Elion wrote later, "and that one could capitalize on the differences between the viral and cellular enzymes." The basic research strategy which Elion employed was also used to develop AZT, the first powerful drug used in treating the human immunodeficiency virus which causes AIDS.

After receiving the Nobel Prize in 1988, Elion became an eminent personality in American science. Retired in 1983, she has since served as a consultant for Burroughs Wellcome, lectured widely, taught at Duke University and other colleges, and served in a host of capacities in a variety of organizations. She was elected to the National Academy of Sciences in 1990 and was awarded the National Medal of Science in 1991. Elion never married after the death of her fiancé in the 1930s but maintained close ties to her family. Eleven members of her family accompanied her to the Nobel awards ceremony in Stockholm. Although her lack of a formal doctorate made her a rare laureate, Elion since 1969 has been awarded no fewer than twenty honorary degrees.

86

Hans Selye
and the Stress Concept

1907–1982

The concept of stress is simple to grasp. In a single word it expresses the penalties of life in an uncertain world. With hundreds of ways to accumulate it, and everything from massage therapy to vitamins to meditation employed to combat its ill effects, stress has become an everyday concept. It is democratic and can afflict all but the cloistered and blessed. It can be discussed without embarrassment by everyone, and can be held at least partly responsible for almost everything bad that can happen to a person. Stress is so popular, in fact, that it is often forgotten that it has a strong basis in scientific medicine, has inspired much research, and forges a once-neglected alliance

between medicine and psychology. It is also a provocative coun-
terbalance to the severe reductionism of much medical and
biological research, providing a perspective which is holistic in
the best sense of the term. The originator of the stress concept
was the Viennese-born physician Hans Selye.

Hans Hugo Bruno Selye was born on January 26, 1907, in
Vienna, the son of Maria Felicitas Langbank and Hugo Selye, a
well-known surgeon, himself from a medical family. Selye's early
education took place at home with a governess, and he later
attended the College of the Benedictine Fathers. In 1924 he began
medical studies at the German University of Prague, spending a
year abroad at the universities of Paris and Rome before taking
his medical degree in 1929. Selye continued his postgraduate
studies in organic chemistry, receiving a Ph.D. in 1931. Migrating
to the United States, Selye spent a year at Johns Hopkins
University then went on to McGill University in Montreal, where
he took a position as a lecturer in biochemistry in 1933.

Selye often recounted the genesis of the concept of stress,
which is a curious scientific tale of discovery, disappointment,
and revelation. His first glimpse of the idea dates to 1925, while
he was still a medical student. During clinical presentations, Selye
was led to wonder why so many patients in the early phases of
various diseases were affected by the same symptoms. Coated
tongues, generalized aches and pains, stomach problems, weight
loss, and other symptoms were characteristics of many illnesses
that professors commonly pointed out but to which they paid
little attention. Rather, the focus was on the specific signs of a
particular disease—the swelling of the parotid glands in mumps,
for example. Selye wondered in passing why such a great variety
of diseases would actually share so many of the same symptoms,
especially in their early stages.

Although Selye lost sight of this "syndrome of just being
sick" for a decade as he pursued his studies, he recovered it again
in 1935. In search of a new bovine hormone—endocrinology was
a new and expanding field—Selye injected extracts of cows'
ovaries into rats. This provoked a characteristic set of reactions in
the animals. The outer layer of the adrenal cortex became
enlarged, while the thymus shrank, and bleeding ulcers appeared
in the stomach and intestines. No such group of symptoms had
ever been observed before, and at first, believing he might have
discovered a new sexual hormone, Selye was excited.

But his elation was not to last. Injecting the rats with all sorts of organ extracts—from placenta, spleen, kidney—produced the same triad of symptoms. His hope for a new hormone vanished, and Selye was in despair until, as he wrote later, "My eyes fell on a bottle of formalin which happened to be on the shelf in front of me." A poisonous substance used to preserve tissue, Selye now injected *that* into his laboratory animals—with the same results. *Anything toxic,* it seemed, would lead to the same set of reactions. "I do not think I have ever been more profoundly disappointed. Suddenly all my dreams of discovering a new hormone were shattered."

Then he had a flashback to his days as a medical student. He recalled the early symptoms produced by so many of the infectious diseases. He recognized something similar in his rats' enlarged adrenal, shrunken thymus, and in the bleeding ulcers. It also occurred to him that many treatments for various diseases were essentially the same: Patients were advised to rest, eat simple foods, and stay warm. "If we could prove that the organism had a general nonspecific reaction-pattern," wrote Selye, "with which it could meet damage caused by a variety of potential disease-producers, this defensive response would lend itself to a strictly objective, truly scientific analysis." The concept of stress was born.

Selye's first paper on stress was published in *Nature* as a letter to the editor in 1936. He soon developed the notion of the *General Adaptation Syndrome* (G.A.S.), to which he gave a three-stage explanation of the stress response. The first stage of stress, the *alarm reaction,* was followed by a *stage of resistance* and, finally, a *stage of exhaustion.* These were not impressionistic terms but rather associated with the way the body discharges its available cortical hormones, replenishes them, and finally exhausts them. Selye first saw stress reactions as purely hormonal. Later, the great importance of the pituitary gland, which is attached to the hypothalamus in the brain, was recognized and seen to play a role in the stress response. Currently it is supposed that neurotransmitters govern the secretion of neurohormones, which in turn regulate release of the adrenocorticotrophin hormone (ACTH), which invokes the stress response. As with everything related to the brain, the full chemistry of stress awaits greater clarification.

The theory of stress did not win immediate acceptance. The concept was criticized by the eminent Walter B. Cannon, who had developed the modern concept of homeostasis, and Selye later said, "So few among the recognized, experienced investigators whose judgment I could trust, agreed with my views and, after all, was it not silly and presumptuous for a beginner to contradict them? Perhaps I had just developed a warped point of view, perhaps I was merely wasting my time?" However, Selye did secure the help of Sir Frederick Banting; the Canadian who had pioneered the use of insulin for diabetes helped him win a small research grant. Although resistance to the stress concept continued for some years, Selye's 1950 monograph *Stress* brought together an impressive array of experimental evidence. Selye began publishing an annual devoted to stress, and new discoveries in endocrinology tended to confirm the theory.

Through research which he and many others conducted, Selye eventually came to identify a stress component in a great number of disorders: cardiovascular disease and heart-related problems of all sorts; inflammatory diseases, including allergic reactions; and even in infectious diseases such as the common cold. Psychosomatic disorders of various kinds, from digestive problems to obesity to sexual disorders, are frequently related to stress. By 1975 Selye could boast that there were one hundred ten thousand publications on stress, and he himself eventually authored over thirty books and fifteen hundred papers.

Selye also wrote popular and even inspirational books in addition to his academic writings. *The Stress of Life* appeared first in 1956 and became a widely read classic, and some years later Selye published *Stress Without Distress*. Selye, aware of the importance of self-expression and creativity, discussed transcendental meditation and Hare Krishna. A distinctively *haute-bourgeoise* character pervades his writings, and he is sometimes highly didactic. He tells people how to sleep and to take life as it comes. He even wrote an instruction manual for scientists, *From Dream to Discovery*, telling them "How to Behave," "How to Think," and "How to Work." Selye held to an anachronistic view of "purposeful causality" and agreed with fellow Viennese KONRAD LORENZ [82] in "species-maintaining purposeful teleonomy." Such formulations could find little support in science, then or now.

Although well established, the stress concept has been challenged in recent years in various ways. Today, stress researchers sometimes distinguish social, physiological, and psychological stress, and the newer concept of "coping" has become important. Pointing out the high sensitivity of the hormonal system to emotional stimuli, stress researcher Richard S. Lazarus and others have contested the basic idea that stress occurs as a purely nonspecific reaction to a stressor. Thus, being *cold* does not necessarily evoke the same stress as being *unpleasantly cold.* But this is only a change of emphasis, reflecting the interest which psychologists have paid to the concept and the growing importance of various kinds of stress management.

An energetic scientist who kept trim and fit throughout his life, and who spoke ten languages, Selye, from 1945 until his retirement in 1977, was professor and director at the University of Montreal's Institute of Experimental Medicine and Surgery. He also served as president of the International Institute of Stress, which he had founded in 1976. Selye was married to Frances Rebecca Love in 1930, Gabrielle Grant in 1949, and his third wife, Louise Drevet, in 1978. A compulsive worker and, to judge by snippets of diary in his autobiography, *The Stress of My Life,* not easy to live with, Selye felt that few scientists "[spend] as much time with their families or [give] as much attention to political problems as the average good citizen should." Like many of the stress researchers who followed him, he was, however, moved by an abstract but genuine sympathy: "To my mind," he wrote, "the highest qualities of mankind are a warmhearted attitude toward our kin, and particularly compassion for all who suffer from disease, poverty or oppression." Hans Selye died on October 16, 1982.

87

J. Robert Oppenheimer
and the Atomic Era

1904–1967

The effort to build an atomic bomb during World War II was headed by the American theoretical physicist J. Robert Oppenheimer. "It is generally agreed," writes Gerald Holton, "that no one else could have directed so well the large group of prima donna scientists assembled at Los Alamos under the difficult and panic-evoking conditions of war." Subsequently, Oppenheimer became an important spokesman for the international scientific community, but in the 1950s he lost much of his influence in government. He opposed the evolving arms race with the Soviet Union and was not in favor of building the hydrogen bomb. Oppenheimer responded to the first test explosion of the

A-bomb in July 1945 with words which became famous: "We knew the world would not be the same" and recalled a line of Hindu scripture, "Now I am become Death, the destroyer of worlds." His career is a potent illustration of the interplay between science, technology, and the aims of government.

J. Robert Oppenheimer was born on April 22, 1904, in New York City, the eldest son of Julius Oppenheimer and Ellie Friedman. An immigrant Jew from Germany who arrived in the United States in 1888, Julius was a successful businessman, and his wife was a teacher and painter. Robert Oppenheimer enjoyed a privileged childhood, attending the private Ethical Culture School in Manhattan. Like many gifted children, he was more comfortable with grown-ups than his peers, and at age twelve, he was accepted into the New York Mineralogical Society, where members assumed from his letters that he was an adult. He had an extraordinary memory, learned a number of languages in high school, and graduated valedictorian in 1921.

At Harvard University, where he was accepted in spite of a prevalent anti-Semitism, Oppenheimer was initially a chemistry major but, under the influence of Percy Bridgman, became interested in physics before graduating summa cum laude in 1925. Oppenheimer went on a fellowship to Cavendish Laboratory, in Cambridge, but his sojourn in England was not happy and was marked by emotional instability. He did learn, however, that he was not an experimentalist, and thenceforth he concentrated on theoretical physics.

Moving on to the University of Göttingen in 1926, Oppenheimer met some of the major figures who were reshaping the theory of quantum mechanics: MAX BORN [32], WERNER HEISENBERG [15], and Wolfgang Pauli. After receiving his Ph.D. in 1927, Oppenheimer remained in Europe, and became one of the first to work on the quantum theory as it applied to electrodynamics. His most important work, with Max Born, led to the development of a theory of molecular behavior which came to be called the Born-Oppenheimer approximation. It is interesting to note that Born found young Oppenheimer arrogant and disliked him.

By the time Oppenheimer returned to the United States in 1929, he had a reputation as a leading American authority on the new quantum physics. Taking a post as professor at both the University of California, Berkeley, and the California Institute of Technology in Pasadena, Oppenheimer eventually became an

outstanding teacher who attracted a long list of successful graduate students and postdoctoral fellows. According to his friend
HANS BETHE [35], at Caltech "Oppenheimer created the greatest
school of theoretical physics that the United States has ever
known." He bought a ranch in New Mexico and cultivated the
image of an outdoorsman, compensating for a certain frailty as a
youth. During the 1930s Oppenheimer's scientific contributions
included significant papers on the theory of the positron, the
first "antiparticle"—the counterpart to the electron which PAUL
DIRAC [20] had predicted in 1930 and which was verified by
experiment in 1932. Generally, Oppenheimer showed a capacity
for envisioning relationships between theoretical and experimental physics which would serve him well in what became the
principal task of his career.

   With the beginning of World War II in Europe, consideration was given to building a nuclear fission bomb; this idea
gained momentum when the United States entered the war at the
end of 1941. By this time Oppenheimer had already begun
nuclear research, and one of his first accomplishments was to
estimate the amount of the uranium isotope U-235 needed to
make an atomic bomb.

   Late in 1942 Oppenheimer became director of the new
research facility at Los Alamos, the top-secret laboratory associated with the Office of Scientific Research and Development,
where the atomic bomb was developed and built. Oppenheimer
was able to gain the confidence of scientists, including many
European emigrés, and his capacity for bringing practical results
from theory impressed the U.S. military. Although he did not
have a background in administration, he turned out to possess
considerable organizational capabilities and understood how to
usefully coordinate work with universities. Known by the code
name Mr. Bradley, he directed operations of about forty-five
hundred individuals. One drawback for the government was
Oppenheimer's political conscience: until the war he had considered himself a pacifist.

   On July 16, 1945, at 5:29 A.M., Fat Man, the first nuclear
bomb, was detonated in the New Mexico desert, melting the sand
and creating an enormous crater. Oppenheimer belonged to a
panel of four scientists which recommended, after some consideration, that the bomb be used on Japan, a decision he later
regretted. On August 6 the United States dropped an atomic

bomb on Hiroshima, followed three days later by a second on Nagasaki. On August 10, the war ended with Japan's surrender. The death toll from the two atomic bombs was about 140,000 in 1945, and another 60,000 deaths from the long-range effects occurred over the next five years.

In 1946 Oppenheimer was awarded the Presidential Medal of Merit by Harry S Truman. Oppenheimer became for a time an important maker of scientific policy, and, writes sociologist Philip Reiff, "became a symbol of the new status of science in American society. His thin handsome face and figure replaced Einstein's as the public image of genius." However, Oppenheimer opposed building further nuclear arms and, at a meeting, told Truman that "I have blood on my hands." This led the president to characterize Oppenheimer as a "crybaby scientist" and to say, "Don't ever bring that damned fool in here again. He didn't set that bomb off—I did. This kind of snivelling makes me sick."

In 1947 Oppenheimer was appointed director of the Institute for Advanced Study in Princeton, New Jersey, and there he remained until the end of his life. It was in his capacity as chairman of the Atomic Energy Commission's board of advisers, from 1947 to 1952, that Oppenheimer came into conflict with proponents of U.S. nuclear arms buildup. He did not like the increasingly paranoid style of American government, and he advocated a policy of openness instead of secrecy. Oppenheimer stood in favor of peaceful applications of nuclear energy and reduced spending for weapons research—largely in consonance with the views of NIELS BOHR [3] and many European physicists. A vocal critic, Oppenheimer therefore tangled with the military. Unlike his friend and colleague at Princeton, JOHN VON NEUMANN [51], who was solicitous of army generals, Oppenheimer could be contemptuous and even sarcastic, and he earned their enmity.

In retaliation for his antimilitarist stance, Oppenheimer was beset with charges of disloyalty, and a campaign was mounted against him within the Atomic Energy Commission (AEC). In 1953 the AEC suspended his security clearance, a move that would effectively remove him from his position as adviser. At a 1954 hearing, he was supported by a number of fellow scientists, who testified to his integrity and loyalty, but one important exception was EDWARD TELLER [88]. In addition, in the redbaiting climate of the 1950s, Oppenheimer could not overcome the suspicions aroused by his affiliations with leftists as a university professor. He not only lost his security clearance, he was pilloried in the popular press. He made his case as best he could in lectures and books, including *Science and the Common Understanding*, published in 1954, and *The Open Mind*, from 1955. He continued teaching at Princeton, although he had ceased doing original research. A political rehabilitation of sorts came in 1963 when Oppenheimer was awarded the AEC's Enrico Fermi Award for Science.

Throughout his life, Oppenheimer cultivated a wide variety of interests in the world outside physics. He was interested in psychoanalysis; he studied Sanskrit and ancient Greek, and his mildly left-wing inclinations were characteristically serious and by no means unusual in the 1930s. His wife, Katherine Puening Harrison, whom he married in 1940, was the widow of a Communist killed in the Spanish Civil War. Only in the changed world of the 1950s did this cosmopolitan stance cause him problems. Oppenheimer's generosity was a notable trait: He gave frequent parties for his students and treated them to dinners at fine restaurants. So popular was Oppenheimer with his students that they sometimes adopted his mannerisms, his accent, and his pipe. The latter proved fatal. In 1966 he was diagnosed as suffering from cancer of the throat, and he died on February 18, 1967.

88

Edward Teller
and the Bomb
1908–

The history of nuclear physics is closely bound up with weapons of mass destruction. No individual scientist better illustrates this than Hungarian-born Edward Teller. After working on the development of the atomic bomb, Teller was widely known from the 1950s as the "father of the H-bomb." He was tireless in his advocacy of national defense, and in the 1980s he largely conceived and promoted the concept of "Star Wars," a costly space-based defense system, to protect the United States from nuclear attack. Because of his political leverage as well as his accomplishments in physics, Teller is considered to be one of the most influential scientists of the twentieth century. He is viewed as a very thoughtful man by some, dangerous by others. "Mankind is still wrestling with Teller's legacy," writes William J. Broad, "still trying to sort through the projects and ideas he championed."

Edward Teller was born in Budapest, Hungary, on January 15, 1908, the son of Max Teller, a lawyer, and Ilona Deutsch Teller. The Tellers were prosperous, assimilated Jews whose fortunes suffered under the brief Communist regime of Béla Kun after World War I. Gifted in math, Edward was said to put himself to sleep by counting multiples, such as "Sixty seconds to a minute, thirty-six hundred seconds in an hour, eighty-four thousand six hundred seconds in a day." He was entranced as a child by the writings of the French novelist Jules Verne, and he was a gifted pianist. Attending the well-known Minta Gymnasium, Edward came to prefer mathematics, but at his father's urging he studied chemical engineering with a view toward a practical career. But at the universities of Budapest and Karlsruhe, he continued to read mathematics on his own, and he became interested in quantum mechanics. He moved to the University of Munich in 1928, where he lost his right foot in a streetcar accident. But this did not prevent him from receiving his doctorate in 1930 from the University of Leipzig, where he studied with WERNER HEISEN-BERG [15].

In 1931 Teller began teaching at the University of Göttingen, but two years later he quickly recognized the implications of the Nazi's rise to power. He wrote in his autobiography: "The hope of making an academic career in Germany for a Jew existed before Hitler came—and vanished the day he arrived." Receiving a Rockefeller Foundation grant, Teller soon moved to the University of Copenhagen, spent a brief period in London, and came to the United States in 1935.

As professor of physics at George Washington University, Teller at first pursued his original interests in the behavior of molecules. He also collaborated with George Gamow, the imaginative Russian physicist, in deriving the rules of beta decay. But, more significant, Teller shared Gamow's growing interest in astrophysics. On account of the revolutionary developments in twentieth-century physics, an explanation of stellar energy had become, by the 1930s, a plausible subject for investigation. Teller and Gamow published a paper on thermonuclear energy in 1937, and in 1938 it was the major topic of the Washington Conference on Theoretical Physics. In 1939, a few days before the next

Washington conference, NIELS BOHR [3] announced that German scientists Fritz Strassmann and Otto Hahn had succeeded in splitting the atom. The potential significance of this event, in light of the political climate of the time, was not lost on many physicists, and for Edward Teller it determined much of the rest of his career.

By the early 1930s physicists had been aware that splitting the atom was possible, and at the onset of World War II it became clear that U-235, a uranium isotope, could be used to create a sustained chain reaction leading to the release of enormous amounts of energy. In the genesis of the atomic bomb, Edward Teller "was present," writes William Broad, "at every critical juncture." He was with physicist Leo Szilard when ALBERT EINSTEIN [2] was asked to lend his prestige to the atomic bomb project, and subsequently Teller joined the Manhattan Project. He worked with ENRICO FERMI [34] at the University of Chicago and later moved to Los Alamos, where the bomb was constructed. In addition, in 1941 Fermi suggested to Teller in a conversation, "Now that we have such a good prospect of developing an atomic bomb, couldn't such an explosion be used to start something similar to the reactions in the sun?" Fusion, the energy produced by the sun and other stars, is far more powerful than fission. This was the first conception of the hydrogen bomb. And even while the atomic bomb project progressed, Teller continued to think about it.

The significance of Teller's work on the atomic bomb at Los Alamos is a subject of some dispute. Teller has often been described as being uncooperative by HANS BETHE [58], head of the theoretical division; he was reluctant to perform crucial but onerous calculations concerning the implosion device, one of the methods used to detonate the bomb. Teller, who had been friends with Bethe, has disputed this assessment. In 1944 J. ROBERT OPPENHEIMER [87] relieved Teller of responsibility for the implosion calculations but persuaded him to remain at Los Alamos to work on a preliminary study of the feasibility of a hydrogen bomb. Teller's biographers, Stanley A. Blumberg and Louis G. Panos, conclude: "First, Teller made important contributions to the Los Alamos project; and second, he might have contributed more if he had been 'a team man' and had set aside his differences with Bethe and Oppenheimer." According to Daniel Kevles in *The Physicists,* Teller "was apt to spend his leisure in long walks, insisted at work upon pursuing his own scientific demon, a thermonuclear weapon, and drove his neighbors to distraction by rhapsodizing on the piano at odd hours of the night."

After World War II ended, Teller pursued the possibility of an H-bomb with great vigor in spite of initial reluctance on the part of a number of leaders in the scientific community. After the Soviet Union developed its own atomic weapon in 1949, the prospect of a superpotent device became highly attractive to the United States. Teller's advocacy of the bomb was initially based on unreliable calculations—a long-classified fact which for years rankled Hans Bethe. Bethe was finally able to reveal that Teller "proposed a number of complicated schemes...none of which seemed to show much promise." But with the help of Stanislaw Ulam, a mechanism was finally conceived that used X rays to ignite the nuclear fuel. A thermonuclear device, named Mike, was exploded on a barren atoll in the South Pacific in December 1952. Its yield exceeded all expectations, leaving a huge crater in place of the former island of Elugelab. Teller, who did not attend the blast, sent a coded telegram telling of its success: "It's a boy."

One of Teller's triumphs and personal tragedies involved an extrascientific debate over the loyalty of J. Robert Oppenheimer. Teller was concerned and angry lest Oppenheimer's negative assessment of the hydrogen bomb impede its construction. At a hearing of the Atomic Energy Commission in 1954, Teller told the committee, which was investigating Oppenheimer as a cold-war security risk, "If it is a question of wisdom and judgment...then I could say one would be wiser not to grant clearance." The testimony was important in bringing down the highly respected Oppenheimer, but it also cost Teller many friends among the nation's senior physicists.

As head of the Lawrence Livermore Laboratory, which was associated with the Berkeley Radiation Laboratory at the University of California, Teller remained a powerful figure for another four decades. He became the most widely known scientist-advocate of the H-bomb, nuclear testing, and missile development. He wielded considerable power in the ensuing arms race between the United States and the Soviet Union. He also coauthored such books as *Our Nuclear Future* in 1958 and *The Legacy of Hiroshima* in 1962, and he was frequently profiled in popular magazines. He weighed in often and determinedly against the notion of a ban on nuclear weapons tests, and he touted an atomic engineering project in Alaska.

Although the cold war favored Teller's views, he is also said to have had a unique gift for befriending political figures. According to Herbert F. York, he "exuded a sort of boyish enthusiasm which, coupled with a typically central European charm and even diffident manner, favorably impressed most people, especially politicians and statesmen, and predisposed them to believe what he was telling them." (Teller considers this view ridiculous.) He courted, and to some extent appears to have misled, President Dwight D. Eisenhower with the optimistic prospect of a "clean" fusion bomb—one without radioactive consequences.

Teller's influence, whatever its source, had a specific aim. According to Ray E. Kidder, Teller "was possessed with the threat of Soviet world domination. It consumed him entirely for the second half of his life. He *knew* he was right, and anybody who failed to understand the enormity and primacy of this threat was simply a fool unworthy of serious consideration." In the 1970s Teller's book *Energy from Heaven and Earth* defended the use of nuclear energy, and he considered running for the U.S. Senate before a heart attack compelled him to reduce his workload. While remaining associate director of Lawrence Livermore Laboratory, from 1963 Teller was also professor of physics at the University of California. Upon his retirement in 1975 he became a research fellow at the Hoover Institute on War, Revolution and Peace at Stanford University.

When Ronald Reagan was elected president of the United States in 1980, Teller gained a strong ally. Characterizing Reagan's election as a "miracle," Teller did not need to convince him of the military threat posed by the Soviet Union. Meeting Reagan in 1982, Teller outlined his proposal for a "third generation" antimissile system and asked for more funding for an X-ray laser program. Early in 1983 President Reagan told the nation that the time had come to begin a massive program for a space-based system of nuclear defense. Billions of dollars were soon poured into a not fully conceived and to some extent unworkable system of defensive weapons. The Strategic Defense Initiative (SDI) was to include an array of weapons based both on the ground and in space, including sophisticated X-ray lasers and particle beams. This "Star Wars" plan was effectively abandoned ten years later after $36 billion had been spent. Not a single working system of defense had been put in operation.

The expense of the Strategic Defense Initiative may have been its undoing, but the program well expressed Teller's basic view of the uses of science. "We would be unfaithful to the tradition of Western civilization if we shied away from exploring what man can accomplish, if we failed to increase man's control over nature," asserted Teller in 1987 in his *Better a Shield Than a Sword*. From a historical perspective, arguments concerning the conflicting moral obligations of humankind to nature go back to the Enlightenment. The conviction that mankind ought to aim at conquering and controlling it has perhaps been dominant. Although this is not the only view found in science, it would appear to have been a motivating assumption behind the career of Edward Teller.

An extraordinarily durable personality in American science, Edward Teller was married to Augusta Maria Harkyani, known as Mici, in 1934, and they had two children, Paul and Susan. With the collapse of Communist governments in Eastern Europe in the late 1980s, Teller was able to revisit his native Hungary. He remained director emeritus of Lawrence Livermore Laboratory and continued, into the 1990s, to offer his advice and counsel on problems of nuclear energy and defense.

Willard Libby
and Radioactive Dating

1908–1980

A half century ago, soon after the end of World War II, the development of radiocarbon dating provided a means for examining the natural history and cultural past of mankind. It became possible to date with general accuracy many thousands of artifacts, from ancient corncobs found in New Mexico caves to the Dead Sea Scrolls. A development of nuclear physics, the new technique had great impact on the disciplines of archaeology, anthropology, and geology. Radiocarbon dating was more than a new technology, however, for it evolved from basic ideas about the chemical composition of the universe. It opened a window on the distant past of mankind and a perspective on the furthest galaxies. It is the major contribution of an American physicist, Willard Frank Libby.

The rare great physicist with a rustic background, Willard Frank Libby was born on December 17, 1908, in Grand Valley, Colorado. His father, Ora Edward Libby, was a farmer whose education had terminated at third grade, and his mother was Eva May Rivers. When Willard was five years old, the family relocated to an apple ranch in northern California, where Willard attended grammar and high school, graduating in 1926. Encouraged by his parents, he continued his education at the University of California at Berkeley. He initially planned to become a mining engineer but found himself drawn to chemistry, mathematics, and physics. He graduated in 1931. Within two years of receiving his Ph.D., Libby was already involved in the field of low-energy, radioactive nuclei and had built a sensitive Geiger counter for detecting low-level radiation. He remained at Berkeley as an instructor from 1933 until 1940.

During World War II Libby moved to the War Research Division of Columbia University, where he worked on the development of atomic energy for the Manhattan Project. His major contribution involved producing the means of separating the uranium isotopes needed to create the atomic bomb. This essential step involved some of the same principles which Libby would invoke in his work on radiocarbon dating. After the war, Libby moved to the Institute for Nuclear Studies at the University of Chicago, directed by ENRICO FERMI [34].

Recognition that radioactivity bore upon the age of the earth did not originate with Libby. It had been recognized from the turn of the century that nuclear decay, over a measurable period of time, transformed unstable, radioactive elements into stable, ordinary elements. As early as 1904 ERNEST RUTHERFORD [19] had recognized that radioactivity could suggest an age for the earth. An American chemist, Bertram Borden Boltwood, began to devise a method for computing this process in 1905, and he arrived at a theory which gave 2.2 billion years for the age of the earth, at the very least, and 5 billion years for the age of the solar system.

Libby's signal contribution to these developing hypotheses was to recognize the significance of cosmic-ray bombardment, which was discovered in 1939. Cosmic rays, subatomic nuclear particles continually arriving from outer space, strike and combine with nitrogen, the element which comprises nearly four-fifths of the atmosphere. Some nitrogen atoms, Libby supposed, would be transformed into radioactive carbon, or carbon-14. This isotope of carbon would in turn be quickly taken up by carbon dioxide, which is absorbed by plants.

Thus, all living things would ingest carbon-14 naturally in the food chain. Libby found it reasonable to suppose that the level of carbon-14 would remain fairly constant in the organism throughout its life cycle—so long, that is, as it continued to absorb nutrients. After death, however, the carbon-14 remaining in the plant or animal would eventually decay, and its presence in the organism would gradually diminish. While the half-life of uranium is four and a half billion years, the half-life of carbon-14, so it was discovered about 1940, is approximately 5,730 years, a relatively short period. "It should be possible," wrote Libby, "by measuring the remaining activity, to determine the time elapsed since death, if this occurred during the period between approximately 500 and 30,000 years ago."

Building a special Geiger counter that he encased in thick lead to keep out ordinary radiation, Libby developed a baseline for a dating process by first burning natural substances, such as redwood trees, whose ages were known by other means. He later tested wood from the deck of the funerary boat of King Sesostris of Egypt, for example, and was able to show excellent accord between predicted and experimental results. To Libby's laboratory came other items: charcoal burned by early humans at Stonehenge, England and from the Great Pyramid of the Sun in Mexico, not to mention ancient sloth dung from Chile. Libby also was able to date the oldest human communities and to suggest that the last Ice Age ended some 10,000 years ago—far later than previously thought. Carbon-14 dating eventually became useful for items from about 500 to 70,000 years old. Libby's *Radiocarbon Dating* was published in 1952, and in 1960 he received the Nobel Prize for chemistry.

Libby became a fairly influential figure in American physics. In 1954 he took a leave from the University of Chicago to serve on the Atomic Energy Commission. An appointee of President Dwight D. Eisenhower, Libby was regarded as a cold warrior and, by some, a dupe of government policy. Supporting arms buildup, he held the view "that the risks are minimal in comparison with the risk resulting from an inadequate nuclear arsenal." During the 1950s Libby was a strong advocate of backyard "fallout shelters," which were supposed to protect people from deadly radiation in an atomic war. He had a remarkably sanguine view of radioactivity and was a strong proponent of nuclear arms testing, writing that "we really cannot say that testing is in any way likely to be dangerous...." Libby worked in the chemistry department at UCLA in the last phase of his career and served as the director of the Institute of Geophysics and Planetary Physics.

Libby was married to Leonor Lucinda Hickey, and they had twin daughters, Susan and Janet. After their divorce in 1966, Libby married Leona Woods Marshall. Tall and imposing, with red hair, Libby was known as "Wild Bill" throughout his life. He was considered an effective teacher who tried to be especially tough on his graduate students. His view of the requirements of his profession was not atypical of his era: "A scientist has to be a man," he told Theodore Berland. "Most people are not, in the sense that they are leaning on others. They are part of a group. A scientist must be able to work as an individual, to do his own work." Libby retired in 1976. He died on September 8, 1980, of complications from pneumonia.

Since Libby's discovery of carbon-14 dating, a whole field of radiometric testing has developed, using methods that are increasingly sophisticated, precise, and significant. New procedures, such as the K-Ar method, for example, which uses radioactive potassium-40, have been instrumental in dating continents and geological structures; and the Rb-Sr method uses rubidium atoms to date rocks from the moon. All such methods, it should be added, hold exceptional implications for biblical literalists. Subatomic particles link the history of mankind to the history of the universe and locate human history in a geological time frame. Such an interface with human civilization, found also in microbiology, is one of the major contributions of physics to cultural enlightenment.

90

Ernst Haeckel
and the Biogenetic Principle

1834–1919

Not many people besides biologists today will recognize the name of Ernst Haeckel, the German botanist and evolutionary thinker. But he was a pivotal and controversial figure who helped shape biological investigation after CHARLES DARWIN [4], expanding its range by bringing to bear studies of embryology, morphology, and cell theory. He also raised and discussed many issues which are still alive today and coined the term *ecology*, which he defined as the scientific investigation of the relationship between organism and environment. Stephen Jay Gould has recently documented his extensive historical significance, and some years ago Erik Nordenskiöld could write that "there are not many personalities who have so powerfully influenced the development of human culture—and that, too, in many different spheres—as Haeckel."

Ernst Heinrich Philipp August Haeckel was born on February 16, 1834, at Potsdam, in Prussia, today a part of Germany. Although his parents' background was allied to the Prussian bureaucracy, the household was liberal and middle class. Encouraged by his mother, Charlotte Sethe Haeckel, Ernst collected and classified plants as a youngster and developed a strong and romantic love of nature. At the gymnasium he had a classical education, with little attention to mathematics, read Goethe and Alexander von Humboldt, and desired to make a career in botany. His father, Carl Haeckel, a civil servant, wanted him to become a physician, and Ernst took a medical degree at the University of Berlin in 1857. But he never lost sight of his major interest and practiced medicine for only a short time before becoming professor of zoology and comparative anatomy at the University of Jena in 1862.

While still a student, Haeckel had been introduced to marine biology and became a devoted microscopist. During 1859 and 1860, he went on a botanical expedition to the Mediterranean to study the peculiar one-celled organism, the Radiolaria. He collected thousands of specimens and discovered 144 new species of these protozoa. With their complex external skeletons, they are some of the most delicately beautiful things found in nature. Haeckel was an accomplished draughtsman, and his monograph from 1862, *Report on the Radiolaria,* is still considered a highly valuable contribution. Over the next decade Haeckel worked to classify the sponges and the medusae, or jellyfish, eventually describing some four thousand species. Haeckel's work in marine biology led him to propose a new three-kingdom system of classification which recognized that certain of the smaller organisms were neither plants nor animals. In the twentieth century this system has been taken up and advanced by others, including, most recently, LYNN MARGULIS [80].

The determining event in Haeckel's thought, apparent even in these early works, was the publication of *The Origin of Species* by CHARLES DARWIN [4], which he read soon after its appearance in Germany. In 1863 Haeckel gave an influential lecture which both summarized Darwin's theory and annealed it to several aspects of his own original, emerging ideas. Haeckel found in the notion of descent the very attractive idea that progress is "a natural law which no human power, neither the weapons of tyrants nor the curses of priests, can ever succeed in suppressing." Haeckel regarded his work within the context of German romantic natural philosophy and viewed such thinkers as Goethe as precursors to Darwin.

Haeckel's *General Morphology,* published in 1866, contains the major statement of his scientific thought. He would elaborate it over the next forty years. Using Darwinian ideas to explain the forms of all the various organisms, Haeckel distinguished the science of anatomy and of emerging forms, which he called ontogeny (development of individuals) and phylogeny (evolution of species). He called his approach "monism" because he rejected the Cartesian dualism of mind and matter and did not believe in any absolute difference between the organic and the inorganic. Haeckel also adopted Lamarckian ideas, believing that acquired characteristics could be passed on to succeeding generations through what he called "progressive heredity." By this amalgamation Haeckel believed that he was expanding Darwinism; however, his extravagant philosophical basis prevented him from appreciating the value of Mendelian ideas when they were re-discovered in 1900.

Yet one of Haeckel's ideas, which he called the "biogenetic principle," became particularly influential. This is the notion that "ontogeny recapitulates phylogeny"—that each individual in the course of its development passes through the stages which the entire species has undergone in the course of its evolution. Although this idea did not originate with Haeckel, he gave it the most prominent place in his biological system. He used it in developing his famous, imaginative genealogical trees for the various species. In man's evolution, for example, one begins, at the base of the tree, with the one-celled creatures because the fertilized ovum is single-celled. Rising toward the tree's top, Haeckel postulated the existence of a *nonverbal* ape-man, based in part on the fact that infants are born without speech.

Although it seems less than completely solid today, Haeckel's biogenetic principle was enormously influential. In *Ontogeny and Phylogeny,* Stephen Jay Gould has argued its significance not only for biology but for theories of race, criminal anthropology, and education, as well as psychoanalysis and child development. Both SIGMUND FREUD [6] and JEAN PIAGET [77] were influenced by this idea, which, Gould argues, did not perish so much as become unfashionable and, eventually, incompatible with Mendelian genetics.

Haeckel's influence outside science was also great. In 1868 he published *The History of Creation,* followed six years later by *The Evolution of Man.* In these popular books Haeckel presented his system for a lay audience, emphasizing the system's philosophical implications. Anticlerical and pantheistic, Haeckel was attacked by organized religion, which he detested. But he found a receptive audience in 1899, when he wrote *The Riddle of the Universe.* Widely translated, highly popular, and often confused, the book discussed the broadest issues of science in sections on cosmology, psychology, theology, and anthropology. Like many other grandiose texts that mingle science with philosophical speculation, *The Riddle of the Universe* was highly popular and eventually led to the formation of the Monist League. Although his belief in progress and his anticlericalism appealed to liberals, Haeckel's quasi-mystical leanings and belief in such concepts as racial purity led his followers, in the years after his death, to support the aims of National Socialism.

Haeckel married a cousin, Anna Sethe, in 1862. Her death just two years later caused him enormous pain but did not prevent him from working. He subsequently married Anna Huschke, the daughter of a well-known anatomist. A robust man who would break away from periods of intense work for cross-country hikes, Haeckel retired in 1909 from the University of Jena. His last years were not happy, and he was especially upset by the onset of World War I, when England—Darwin's country—fought against Germany. He died on August 9, 1919.

91

Jonas Salk
and Vaccination

1914–1995

Three names are closely associated with the conquest of epidemic polio. Albert Sabin unlocked the mystery of the polio virus's transmission and eventually developed an oral vaccine used the world over. John Enders made a Nobel Prize-winning contribution by finding a way to grow virus in a test tube. But it was Jonas Salk who made the historic breakthrough: the first vaccine to induce immunity to the disease. The story of the Salk vaccine has all the indicia of other great medical discoveries to combat against killer diseases: public fear, adulation of the bold superman, doubts among a minority, wariness among peers, and bitter rivalry between colleagues.

Jonas Salk was born in New York City on October 28, 1914, the eldest of three sons of a garment worker, Daniel Salk, and Dora Press. A gifted and studious child growing up in an Orthodox Jewish home, Jonas attended Townsend Harris High School, which was designed for exceptional students, and graduated at age fifteen. He went on to the tuition-free City College of New York, from which he graduated in 1933. Originally Salk was not interested in science: he intended to become a lawyer. But work as a laboratory technician and several courses taken to satisfy his curiosity changed his mind. He attended the New York University School of Medicine with the help of fellowships and received his medical degree in 1939. In 1942, after interning at Mount Sinai Hospital, he joined Thomas Francis Jr., a virologist under whom he had worked in medical school, at the University of Michigan's School of Public Health.

Salk's early work, at the onset of World War II, involved efforts to develop an influenza vaccine. This research was supported by the U.S. Army, whose soldiers were falling ill from Sicily to the Philippines, in an era when many could still recall the devastation wreaked by the flu after World War I. Salk eventually did play a role in developing the vaccine which became, and long remained, the principal means to avoid the full-scale illness. In the late 1940s his work on influenza brought him a reputation as an important young researcher.

At war's end, Salk was increasingly drawn to research on polio, as the disease was becoming disturbingly common; fifty-eight thousand cases were reported in 1952. Knowledge of the disease accumulated slowly, as it became understood that the virus entered the bloodstream through the digestive tract. Some people with the virus—most often children—were affected by fever, headache, malaise, and a few other symptoms which, in most cases, disappeared in a short time. However, in about two percent of those affected, the virus went on to invade the membrancs around the brain, damaging cells which control the peripheral nerves or other functions. Paralysis in various degrees, and sometimes death, was the result. Victims who survived were frequently crippled or confined to "iron lungs" and needed respiratory help until the end of their lives.

In 1947 Salk joined the University of Pittsburgh's School of Medicine as associate professor and director of the Virus Research Laboratory. He soon attracted the interest and financial support of the National Foundation for Infantile Paralysis, which was responsible for the March of Dimes charity drives, and Salk's early work involved typing the virus; it turned out to have three strains, named Brunhilde, Lansing, and Leon.

The polio virus has an interesting natural history. Some evidence suggests that it existed in ancient Egypt, but the first documented epidemic swept Sweden in 1887. Polio appeared in the United States in 1894, with an epidemic in Rutland County, Vermont, and in 1916 its incidence suddenly quadrupled to some twenty-seven thousand cases, six thousand of which were fatal. It was believed for a time that the virus was transmitted through the air or carried by insects, and immigrants and the urban poor were taken to be responsible. In fact, the virus turned out to be intestinal, and the epidemic resulted in part from unprecedented social emphasis on hygiene. For centuries most children had acquired immunity through breast-feeding or had been exposed to the virus while young, with fewer consequences. But improved sanitation and cleanliness as well as a misplaced medical passion for bottle feeding, meant a lack of acquired immunity and greater vulnerability when older children or adults ingested the virus.

Salk's development of a vaccine depended on several key events. The first came in 1949 at Harvard University, where John Enders discovered how to grow the mumps virus in animal tissue. Salk adapted the technique to polio, eventually using the kidneys of monkeys to grow all three strains of the virus. Then, at Johns Hopkins University, it was found that a killed form of the virus stimulated antibody production in experimental monkeys. This led Salk to suspect that a polio vaccine might be developed using totally inactivated virus—a concept which ran counter to accepted wisdom. The view that a crippled microbe stimulates better immunity than a dead one goes back to the days of LOUIS PASTEUR [5] and was open to debate.* Salk's espousal of the killed virus concept, and his vigorous pursuit of such a vaccine in the face of considerable opposition, was the source of his triumph.

With the support of the National Foundation for Infantile Paralysis—which wanted a vaccine as quickly as possible—Salk developed the vaccine that was to make him famous. Using all three types of the virus, which he killed with formaldehyde, he

---

*Recall that Pasteur, Gerald L. Geison has recently suggested, appears to have lied about using an attenuated virus to make an anthrax vaccine, and in fact, used a killed virus.

created an injectable brew. He then tested the vaccine on monkeys before clinical trials with about one hundred children and adults began in 1952. To bolster confidence in the vaccine, Salk vaccinated himself, his wife, and his children. The following year he directed a trial of five thousand children, and in 1954 he began the famous mass field trials in which over two hundred thousand children were vaccinated. A year later, on April 12, 1955, came the announcement that the vaccine was safe and effective, and within a few years some two hundred million shots had been administered. The number of new cases of polio dropped rapidly.

The Salk vaccine brought its maker the status of hero, proof of which came when Hollywood sought Marlon Brando for the title role in *The Jonas Salk Story*. Salk and his family were brought to the White House, where President Eisenhower called him a "benefactor of mankind" and gave his little boys pen knives. Drug companies offered to make him a rich man many times over. He was beset with people expressing their gratitude and with newspapers vulgarizing his achievement. "The worst tragedy that could have befallen me was my success," Salk said later. "I knew right away that I was through, cast out."

This was overstated but not entirely false. Salk was not an establishment figure—indeed, he had experienced a certain amount of anti-Semitism—and was not elected to the National Academy of Sciences or awarded the Nobel Prize. Even before the vaccine was tested, Salk's notion of using a killed virus was strongly opposed by Albert Sabin, an eminent researcher who had discovered much about how the disease was transmitted. The rivalry between the two men intensified when Sabin made efforts to block the mass trials in 1952 and later tried to have the vaccine banned when a botched batch caused several deaths.

When Sabin developed his own vaccine, which was administered orally, he made it available to the Soviet Union in 1959, and its popularity eventually rivaled and surpassed the Salk vaccine, even in the United States. Attending medical conferences while the Sabin vaccine was gaining ground was, Salk later said, "like sitting in on plans for one's own assassination." Eventually Salk came to believe he should have made a greater effort to capture more of the world's market for the killed vaccine. In an article in the *New York Times* in 1973, he warned of dangers associated with the Sabin vaccine, but his plea went unheeded.

Salk's later career was distinguished by his founding of the institute which bears his name. Built according to his own specifications, and opened in 1963, the Salk Institute for Biological Studies at La Jolla, California, became a prestigious, well-endowed institution able to attract an impressive array of scientists. Salk himself continued original research into multiple sclerosis and cancer. In the early 1970s, he wrote a series of books with philosophical themes: *Man Unfolding, Anatomy of Reality, The Survival of the Wisest,* and *How Like an Angel.* "Wisdom, understood as a new kind of strength," Salk wrote, "is a paramount necessity for man. Now, even more than before, it is required as a basis for fitness, to maintain life itself on the face of this planet, and as an alternative to paths toward alienation and despair." In the last decade of his life, Salk directed research on a vaccine for the human immunodeficiency virus (HIV).

It is appropriate for a medical hero to be a workaholic as well as devoted to his family, and so it was with Salk, whose wife was quoted in *Time* magazine: "Why, Jonas, you're not listening to me at all!" Salk married Donna Lindsay when he graduated from medical school in 1939, and they remained close even after their divorce in 1968. In 1970 Salk married Françoise Gilot, an artist and former mistress to Pablo Picasso. On June 24, 1995, Jonas Salk died from heart failure.

92

Emil Kraepelin
and Twentieth-Century Psychiatry

1856–1926

Modern psychiatry took shape in the late nineteenth century, and its leading figure was the German Emil Kraepelin. Adopting scientific and emergent medical principles to the observation of mental illness, Kraepelin developed a classification that is still the basis of contemporary diagnostics. His method was descriptive, applied to the severest forms of psychiatric disorders, and based on a belief in some underlying hereditary, constitutional, or physiological abnormality. Arising from neuroanatomy, Kraepelin's psychiatry offered its patients gloomy prospects for recovery, and he hoped for chemical solutions, which eventually came about in the form of antipsychotic and psychotropic drugs.

The limitations of this approach were, and are, that it is difficult for an explanation of mental disorders to progress much beyond the description and treatment of symptoms.

Emil Kraepelin was born on February 15, 1856, in Neustrelitz, the capital of the German free state of Mecklenberg-Strelitz. His father was a civil servant, and Emil became interested in biology through an older brother, Karl, who later became a well-known zoologist. At the University of Würzburg, Emil studied medicine, receiving his degree in 1878. The following year, his interest in mental disease was evident in his dissertation "The Place of Psychology in Psychiatry." He studied neuroanatomy in Munich and was particularly interested in cases of organic brain disease. Kraepelin had also spent the summer of 1876 at the University of Leipzig and was so taken with the experimental psychology of WILHELM WÜNDT [99] that in 1882 he returned to work with that eminent figure. Kraepelin was impressed by the chemical effects of drugs on behavior, although they had no application to psychiatry at the time.

During the late 1880s Kraepelin held positions in clinical psychiatry at mental hospitals in Munich, Leubus, and Dresden. In 1886, he was made professor at the University of Dorpat, where four years later he was asked to head the department of psychiatry at the University of Heidelberg. It was from this position, over the next fourteen years, that Kraepelin achieved his international reputation.

Kraepelin's great influence is derived from his diagnostic breakdown of mental illness, which he initially presented in 1883 in the first edition of his *Kompendium der Psychiatrie*. This book, originally 400 pages, underwent extensive revisions over the years until by the ninth edition, in 1927, it comprised four volumes and came to 2,425 pages. In the *Kompendium*, translated into English as *Textbook of Psychiatry*, Kraepelin set out his belief that mental processes could "be deduced from certain external manifestations such as the manner of speech, gestures, and actions." He laid down the view, which could have been etched in stone for its durability, that "mental disorders are diffuse illnesses of the cerebral cortex" and psychiatry was a branch of neuropathology.

In general, the classification of the severe mental disorders is Kraepelin's signal achievement. Through successive editions of the *Kompendium* he gradually distinguished the forms of dementia praecox, which later was called schizophrenia, to include manic-depressive illness and paranoia. Kraepelin also classified subtypes, such as hebephrenia, which involves bizarre verbal behavior and has been responsible for some great anonymous poetry in the clinical literature: "The mountains which are outlined in the swellings of the oxygen" and "In Switzerland, it is not permitted to do mischief with human flesh!" It is interesting to note that the adaptive context of language in schizophrenic patients was entirely lost upon Kraepelin and his colleagues; only with SIGMUND FREUD [6] are such utterances revealed to possess psychological meaning.

Not surprisingly, Kraepelin also took an interest in what today are considered purely neurological problems, such as Alzheimer's disease, and he was an activist against alcoholism, which he viewed as a terrible scourge that could provoke schizophrenic reactions in susceptible people. He made studies of the effect of alcohol on the body, but they did not form part of his major work.

For much of his career Kraepelin believed that the psychoses were all due to heredity and largely irreversible, although he eventually came to think that some cases might be due to disorders of metabolism. Of several notable aspects of Kraepelin's classification, the most severe was its Calvinist destiny. People with severe mental disorders Kraepelin believed incurable, and a diagnosis of schizophrenia was a life sentence. In theory, "Kraepelin finally succeeded," wrote his eminent student, Eugen Bleuler, "in isolating a number of symptoms which were present in maladies with very poor prognoses while absent in other disease-groups." But the practical result was "a basis on which to make predictions in a large number of cases as to acute attacks, and terminal state."

Kraepelin's pessimism shaped many subsequent custodial-like treatment strategies, unfortunate in light of present-day psychiatry which regards about one-third of all schizophrenics as subject to full remission. The Kraepelinian viewpoint led Bleuler, for example, to bemoan the oversurveillance of schizophrenics, which he believed only aggravated their illness and even their desire to commit suicide. The "back ward" character of schizophrenia persisted through the 1960s, when new generations of antipsychotic drugs made it both plausible and economically desirable to release large numbers of hospitalized patients into the general population.

In 1904 Kraepelin became professor at the University of Munich and director of the city's new psychiatric clinic. The clinic's efficiency, and its atmosphere, which was conducive to instruction, enhanced his reputation as a teacher. He opened a museum of psychiatry, which showed some of the cruelties the insane had been subjected to in the past. "We must not lose sight of the enormous impact that Kraepelinian psychiatry had in its own time," write Franz Alexander and Sheldon Selesnick in *The History of Psychiatry*. "Like Pinel and Esquirol, he demonstrated repeatedly the importance of utilizing in psychiatry the medical approach of detailed observation, careful description, and precise organization of data. Without this orientation psychiatry could never have become a clinical, disciplined specialty of medicine." At the same time, Kraepelin has also been severely criticized, sometimes viewed as only repaving the Greek rationalism in psychiatry which dates to Aretaeus of Cappadocia in the second century A.D. "A closer look at the historical picture," writes psychoanalyst Reuben Fine, "reveals that Kraepelin was merely partially redressing the massacres and tortures that the mentally ill had been subjected to through the centuries, quite often at the hands of the church."

Away from the clinic, though not excessively garrulous or outwardly expressive, a love of nature combined in Emil Kraepelin with a desire to write poetry, and in 1933 some of his verse was translated for an article in the *Journal of Nervous and Mental Diseases*. "Far to the east in glacier ice," Kraepelin wrote of Voringfoss, a beautiful waterfall which drops 600 feet off the Bjoreia river in Norway,

> Lusty the young stream has its birth;
> Out from the crystal gates with mirth,
> Free in its life course from its rise.
> Merry is its play of youth;
> See it sparkle, bubble, foam—
> Dreams it darkly of a home.
> Striving toward a goal, in truth?

Emil Kraepelin died on October 7, 1926.

93

Trofim Lysenko
and Soviet Genetics

1898–1976

During more than a generation Trofim Lysenko was the foremost figure in agriculture in the Soviet Union, and for many years he dominated the biological sciences as well. He distrusted Western biology—much as today in the United States "creation science" despises neo-Darwinism—and was responsible for its long and destructive suppression. Although his authority is widely considered to have been noxious, Lysenko's significance scarcely goes unrecognized. He is the subject of a considerable literature and has earned a place in the *Dictionary of Scientific Biography*. Among scientists he is often held up as an object of ridicule. "All this DNA, DNA!" he used to say. "Everybody speaks about it, nobody has seen it!" But in spite of his ignorance, the deeper significance of Lysenko as a figure in the history of science is clear. "Lysenkoism showed how a forcibly instilled illusion," writes Valery Soyfer, "repeated over and over in meetings and in the media, takes on an existence of its own in people's minds, despite all realities."

The son of Denis and Oksana Lysenko, Trofim Denisovich Lysenko was born in Karlovka on September 29, 1898, in Poltava, a Ukrainian province of Russia. Because his parents were peasants, he learned to read and write only at about age thirteen, when he attended a local school for two years. Lysenko subsequently graduated from the Poltava Horticultural School, which mainly produced gardeners for rich landowners, and in 1917 he went on to study at the agricultural institute in Uman. In 1922 he began attending the Kiev Agricultural Institute, from which he received a degree as an agronomist in 1925. (He did not receive a doctorate, as is sometimes reported.) He published two articles in 1923 concerning tomato breeding and sugar beet grafting.

Lysenko's rise to prominence in the Soviet Union comes with the ascendancy of Stalin following the death of Lenin in 1924. While working at the Ordzhonikidze Central Plant-Breeding Station from 1925 to 1929, he introduced some varieties of peas, which brought him to the attention of the press. He was feted in popular magazine articles as a proletarian hero who smiled only when he thought of his mother's cherry dumplings. Subsequently Lysenko studied the influence of temperature on ripening and in 1928 suggested that there was merit in subjecting seeds to cold before planting. He claimed that wheat which was "vernalized" in this way brought a better harvest. Effectively an adaptation of an older method known to peasants for centuries, his "vernalization" was praised by such legitimate scientists as Nikolai Vavilov, who may have hoped to explain the limited value of the technique in terms of ordinary agronomy.

Immeasurably aided by the disorganization of Soviet agriculture, which invoked bureaucratic desperation, Lysenko's work was popularized by the Ministry of Agriculture. As was to happen later under Mao Zedong in China, general ignorance among the peasantry provided a populist basis for denigrating "experts" and bourgeois specialists and adapting inexpensive—and ineffective—techniques. In 1934 Lysenko was named director of the agronomy institute in Odessa, from which position he directed a wide variety of experimental projects.

Although poor agricultural yields plagued the Soviet government through the 1930s, as Josef Stalin became increasingly grandiose, vicious, persecutory, and paranoid, Lysenkoism thrived. While in the early phase of his career Lysenko had promoted vernalization as a method, he began about 1935 to develop an overarching theoretical framework in which he made larger claims for an underlying theory. Together with philosopher I. I. Prezent, Lysenko proposed a definition of heredity as "the property of a living body to require definite conditions for its life and development and to respond in a definite way to various conditions." He also began describing his approach as "Michurinist" after the late, renowned Russian horticulturist Ivan V. Michurin; this may be fairly described as a propagandist strategem with nativist overtones. Lysenko contrasted Michurin to GREGOR MENDEL [60], whom he denigrated as representative of "bourgeois" and "capitalist" science.

Prior to and following World War II, Lysenko consolidated his hold on the bureaucracy of Soviet agriculture. During the period of Stalin's great purges in the late 1930s, Lysenko became president of the Lenin All-Union Academy of Agricultural Sciences (VASKhNIL); and after his scientific opponent, Vavilov, was arrested in 1940, Lysenko became head of the Institute of Genetics of the Soviet Academy of Sciences in Moscow. This post he held until 1965.

In addition to his hold on agronomy, in August 1948, with Stalin's imprimatur, Trofim Lysenko expanded his control to encompass all of Soviet biology. Lysenko supported a so-called Lamarckian conception of heredity in which the organism transmits acquired characteristics to its offspring. He also turned to theories of spontaneous generation and other obsolete notions, which he viewed as congruent with his own. Stalin himself carefully edited Lysenko's 1948 report, "Situation in Biological Science," which was published with considerable fanfare in the newspapers. It described Michurinism as "the only acceptable form of science because it is based on dialectical materialism and on the principle of changing nature for the benefit of the people." As a consequence, Soviet biology was thoroughly politicized and reorganized, and hundreds of scientists were dismissed from their posts.

Nature itself presented the greatest obstacle to the success of Lysenkoism in the Soviet Union. His methods never achieved the promised results, and there were particularly embarrassing failures in forestry in the late 1940s. In addition, discovery of the structure of DNA in 1953 aroused great interest among some Soviet scientists, including prestigious chemists, physicists, and mathematicians. This was also a factor in putting an end to efforts to defend Lysenko in the West, such as Alan G. Morton's *Soviet Genetics*, published in 1951, in which Lysenkoism was touted as "a revolutionary event in the history of the world." In 1953, too, Josef Stalin died, and Lysenko lost a great friend. By the mid-1950s attacks on Lysenko's methods and his science began to appear in the Soviet press.

Remarkably, Lysenko had not one but two downfalls. As a result of his ruinous policies, which were widely discussed, he resigned as president of the Academy of Agricultural Sciences in 1956. But he made a phoenixlike reappearance several years later. Appearing at the twenty-first Party Congress in 1959, Lysenko made a fervid appeal on behalf of his form of "creative Darwinism" and managed to win the support of Premier Nikita Khrushchev. Convincing the Soviet leader that the lack of success in agriculture was the fault of bureaucrats and academics, Lysenko managed to be reappointed director of VASKhNIL. Before being forced to resign for political reasons in 1964, Khrushchev, as a supporter of Lysenko, found himself at serious odds with the Academy of Science over agricultural reform.

In 1965 Lysenkoism was finally interred for scientific purposes, with a long official critique in the magazine *Science and Life*. A period of discussion within the Soviet Union was followed by official silence. However, not even in the 1970s was the influence of Lysenkoism totally extinguished. Lysenko remained a political appointee until he died on November 20, 1976.

In spite of his obviously inadequate education, Lysenko was said to be a quick study with a good memory. He was generous with money, witty, and lacking in personal vanity. Tales of his scientific illiteracy abound. When Vladimir Engelhardt showed Lysenko a preparation of deoxyribonucleic acid (DNA), the Soviet geneticist laughed in his face. "Ha!" Lysenko told Engelhardt. "You are speaking nonsense. DNA is an acid. Acid is a liquid. And that's a powder. That can't be DNA!"

More seriously, the story of Trofim Lysenko cuts to the heart of science and the conflicting claims of ideology and culture. Indeed, the same phenomenon exists in the United States today, although on a populist rather than a top-down basis. Beginning in the 1980s, with a conservative backlash felt throughout the political spectrum, "creation science" proposed to dethrone the theories of evolution and natural selection. Rooted in religious fundamentalism, creationists were willing to take advantage of technological advances such as the computer and television, instruments which were based on science they effectively claimed was fallacious. Today the "battle against evolution," writes Ronald W. Clark, "is as real and earnest as it was when Clarence Darrow reduced Bryan to incoherence [in the Scopes 'monkey' trial] more than half a century earlier." It has resulted in court battles, de facto censorship, and the manufacture of scientific ignorance in the United States, in the late twentieth century, on a grand scale.

Indeed, the story of Trofim Lysenko is prized by American science, for it is a cautionary tale, resonant with the values of a whole culture.

94

Francis Galton
and Eugenics

1822–1911

One of the last of the "gentleman scientists," Francis Galton made a variety of contributions to meteorology and experimental psychology, and among his lasting accomplishments is the fingerprint classification system used to track down criminals. But he is best remembered for founding and passionately promulgating eugenics, a theory and program which proposed that human beings might be bred like animals to favor "good" traits and suppress unwanted inheritances. These views became popularly discussed and were taken up by, among others, the Nazis. Eugenics, although discredited, has persisted throughout the twentieth century in various guises, and its history makes a strong case for discretion in the emerging sciences of genetic manipulation. With interesting limitations, however, Francis Galton was a "Victorian genius" whose most important contribution, David Depew and Bruce Weber argue, was to be the first to view Darwinism "as a theory in which statistical arguments...acquire explanatory power and fecundity in their own right."

Francis Galton was born on February 16, 1822, near Birmingham, England, to Samuel Tertius Galton, a banker, and Violetta Darwin Galton, a daughter of Erasmus Darwin. The youngest of seven children, Francis proved to be a prodigy able to read and do sums when he was four years old. (His I.Q. was once estimated to be 200, which would make him 75 points smarter than RICHARD FEYNMAN [52], but this seems unlikely.) Galton's parents initially planned that he would study medicine, and at age sixteen he began studying at Birmingham General Hospital and then King's College, in London. At Trinity College, Cambridge, he worked for high honors but suffered a nervous breakdown from overwork. He took his B.A. in January 1844, but soon thereafter his father passed away, and Galton decided not to continue in medicine. The death of his father was an important event in Galton's life, not least because it brought him a substantial inheritance that enabled him to pursue his own interests.

The mushrooming of the British empire made exotic travel a distinct possibility for a young man such as Galton, and in 1845 he journeyed to Africa, where he sailed up the Nile, crossed the Sahara Desert, and visited Beirut and Jerusalem. He returned to England in 1846. He took another trip in 1850 and in 1853 published a spirited account of his voyages in *Tropical South Africa*. Two years later *The Art of Travel; or, Shifts and Contrivances Available in Wild Countries* proved an enduring bestseller. It is interesting to speculate as to what influence the voyages of CHARLES DARWIN [4] on the *Beagle* may have had upon Galton's own desire to travel. Some thirteen years Darwin's junior, Galton was a great admirer of his cousin, as much of his scientific work attests.

Settling down to domestic life after marrying Louise Butler in 1853, Galton made a study of meteorology. He was responsible for some of the first extensive efforts to map the weather, and to Galton we owe the term "anticyclone" to designate a high pressure system. But by the mid-1860s Galton grew less interested in geography and meteorology and became more preoccupied by heredity. According to his biographer, D. W. Forrest, Galton's interest in heredity "dates from about the time when it was evident that his marriage was likely to prove infertile." It appears that Galton's marriage was not an excellent one and that sexual frustration was a strong component. As an adult, he suffered from attacks of dizziness and anxiety, and throughout his life was subject to obsessional symptoms. Apart from these presumed psychological factors, it is unclear exactly why Galton turned to the study of heredity, but when he did, it was with great enthusiasm and religious fervor.

Galton wrote his first articles on inheritance in 1865, and his book *Hereditary Genius* was published in 1869, followed by *English Men of Science* in 1874. In these and other works he was guided by his conviction that, like physical traits, intelligence and temperament were inherited and that "heredity was a far more powerful agent in human development than nurture." Influenced by his travels in colonial Egypt and elsewhere, Galton believed that non-European peoples were inferior, and he was concerned about their higher birth rates. "It is in the most unqualified manner," wrote Galton, "that I object to pretensions of natural equality." The solution, he believed, was through manipulation of human breeding stock. "It would seem as though the physical structure of future generations was almost as plastic as clay, under the control of the breeder's will," wrote Galton. "It is my desire to show...that mental qualities are equally under control."

In his 1883 book *Human Faculty*, Galton coined the word *eugenics*, which, as he later defined it, was "the science which deals with all the influences that improve the inborn qualities of a race; also with those that develop them to the utmost advantage." A form of social Darwinism with the preconceived notion that the rich are genetically superior to the poor, as the Caucasian is to the nonwhite, eugenics became an important movement in England, the United States, and Europe. Until recently a form of social amnesia has obscured its popularity, together with its spuriousness. In the United States, beginning in 1911, some twenty-four states passed compulsory sterilization laws. Eugenics was also an intellectual motor behind legislation outlawing interracial marriage. "Since Galton's day," writes Daniel Kevles, "'eugenics' has become a word of ugly connotations—and deservedly." It should be noted that Galton was working with a defective theory, known as the "ancestral law of heredity." He believed that each parent contributed one-quarter of an offspring's traits, and ancestors on

both sides the rest. This theory was show to be invalid with the rediscovery of the work of GREGOR MENDEL [60]. Intriguingly, Galton had briefly considered a theoretical approach similar to Mendel's, in an 1875 letter to Charles Darwin, but carried it no further.

Galton was familiar with the "gaussian" or "bell curve," and he became one of the founders of biometrics. He opened the Anthropometric Laboratory in 1884 at the International Health Exhibition held in South Kensington, where he measured visitors' weight, height, breathing capacity, strength, sight and hearing, and other variables. To better society, he suggested a means of measuring intellectual capacity and had some influence upon Alfred Binet's general intelligence test.

In 1884 Galton gave a lecture, retrospectively quite important, on the assessment of personality. "We want lists of facts," he said, "every one of which may be separately verified, valued and revalued, and the whole accurately summed" to give a measure of character. His work was shaped by the view, still found today in sociology as well as in epidemiology and several other sciences, which overvalues statistics and sheathes preconceptions in numbers. In Galton the normal interplay in science of induction and rationality becomes entangled in cultural variables.

Today Galton is widely characterized as having possessed an obsessional character, ready to measure anything. He quantified the boredom of an audience by counting people's fidgeting and attempted to gauge the efficacy of prayer; his most famous and symptomatic measure was his "beauty map" of Great Britain. Visiting various cities, Galton kept a piece of paper in his pocket, into which he pricked holes to record the relative allure of women he passed. He found the greatest number of pretty girls in London, the least in Aberdeen.

Other of Galton's writings—he had over three hundred publications—had great breadth and represented unbridled curiosity. He was an acute observer in many ways, and in his wide travels he became an excellent armchair anthropologist. He describes Americans, for example, as "enterprising, defiant, and touchy; impatient of authority, furious politicians, very tolerant of fraud and violence, possessing much high and generous spirit, and some true religious feeling, but strongly addicted to cant." Before his death he wrote a utopian fantasy, "The Eugenic College of Kantsaywhere," parts of which appeared in the biography written by his disciple Karl Pearson.

Galton was knighted in 1909, a year after the appearance of *Memories of My Life*. He died on January 17, 1911. He still has a following. The Eugenics Society which he founded was succeeded in 1989 by the London-based Galton Institute. The Anthropometric Laboratory was later renamed the Galton Laboratory and is connected today to University College, London, which was endowed with a chair of eugenics in his will.

95

Alfred Binet
and the I.Q. Test

1857–1911

The quantification of intelligence arose with Alfred Binet, the eminent French psychologist who, in the first decade of the twentieth century, developed a scale to measure the mental age of children. Initially devised to distinguish feeblemindedness, it was revised by Lewis Terman as the Stanford-Binet scale and achieved a high profile when used by the U.S. Army during World War I. The flexibility and spare theoretical basis of the Intelligence Quotient (I.Q.) insured the test's widespread use and ultimately stirred a wasps' nest of conflict and controversy. "I.Q. testing," writes Stephen Jay Gould, "has had momentous consequences in our century." With the unwarranted presumption of the strong heritability of intelligence, the I.Q. test provides a scientifically reliable staple which has nourished nativism and racism in ways which would undoubtedly horrify its creator. A reformer and activist, Alfred Binet stands as one of the important early psychologists; he was, JEAN PIAGET [77] observes, "a subtle analyst of thought processes,... more aware than anybody of the difficulties of arriving, through his measurements, at the actual mechanism of intelligence."

Alfred Binet was born on July 11, 1857, in Nice, France. His father and grandfather were physicians, but his parents appear to have separated when he was a child, and he was raised by his mother, Madame Moïna Binet. Not a great deal is known about his childhood. His biographer, Theta Wolf, believes that his father, hoping to remedy his timidity, may have once taken him to a mortuary and made him touch a cadaver, and as a consequence he later renounced medicine as a career. In 1872 he entered the prestigious Lycée Louis-le-Grand, from which he graduated in 1875. He initially studied law, and received his *license* in jurisprudence in 1878. He did not continue to work toward a doctorate in law, however. About 1880 he began spending his time at the Bibliothèque Nationale, and there became interested in psychology, then an emerging and much discussed discipline in France, England, and Germany. Much later, in 1894, Binet received a *license* in natural science, but he was not, as sometimes is reported, a physician.

Early papers by Binet, which extended the unfruitful psychological thought of John Stuart Mill, nevertheless brought him encouragement and, in 1882, a place in the laboratory of the eminent Jean Martin Charcot. He remained seven years, observing hysterics. His first book, *La psychologie du raisonnement,* was a study of the principles of association, published in 1886. In 1892 Binet joined the new Laboratory of Physiology and Psychology at the Sorbonne, and four years later, with the death of Henri Beaunis, he became its director, a position he held until his death. In 1895 he was one of the main founders of the first—and for many years foremost—French psychology review, *L'Année psychologique.* He later became the journal's editor in chief, which constituted for him a lifelong task.

A contemporary of WILHELM WUNDT [99], the first of the experimental psychologists, Binet undertook some studies in tactile sensitivity—blindfolding his subjects, for example, and pressing the skin with two blunt points—and in the phenomena of optical illusion. But in general, his interests ranged widely and focused upon larger issues. Like many French psychologists of the nineteenth century, he studied and speculated upon the higher mental processes, such as the thought processes of chess players and natural calculators. He published several books on hypnotism and was moved to study graphology, which he took quite seriously. Binet believed that "assuredly there is something in graphology," and in France today, corporations still regularly use handwriting analysis to evaluate potential employees.

In 1890 Binet published the results of experiments he had undertaken with his young daughters, and in 1903 published further studies, in which he analyzed their problem-solving techniques. In using his own children, Binet clearly prefigures the early work of Jean Piaget, and his *Étude expérimentale de l'intelligence* is sometimes considered Binet's greatest work. In this study, he was impressed by the fact that his daughters could not report all they thought in terms of images, which was a limitation of introspectionism as a means of arriving at generalizations in psychology. Florence Goodenough called this work "one of the most convincing pictures of personality differences that has ever appeared."

Binet's conceptualization of intelligence, and a means of testing it, developed over a period of fifteen years from about 1890. He suggested that a place ought to be made for measuring the "superior processes" which generate individual differences. Intelligence is a synthetic function, he argued, comprising a number of faculties, such as memory, attention, and imagination. Thus, Binet was a critic of various methods of the era which employed quantitative approaches. With his close colleague Théodore Simon, Binet made various attempts to find physical signs of intelligence. He made fruitless efforts, as Stephen Jay Gould has recounted in *The Mismeasure of Man,* at measuring the hand and employed "craniometry" in an attempt to discover a physical correlate with intelligence. One of Binet's important findings—a mark of his ability and subtlety as a scientist—was that these methods consistently supported the null hypothesis: There is no difference in intelligence due to physical conformation.

In 1904, asked to find a means for identifying backward or feebleminded schoolchildren, Binet recognized the importance of establishing some kind of benchmark of normalcy; and from

Binet's daughters.

this insight derives what came to be called the I.Q. test. Binet was not himself interested in ranking children on a numerical scale, but he did develop a series of simple tests devised to measure memory, attention, comprehension of sentences, moral judgments—in effect, all complex variables. A child at age three could point out parts of its body; at age twelve, he or she could repeat a sentence of twenty-six syllables. Questions were devised and carried out empirically with children. It is interesting to note that Binet and Simon were aware of the negative influence of environment from infancy. Examining children from three months to two years old in a nursery setting, they wrote, "even from this age, extreme poverty, the absence of fondling and being played with, already makes its marks and retards the awakening of intellectual faculties."

The 1905 test to measure feeblemindedness was revised by Binet and Simon over the next three years, when it became a scale for measuring "the development of intelligence among children," and another revision was made in 1911. In 1914 the German psychologist Wilhelm Stern suggested a quantified scale in which the mental age was related to chronological age, with the quotient of a normal child unity, or 1.0. In this form, which gave greater precision than Binet or Simon believed was warranted, the scale gained almost immediate popularity, and by 1915 one of its early backers, H. H. Goddard, wrote that "the whole world speaks now of the Binet-Simon scale." In 1916, Lewis Terman published the "Stanford Revision and Extension of the Binet-Simon Intelligence Scale," which provided the basis for tests given today.

With Terman came the assumption of strong heritability of intelligence, bound up with ideological claims, and no one better than he illustrates that, over the years, the worst enemies of I.Q. tests have frequently been their proponents. Terman found lower scores among Hispanics and blacks and held an opinion about these groups that National Socialists later believed of the Poles: "They cannot master abstractions, but they can often be made efficient workers...." Another researcher, Sir Cyril Burt, a British proponent of the I.Q. test, published totally fabricated data over a period of many years; his work, which had a good fit with preconceptions, went long unquestioned by his colleagues. Equally unnerving have been psychologist Leon Kamin's investigations of the actual circumstances behind data gathering in which, for example, researchers concoct I.Q. scores for illiterate adults, using tests not designed for numerical conversions. The I.Q. controversy at century's end took place around *The Bell Curve*, a bestselling book by Richard J. Hernstein and Charles Murray. But both the book and the debate which followed in its wake were so contaminated by political agendas that scientific insight did not apply.

Alfred Binet married Laure Balbiani, the daughter of an embryologist, in 1884. Their two daughters, Madeleine and Alice, were called Marguerite and Armande in Binet's studies on intelligence. Energetic and austere, Binet was somewhat aloof, more admired than loved by his friends. But his daughter Madeleine wrote that her father "was above all a lively man, smiling, often very ironical, gentle in manner, wise in his judgments, a little skeptical of course—moderate, ingenious, clever and imaginative." Unfortunately, he did not live to arbitrate the I.Q. controversy. His death, reported to be due to "cerebral apoplexy," came on October 18, 1911.

96

Alfred Kinsey
and Human Sexuality

1894–1956

Sexuality as a focus of scientific interest developed only in the twentieth century, as people in advanced industrial societies became accustomed to leisure as well as work and to romantic attachments before, during, and sometimes outside marriage. Psychoanalysis, with borrowings from biology, discovered sexuality in children and emphasized its importance for the interior life of adults. But the actual copulative and autoerotic behavior of men and women remained largely a mystery until, in two books published after World War II, Alfred Kinsey provided revealing statistical profiles. His work became of great significance in the development of a new discourse on sexuality in the following decades. Kinsey "does not command our attention because of the profundity or elegance of his thought," writes historian Paul Robinson. "Rather, he is important because he has been influential, more influential than any other sexual thinker" in the second half of the twentieth century.

Alfred Kinsey was born in Hoboken, New Jersey, on June 23, 1894, the son of Alfred Seguine Kinsey Sr. and Sarah Ann Charles. Although his mother, of pleasant disposition, had limited education, his father was a professor of engineering at Stevens Institute of Technology and a straitlaced, strict disciplinarian. In an anecdote which still resonates today, the senior Kinsey would send his son to purchase cigarettes, which could not be legally sold to minors, then notify the authorities so that the unfortunate shopkeeper could be punished. Although Kinsey was physically frail as a child, he came to enjoy the outdoors as an adolescent and joined the Boy Scouts, eventually becoming an Eagle Scout. He was shy around girls and quoted *Hamlet* in his senior yearbook: "Man delights not me; no nor woman either."

After graduating from high school, Kinsey initially followed his father's wishes and attended Stevens Institute, intending to study mechanical engineering. But at age twenty he announced he planned to study biology and, with the help of a scholarship, transferred to Bowdoin College, in Brunswick, Maine. Kinsey's educational switch caused a rupture with his father, who terminated financial support for his son with the gift of a twenty-five-dollar suit. After graduating from Bowdoin in 1916, Kinsey went on to study taxonomy at the Bussey Institute of Harvard University, receiving his D.Sc. degree in 1920. Here he became interested in the gall wasp, which has a great range in the United States, and he traveled all over the country collecting specimens. The gall provided clear evidence of evolution and, to record the various measurements, Kinsey developed a code which he would later adapt in his sexual history interviews.

At Indiana University, where he began to teach in 1920, Kinsey established a firm reputation over the next two decades as a family man and professor. In 1921 he married Clara Bracken McMillen, with whom he raised four children. In his professional life he became the world's greatest authority on gall wasps, amassing a collection of over four million specimens, which he eventually donated to the American Museum of Natural History in New York. He also wrote several textbooks, including *An Introduction to Biology*.

The sexual focus of Kinsey's professional interest emerged in 1938 when the university asked him to coordinate a course on marriage. To his surprise, he found relatively little statistical data on sexual behavior. As he wrote later, "In many of the published studies on sex there were obvious confusions of moral values, philosophic theory, and the scientific fact." His attempts to discover more about adolescent sexuality by conducting interviews with his students became the basis of his later studies.

Kinsey's frank efforts to seek objective data led the university to ask him to relinquish the marriage course if he were to continue his basic research into sex. He had soon compiled several hundred interviews. In 1941 he enlisted the support of the Rockefeller Foundation (which had been interested in the study of sexuality since the 1920s) and added to his team anthropologist Paul Gebhard, statistician Clyde Martin, and psychologist Wardell Pomeroy. Kinsey interviewed a large number of students at first, but as news of his project spread by word of mouth, he developed a more representative sample which was, however, still heavily weighted with prisoners and homosexuals. Kinsey was exceptionally tolerant of homosexuality for his time, rejecting the predominant view that it was an inherited abnormality, as well as the psychoanalytic nosology, which viewed it as caused partially by upbringing. He developed a behavioral program, however, for homosexuals who wished to change orientation.

Although he set an unreachable goal of one hundred thousand case histories, Kinsey eventually managed some eighteen thousand, a striking achievement. His questionnaire consisted of upward of three hundred fifty items, depending on the subject's proclivities, and covered socioeconomic issues as well as physical data and sexual history. Into their interview technique Kinsey and his colleagues built a variety of mechanisms to insure validity. Interviewers—all married, all male, none politically radical— assumed from the outset that their subjects had engaged in every form of sexual behavior. They asked questions rapidly and impersonally, and they abstained from all moral judgment. When interviewers were sexually approached, as they sometimes were, Kinsey counseled total passivity as the best form of cooling off the seducer.

Sexual Behavior of the Human Male was published in 1948 to a generally positive public response, eventually entailing much commentary and criticism from physicians, psychiatrists, social scientists, and even literary critics. *Sexual Behavior of the Human Female,* published in 1954, evoked more wrath from religious quarters as well as from some scientists, with Margaret Mead, the anthropologist, arguing that it should not become a bestseller because young people ought to be protected from its findings. Some of the clergy found the book Communist-inspired, while Communists found it reactionary. The Rockefeller Foundation suspended its support, and, by Ward Pomeroy's account in his excellent biography, *Dr. Kinsey and the Institute for Sex Research,* "The year and a half before [Kinsey] died was a dark period indeed." After a 1955 European trip, Kinsey suffered a coronary embolism and passed away on August 25, 1956.

Although Kinsey remains a controversial figure, Ward Pomeroy has suggested that Kinsey made no fewer than eight major contributions. The research itself was a landmark, Pomeroy has pointed out, as was the establishment of the Kinsey Institute. Kinsey developed statistical baselines for premarital and extramarital intercourse and masturbation. His 0–6 scale for homosexual behavior has proved useful, as has his notion of a person's "total outlet" for sexuality. Kinsey's recognition that sexual behavior changes with social class was revealing, as was his discovery that sexual response can continue into old age.

But most significant of all is Kinsey's revelation of the range of individual variation in human sexual behavior. Recording the great variability of men and women both in their sexual orientation and specific practices is Kinsey's great scientific contribution. Extramarital intercourse, homosexuality, and animal contacts were all received by Kinsey and his associates with the same cool reserve. At a time when masturbation was official cause for rejection from the U.S. Naval Academy, Kinsey's research on its prevalence was an exceptional example of science as demystification. It may be said that Kinsey was not a great theoretician and that his studies are striking for not addressing issues of psychological conflict or emotional satisfaction. As a collector of data concerning something so significant as sexuality, however, his importance cannot be contested.*

---

*Kinsey may be the collector's equivalent of FRANCIS GALTON [94], whose desire to quantify outstripped all plausibility. As a boy Kinsey collected stamps, and as an adult the gall wasp and sexual histories. He believed in the usefulness of collecting anything. Kinsey amassed the largest number of penis measurements in the world and made an effort, not entirely successful, to compile measurements of the clitoris.

Although Kinsey's work provided, as Gerhard Brand writes, "a monumental amount of information regarding sexual behavior in the United States," his heritage has been decidedly mixed. Some years after his death, the Kinsey Institute entered a period of decline, and a new report was scuttled in the 1970s by disagreement among researchers. When the Kinsey Institute issued its report for the 1990s, it was a self-help manual designed for the general public. Meanwhile, studies by William H. Masters and Virginia Johnson during the 1960s on "human sexual response" were logical extensions of Kinsey's work, but their clinical descriptions of the sexual act proved to be more pretext than science, oriented toward defining moral and behavioral norms. It is not too much to say that the scientific intent behind much of Kinsey's work has been, a generation after his death, too often subverted by ideology and a new obscurantism.

97

Alexander Fleming
and Penicillin

1881–1955

Penicillin, the first efficient antibiotic, has saved millions of lives since its introduction during World War II. Not only was it crucial to reducing risk of infection in wound treatment and surgery, it greatly decreased the mortality of formerly fearsome diseases such as pneumonia. As a potent remedy for syphilis, it was one of two recent medical advances (the other is the birth control pill) to lead to profound social changes. The overuse and misuse of antibiotics in agriculture as well as medicine, and the development of drug-resistant strains of bacteria, should not obscure its significance. Penicillin was first isolated and produced in concentrated form by Howard Florey and Ernst Chain in 1940.

But it was discovered by, and brought remarkable fame to, the Scottish physician Alexander Fleming.

Indeed, following World War II, Fleming became the focus of such adulation as befits a movie star today; he was the recipient of honors galore, including the Nobel Prize. However, the magnitude of Fleming's actual contribution is questionable. Although he was a skilled bacteriologist with solid accomplishments, his range as a scientist was limited. His biographer Gwynn Macfarlane puts it bluntly: To class Fleming as a towering genius, as was done beginning in the 1940s and as persists in popular histories today, is a symptom of "mass hysteria."

A Scot from Lochfield, Ayrshire, Alexander Fleming was born on August 6, 1881, to Grace Morton and Hugh Fleming, a hardworking, elderly farmer. Alexander's father died when he was seven, and after elementary school he went to London in 1895 to live with his brothers; there he attended Regent Street Polytechnic for two years, where he excelled. He worked for a time as a clerk, and in 1900 he enlisted with the London Scottish Rifle Volunteers to fight in the Boer War. Although not sent overseas, he remained active in his regiment for many years. At age twenty, after coming into a small inheritance, he entered St. Mary's Hospital Medical School, in Paddington, in 1901, where he became a fine student and qualified for a conjoint degree in 1906. Two years later he took his bachelor's exams, which he passed with honors, receiving his M.B. and M.S. degrees. He also won a gold medal for an essay entitled "The Diagnosis of Acute Bacterial Infection." In 1909, he qualified as a surgeon.

Rather than practice medicine, however, Fleming had decided upon a career in research, after coming under the influence of Almroth Wright, a well-known professor of pathology at St. Mary's Hospital. Fleming soon gained respect for his skill and common sense, and he published exemplary work on such diseases as acne and syphilis. Working before drugs were tested in organized clinical trials, Fleming liked to inoculate himself, and he put together vaccines whenever one of his own family came down ill with any of the simple ailments such as a sore throat or a cold.

During World War I Fleming studied antiseptics. Posted to France, he showed that gangrene and tetanus, which commonly resulted from wounds, were due to organisms found in farmers' fields which the war had turned to killing grounds. Together with

Wright, he demonstrated that the ordinary antiseptics in use at the time were not able to thoroughly penetrate wounded tissue—how, indeed, they reduced the natural antibacterial reaction in blood. He also developed techniques to combat infection. During the war, this work received less attention than it ought, but it was gradually absorbed into standard procedures for cleanliness and treatment. Fleming was impressed and disturbed by the human devastation of the war, all the more that so much suffering followed from infections which were in principle preventable or remediable.

During the 1920s Fleming made his major discoveries. In 1921—working with his own nasal secretions while he suffered from a head cold—he discovered lysozyme, a bacteria-destroying enzyme, first in nasal mucus, then in a whole variety of body fluids and other substances. Although this work turned out to be the most important of Fleming's career up to that time, he was not able to isolate the substance. This was unfortunate, because other researchers were less prone to investigate it. The significance of lysozyme was considerable because it did not destroy living tissue, but this remained unclear for some years. Fleming did publish his results, however, and lysozyme was eventually purified.

In September 1928 Fleming made one of the great observations in Western medicine. He had been working with staphylococcus—found in abscesses, boils, and various other infections—and noticed that a mold of some kind was killing off the bacteria on one of the petri dishes in his laboratory. He subsequently performed experiments with the mold, which was (and remained) of unknown origin. He discovered it had some interesting properties. Notably, it was harmless to blood cells while killing bacteria more readily than carbolic acid. However, Fleming did not immediately recognize its therapeutic importance when he described the "penicillin effect" and published his first results in 1929. Nor did others. The paper attracted little interest then or for some years to come. Indeed, similar observations on the destructive effects of mold on bacteria could be found in the medical literature dating back to the 1870s.

The crucial work in the development of penicillin as a drug was undertaken in the shadow of World War II by Howard Walter Florey and Ernst Boris Chain. Beginning in 1938, Florey and Chain began to test penicillin as part of a larger effort to find natural antibacterial agents. By 1939 it was clear that the potential for penicillin was great. Over the next two years it was tested, and the first clinical trials were completed in mid-1941. "There is no doubt," writes Trevor I. Williams, "that it was Florey and Chain who jointly set in train the research programme that made penicillin available to the world as a chemotherapeutic agent of unrivalled excellence." World War II provided more than sufficient casualties to test the drug's worth, and large-scale manufacture began in England and the United States.

Given the disastrous effects of infection in previous warfare (which had become extremely bloody in the nineteenth and twentieth centuries), the huge public admiration of penicillin is fully understandable. More curious is the veneration that was settled upon Alexander Fleming. Even during the war he became the object of adulation. He was elected to the Royal Society in 1943 and knighted in 1944. In 1945 he shared the Nobel Prize with Chain and Florey and took the occasion to say, "My only merit is that I did not neglect the observation and that I pursued the subject as a bacteriologist." Later claims by Fleming were somewhat less modest, and both his Nobel corecipients regarded them as exaggerated.

Until the end of his life, Fleming remained a figure of tremendous renown. He was aware of the great gulf between his accomplishment and the idolization that came his way, and he preserved a scrapbook entitled "Fleming Myth." Personable, kind, unpretentious in bearing, according to a colleague Fleming once said "that he didn't deserve the Nobel Prize, and I had to bite my teeth not to agree with him." Nevertheless, Fleming was comfortable with his celebrity, which lasted until the end of his life.

Fleming married Sarah Marion McElroy in 1915, and they had one son. After Sarah's death in 1949, he married Amalia Voureka Coutsouris, a bacteriologist. Fleming's death was exceptional for a physician. On March 11, 1955, he was to have dinner with the famous actor Douglas Fairbanks Jr. and Eleanor Roosevelt. Ill that morning, Fleming refused to see a doctor. When his wife found him in bed, he asked if she would comb his hair. He was in a cold sweat, with a pain in his chest, but believed that nothing was the matter with his heart. He then bowed his head and died. He was mourned the world over and is buried in St. Paul's Cathedral in London.

98

B. F. Skinner
and Behaviorism

1904–1990

For half a century, American psychology was dominated by behaviorism, and its most prominent proponent was B. F. Skinner. Behaviorism was rooted in the failure of introspection to yield reliable data and, nourished by the aims of logical positivism, it gained an impressive grip on academic psychology which lasted through the 1960s. A Harvard professor whose "operant behaviorism" was a successor to behaviorist programs advanced earlier in the century by Edward Thorndike and John Watson, Skinner eschewed theory in favor of purely quantified results. In addition, in later life he had a career as a popular philosopher while his followers applied techniques of conditioning and reinforcement in the fields of education, linguistics, law enforcement, and psychotherapy. Today behaviorist influence has diminished, and Skinner, like many other academic psychologists, has faded from once great prominence.* In 1974 he could be called "easily the most prestigious and certainly the most controversial living American psychologist." Less than twenty years later, Howard Gardner would write that "today the theoretical claims of behaviorism (though not its various applied achievements) are largely of historical interest."

Burrhus Frederic Skinner was born on March 20, 1904, in Susquehanna, Pennsylvania, the son of Grace Madge Burrhus and William Arthur Skinner, a lawyer. Interested as a boy in mechanical gadgetry, Skinner acquired skills of carpentry which he later put to considerable use in devising experiments. "I was always building things," he wrote in his autobiography. "I made tops, diabolos, model airplanes driven by twisted rubber bands, box kites and tin propellers which could be sent high into the air with a spool-and-string spinner. I tried again and again to make a glider in which I myself might fly."

After graduating from high school in 1922, he attended Hamilton College in Clinton, New York, where he majored in English and nurtured ambitions of a literary career. After graduation in 1926, Skinner spent a year trying to become a writer before, as he later said, discovering "the unhappy fact that I had nothing to say." Inspired by Bertrand Russell, who wrote favorably on behaviorism, and by the works of John B. Watson, Skinner decided to return to school for graduate work. He attended Harvard, receiving his master's degree in 1930 and his Ph.D. the following year.

During the 1930s, at Harvard, where he remained as a postdoctoral fellow until 1936, Skinner developed the major principles of what he came to call "operant conditioning." The Russian physiologist Ivan Pavlov had previously discovered the

---

*Skinner is not the most spectacular example in psychology of a reputation curtailed by death. Vernon J. Nordby and Calvin S. Hall, in their 1974 *Guide to Psychologists and Their Concepts*, devote a chapter to W. H. Sheldon—whose work is "for many psychologists the most successful" effort to link physique to psychology. Inspired by FRANCIS GALTON [94], over many years Sheldon took thousands of "posture photographs" of unclothed undergraduates at Yale, Vassar, and other universities. He published *An Atlas of Men*, and planned an *Atlas of Women*. By 1995, his work was so little valued that a large cache of his nude photos, considered to have no redeeming scientific merit but considerable capacity to embarrass, was destroyed.

principle of stimulus-response, conditioning in famous experiments eliciting reflexive behavior in dogs. By contrast, Skinner's method involved isolating and describing behavior which operated upon the environment. Rather than send rats through mazes, as is often done in experimental psychology, he developed a box with an apparatus for dispensing pellets of food when a rat pressed a lever. Eventually connected to a recording system, the "Skinner box" could provide a schedule of learned behavior.

The behaviorist project elaborated by B. F. Skinner differed in several ways from earlier behaviorism and strongly reflected the character of operationalism and logical positivism, two schools of thought which during the 1920s had distilled the presumed precepts of scientific method. Skinner, who began teaching at the University of Minnesota in 1936, published *The Behavior of Organisms,* an introduction to the principles of operant conditioning and the notion of learning through reinforcement, in 1938. The book offered basically a methodology for investigating an organism's interaction with its environment, for Skinner wished to make no assumptions about nonobservable mental operations. He employed only the postulate that experimental data will be regular and in some way lawful.

After World War II—during which Skinner showed that pigeons might be taught to direct a guided missile—the program of operant behaviorism emerged in full flower at the Conference on the Experimental Analysis of Behavior in 1946, while Skinner was teaching at Indiana University. He returned to Harvard as professor of psychology in 1947. He soon published his novel *Walden Two,* about a utopian experiment based on operant behaviorist principles, which psychology students read and discussed in university courses for decades afterward. During the 1940s Skinner also developed an air-conditioned, soundproof crib for his daughter, Deborah, which was featured in the *Ladies' Home Journal* and manufactured as the "Aircrib." In later years it was confused with the Skinner box, and the mythic assumption arose that Skinner had raised his child in a stimulus-reward environment, like a rat. There were rumors that Deborah had gone mad or killed herself. This was not the case, although the story itself resonates with the banality which plagued the whole behaviorist project.

To attempt to extrapolate lessons of operant conditioning to larger issues, Skinner wrote *Science and Human Behavior* in 1953. His *Schedules of Reinforcement,* written with Charles Ferster and published in 1957, contained the results of his experiments with pigeons. In the same year there appeared *Verbal Behavior,* which Skinner had begun many years earlier; it presented an analysis of language acquisition as a process of operant conditioning. Behaviorists believed, for a time, that they had somehow succeeded in changing the course of linguistics. But Noam Chomsky's scathing review of *Verbal Behavior* in 1959 was the first of many serious challenges to Skinner's work.

From the late 1950s behaviorist psychology became increasingly important in universities, and Skinner's Harvard mantle—from 1958 he was the Edgar Pierce Professor of Psychology—helped to sustain his enterprise for some years. He published a controversial and popular book, *Beyond Freedom and Dignity,* in 1971. Several years later, *About Behaviorism* appeared. In these works he argued for social engineering through management of the human environment. He and his followers succeeded in having a long-term influence in education—particularly special education—and in psychotherapy, where a behaviorist approach can prove effective for some cases of phobia and certain other problems. In general, the concept of reinforcement retains some importance for education, and conditioning is used for various kinds of therapy. Both applications are of limited scope.

B. F. Skinner married Yvonne Blue in 1936 after a romantic engagement, but their marriage, although it endured, appears to have been painful on both sides. Skinner had a warm relationship with both his daughters, Deborah and Julie; and the latter became a professional behaviorist. When Skinner retired from Harvard in 1974, he went on to write a three-volume autobiography, *Particulars of My Life, Shaping of a Behaviorist,* and *A Matter of Consequences.* This extravagance represented what must be considered the fulfillment of a mission, for he had written years before, "Whether from narcissism or scientific curiosity, I have been as much interested in myself as in rats and pigeons. I have applied the same formulations, I have looked for the same kinds of causal relations, and I have manipulated behavior in the same way and sometimes with comparable success."

More recently, Skinner has been the object of a biography by Daniel W. Bjork, who suggests that Skinner belongs to a broad tradition of such intellectual stars in the United States as Jonathan Edwards, Henry David Thoreau, and John Dewey. He was, suggests Bjork, "an American original, adding a fresh twist to the American scientific, intellectual, and social heritage."

B. F. Skinner died on August 18, 1990.

99

Wilhelm Wundt
and the Founding of Psychology

1832–1920

Psychology did not emerge as a discipline separate from philosophy until the late nineteenth century, and from the beginning it embraced both the higher thought processes and basic elements of perception. Such figures as William James wrote perceptive explorations of the human psyche, upon which philosophy had ever more reduced claims, while the studies of HERMANN HELMHOLTZ [63] and Gustav Fechner's psychophysics laid the groundwork for a new experimental science. It is in this context that Wilhelm Wundt emerges as the founder of academic psychology. This famous and prolific German "was not an undoubted genius," writes Paul Fraisse, "but his prodigious output, erudition, efficiency and influence made him the initiator of experimental psychology."

Wilhelm Max Wundt was born on August 16, 1832 in Neckarau, near Mannheim, which then belonged to Baden in the Germanic Confederation. His father, Maximillian Wundt, was a loving parent but a somewhat ineffective minister who carried on—unwillingly, according to his son—a family tradition of pastoral service. His mother, Maria Friederike Arnold, was from a cultivated, bourgeois family. Wundt took an early interest in books, and he developed an inner life of daydreams and fantasy. In 1848 he became a young supporter of the Vienna uprising and watched with his comrades as the Prussian army put an end to the Republic of Baden. Wundt later described his adolescent revolutionary activities as one of the peak experiences of his life.

Wundt attended the universities of Tübingen and Heidelberg, from which he received a medical degree in 1855. He was not committed to practicing medicine; instead, in 1857, he began to teach physiology at the University of Heidelberg, where he also became an assistant in the laboratory of Hermann Helmholtz. After a mysterious illness, which may have involved depression, Wundt recovered with a fresh outlook on life and a new productive zeal. His first book, issued in 1858, concerned the mechanics of muscular movement. But he then moved toward issues that would one day become part of the curriculum of academic psychology.

Like other early psychologists, Wundt's training in physiology was a fundamental influence which becomes apparent in any survey of his work. His *Beiträge zur Theorie der Sinneswahrnelmung* (*Contributions to a Theory of Sensory Perception*) was published in 1862 and is considered the founding work of experimental psychology. In 1863 came *Vorlesungen über die Menschen und Thierseele* (*Lectures on Human and Animal Psychology*). Still, Wundt published the first edition of his *Textbook of Human Physiology* in 1865. And one of his most valuable and successful contributions was the series of lectures constitute *Gründzuge der physiologischen psychologie* (*Principles of Physiological Psychology*) in 1873–74. This book, according to a contemporary review, delivered a much needed "specialized scientific treatment of the actual relations between body and consciousness."

In 1875 Wundt accepted a chair in philosophy at the University of Leipzig, offered because of his background in natural science. The match between academy and scholar was excellent, and Wundt remained at Leipzig for the next forty-five years. There he became a highly prolific institution unto himself and his laboratory a mecca for students from the United States and other countries, including Russia. Indeed, a great part of Wundt's influence stems from his teaching. He is said to have supervised about two hundred doctoral dissertations, and he influenced a whole generation of the most significant academic psychologists in the United States, including G. Stanley Hall, James Cattell, and Edward Titchener.

Most significant for Wundt's future influence was his reliance upon experiment. In 1879 he officially set up the Institute of Experimental Psychology, not unlike the Anthropometrics Laboratory founded about the same time by FRANCIS GALTON [94]. In his journal *Philosophische Studien (Studies in Philosophy)*, Wundt and his students published results of experiments. Working with real subjects, they measured and recorded and set in motion a statistical trend in psychology which has not abated to the present day. Although Wundt relied partly on introspection, which later would be abandoned by psychologists, many of his investigations into various aspects of perception, expression, and other topics made use of controls and various mechanisms to generate objective results.

Wundt was aware of the limitations of experiment. He developed a second approach to psychology, examining the higher thought processes, and it is an important part of his legacy. Emphasizing social context and cultural analysis, as well as a study of language, Wundt became an early combination of social psychologist, cultural anthropologist, philosopher, and sociologist. He had published a book on ethics, *Ethik*, in 1886, and in 1889, *System der Philosophie*. In 1900, at age sixty-eight, he published the first volume of his *Völkerpsychologie*, and over the next twenty years added nine volumes more. The title, which translates as *Folk Psychology*, is a misnomer; Wundt's objective was to probe myths, customs, and the use of language in cultural and historical context. Although Herman K. Haeberlin considers it an "ingenious attempt," he writes that Wundt's scheme "breaks down when applied." It was not well received by experimental psychologists, who regarded it as too metaphysical.

Wundt's influence upon psychology is to some extent more symbolic than real, and yet he cannot be ignored. His name "remains indissolubly linked to the origins of experimental psychology," Kurt Danziger asserts in a perceptive article, adding, "This is so even though he cannot be credited with a single scientific discovery, any genuine methodological innovation or any influential theoretical generalization." The fact that Wundt's influence was great but his legacy nil is not unique in the history of psychology. The same fate has awaited a whole legion of psychologists, whose careers are scarcely finished before relative obscurity sets in. B. F. SKINNER [98], whose prestige two decades ago was enormous, is only one example.

Among Wilhelm Wundt's experimental apparatuses was a "thought meter," with which he attempted to test the perception of time. It was characteristic of Wundt that he was also disturbed by the way people in the modern world were becoming enslaved by the clock. The clock, he wrote, was "the first policeman," and "brought with it all those limitations of personal freedom." He added, "A natural instinct leads people to struggle against any power that tends to repress their independence. We can love everything, people, animals, flowers, stones—but nobody loves the police! We are also engaged, some more, some less, in never-ending conflict with the clock....[It] is I who sometimes flies with the wings of a bird and sometimes creeps like a snail, and...when I think I am killing time, I am really killing myself."

Wilhelm Wundt died on August 31, 1920.

100

Archimedes
and the Beginning of Science

c. 287–212 B.C.

A clear anticipation of modern science is found in the works of Archimedes. An engineer and one of the greatest mathematicians in history, he is the only ancient Greek to have made significant, direct, and lasting contributions to mechanics. His particular interest for science today resides in his use of experiment or invention to test theory and his recognition that basic principles, which can be described mathematically, underlie physical phenomena. Archimedes was, with EUCLID [59] and LUCRETIUS [73], a strong and positive influence on figures such as GALILEO GALILEI [7] and ISAAC NEWTON [1]. Plutarch encapsulated him a thousand years ago as possessed "of such a lofty spirit, so profound a soul, and such a wealth of scientific theory."

A fair amount is known about the life of Archimedes, making him an exception to many other learned ancients. At the Sicilian port of Syracuse, on the Ionian Sea, where he grew up and spent much of his life, it is still possible to see walls, fortifications, and aqueducts of the ancient city. Born about 287 B.C., Archimedes was the son of an astronomer, Phidias, and he was a friend and possibly kinsman of King Hieron II, the despot of Sicily who ruled from about 270 B.C. At some point, Archimedes traveled to Egypt and studied at Alexandria, then the center of Greek culture and scholarship, home to a great library of the ancient world, where Euclid had established his academy a generation earlier.

The accomplishments of Archimedes include both his mathematical treatises, his practical inventions, and the anecdotal accounts of his experiments. Several of his books on mechanics have been lost, but his treatises on geometry—the Greeks' form of mathematical discourse—are all written in a lucid and economical style. In *On the Equilibrium of Planes,* Archimedes proved the law of the lever and investigated the center of gravity. In *On the Sphere and Cylinder* he discovered formulas for the volume and surface area of a sphere. He came close to inventing a calculus, and his work became part of the tradition available to Newton and Leibniz in the seventeenth century. In *The Sand Reckoner,* one of his last works, Archimedes almost invented logarithms and used a scientific notation for large numbers. He estimated, for example, that about 10^{63} grains of sand would fill up the universe.

Archimedes' principle—his famous law of buoyancy—is discussed in his *On Floating Bodies.* The principle states that when a body is submerged in a fluid, it is subject to a vertical force of buoyancy equal to the weight of the fluid which it displaces. A small stone will weigh more than the tiny amount of water it displaces, and sinks. But a large ship is buoyed up by the tremendous weight of water which it displaces, and so it floats. Archimedes' principle explains flotation and is one of the founding principles of hydrostatics.

Another consequence of Archimedes' principle is contained in a famous and probably apocryphal story. King Hieron was suspicious that a wreath (not a crown, as is often stated) that had been made for him was not forged of solid gold but also contained silver. Without destroying the wreath (which would be a sacrilege), Archimedes was to discover whether this was the case. Pondering the problem while bathing, "as he was sitting down in the tub," wrote the Roman architect, Marcus Vitruvius, about two hundred years after Archimedes death, "he noticed that the amount of water which flowed over by the tub was equal to the amount by which his body was immersed. This indicated to him a method of solving the problem, and he did not delay, but in his joy leapt out of the tub, and, rushing naked towards his home, he cried out in a loud voice that he had found what he sought, for as he ran he repeatedly shouted in Greek, *heurēka, heurēka*."

Archimedes had recognized that he could discover the weight density of an object with an irregular shape. To test the King's wreath, he submerged it in water and measured the fluid it displaced. When an equal weight of gold was shown to displace less water, it was clear that the wreath was a fraud.

Archimedes is also credited with a number of practical inventions. The most famous is undoubtedly the "endless screw," a spiral pipe traditionally used for raising underground water. He also created an orrery, that is, a planetarium-like apparatus which mechanically shows the movements of the heavenly bodies. Archimedes also seems to have invented a diopter, an instrument for measuring the diameter of the sun.

Plutarch depicts Archimedes as proverbially focused on mathematics, absent-minded, and neglectful of his appearance and hygiene. "He used to trace geometrical figures in the ashes of the fire, and diagrams in the oil on his body, being in a state of entire preoccupation, and, in the truest sense, divine possession with his love and delight in science." Archimedes was not without a sense of humor, and told of sending false theorems to friends in Alexandria to show "how those who claim to discover everything, but produce no proofs of the same, may be confuted as having actually pretended to discover the impossible."

Archimedes was killed by the Romans in 212 B.C. during the invasion of Syracuse. According to three historians—Polybius, Livy, and Plutarch—Archimedes played an important role in defending the city from the invaders. They describe his ballistics machines as hurling rocks at ships, and cranes as dropping large stones on them. One story has a great iron hand lifting a Roman boat out of the water. The story that Archimedes constructed large mirrors to set boats afire is undoubtedly false, but it is no surprise that the Romans succeeded in defeating Syracuse only after a long siege. Plutarch quotes Marcellus, the general in charge of the mission, as saying to his engineers, "Shall we not make an end of fighting against [Archimedes]...who uses our ships to ladle water from the sea, who...by the multitude of missiles that he hurls at us all at once outdoes the hundred-armed giants of mythology?"

Although Marcellus understandably wanted Archimedes to be taken alive, the soldier sent off to husband his intellect ended by dispatching it. Marcellus was distraught, although the philosopher Alfred North Whitehead later turned the story to good, if exaggerated, account when he stated that this showed that the Romans lacked a contemplative nature.

Archimedes's favorite proof involves the relationship of cones, cylinders, and spheres. He showed that if these figures have the same base and height—imagine a cone inscribed in a hemisphere which itself is inscribed within a cylinder—the ratio of their volumes will be 1: 2: 3. In addition, the surface of the sphere is equivalent to two-thirds the surface of the cylinder which encloses it. This relation of sphere and cylinder so enchanted Archimedes that he wished that his grave be marked by a representation of it. Over a century after his death Cicero, the Roman statesman, serving as an administrator in Sicily, sought out Archimedes's grave, "and found it enclosed all around and covered with brambles and thickets...," he wrote. "I noticed a small column arising a little above the bushes, on which there was the figure of a sphere and a cylinder."

Although Archimedes was not the first to invent the lever, as is sometimes stated, he is supposed to have elucidated the principle of the compound pulley with the proverbial saying, "Give me a single place to stand, and I will move the Earth." And so he takes his place at the end of a list, following ninety-nine scientists who came after him—almost all of them, in some measure, in his everlasting debt.

INEXCUSABLE OMISSIONS, HONORABLE MENTIONS, AND ALSO-RANS

Some explanation is in order for those famous and influential scientists not included in this book. Above all, the decision to begin with Isaac Newton imposed a structure which restricted earlier figures to those who made specific accomplishments and revolutionary advances—Nicolaus Copernicus and Johannes Kepler, for example. *Aristotle* is of the greatest importance in the history of science, but his contributions are due to his pervasive and historical, rather than direct, influence. Similarly, the omission of *René Descartes*. He certainly would belong in this book for his overall significance and contribution to method, but no major enduring discovery belongs to him. About the same may be said of *Francis Bacon*, who until the twentieth century was considered among the greatest scientists ever.

British science, particularly, offers many examples of scientists before Newton of formidable influence but who receive only a mention here, including *Robert Boyle, William Gilbert, Henry Cavendish,* and *Edmond Halley.* Further back in history, there is a class of scientific pioneers whose absence should not go without mention. Just to name a few: *Hippocrates, Galen, Ptolemy,* and *Paracelsus,* along with the great figure of Arab science, *Alhazen.*

Omissions in physics are many. Nothing can adequately explain the absence of *Josiah Gibbs* or *Lord Kelvin,* unless you asked Charles Darwin, who liked to call the latter an "odious scepter" for his pious views on the age of the earth. *Heinrich Hertz* and *Alessandro Volta* had units of electricity named after them, which surely ought to be sufficient to earn them a place in the centumvirate—but wasn't. The major architects of quantum theory are included—with exceptions, such as *Wolfgang Pauli.*

471

Richard Feynman is here, but not *Julian Schwinger* or *Sin-Ituro Tomonaga,* the two other major theorists behind renovated quantum electrodynamics. A few omissions have not only the consolation of the Nobel Prize but also pride of kinship, such as *William Henry Bragg* and his son, *Sir Lawrence Bragg.*

Francis Crick once remarked that of all the physical sciences, chemistry is most resistant to popular treatment. Not to be gainsaid by this book, in which neither *Claude Berthollet* nor *Jons Berzelius* nor *Joseph Priestley* is included. In the twentieth century, it is remarkable but true that no place was available for either the prolific organic chemist *Derek Barton* or *Gilbert N. Lewis,* whose work on the atom meant much to Linus Pauling.

Astronomy, by contrast, has always had its great figures who were also popular and widely beloved, such as Stephen Hawking. It is unfortunate that *Roger Penrose* could not be included, nor *Fred Hoyle,* nor *John Wheeler.*

The various branches of biology have produced a pantheon of remarkable figures. Before Darwin, *Louis Agassiz,* for discovering the ice age, and *Georges Cuvier,* for comparative anatomy and paleontology, were exceptionally significant. Following *The Origin of Species, Hugo de Vries,* who rediscovered Gregor Mendel and suggested the theory of mutations, is a notable omission, but there are many others: *J. B. S. Haldane* and *Julian Huxley,* for example. Among contemporary figures it is unfortunate a place could not be found for, among others, *Stephen Jay Gould* or *Richard C. Lewontin.*

What holds for physics is true of molecular biology. But if *George Gamow,* who worked in both disciplines, is not here, it might be understood that there was no room either for *Salvador Luria, Oswald Avery,* or *Jacques Monod.* Although Frederick Sanger is included for his basic contribution to unbuttoning the human genome, why not *Walter Gilbert?*

Finally, it should be obvious that only certain figures in the history of medicine can be found here. The discovery of insulin by *Frederick Banting* and *Charles Best* has often been told but is here neglected. *John Enders* deserved to be included for his work on immunology, and I especially regret the space not accorded *Gerald Edelman,* whose fascinating research in brain science has augmented his great discoveries in immunology. It was also painful to exclude *Henry Dale,* who discovered acetylcholine, as well as *Rita Levi-Montalcini,* who discovered nerve growth factor. From the chapter on Jonas Salk, the absence of *Albert Sabin* should be apparent.

These are only a few of the omissions from that class of scientists whose long reach into nature extends beyond the laboratory bench and scholarly enclave, not only to experiment, observe, and demonstrate, but even to shape our perception of the world.

PICTURE ACKNOWLEDGMENTS

Every effort has been made to locate the copyright holder of the photos used in *The Scientific 100*. Some illustrations and photos are in the public domain.

Courtesy Austrian Institute: Ludwig Boltzmann, Sigmund Freud, Erwin Schrödinger

Courtesy Bantam Books: Stephen Hawking

Courtesy Biographees: Noam Chomsky, Claude Lévi-Strauss, Lynn Margulis, Frederick Sanger

Courtesy Burroughs-Wellcome: Gertrude Belle Elion

Courtesy Fermilab: Footprint of Fermilab.

Courtesy German Information Center: Max Born, Paul Ehrlich, Werner Heisenberg, Johannes Kepler, Gustav Kirchhoff, Robert Koch, Max von Laue, Justus Liebig, Max Planck, Rudolf Virchow, Alfred Wegener

Courtesy Harvard University: Sheldon Glashow, Ernst Mayr, B. F. Skinner, Edward O. Wilson

Courtesy Kamerlingh Onnes Laboratory: Heike Kamerlingh Onnes

Courtesy Linus Pauling Institute of Science and Medicine: Linus Pauling

Courtesy New York Public Library: Claude Bernard, Franz Boas, Comte de Buffon, Tycho Brahe, Nicolaus Copernicus, Marie Curie, John Dalton, Albert Einstein, Euclid, Leonhard Euler, Michael Faraday, Alexander Fleming, Ernst Haeckel, Albert von Haller, William Harvey, Edwin Hubble, Christiaan Huygens, August Kekulé, Emil Kraepelin, Lucretius, Trofim Lysenko, Marcello Malpighi, Louis Pasteur, J. J. Thomson, Andreas Vesalius

Courtesy Royal Danish Embassy: Niels Bohr

Courtesy Salk Institute: Francis Crick, Jonas Salk

Courtesy Santa Fe Institute: Murray Gell-Mann

Courtesy University of California Press: George Gaylord Simpson

Courtesy University of Chicago: Willard Libby

Courtesy University of Illinois at Urbana–Champaign Department of Physics: John Bardeen

© The Nobel Foundation: Louis Victor de Broglie, Max Delbrück, Paul Dirac, Arthur Eddington, Albert Einstein, Enrico Fermi, Richard Feynman, Emil Fischer, Frederick Gowland Hopkins, Konrad Lorenz, Karl Landsteiner, Thomas Hunt Morgan, Ernest Rutherford, Charles Sherrington, James Watson

Université de Genève/Photo by Landenberg: Jean Piaget

Rockefeller University Archives: Theodosius Dobzhansky

I also wish to thank:

Kinsey Institute for Sex Research/Dellenback: Alfred Kinsey

Los Alamos National Laboratories: Hans Bethe, Enrico Fermi, John von Neumann, J. Robert Oppenheimer, Edward Teller

McGill University Archives: Hans Selye

474

SOURCE NOTES

See the bibliography for complete references to the citations.
Abbreviations: *CB* = *Current Biography Yearbook; DSB* = *Dictionary of Scientific Biography; NPW* = *Nobel Prize Winners*

Introduction
xvi "the sole test": R. Feynman, *Physics: 1920 to Today,* p. 227.
xvi "as if you had": quoted in A. E. E. McKenzie, *The Major Achievements of Science,* p. 293.
xvii "One tends": G. Holton, *Einstein, History, and Other Passions,* p. 134.
xix "sooner or later": G. Sarton, *The History of Science and the New Humanism,* p. 47.

1 Isaac Newton
4 "Threatening my father": G. Christianson, *In the Presence of the Creator,* p. 7.
5 "I was in": ibid., p. 74.
6 "Newton a magician": quoted in J. Fauvel et al. (eds.), *Let Newton Be!* p. 61.
7 "Newton explored": ibid., p. 227, p. 1.

2 Albert Einstein
8 "The imprint": G. Holton, *Einstein, History, and Other Passions,* p. 3.
10 "flamed with": E. Segrè, *From X-Rays to Quarks,* pp. 87–88.
13 "I still believe in": N. Herbert, *Quantum Reality,* p. 24.
14 "One may not": A. Pais, *Niels Bohr's Times,* p. 225.
14 "I want to go": A. Pais, *Subtle Is the Lord...,* p. 477.

3 Niels Bohr
16 "It is wrong": quoted in R. Rhodes, *The Making of the Atomic Bomb,* p. 77.
16 "that something was expected": A. Pais, *Niels Bohr's Times,* p. 44.
17 "[in] retrospect": ibid., p. 21.
20 "We see him": V. Weisskopf, *Niels Bohr, the Quantum, and the World,* p. 586.
20 "Bohr's contributions": R. Rhodes, *The Making of the Atomic Bomb,* p. 54.

4 Charles Darwin
22 "Darwin is arguably": A. Desmond and J. Moore, *Darwin,* p. xxi.
22 "The passion for": C. Darwin, *Autobiography,* p. 23.
23 "a man physically vigorous": L. R. Stevens, *Charles Darwin,* p. 27.
23 "I am become": in R. Clark, *The Survival of Charles Darwin,* p. 28.
23 "I have always felt": ibid., pp. 34–35.
26 "by reason of A. E. E. McKenzie, *The Major Achievements of Science,* p. 203.
26 "genius who though fallible": G. Simpson, *Book of Darwin,* p. 17.

5 Louis Pasteur
29 "That there is": in J. Nicolle, *Louis Pasteur,* p. 51.
31 fn. "In 1940": R. Dubos, *Pasteur and Modern Science,* p. 119.
32 "His remarkable talent": J. Nicolle, *Louis Pasteur,* p. 205.

475

32 "Pasteur's scientific work": G. Geison, *The Private Science of Louis Pasteur*, pp. 277, 278.

6 Sigmund Freud

34 "continuing extremes": I. B. Cohen, *Revolution in Science*, p. 353.
36 fn. "What will the Professor's": H. Deutsch, *Confrontations with Myself*, p. 132.
38 "an inscrutable face": K. R. Eissler, *Sigmund Freud*, p. 23.
39 "the most stupendous": quoted in E. F. Torrey, *Freudian Fraud*, p. 236.
39 "It would be": R. Holt, *Freud Reappraised*, p. 3.
39 "It is commonplace": P. Gay, *Freud*, p. xvii.
39 "Sigmund Freud was clearly": E. Wigner, *The Recollections of Eugene P. Wigner*, p. 67.

7 Galileo Galilei

42 "perhaps the greatest": J. R. Ravetz, *The Copernican Revolution*, p. 210.
44 "After 350 Years": in J. Reston, *Galileo*, p. 284.
44 "that a coherent depiction": S. Drake, *Galileo*, p. 6.

8 Antoine Lavoisier

45 "what Newton had": D. McKie, *Antoine Lavoisier*, p. 35.
48 "in order to link": quoted in W. Brock, *Norton History of Chemistry*, p. 104.
48 fn. "an important source": F. Holmes, *Lavoisier*, p. 491.
49 "We must trust": quoted in G. Kauffman, "The Making of Modern Chemistry," p. 700.

9 Johannes Kepler

51 "I have attested": quoted in M. Kline, *Mathematics and the Physical World*, p. 124.
54 "I take religion": quoted in G. Holton, *Thematic Origins of Scientific Thought*, p. 70.
54 "Kepler was one": A. Einstein, *Out of My Later Years*, p. 224.

10 Nicolaus Copernicus

56 "The earth": A. E. E. McKenzie, *The Major Achievements of Science*, p. 353.
58 "Copernicus did not": quoted in I. B. Cohen, *Revolution in Science*, p. 125.
58 "One can easily": O. Gingerich, *The Eye of Heaven*, p. 201.
58 "I cannot hear": F. Hoyle, *Nicolaus Copernicus*, p. 286.

11 Michael Faraday

61 "altered the history": I. McCabe and J. Thomas, "Bicentenary of the Birth of Michael Faraday," p. 136.
62 "I know not": quoted in M. Kaku, *Hyperspace*, p. 25.
63 "that the various": M. Faraday, *Diary*, paragraph 2146, quoted in E. Segrè, *From Falling Bodies to Radio Waves*, p. 149.

12 James Maxwell

64 "The most significant": quoted in I. Tolstoy, *James Clerk Maxwell*, p. 2.
65 "Oh, I'm so glad": quoted in ibid., p. 14.
66 "The velocity is so nearly": in D. Runes, *A Treasury of World Science*, p. 700.
67 "cornerstone of the nineteenth": I. Tolstoy, *James Clerk Maxwell*, p. 141.
67 "James, you're beginning": quoted in ibid., p. 155.

13 Claude Bernard

69 "His philosophy": in H. Parvez and S. Parvez, *Advances in Experimental Medicine*, p. 1.
70 "They had the greatest": J. Fruton, "Claude Bernard the Scientist," p. 39.
71 "clearly pointed out that": in H. Parvez and S. Parvez. *Advances*, p. 43.

14 Franz Boas

72 "was one of these": C. Lévi-Strauss and D. Eribon, *Conversations with Claude Lévi-Strauss*, p. 36.
73 "the intelligent understanding": M. Herskovits, *Franz Boas*, p. 10.
74 "More than any": M. Hyatt, *Franz Boas*, p. 98.
75 "not even those": ibid., p. 109.
76 "almost single-handedly": quoted in H. Gardner, *The Mind's New Science*, p. 232.
76 "marked a transformation": G. Stocking, *A Franz Boas Reader*, p. 157.
76 "an old fur hat": C. Lévi-Strauss and D. Eribon, *Conversations*, p. 37.

15 Werner Heisenberg

78 "Werner Heisenberg, born of": D. Cassidy, *Uncertainty*, p. ix.
78 "They adhered.": D. Cassidy, "Heisenberg, Uncertainty and the Quantum Revolution," p. 107.
80 "game of chess": E. Heisenberg, *Inner Exile*, p. 155.

80 "do my bit": W. Heisenberg, *Physics and Beyond*, p. 154.
81 "We will have": W. Heisenberg, *Tradition in Science*, p. 17.

16 Linus Pauling
84 "If one wished": T. Goertzel and B. Goertzel, *Linus Pauling*, pp. 74–75.
85 "By 1935": L. Pauling, "Fifty Years of Progress in Structural Chemistry and Molecular Biology," p. 291.
86 "the *general* relation between": quoted in H. F. Judson, *The Eighth Day of Creation*, p. 84.
87 "accepts as members": quoted in T. Goertzel and B. Goertzel, *Linus Pauling*, p. 240.

17 Rudolf Virchow
89 "Germany would": E. Ackerknecht, *Rudolf Virchow*, p. 3.
90 "Democracy, education": quoted in J. Bendiner and E. Bendiner, *Biographical Dictionary of Medicine*, p. 248.
90 "Are the triumphs": quoted in H. Sigerist, *Great Doctors*, p. 339.
90 "Experiment": quoted in S. Nuland, *Doctors*, p. 313.
91 "Development cannot cease to": R. Virchow in E. Carlson, *Modern Biology*, p. 25.
91 "What Virchow accomplished": S. Nuland, *The Doctors*, p. 325.
91 "It is too often": E. Carlson, *Modern Biology*, p. 22.
92 "showed the body": quoted in I. B. Cohen, *Revolution in Science*, p. 317.
92 "Physical anthropology and": in G. Stocking, *A Franz Boas Reader*, p. 41.
92 "Our society": E. Ackerknecht, *Rudolf Virchow*, p. 166.

18 Erwin Schrödinger
94 "Everybody read": H. F. Judson, *The Eighth Day of Creation*, p. 244.
94 "friend, teacher": quoted in DSB.
95 "The power": D. Cassidy, *Uncertainty*, p. 212.
96 "I should be": in W. Heisenberg, *Physics and Beyond*, p. 75.
97 "a second flowering of": C. Kilmister, *Schrödinger*, p. 2.
97 "represents": R. Penrose, Foreword to E. Schrödinger, *What Is Life?* p. x.
97 fn. "I would have": E. Schrödinger, "Autobiographical Sketches," in *What Is Life?* p. 184.

19 Ernest Rutherford
100 "Newton": R. Rhodes, *The Making of the Atomic Bomb*, p. 230.
100 "jolly little beggars": D. Wilson, *Rutherford*, p. 114.
101 "laid down the fundamental": quoted in ibid.
101 "surrounded by a..."D. Wilson, Rutherford, p. 298.
101 "It was as if": quoted in A. E. E. McKenzie, *The Major Achievements of Science*, p. 293.
102 "surrounded by a": Wilson, *Rutherford*, p. 298.
102 "If, as I": ibid, p. 405.
103 "when he came": ibid, p. 35.
103 "He was": E. N. da C. Andrade, quoted in A. Pais, *Niels Bohr's Times*, p. 129.

20 Paul Dirac
104 "Enter Dirac": A. Pais, *Niels Bohr's Times*, p. 351.
105 "The result was": E. Wigner, quoted in B. Kursuhoglu and E. Wigner, *Dirac*, p. 93.
105 "I feel much": M. Dirac, "Thinking of My Darling Paul," p. 5.
106 "has no idea": in H. Kragh, *Dirac*, p. 37.
107 "a self-consistent": in S. Glashow, *Interactions*, p. 129.
107 "Dirac had set": R. Crease and C. Mann, *The Second Creation*, pp. 182–83.
108 "shy as": quoted in H. Kragh, *Dirac*, p. 116.
108 "I think one": R. Peierls, "Dirac's Way,": p. 44.
108 "the mid-1930s": H. Kragh, *Dirac*, p. 292.
108 "definitive form": in R. Feynman and S. Weinberg, *Elementary Particles and the Laws of Physics*, p. vii.

21 Andreas Vesalius
110 "I could": in C. D. O'Malley, *Andreas Vesalius of Brussels*, p. 222.
110 "Everything": in D. Runes, *A Treasury of World Science*, p. 955.
111 "I urge": quoted in C. D. O'Malley, *Andreas Vesalius*, p. 239.
111 "When the remaining": ibid., p. 239.
111 "By the beginning": *DSB*.
113 "no fighter": G. Zilboorg, "Psychological Sidelights on Andreas Vesalius," p. 565.
113 "Dissection gained a good": L. Bragman, "A Rhymed History of Medicine," pp. 31–32.

22 Tycho Brahe

114 "If Copernicus was the greatest": T. Kuhn, *The Copernican Revolution,* p. 200.
115 "I noticed that a new": in D. Runes, *A Treasury of World Science,* p. 102.

23 Comte de Buffon

120 "Nearly all cultivated persons": J. Browne, "Georges-Louis Leclerc, Comte de Buffon," p. 86.

24 Ludwig Boltzmann

123 "the one who": E. Broda, *Ludwig Boltzmann,* p. 83.
123 "This development": A. Pais, *Niels Bohr's Times,* p. 82.
123 "precise preparation": G. Holton, *Einstein, History, and Other Passions,* p. 288.
125 "We are ready": in E. Broda, *Ludwig Boltzmann,* p. 46.
125 "Despite his great": ibid., pp. 29–30.

25 Max Planck

126 "has given one": quoted in L. Motz and J. Weaver, *The Story of Physics,* p. 190.
126 "A firm conservative": E. Segrè, *From X-Rays to Quarks,* p. 76.
127 "the quest": quoted in R. Rhodes, *The Making of the Atomic Bomb,* p. 30.
129 "transitional figure": A. Pais, *Niels Bohr's Times,* p. 84.

26 Marie Curie

130 "a driven and probably obsessive": A. Pais, *Inward Bound,* p. 55.
131 "We began a": S. Quinn, *Marie Curie,* p. 115.
132 "one could not": A. Pais, *Inward Bound,* p. 53.
132 "extremely handicapped": quoted in S. Quinn, *Marie Curie,* p. 154.
133 "What is the": ibid., p. 159.
133 "From this stark": R. Pflaum, *Grand Obsession,* p. 66.
133 "furnished proof": quoted in S. Quinn, *Marie Curie,* pp. 329–30.

27 William Herschel

136 "I was even obliged": quoted in J. Sidgwick, *William Herschel,* p. 57.

28 Charles Lyell

140 "Lyell must be": L. Eiseley, *Darwin's Century,* p. 98.
141 "It cannot easily be": in L. Wilson, *Charles Lyell,* p. 271.
141 "uninterrupted succession of": ibid., p. 200.

29 Pierre Simon de Laplace

143 "The age of": R. Fox, "Laplacian Physics," p. 291.
144 "the greatest scientist": M. Kline, *Mathematics and the Physical World,* p. 419.
144 "the skeleton of his": J. North, *Norton History of Astronomy and Cosmology,* p. 394.
145 "without feeling sure": J. Newman, "Laplace," p. 53.
146 "What we know": quoted in ibid., p. 58.

30 Edwin Hubble

148 "a particularly interesting": R. Smith, "Edwin P. Hubble and the Transformation of Cosmology," p. 56.
149 "Here is the": quoted in G. Christianson, *Edwin Hubble,* p. 159.
150 "catapulting Hubble into": ibid., p. 209.
150 "The universe": quoted in ibid., p. 210.
150 "Not until the empirical": quoted in ibid., p. 248.
151 "Most would admit": T. Ferris, *The Red Limit,* p. 44.

31 Joseph J. Thomson

154 "[The] carriers of electricity": quoted in *NPW.*
155 "The scientific world": A. Schuster, quoted in *DSB.*
155 "Thomson's success": A. E. E. McKenzie, *The Major Achievements of Science,* p. 279.

32 Max Born

156 "Born's work was": J. Gribbin, *In Search of Schrödinger's Cat,* p. 71.
157 "I loved to listen": M. Born, *My Life,* p. 13.
158 "The time is perhaps": quoted in D. Cassidy, *Uncertainty,* p. 146.
159 "simply ridiculous": M. Born, *My Life,* p. 238.
159 "I never liked": *NPW.*

33 Francis Crick

161 "No one man": in H. F. Judson, *The Eighth Day of Creation*, p. 109.
162 "A knowledge of the true": F. Crick, *What Mad Pursuit*, p. 11.
163 "Jim and I": ibid., p. 64.
164 "It has not": quoted in H. F. Judson, *Eighth Day*, p. 198.
164 "your joys and your sorrows": F. Crick, *The Astonishing Hypothesis*, p. 3.
164 "It is clear": R. Olby, "Francis Crick, DNA, and the Central Dogma," p. 267.
164 "The discovery of the double": F. Crick, *Pursuit*, p. 67.
165 "You were always": ibid., p. 77.

34 Enrico Fermi

167 "With his superb": L. Motz and J. Weaver, *The Story of Physics*, p. 315.
170 "he was measuring": See E. Segrè, *Enrico Fermi*, p. 184.

35 Leonard Euler

172 "This is indeed": L. Euler, *Letters of Euler to a German Princess*, p. 330.
173 "In all his": Introduction, ibid., p. x.

36 Justus Liebig

175 "Liebig is": quoted in G. Cannon, *Great Men of Modern Agriculture*, p. 150.
177 "If I can": quoted in ibid., p. 159.
177 "Such was the esprit": J. B. Morrell, "The Chemist Breeders,": p. 48.

37 Arthur Eddington

179 "acted as an": J. North, *Norton History of Astronomy and Cosmology*, p. 487.
180 "Once championed": M. Bartusiak, *Through a Universe Darkly*, p. 159.
181 "foremost popularizer of his time": L. Motz and J. Weaver, *The Story of Physics*, p. 367.
181 "queer; he is like": quoted in G. Christianson, *Edwin Hubble*, p. 257.
181 "The idea of a": A. Eddington, *The Nature of the Physical World*, p. 338.
182 "Space seems to be": quoted in T. Ferris, *The Red Limit*, p. 118.

38 William Harvey

185 "enough to overturn": Raffaello Magiotti quoted in I. B. Cohen, *Revolution in Science*, p. 85.
186 "passes all the": ibid., p. 189.
186 "I do not": quoted in D. Boorstin, *The Discoverers*, p. 367.
186 "pretty young wench": quoted in S. Nuland, *Doctors*, p. 143.

39 Marcello Malpighi

188 "might have been": D. Boorstin, *The Discoverers*, p. 376.
188 "I could clearly see": quoted in ibid., pp. 379–80.
189 "anatomized all phases": quoted in H. Adelman, *Marcello Malpighi. and the Evolution of Embryology*, v. 1, p. 344.

40 Christiaan Huygens

192 "showed a complete": J. Yoder, *Unrolling Time*, p. 178.
193 "that otherwise our Earth": quoted in J. V. Nash, "Some Seventeenth-Century Cosmic Speculations," p. 487.

41 Carl Gauss

194 "Even today": M. Kaku, *Hyperspace*, p. 32.
196 "There are enough": S. Hollingdale, *Makers of Mathematics*, p. 316.
197 "one might expect": *DSB*.
197 "closed the angel": ibid.

42 Albrecht von Haller

201 "Whoever writes a": in S. Roe, *Matter, Life, and Generation*, p. 96.
202 "devoid of any": H. Sigerist, *The Great Doctors*, p. 204.
203 "as leading toward": S. Roe, *Matter, Life, and Generation*, p. 92.

43 August Kekulé

205 "most brilliant piece": quoted in W. Brock, *Norton History of Chemistry*, p. 269.
206 "through the deserted": quoted in A. Findlay, *A Hundred Years of Chemistry*, p. 38.
207 "Just as Picasso": W. Brock, *Norton History of Chemistry*, p. 269.
207 "Sometimes said not": This judgment is common in the historical literature, but not necessarily true. Prof. Alan Rocke, who reviewed this chapter, disagrees.

44 Robert Koch
210 "I beg": P. de Kruif, *The Microbe Hunters*, p. 144.
212 "Koch's announcement": V. Robinson, "Robert Koch," p. 135.
213 "The Faustian": *DSB*.

45 Murray Gell-Mann
215 "Ben and I": M. Gell-Mann, *The Quark and the Jaguar*, p. 14.
217 "have all been": ibid., p. 186.

46 Emil Fischer
219 "did not live to see his impractical son": T. Williams, *Biographical Dictionary of Scientists*, p. 180.
219 "perhaps the greatest": ibid.
220 "By the end": A. Findlay, *A Hundred Years of Chemistry*, p. 165.
220 "The veil": *NPW*.

47 Dmitri Mendeleev
224 "But nothing": quoted in W. Brock, *Norton History of Chemistry*, p. 311.
224 "the size": in D. Runes, *A Treasury of World Science*, p. 741.
224 "Among the ordinary": ibid., p. 744.
225 "Mendeleev has two": quoted in E. Farber, *Great Chemists*, p. 726.

48 Sheldon Glashow
227 "The theory": S. Glashow, *Interactions*, p. 277–278.
227 "He asked me": in R. Crease and C. Mann, "How the Universe Works," p. 72.
228 "a fully acceptable": ibid., p. 73.
228 "The weak and electromagnetic": ibid., p. 77.
228 "Charm": Glashow, *Interactions*, p. 213.
229 "One, charm is not": R. Crease and C. Mann, *The Second Creation*, p. 358.
230 "appears to offer": S. Glashow, *The Charm of Physics*, p. 8.

49 James Watson
232 "I don't think": quoted in H. F. Judson, *The Eighth Day of Creation*, p. 195.
232 "I became": ibid., p. 47.
233 "Suddenly I was excited": quoted *CB* 1990.
233 "Mr. Crick was thirty-five": H. F. Judson, *Eighth Day*, p. 111.
234 "Suddenly I became": quoted *CB* 1990.
235 "sort of completed": quoted in S. Hall, "Old School Ties," p. 1533.

50 John Bardeen
238 "John passionately aspired": C. Herring, "Recollections from the Early Years of Solid-State Physics," p. 32.
239 "my quantum mechanic": quoted in B. Schechter, *Path of No Resistance*, p. 219.

51 John von Neumann
243 "The visionary part": N. Macrae, *John von Neumann*, p. 285.
243 "von Neumann's genius": quoted ibid., pp. 287–88.
244 "The view of von Neumann": S. Heims, *John von Neumann and Norbert Wiener*, p. 368.
244 "mathematical axiomatic approach": D. Noble, *Forces of Production*, p. 71.
245 "mostly saw women": quoted in S. Heims, *John von Neumann and Norbert Wiener*, p. 350.

52 Richard Feynman
247 "that transcended any raw": J. Gleick, *Genius*, p. 9.
247 "Every puzzle that": R. Feynman, *Surely You're Joking, Mr. Feynman*, p. 9.
248 "combined brilliance with greatness": quoted in J. Horgan, "Illuminator of the Stars," p. 40.
248 "a kind of": in C. Sykes, *No Ordinary Genius*, p. 58.
248 "When you went": quoted in Omni.
249 "the first time": R. Feynman, *Surely You're Joking, Mr. Feynman*, p. 229.
250 "It doesn't seem": quoted in J. Gleick, *Genius*, p. 372.

53 Alfred Wegener
253 "Doesn't the east": in M. Schwarzbach, *Alfred Wegener*, p. 76.
254 "The Newton of the": quoted in ibid., p. 82.
254 "two halves of the same": ibid., p. 180.
255 "Wegener, working in": M. Greene, "Alfred Wegener," p. 761.

54 Stephen Hawking

257 "I knew": S. Hawking, *A Brief History of Time,* p. 11.

257 "The big": *CB* 1984.

258 "is regarded": J. Gribbin, "Brief History of Stephen Hawking," p. 41.

259 "With all these": H. Pagels, *Perfect Symmetry,* p. 73.

260 "And this": in S. Hawking, *A Brief History of Time,* p. x.

55 Anton van Leeuwenhoek

261 "It would be": B. Ford, *Single Lens,* p. 79.

263 "the most wretched": in A. E. E. McKenzie, *The Major Achievements of Science,* pp. 394–95.

263 fn. "had too little,": P. de Kruif, *The Microbe Hunters,* p. 22.

264 "so delighted the Prince": in C. Dobell. *Antony von Leeuwenhoek,* p. 55.

56 Max von Laue

266 "one of the": *NPW.*

57 Gustav Kirchhoff

270 "strove for clarity": *DSB.*

271 "Their results": A. Pais, *Niels Bohr's Times,* p. 140.

271 "It is plausible": ibid., p. 140.

272 It is a highly": quoted in ibid., p. 77.

273 "a perfect example": R. von Helmholtz, "A Memoir of Gustav Robert Kirchhoff," p. 532.

273 "despite its simplicity": L. Motz and J. Weaver, *The Story of Physics,* p. 124.

58 Hans Bethe

274 "macroverse and microverse": S. Glashow, *The Charm of Physics,* p. 193.

275 "My life was spent": J. Bernstein, *Prophet of Energy,* p. 9.

276 "I went systematically": H. Bethe, *From a Life of Physics,* p. 12.

277 "resembled": R. Feynman paraphrased in D. Kevles, *The Physicists,* p. 331.

278 "I feel the.": H. Bethe, "Open Letter From Hans Bethe," April 30, 1996.

278 "There is nothing": quoted in J. Horgan, "Illuminator of the Stars," p. 32.

59 Euclid

279 "bears the same": S. Hollingdale, *Makers of Mathematics,* p. 35.

281 "an aggravated case": W. Birdwood, *Euclid's Outline of Sex,* p. 19.

60 Gregor Mendel

282 "priest who held": L. Eiseley, *Darwin's Century,* ch. 8.

284 "It requires": in G. Mendel, "Experiments in Plant-Hybridization," pp. 705–6.

284 "which he said": in R. Olby, *The Origins of Mendelism,* p. 104.

285 "was a stepping stone": P. Bowler, *From the Mendelian Revolution,* p. 1.

61 Heike Kamerlingh Onnes

287 "lift the veil": *NPW.*

288 "introduced sound engineering": E. Segrè, *From Falling Bodies to Radio Waves,* p. 247.

288 "With this liquefaction": *DSB.*

62 Thomas Hunt Morgan

291 "It is notorious": in G. Allen, "Thomas Hunt Morgan," p. 719.

292 "And how is": in R. Clark, *Survival of Charles Darwin,* p. 261.

292 "some of the": D. Depew and B. Weber, *Darwinism Evolving,* p. 230.

293 "compounded with enthusiasm": A. Sturtevant quoted in G. Allen, "Thomas Hunt Morgan," p. 731.

293 "In his strong": ibid., p. 738.

63 Hermann von Helmholtz

295 "Helmholtz also": R. Kremer, *Letters of Hermann von Helmholtz to His Wife,* p. xi.

296 "had not asked": quoted in H. Sigerist, *The Great Doctors,* pp. 325–26.

296 "the most influential": *DSB.*

297 "If we accept": in S. Mason, *History of the Sciences,* p. 549.

297 "Gentlemen!": quoted in J. Mulligan, "Hermann von Helmholtz and His Students," p. 72.

298 "When during a conversation": quoted in ibid., p. 69.

298 "It was obvious": quoted in G. Holton, *Einstein, History, and Other Passions,* p. 292.

298 "the last scholar": *DSB.*

64 Paul Ehrlich

300 "[magic] bullets": quoted in I. Galdston, *Behind the Sulfa Drugs,* p. 103.
310 "Here he crowned": ibid., p. 101.
302 "the chairs and tables": G. Lapage, "Paul Ehrlich," p. 162.
302 "He was loath": I. Galdston, *Behind the Sulfa Drugs,* p. 124.

65 Ernst Mayr

304 "one of the founders": quoted in J. Rennie, "Darwin's Current Bulldog,": p. 24.
304 "Our greatest living": quoted in *Notable Twentieth-Century Scientists.*
305 "I collected 137": P. Weintraub, *Omni Interviews,* p. 42.
305 "groups of actually": *CB* 1984.
306 "strictly physico-chemical nature": Personal Communication, January 31, 1996.
306 "Ah, Francis Crick": P. Weintraub, *Omni Interviews,* p. 55.
306 "The majority of people": ibid., p. 49.
307 "neatly-dressed, grey-haired": J. Rennie, "Darwin's Current Bulldog,": p. 25.

66 Charles Sherrington

310 "The whole quantitative": *NPW.*
311 "We have to": quoted in W. Penfield, "Sir Charles Scott Sherrington," p. 882.
311 "The wide emotional": R. Granit, *Charles Scott Sherrington,* p. 18.

67 Theodosius Dobzhansky

312 "The most important": E. Boesiger, "Evolutionary Theories After Lamarck and
   Darwin," p. 38.
314 "My interest in genetics": G. Allen, "Theodosius Dobzhansky," p. 94.
314 "a connected story": T. Dobzhansky, *Genetics and the Origin of Species,* p. 13.
315 "signalizes very clearly": L. Dunn, Introduction to ibid., p. vii.
315 "For the first time": E. Wilson, *Naturalist,* p. 112.
315 "saw himself as aiding": C. Krimbas, "The Evolutionary Worldview of Theodosius
   Dobzhansky," p. 190.
316 "man, this mysterious": T. Dobzhansky, *The Biology of Ultimate Concern,* p. 7.

68 Max Delbrück

318 "the pioneer of a new": W. Hayes, "Max Delbrück and the Birth of Molecular Biology,"
   p. 663.
319 "fastidious aesthetician": H. F. Judson, *The Eighth Day of Creation,* p. 25.
319 "manifesting subconscious hatred": E. Fischer and C. Lipson, *Thinking About Science,* p.
   21.
320 "This seemed": W. Hayes, "Max Delbrück," p. 647.
321 "the phage group's Vatican": G. Stent quoted in ibid., p. 653.
321 "one of the rare": H. F. Judson, *Eighth Day,* p. 65.
321 "make themselves known": quoted in ibid., p. 51.
322 "I have the feeling": ibid., p. 230.
312 "quick, courteous": ibid., p. 61.

69 Jean Baptiste Lamarck

324 "One wishes": L. Eiseley, *Darwin's Century,* p. 204.
325 "He continued his work": *Encyclopédie universalis* (my translation).

70 William Bayliss

327 "Bayliss was the more": *DSB.*
328 "It was a": L. Bayliss, "William Maddock Bayliss," p. 472.
329 "a small brown": ibid., p. 465.
329 "revelation of the": ibid., p. 475.
329 "One of the": ibid., p. 475.

71 Noam Chomsky

331 "higher than that": R. Robins, *A Short History of Linguistics,* p. 228.
331 "a spoken language": N. Chomsky, Personal Communication, January 9, 1996.
331 "I therefore dropped": Ibid.
332 "to find a system": N. Chomsky, *Logical Structure of Linguistic Theory,* p. 25.
332 "One could have": N. Chomsky, *Language and Responsibility,* p. 129.
332 "for a more": N. Chomsky, *Syntactic Structures,* p. 208.

334 "After a decade": N. Smith, "Chomsky's Revolution," p. 521.
334 "international law": quoted in M. Haley and R. Lunsford, *Noam Chomsky*, p. 187.

72 Frederick Sanger
337 "Thus, perhaps more": C. Wills, *Exons, Introns, and Talking Genes*, p. 26.
337 "The idea that biology": F. Sanger, "Sequences, Sequences, and Sequences," p. 2.
339 "the best idea": ibid., p. 22.
340 "The possibility seemed": ibid., p. 26.

73 Lucretius
342 "Show many glimpses": quoted in *DSB*.
343 "You must not": Lucretius, *On The Nature of the Universe*, p. 156.
343 "the thing born": ibid., p. 156.
343 "It may also happen": ibid., p. 168.
344 "Though not a scientist": G. Hadzsits, *Lucretius and His Influence*, pp. 333–34.

74 John Dalton
345 "solid, massy, hard": Isaac Newton's formulation from his *Opticks*, quoted in E. Patterson, *John Dalton and the Atomic Theory*, p. 107.
346 "a bridge": W. Brock, *Chemistry*, p. 135.
348 "we have made": F. Greenaway, *John Dalton and the Atom*, p. 7.

75 Louis Victor de Broglie
349 "Today in the autumn": L. de Broglie, *Certitudes et incertitudes de la science*, p. 22 (my translation).
350 "I was nineteen": ibid., p. 13.
351 "After long reflection": quoted in A. Pais, *Subtle Is the Lord...*, p. 435.
351 "Read it": quoted in D. Kevles, *The Physicists*, p. 164.

76 Carl Linnaeus
353 "Anyone who knows": H. Goerke, *Linnaeus*, p. 108.
354 "a prospectus for": D. Boorstin, *The Discoverers*, p. 437.
356 "gross prurience of": quoted in ibid., p. 439.
356 "his lectures were": G. Cannon, *Great Men of Modern Agriculture*, p. 67.

77 Jean Piaget
358 "was the greatest": M. Hunt, *Story of Psychology*, p. 354.
358 "It was at this": D. Cohen, *Piaget*, p. 13.
361 "Piaget's grandiose": H. Gardner, *The Mind's New Science*, p. 118.

78 George Gaylord Simpson
363 "brought paleontology back": N. Eldredge, *Time Frames*, p. 96.
363 "an uncontrollable drive": G. Simpson, *Concession to the Improbable*, p. 274.
363 "I only regret": quoted in *Notable Twentieth-Century Scientists*.
363 "of greatest value": G. Simpson, *Concession*, p. 63.
364 "fossil animals cannot": G. Simpson, *Tempo and Mode in Evolution*, pp. xvi, xvii.
365 "I am slowly": L. Laporte, *Simple Curiosity*, p. 327.
366 "I do not value": G. Simpson, *Concession*, p. 178.
366 "themes of loneliness": S. J. Gould, Afterward to G. Simpson, *The Dechronization of Sam Magruder*, p. 210.

79 Claude Lévi-Strauss
369 "The vogue for structuralism": C. Lévi-Strauss and D. Eribon, *Conversations with Claude Lévi-Strauss*, p. 68.
369 fn. "probably the only": quoted in D. Pace, *Claude-Lévi-Strauss*, pp. 153–54.
369 "projection outside our": quoted in ibid., p. 173.
369 "For twenty years": C. Lévi-Strauss and D. Eribon, *Conversations*, p. 132.
370 "By the late": D. Pace, *Lévi-Strauss*, p. 7.
370 a pivotal contribution": H. Gardner, *The Mind's New Science*, p. 242.
371 "By setting mankind": C. Lévi-Strauss and D. Eribon, *Conversations*, p. 162.

80 Lynn Margulis
373 "The evolution of the": quoted in C. Mann, *Lynn Margulis*,: p. 378.
375 "the major source": C. Mann, ibid., p. 379.
376 "Homo sapiens": L. Margulis, "Personal Statement," p. 39.
376 "rejection of Judeo-Christian": ibid., p. 39.

82 Konrad Lorenz

382 "Konrad...preferred ornithology": quoted in A. Nisbet, *Konrad Lorenz*, pp. 35–36.
382 "was as applicable": *NPW*.
383 "The racial idea": A. Nisbet, *Konrad Lorenz*, p. 82.
384 "domestication threatens": ibid., p. 90.
384 "their discoveries concerning": *NPW*.
384 "the invention of": *NPW*.
385 "claims humility and": A. Nisbet, *Konrad Lorenz*, p. 224.

83 Edward O. Wilson

386 "human nature can be": in C. Barlow, *From Gaia to Selfish Genes*, p. 242.
387 "I grew up": E. Wilson, *Naturalist*, p. 15.
387 "under the microscope": ibid., p. 133.
387 "was my destiny": ibid., p. 132.
388 "physically trapped": ibid., p. 231.
389 "A congenital synthesizer": ibid., p. 312.
389 "It may not": E. Wilson, *Sociobiology*, p. 4.
390 "[tends] to": quoted in A. Fisher, p. 74.
390 "withstood these assaults": A. Montagu quoted in C. Barlow, p. 190.
390 "A society that chooses": E. Wilson and C. Lumsden, *Promethean Fire*, p. 184.
391 "When sociobiology is": S. J. Gould quoted in C. Barlow, *From Gaia*, p. 191.
391 "Both radical environmentalism": M. Lind, "Brave New Right," p. 24.

84 Frederick Gowland Hopkins

393 "I felt in": *DSB*.
394 "when fed upon..": quoted in J. Talbott, *Biographical History of Medicine*, p. 912.
394 "It was only": *DSB*.
395 "a classic statement": N. Morgan, "From Physiology to Biochemistry," p. 497.

85 Gertrude Belle Elion

387 "War changed everything": quoted in A. Macdonald, *Feminine Ingenuity*, p. 360.
399 "stresses the importance": B. Chabner, "In Celebration of a Nobel Prize," p. 1513.
399 "We had finally": *CB* 1995.

86 Hans Selye

402 "syndrome of just": quoted in A. Monat and R. Lazarus, *Stress and Coping*, p. 19.
403 "My eyes fell": H. Selye, *In Vivo*, p. 43.
403 "If we could": H. Selye, *The Stress of Life*, p. 31.
404 "So few among": H. Selye, *In Vivo*, pp. 48–49.
405 "[spend] as much": H. Seyle, *From Dream to Discovery*, p. 30.
405 "To my mind": ibid., p. 30.

87 J. Robert Oppenheimer

406 "It is generally": G. Holton, *Einstein, History, and Other Passions*, p. 205.
407 "Now I am": in R. Rhodes, *The Making of the Atomic Bomb*, p. 676.
408 "Oppenheimer created": in A. Pais, *Inward Bound*, p. 369.
409 "became a symbol": quoted in D. Kevles, *The Physicists*, p. 377.
409 "I have blood": quoted in G. Holton, *Einstein, History, and Other Passions*, p. 219.
409 "crybaby scientist": R. Erwin, "Oppenheimer Investigated,": p. 41.
409 "Don't ever bring": quoted in G. Holton, *Einstein, History*, p. 219.

88 Edward Teller

412 "Mankind is still": W. Broad, *Teller's War*, p. 290.
412 "The hope": *CB* 1983.
413 "Now that we have": R. Clark, *Greatest Power on Earth*, p. 260.
413 "First, Teller": S. Blumberg and L. Panos, *Edward Teller*, p. 260.
413 "was apt to": D. Kevles, *The Physicists*, p. 330.
414 "proposed a number": quoted in R. Rhodes, *The Making of the Atomic Bomb*, p. 772.
414 "If it is": W. Broad, *Teller's War*, p. 44.
415 "exuded a sort": H. York, *The Advisors*, p. 4.
415 "Teller considers": Personal Communication, March 18, 1996.
415 "was possessed": in W. Broad, *Teller's War*, p. 282.
416 "We would be": S. Blumberg and L. Panos, *Edward Teller*, p. 141.

89 Willard Libby
419 "It should be": *NPW.*
420 "A scientist has to be": T. Berland, *The Scientific Life,* pp. 24–25.

90 Ernst Haeckel
421 "there are not": E. Norkenskiöld, *The History of Biology,* pp. 505–6.
423 "a natural law which no human power": quoted in ibid., p. 51.

91 Jonas Salk
428 "the worst tragedy": quoted in R. Rapoport, *The Super-Doctors,* pp. 244–45.
428 "like sitting in on": quoted in ibid., p. 246.
429 "Wisdom, understood as": J. Salk, *The Survival of the Wisest,* p. 124.
429 "Why, Jonas": *CB* 1954.

92 Emil Kraepelin
431 "be deduced from": J. Talbott, *Biographical History of Medicine,* p. 866.
432 "The mountains which": E. Bleuler, *Dementia Praecox,* p. 19, 20.
432 "Kraepelin finally": ibid., p. 3.
433 "Like Pinel": F. Alexander and S. Selesnick, *History of Psychiatry,* p. 165.
433 "A closer look": R. Fine, *A History of Psychoanalysis,* p. 8.
433 "Far to the": in J. Talbott, *Biographical History,* p. 866.

93 Trofim Lysenko
434 "All this DNA": H. F. Judson, *The Eighth Day of Creation,* p. 468.
435 "Lysenkoism showed": V. Soyfer, "Lysenko and the Tragedy of Soviet Science": p. 3.
436 "The property": quoted in A. E. E. McKenzie, *The Major Achievements of Science,* p. 504.
436 "The only acceptable": Statement of the Praesidium of the U.S.S.R Academy of Sciences, 1948, quoted in McKenzie, *Major Achievements,* p. 502.
437 "Ha! You are": H. F. Judson, *Eighth Day,* p. 468.
438 "battle against": R. Clark, *The Survival of Charles Darwin,* p. 340.

94 Francis Galton
440 "as a theory": D. Depew and B. Weber, *Darwinism Evolving,* p. 201.
441 "dates from about": D. W. Forrest, *Francis Galton,* p. 85.
441 "heredity was far more": F. Galton, *Memories of My Life,* p. 266.
441 "It is in the most": in D. W. Forrest, *Francis Galton,* p. 89.
441 "It would seem as though": F. Galton, *Memories,* p. 312–13.
441 "We want lists…": D. W. Forrest, *Francis Galton,* p. 186.
441 "Since Galton's day": D. Kevles, *In the Name of Eugenics,* p. xi.
443 "enterprising, defiant": quoted in ibid., p. 9.

95 Alfred Binet
444 "I.Q. testing": S. J. Gould, *The Mismeasure of Man,* p. 150.
445 "a subtle analyst": quoted in T. Wolf, *Alfred Binet,* p. 331.
446 "one of the most": quoted in ibid., p. 117.
447 "even from this": ibid., p. 177.
448 "They cannot master": quoted in S. J. Gould, *Mismeasure,* p. 191.

96 Alfred Kinsey
449 "does not command": P. Robinson, *The Modernization of Sex,* p. 43.
451 "In many of": A. Kinsey, W. Pomeroy, and C. Martin, *Sexual Behavior in the Human Male,* p. 9.
452 "The year and a half": W. Pomeroy, *Dr. Kinsey and the Institute for Sex Research,* p. 400.
453 "a monumental amount": G. Brand, *Great Scientists,* p. 21.

97 Alexander Fleming
455 "mass hysteria": G. Macfarlane, *Alexander Fleming,* p. 262.
457 "There is no doubt": T. Williams, *Howard Florey,* p. 85.
457 "My only merit": quoted in J. G. Crowther, *Alexander Fleming,* p. 138.
457 "that he didn't": G. Macfarlane, *Alexander Fleming,* p. 271.

98 B. F. Skinner
459 "easily the most": V. Norby and C. Hall, *A Guide to Psychologists and Their Concepts,* p. 155.
459 fn. "for many psychologists": ibid., p. 151.
459 "I was always": in *CB* 1979.

461 "Whether from narcissism": in E. Boring and G. Lindzey, *A History of Psychology in Autobiography,* v. 5, p. 407.

462 "an American original": D. W. Bjork, *B. F. Skinner,* pp. xii–xiii.

99 Wilhelm Wundt

463 "was not an": P. Fraisse, "Evolution of Experimental Psychology," p. 20.

464 "specialized scientific treatment": S. Diamond, "Wundt before Leipzig," p. 59.

465 "ingenious attempt": H. Haeberlin, "Theoretical Foundations of Wundt's Folk Psychology," pp. 248–49.

466 "remains indissolubly linked": K. Danziger, "Wilhelm Wundt and the Emergence of Experimental Psychology," p. 396.

466 "the first policeman": quoted in S. Diamond, "Wundt before Leipzig," p. 40–41.

100 Archimedes

467 "of such a lofty": *DSB.*

469 "as he was sitting": *DSB.*

469 "He used to": quoted in A. Aaboe, *Episodes from the Early History of Mathematics,* p. 76.

469 "how those": Archimedes quoted in ibid., p. 76.

470 "Shall we not": quoted in E.J. Dijksterhuis, *Archimedes,* pp. 27–28.

470 "I noticed a small column": quoted in *DSB.*

BIBLIOGRAPHY

1. General Reference Works

Gillispie, Charles Coulston, ed. *Dictionary of Scientific Biography,* vol. 1–14. New York: Scribner's, 1970.

Graham, Judith, ed. *Current Biography Yearbook, 1940–1995.* New York: H. W. Wilson.

Hellemans, Alexander, and Bunch, Bryan. *The Timetables of Science.* New York: Simon and Schuster, 1988.

McGraw-Hill Modern Men of Science. New York: McGraw-Hill, 1986.

McMurray, Emily J., ed. *Notable Twentieth-Century Scientists.* Detroit: Gale Research, 1995.

Mount, Ellis, and List, Barbara A. *Milestones in Science and Technology.* Phoenix, Ariz: Oryx Press, 1987.

Pelletier, Paul. *Prominent Scientists: An Index to Collective Biographies,* 3rd ed. New York: Neal-Schuman, 1994.

Wasson, Tyler, ed. *Nobel Prize Winners.* New York: H. W. Wilson, 1988.

2. Biographies, Autobiographies, and Other Sources

Aaobe, Asger. *Episodes from the Early History of Mathematics.* Washington, D.C.: Mathematical Association of America, 1964.

Ackerknecht, Erwin H. *Rudolf Virchow: Doctor, Statesman, Anthropologist.* Madison, Wisc.: University of Wisconsin Press, 1953.

————. *A Short History of Psychiatry,* 2d rev. ed. New York: Hafner, 1968.

————. *A Short History of Medicine.* Baltimore: Johns Hopkins University Press, 1982.

Adams, Mark B., ed. *The Evolution of Theodosius Dobzhansky: Essays on His Life and Thought in Russia and America.* Princeton: Princeton University Press, 1994.

Adelman, Howard B. *Marcello Malpighi and the Evolution of Embryology,* 5 vols. Ithaca: Cornell University Press, 1966.

Alexander, Franz G., and Selesnick, Sheldon T. *The History of Psychiatry.* New York: Harper & Row, 1966.

Allen, Garland E. "Thomas Hunt Morgan: Materialism and Experimentalism in the Development of Modern Genetics." *Social Research* 51 (1984): 709–738.

————. "Theodosius Dobzhansky, the Morgan Lab, and the Breakdown of the Naturalist/Experimentalist Dichotomy, 1927–1947," pp. 87–98 in *Evolution of Theodosius Dobzhansky,* ed. Mark B. Adams. Princeton, N.J.: Princeton University Press, 1994.

Armitage, Angus. *Copernicus: The Founder of Modern Astronomy.* New York: A. S. Barnes, 1962.

Baeyer, Hans Christian von. *Taming the Atom.* New York: Random House, 1992.

Bailey, Edward. *Charles Lyell.* Garden City, N.Y.: Doubleday, 1963.

Barlow, Connie, ed. *From Gaia to Selfish Genes.* Cambridge, Mass.: MIT Press, 1991.

Bartusiak, Marcia. *Through a Universe Darkly.* New York: HarperCollins, 1993.

Bayliss, L. E. "William Maddock Bayliss, 1860–1924: Life and Scientific Work." *Perspectives in Biology and Medicine.* Summer (1961): 460–77.

Bayliss, William Maddock. *Principles of General Physiology,* 4th ed. London: Longmans, Green, 1924.

Bendiner, Jessica and Elmer. *Biographical Dictionary of Medicine.* New York: Facts on File, 1990.

Berland, Theodore. *The Scientific Life.* New York: Coward-McCann, 1962.

Bernstein, Jeremy. *Einstein.* New York: Viking, 1973.

————. *Hans Bethe: Prophet of Energy.* New York: Basic Books, 1980.

————. "What Did Heisenberg Tell Bohr About the Bomb?" *Scientific American* 272(5) (1995): 92–97.

Bethe, Hans, et al. *From a Life of Physics.* Singapore: World Scientific, 1989.

Birdwood, Wilbur D. [pseud.]. *Euclid's Outline of Sex.* New York: Henry Holt, 1922.

Bleuler, Eugen. *Dementia Praecox, or the Group of Schizophrenias.* New York: International Universities Press, 1950.

Blumberg, Stanley and Panos, Louis G. *Edward Teller: Giant of the Golden Age of Physics.* New York: Scribner's, 1990.

Boesiger, Ernest. "Evolutionary Theories After Lamarck and Darwin," pp. 21–44 in *Studies in the Philosophy of Biology,* ed. F. J. Ayala and T. Dobzhansky. Berkeley, Calif.: University of California Press, 1974.

Bolles, Robert C. *The Story of Psychology: A Thematic History.* Pacific Grove, Calif.: Brooks/Cole, 1993.

Boorstin, Daniel. *The Discoverers.* New York: Random House, 1983.

Boring, Edwin, and Lindzey, Gardner. *A History of Psychology in Autobiography,* vol. 5. New York: Appleton-Century Crofts, 1967.

Born, Max. *My Life: Recollections of a Nobel Laureate.* New York: Scribner's, 1975.

Boslough, John. *Stephen Hawking's Universe.* New York: Morrow, 1985.

Bowers, Bryan. *Michael Faraday and Electricity.* London: Priory Press, 1994.

Bowler, Peter J. *From the Mendelian Revolution: The Emergence of Hereditarian Concepts in Modern Science and Sociology.* Baltimore: Johns Hopkins Press, 1989.

Bragman, Louis. "A Rhymed History of Medicine." *Medical Life* 39(1) (1932): 5–54.

Brand, Gerhard. "Alfred Charles Kinsey," pp. 14–21, in *Great Scientists,* vol. 5, ed. F. Magill. Danbury, Conn.: Grolier.

Broad, William J. *Teller's War.* New York: Simon & Schuster, 1992.

Brock, William H. *The Norton History of Chemistry.* New York: Norton, 1992.

Broda, Engelbert. *Ludwig Boltzmann.* Woodbridge, Conn.: Ox Bow Press, 1983.

Browne, Janet. "George-Louis Leclerc, Comte de Buffon (1707–88)." *Endeavor* 12(2) (1988): 86–90.

Bruno, Leonard C. *Landmarks of Science.* New York: Facts on File, 1989.

Brush, Stephan G. *The History of Modern Science: A Guide to the Second Scientific Revolution, 1800–1950.* Iowa State University Press.

Buhler, W. K. *Gauss: A Biographical Study.* Berlin: Springer Verlag, 1981.

————. "Should the History of Science Be Rated X?" *Science* 183 (1974): 1164–72.

Cannon, Grant G. *Great Men of Modern Agriculture.* New York: Macmillan, 1963.

Carlson, Elof Axel, ed. *Modern Biology: Its Conceptual Foundations.* New York: Braziller, 1967.

Cassidy, David. "Heisenberg, Uncertainty and the Quantum Revolution." *Scientific American* 266(5) (1992): 106–12.

————. *Uncertainty: The Life and Science of Werner Heisenberg.* New York: W. H. Freeman, 1992.

Chabner, Bruce A. "In Celebration of a Nobel Prize." *Journal of the National Cancer Institute* 80 (1988): 1512–13.

Chomsky, Noam. *Syntactic Structures.* The Hague: Mouton, 1957.

————. *Logical Structure of Linguistic Theory.* New York: Plenum, 1975.

————. *Language and Responsibility.* New York: Pantheon, 1977.

Christenson, Cornelia. *Kinsey: A Biography.* Bloomington, Ind.: Indiana University Press, 1971.

Christianson, Gale E. *In the Presence of the Creator: Isaac Newton and His Times.* New York: Free Press, 1984.

_____. *Edwin Hubble: Mariner of the Nebulae*. New York: Farrar, Straus, 1995.

Clark, Ronald W. *The Survival of Charles Darwin*. New York: Random House, 1984.

Coe, Sophia Dobzhansky. "Theodosius Dobzhansky: A Family Story," pp. 13–29 in *The Evolution of Theodosius Dobzhansky*, ed. Mark B. Adams. Princeton: Princeton University Press, 1994.

Cohen, David. *Piaget: Critique and Reassessment*. London: Croom Helm, 1983.

Cohen, I. Bernard. *Revolution in Science*. Cambridge, Mass.: Harvard Univ. Press, 1985.

Cook-Deegan, Robert. *The Gene Wars*. New York: Norton, 1994.

Crease, R. and Mann, C. "How the Universe Works." *Atlantic* 254(2): 66–93. 1984.

_____. *The Second Creation: Makers of the Revolution of the Twentieth-Century Physics*. New York: Macmillan, 1986.

Crick, Francis. *What Mad Pursuit: A Personal View of Scientific Discovery*. New York: Basic Books, 1988.

_____. *The Astonishing Hypothesis*. New York: Scribner's, 1994.

Crowther, J. G. *Alexander Fleming*. n.p.: Heron Books, 1971.

Danziger, Kurt. "Wilhelm Wundt and the Emergence of Experimental Psychology," pp. 396–409 in *Companion to the History of Modern Science*, ed. R. C. Olby et al. London: Routledge, 1990.

Darwin, Charles. *The Autobiography of Charles Darwin, 1809–1882*. New York: Norton, 1958.

de Broglie, Louis. *Certitudes et incertitudes de la science*. Paris: Albin Michel, 1966.

de Kruif, Paul. *The Microbe Hunters*. New York: Harcourt, Brace, 1926.

Depew, David J. and Weber, Bruce H. *Darwinism Evolving: Systems Dynamics and the Genealogy of Natural Selection*. Cambridge, Mass.: MIT Press, 1995.

Desmond, Adrian and Moore, James. *Darwin*. New York: Norton, 1991.

Deutsch, Helene. *Confrontations With Myself*. New York: Norton, 1973.

Diamond Solomon. "Wundt before Leipzig," pp. 3–70 in *Wilhelm Wundt and the Making of a Scientific Psychology*, ed. R. W. Rieber. New York: Plenum Press, 1980.

Dijksterhuis, E. J. *Archimedes*. Princeton, N.J.: Princeton University Press, 1987.

Dirac, Margit. "Thinking of My Darling Paul," pp. 5–8 in *Paul Adrian Maurice Dirac*, eds. B. N. Kursunoglu and E. Wigner. Cambridge: Cambridge University Press, 1987.

Dobell, Clifford. *Antony van Leeuwenhoek and His "Little Animals."* New York: Dover, 1932.

Dobzhansky, Theodosius. *Genetics and the Origin of Species*. New York: Columbia University Press, 1937.

_____. *The Biology of Ultimate Concern*. New York: New American Library, 1967.

Drake, Stillman. *Galileo: Pioneer Scientist*. Toronto: University of Toronto Press, 1990.

Dreyer, J. L. E. *Tychoe Brahe: A Picture of Scientific Life and Work in the Sixteenth Century*. New York: Dover, 1963.

Dubos, René. *Pasteur and Modern Science*. Madison, Wisc.: Science-Tech Publishers, 1988.

Eagle, Morris N. *Recent Developments in Psychoanalysis*. Cambridge: Harvard University Press, 1984.

Eddington, Arthur. *The Nature of the Physical World*. New York: Macmillan, 1946.

Edelstein, Ludwig. "Andreas Vesalius, the Humanist." *Bulletin of the History of Medicine* 14(5) (1943): 547–61.

Einstein, Albert. *Out of My Later Years*. New York: Philosophical Library, 1950.

_____. *Relativity: The Special and the General Theory*. New York: Crown, 1961.

Eisely, Loren. *Darwin's Century: Evolution and the Men Who Discovered It*. New York: Doubleday, 1958.

Eldredge, Niles. *Time Frames: The Evolution of Punctuated Equilibria*. Princeton, N.J.: Princeton University Press, 1989.

_____. *Reinventing Darwin*. New York: Wiley, 1995.

Elkind, David. *Children and Adolescents: Interpretive Essays on Jean Piaget*. New York: Oxford University Press, 1970.

Erwin, Robert. "Oppenheimer Investigated." *Wilson Quarterly* 18(4) (1994): 34–45.

Euler, Leonard. *Letters of Euler on Different Subjects in Natural Philosophy Addressed to a German Princess*. New York: J. & J. Harper, 1833.

Fairbairn, W. R. D. *Psychoanalytic Studies of the Personality*. London: Routledge, 1952.

Farber, Eduard. *Great Chemists*. New York: Interscience, 1961.

Fauvel, John et al., eds. *Let Newton Be!* New York: Oxford University Press, 1988.

Ferris, Timothy. *The Red Limit*. New York: Quill, 1983.

Feynman, Richard. *The Character of Physical Law.* Cambridge, Mass.: MIT Press, 1967.
————. "Physics: 1920 to Today," pp. 219–235 in *Writing About Science,* eds. M. E. Brown and J. A. Mazzeo. New York: Oxford University Press, 1979.
————. *Surely You're Joking, Mr. Feynman.* New York: Norton, 1985.
————, and Weinberg, Steven. *Elementary Particles and the Laws of Physics.* Cambridge: Cambridge University Press, 1987.
Findlay, Alexander. *A Hundred Years of Chemistry,* 3rd rev. ed. London: Gerald Duckworth, 1958.
Fine, Reuben. *A History of Psychoanalysis.* New York: Columbia University Press, 1979.
Fischer, Ernst Peter. "We Are All Aspects of One Single Being: An Introduction to Erwin Schrödinger." *Social Research* 51 (1984): 809–832.
————, and Lipson, Carol. *Thinking About Science: Max Delbrück and the Origins of Molecular Biology.* New York: Norton, 1988.
Fisher, Arthur. "Sociobiology: Science or Ideology." *Society.* July/August (1992): 67–79.
Ford, Brian J. *Single Lens: The Story of the Simple Microscope.* New York: Harper & Row, 1985.
Forrest, D. W. *Francis Galton: The Life and Work of a Victorian Genius.* New York: Taplinger, 1974.
Fox, Robert. "Laplacian Physics," pp. 278–294 in *Companion to the History of Modern Science,* ed. R. C. Olby et al. London: Routledge (Article from 1974), 1990.
Fraisse, Paul. "The Evolution of Experimental Psychology," pp. 1–90 in *Experimental Psychology: Its Scope and Method,* vol. I. Paul Fraisse and Jean Piaget. New York: Basic Books, 1968.
Fruton, Joseph S. "Claude Bernard the Scientist," pp. 36–40 in *Claude Bernard and the Internal Environment,* ed. Eugene Debs Robin. New York: Marcel Dekker, 1979.
Galdston, Iago. *Behind the Sulfa Drugs.* New York: Appleton-Century, 1943.
Galton, Francis. *Memories of My Life.* London: Methuen, 1908.
Gardner, Howard. *The Mind's New Science: A History of the Cognitive Revolution.* New York: Basic Books, 1985.
Gay, Peter. *Freud: A Life for Our Time.* New York: Norton, 1988.
Geison, Gerald L. *The Private Science of Louis Pasteur.* Princeton, N.J.: Princeton University Press, 1995.
Gell-Mann, Murray. *The Quark and the Jaguar.* New York: W. H. Freeman, 1994.
Gibson, Charles Robert. *Heroes of the Scientific World.* Freeport, N.Y.: Books for Libraries Press, 1970.
Gingerich, Owen. *The Eye of Heaven: Ptolemy, Copernicus, Kepler.* New York: American Institute of Physics, 1993.
Glashow, Sheldon. *Interactions: A Journey Through the Mind of a Particle Physicist and the Matter of This World.* New York: Warner Books, 1988.
————. *The Charm of Physics.* New York: American Institute of Physics, 1991.
Gleick, James. *Genius: The Life and Science of Richard Feynman.* New York: Pantheon, 1992.
Goerke, Heinz. *Linnaeus.* New York: Scribner's, 1973.
Goertzel, Ted, and Goertzel, Ben. *Linus Pauling: A Life in Science and Politics.* New York: Basic Books, 1995.
Goldman, Martin. *The Demon in the Aether: The Life of James Clerk Maxwell.* Edinburgh: Paul Harris, 1983.
Goodstein, Judith R. "Atoms, Molecules, and Linus Pauling." *Social Research* 51(3) (1984): 691–708.
Gould, Stephen Jay. *Ontogeny and Phylogeny.* Cambridge, Mass.: Harvard University Press, 1977.
————. *The Mismeasure of Man.* New York: Norton, 1981.
————. *An Urchin in the Storm.* New York: Norton, 1987.
Granit, Ragnar. *Charles Scott Sherrington: An Appraisal.* Garden City, N.Y.: Doubleday, 1967.
Greenaway, Frank. *John Dalton and the Atom.* Ithaca, N.Y.: Cornell University Press, 1966.
Greene, Mott T. "Alfred Wegener." *Social Research* 51(3) (1984): 739–61.
Gribbin, John. *In Search of Schrödinger's Cat.* New York: Bantam, 1984.
————. "A Brief History of Stephen Hawking." *New Scientist,* March 28, 1992.
Grünbaum, Adolf. *The Foundations of Psychoanalysis: A Philosophical Critique.* Berkeley, Calif.: University of California Press, 1985.

Hadzsits, George Depue. *Lucretius and His Influence*. New York: Cooper Square Publishers, 1963.

Haeberlin, Herman K. "The Theoretical Foundations of Wundt's Folk Psychology," pp. 229–49 in *Wilhelm Wundt and the Making of a Scientific Psychology*, ed. R. W. Rieber. New York: Plenum Press, 1980.

Haley, Michael C., and Lunsford, Ronald F. *Noam Chomsky*. New York: Twayne, 1994.

Hall, Stephen S. "James Watson and the Search for Biology's 'Holy Grail.'" *Smithsonian* 20 (Feb.): 41–50, 1990.

Harré, R. *Early Seventeenth-Century Scientists*. London: Pergamon, 1965.

Hawking, Stephen. *A Brief History of Time*. New York: Bantam, 1988.

Hayes, William. "Max Delbrück and the Birth of Molecular Biology." *Social Research* 51(3) (1984): 641–73.

Heims, Steven J. *John von Neumann and Norbert Wiener: From Mathematics to the Technologies of Life and Death*. Cambridge, Mass.: MIT Press, 1980.

Heisenberg, Elisabeth. *Inner Exile: Recollections of a Life with Werner Heisenberg*. Boston: Birkhauser, 1984.

Heisenberg, Werner. *Physics and Beyond: Encounters and Conversations*. New York: Harper & Row, 1971.

————. *Tradition in Science*. New York: Seabury, 1983.

Helmholtz, Robert von. "A Memoir of Gustav Robert Kirchhoff," pp. 527–40 in *Annual Report of the Board of Regents*. Smithsonian Institution. Washington, D.C.: Government Printing Office, 1890.

Herbert, Nick. *Quantum Reality: Beyond the New Physics*. Garden City, N.Y.: Doubleday, 1985.

Herring, Conyers. "Recollections From the Early Years of Solid-State Physics." *Physics Today*, April 1992: 26–33.

Herskovits, Melville J. *Franz Boas: The Science of Man in the Making*. New York: Scribner's, 1953.

Hodge, M. J. S. "Origins and Species Before and After Darwin," pp. 374–95 in *Companion to the History of Modern Sciences*, ed. R. C. Olby et al. London: Routledge, 1990.

Hollingdale, Stuart. *Makers of Mathematics*. London: Penguin, 1991.

Holmes, Frederic Lawrence. *Lavoisier and the Chemistry of Life*. Madison, Wisc.: University of Wisconsin Press, 1985.

Holt, Robert R. *Freud Reappraised: A Fresh Look at Psychoanalytic Theory*. New York: Guilford Press, 1989.

Holton, Gerald. *Thematic Origins of Scientific Thought*. Cambridge, Mass.: Harvard University Press, 1988.

————. *Einstein, History, and Other Passions*. Woodbury, N.Y.: AIP, 1995.

Hoyle, Fred. *Nicolaus Copernicus: An Essay on His Life and Work*. New York: Harper & Row, 1973.

Hunt, Morton. *The Story of Psychology*. New York: Doubleday, 1993.

Hyatt, Marshall. *Franz Boas, Social Activist: The Dynamics of Ethnicity*. New York: Greenwood, 1990.

Jones, Brian. "The Legacy of Edwin Hubble." *Astronomy* 17(2) (1989): 38–44.

Jones, Ernest. *The Life and Work of Sigmund Freud*, vol. 1. New York: Basic Books, 1953.

Jordanova, L. J. *Lamarck*. New York: Oxford University Press, 1984.

Judson, Horace Freeland. *The Eighth Day of Creation*. New York: Simon & Schuster, 1979.

Kaku, Michio. *Hyperspace: A Scientific Odyssey Through Parallel Universes, Time Warps, and the 10th Dimension*. New York: Oxford University Press, 1994.

Kamin, Leon J. *The Science and Politics of I.Q.* New York: Wiley, 1974.

————. "Behind the Curve." *Scientific American* 272(2) (1995): 99–103.

Kauffman, George B. "The Making of Modern Chemistry." *Nature* 338 (1989): 699–700.

Kevles, Daniel J. *In the Name of Eugenics: Genetics and the Uses of Human Heredity*. New York: Knopf, 1985.

————. *The Physicists: The History of a Scientific Community in Modern America*. Cambridge, Mass.: Harvard University Press, 1995.

Keynes, Milo. *Sir Francis Galton, FRS: The Legacy of His Ideas*. London: Macmillan and the Galton Institute, 1993.

Kilmister, C. W., ed. *Schrödinger: Centenary Celebration of a Polymath.* Cambridge, Mass.: Cambridge University Press, 1987.

Kinsey, Alfred C.; Pomeroy, Wardell B.; and Martin, Clyde E. *Sexual Behavior in the Human Male.* Philadelphia: W. B. Saunders, 1948.

Kline, Morris. *Mathematics and the Physical World.* New York: Thomas Y. Crowell, 1959.

Kragh, Helge S. *Dirac: A Scientific Biography.* Cambridge: Cambridge University Press, 1990.

Kremer, Richard L. *Letters of Hermann von Helmholtz to His Wife 1847–1859.* Stuttgart: Franz Steiner, 1990.

Krimbas, Costas B. "The Evolutionary Worldview of Theodosius Dobzhansky," pp. 179–94 in *The Evolution of Theodosius Dobzhansky,* ed. Mark B. Adams. Princeton, N.J.: Princeton University Press, 1994.

Kuhn, Thomas S. *The Copernican Revolution.* Cambridge, Mass.: Harvard University Press, 1957.

Kursunolgu, Behram N. and Wigner, Eugene P., eds. *Paul Adrien Maurice Dirac.* Cambridge: Cambridge University Press, 1987.

Langone, John. *Superconductivity: The New Alchemy.* Chicago: Contemporary Books, 1989.

Lapage, G. "Paul Ehrlich." *Nature* 169 (1952): 152.

Laporte, Leo F., ed. *Simple Curiosity: Letters from George Gaylord Simpson to His Family, 1921–1970.* Berkeley, Calif.: University of California Press, 1987.

Laudan, Rachel. "The History of Geology, 1780–1840," pp. 314–325 in *Companion to the History of Modern Science,* ed. Olby, R. C. et al. London: Routledge, 1990.

Lear, John. *Kepler's Dream.* Berkeley, Calif.: University of California Press, 1965.

Lee, Thomas F. *Gene Future: The Promise and Perils of the New Biology.* New York: Plenum Press, 1993.

Lévi-Strauss, Claude. *The Elementary Structures of Kinship.* Boston: Beacon Press, 1969.

———, and Eribon, Didier. *Conversations With Claude Lévi-Strauss.* Chicago: University of Chicago Press, 1991.

Libby, Willard. *Radiocarbon Dating,* 2nd ed. Chicago: University of Chicago Press, 1955.

Lind, Michael. "Brave New Right." *New Republic* 211: 24–25, 1994.

Lucretius. *On the Nature of the Universe,* translated by R. E. Latham. New York: Penguin, 1951.

Macdonald, Anne L. *Feminine Ingenuity.* New York: Ballantine, 1992.

Macfarlane, Gwyn. *Alexander Fleming: The Man and the Myth.* Cambridge, Mass.: Harvard University Press, 1984.

Macrae, Norman. *John von Neumann.* New York: Pantheon, 1992.

Mahler, Margaret S.; Pine, Fred; and Bergman, Annie. *The Psychological Birth of the Human Infant.* New York: Basic Books, 1975.

Mann, Charles. "Lynn Margulis: Science's Unruly Earth Mother." *Science* 252 (1991): 378–81.

Margulis, Lynn. "Personal Statement," pp. 39–47 in *Minds for History Directory.* Mayer, Ariz.: Minds for History Institute, 1990.

Mason, Stephen F. *A History of the Sciences.* New York: Collier, 1962.

Mayr, Ernst. *The Growth of Biological Thought: Diversity, Evolution, and Inheritance.* Cambridge, Mass.: Harvard University Press, 1982.

———. *One Long Argument: Charles Darwin and the Genesis of Modern Evolutionary Thought.* Cambridge, Mass.: Harvard University Press, 1991.

McCabe, Irena M., and Thomas, John M. "The Bicentenary of the Birth of Michael Faraday of the Royal Institution of Great Britain," *Endeavor* 15(2) (1991): 363–369.

McDermott, Jeanne. "A Biologist Whose Heresy Redraws Earth's Tree of Life." *Smithsonian* 20(72) (1989): 72–80.

McGrayne, Sharon Bertsch. *Nobel Prize Women in Science.* New York: Birch Lane Press, 1993.

McKenzie, A. E. E. *The Major Achievements of Science.* New York: Simon & Schuster, 1973.

McKie, Douglas. *Antoine Lavoisier: Scientist, Economist, Social Reformer.* New York: Henry Schuman, 1952.

Monat, Alan, and Lazarus, Richard S., eds. *Stress and Coping,* 2d ed. New York: Columbia University Press, 1985.

Moore, Ruth. *Niels Bohr: The Man, His Science, and the World They Changed.* New York: Knopf, 1966.

Moore, Walter. *Schrödinger: Life and Thought.* 1989: Cambridge University Press, 1989.

Morgan, Neil. "From Physiology to Biochemistry," pp. 494–502 in ed. R. C. Olby. *Companion to the History of Modern Science.* London: Routledge, 1990.

Morrell, J. B. "The Chemist Breeders: The Research Schools of Liebig and Thomas Thomson." *Ambix.* 19 (1972): 1–46.

Morton, Alan G. *Soviet Genetics.* London: Lawrence & Wishart, 1951.

Motz, Lloyd, and Weaver, Jefferson Hane. *The Story of Physics.* New York: Plenum, 1989.

Mulligan, Joseph F. "Hermann von Helmholtz and His Students." *American Journal of Physics.* 57(1) (1989): 68–74.

Nash, J. V. "Some Seventeenth-Century Cosmic Speculations." *Open Court.* 51(8) (1927): 467–87.

Newman, James R. "Laplace," pp. 45–58 in *Lives in Science,* ed. Editors of *Scientific American.* New York: Simon & Schuster, 1957.

Nicolle, Jacques. *Louis Pasteur: The Story of His Major Discoveries.* New York: Basic Books, 1961.

Nicolson, Marjorie. "Kepler, The Somnium, and John Donne," pp. 306–27 in *Roots of Scientific Thought,* eds. Philip P. Wiener and Aaron Noland. New York: Basic Books, 1957.

Nisbett, Alec. *Konrad Lorenz.* New York: Harcourt Brace, 1976.

Noble, David. *Forces of Production.* New York: Knopf, 1984.

Nordby, Vernon J., and Hall, Calvin S. *A Guide to Psychologists and Their Concepts.* New York: W. H. Freeman, 1975.

Nordenskiöld, Erik. *The History of Biology.* New York: Knopf, 1928.

North, John. *The Norton History of Astronomy and Cosmology.* New York: Norton, 1995.

Nuland, Sherwin B. *Doctors: The Biography of Medicine.* New York: Knopf, 1988.

O'Malley, C. D. *Andreas Vesalius of Brussels.* Berkeley, Calif.: University of California Press, 1964.

Olby, Robert. "Francis Crick, DNA, and the Central Dogma," pp. 227–80 in *The Twentieth-Century Sciences,* ed. Gerald Holton. New York: Norton, 1972.

————. "The Emergence of Genetics," pp. 521–35 in *Companion to the History of Modern Science,* ed. R. C. Olby et al. London: Routledge, 1990.

Oldroyd, David. "Gregor Mendel: Founding-Father of Modern Genetics?" *Endeavor* 8(1) (1984): 29–31.

Oliphant, Mark. "Rutherford." *Endeavor* 11(3) (1987): 133–36.

Pace, David. *Claude Lévi-Strauss: The Bearer of Ashes.* Boston: Routledge, 1983.

Pagels, Heinz R. *Perfect Symmetry: The Search for the Beginning of Time.* New York: Bantam, 1985.

Pais, Abraham. *"Subtle is the Lord..."* New York: Oxford University Press, 1982.

————. *Inward Bound: Of Matter and Forces in the Physical World.* New York: Oxford University Press, 1986.

————. *Niels Bohr's Times: In Physics, Philosophy, and Polity.* Oxford: Clarendon Press, 1991.

Parvez, H., and S., eds. *Advances in Experimental Medicine: A Centenary Tribute to Claude Bernard.* Amsterdam: Elsevier, 1980.

Patterson, Elizabeth C. *John Dalton and the Atomic Theory: The Biography of a Natural Philosopher.* New York: Doubleday, 1970.

Pauling, Linus. "Fifty Years of Progress in Structural Chemistry and Molecular Biology," pp. 281–307 in *The Twentieth-Century Sciences: Studies in the Biography of Ideas,* ed. Gerald Holton. New York: Norton, 1972.

Peck, James, ed. *The Chomsky Reader.* New York: Pantheon, 1987.

Peierls, Rudolf. "Dirac's Way," pp. 43–45 in *Paul Adrien Maurice Dirac,* ed. Behram N. Kursunoglu and Eugene P. Wigner. Cambridge: Cambridge University Press, 1987.

Penfield, Wilder. "Sir Charles Scott Sherrington," pp. 881–883 in *Dictionary of National Biography, 1951–1960,* eds. E. T. Williams and H. M. Palmer. Cambridge: Oxford University Press, 1971.

Pflaum, Rosalynd. *Grand Obsession: Madame Curie and Her World.* New York: Doubleday, 1989.

Pomeroy, Wardell. *Dr. Kinsey and the Institute for Sex Research.* New York: Harper & Row, 1972.

Poupard, Paul Cardinal. *Galileo Galilei: Toward a Resolution of 350 Years of Debate.* Pittsburgh: Duquesne University Press, 1987.

Quinn, Susan. *Marie Curie: A Life.* New York: Simon & Schuster, 1995.

Rapoport, Roger. *The Super-Doctors.* New York: Playboy Press, 1975.

Rapport, Samuel and Wright, Helen, eds. *Mathematics.* New York: New York University Press, 1963.

Ravetz, J. R. "The Copernican Revolution," pp. 210–16 in *Companion to the History of Modern Science,* eds. R. C. Olby et al. London: Routledge, 1990.

Rayleigh, Robert John. *The Life of Sir J. J. Thomson.* Cambridge: Cambridge University Press, 1943.

Rennie, John. "Darwin's Current Bulldog." *Scientific American* 271(8): 24–25. 1994.

Reston, James Jr. *Galileo: A Life.* New York: Harper Collins, 1994.

Rhodes, Richard. *The Making of the Atomic Bomb.* New York: Simon & Schuster, 1986.

Rieber, R. W., ed. *Wilhelm Wundt and the Making of a Scientific Psychology.* New York: Plenum Press, 1980.

Robin, Eugene Debs (ed.). *Claude Bernard and the Internal Environment.* New York: Marcel Dekker, 1979.

Robins, R. H. *A Short History of Linguistics,* 2nd ed. London: Longman, 1979.

Robinson, Paul. *The Modernization of Sex.* New York: Harper & Row, 1976.

Robinson, Victor. "Robert Koch." *Medical Life* (n.s.) 39(3) (1932): 129–67.

Roe, Shirley A. *Matter, Life, and Generation.* Cambridge: Cambridge University Press, 1981.

Ronan, Colin A. *Science: Its History and Development Among the World's Cultures.* New York: Facts on File, 1982.

Runes, Dagobert D. *A Treasury of World Science.* New York: Philosophical Library, 1962.

Salk, Jonas. *Man Unfolding.* New York: Harper & Row, 1972.

————. *The Survival of the Wisest.* New York: Harper & Row, 1973.

————. *World Population and Human Values: A New Reality.* New York: Harper & Row, 1981.

Sanger, Frederick. "Sequences, Sequences, and Sequences." *Annual Review of Biochemistry* 57 (1988): 1–28.

Sarton, George. *The History of Science and the New Humanism.* Cambridge, Mass.: Harvard University Press, 1937.

Schechter, Bruce. *The Path of No Resistance.* New York: Simon & Schuster, 1989.

Schrödinger, Erwin. *What Is Life?* Cambridge: Cambridge University Press, 1992.

Schuster, John A. "The Scientific Revolution," pp. 217–42 in *Companion to the History of Modern Science,* ed. R. C. Olby et al., London: Routledge, 1990.

Schwarzbach, Martin. *Alfred Wegener: The Father of Continental Drift.* Madison, Wisc.: Science Tech, 1986.

Segrè, Emilio. *Enrico Fermi: Physicist.* Chicago: University of Chicago Press, 1970.

————. *From X Rays to Quarks: Modern Physicists and Their Discoveries.* San Francisco: W. H. Freeman, 1980.

————. *From Falling Bodies to Radio Waves: Classical Physicists and Their Discoveries.* New York: W. H. Freeman, 1984.

Selye, Hans. *From Dream to Discovery.* New York: McGraw-Hill, 1964.

————. *In Vivo: The Case for Supramolecular Biology.* New York: Liveright, 1967.

————. *The Stress of Life,* rev. ed. New York: McGraw-Hill, 1976.

Serafini, Anthony. *Linus Pauling: A Man and His Science.* New York: Paragon House, 1989.

Sidgwick, J. B. *William Herschel: Explorer of the Heavens.* London: Faber and Faber, 1954.

Sigerist, Henry E. *The Great Doctors: A Biographical History of Medicine.* New York: Norton, 1933.

Simpson, George Gaylord. *The Dechronization of Sam Magruder.* New York: St. Martin's Press, 1996.

————. *Tempo and Mode in Evolution.* New York: Columbia University Press, 1944.

————. *Concession to the Improbable.* New Haven: Yale University Press, 1978.

————. *The Book of Darwin.* New York: Washington Square Press, 1982.

Smith, Neil. "Chomsky's Revolution." *Nature* 367 (1994): 521.

Smith, Robert W. "Edwin P. Hubble and the Transformation of Cosmology." *Physics Today* 43(4) (1990): 52–58.

Sourkes, Theodore, ed. *Nobel Prize Winners in Medicine and Physiology, 1901–1965, rev. ed.* New York: Abeldard-Schuman, 1966.

Soyfer, Valery N. *Lysenko and the Tragedy of Soviet Science.* New Brunswick, N.J.: Rutgers University Press, 1994.

Spielberg, Nathan, and Anderson, Bryon. *Seven Ideas That Shook the Universe.* New York: Wiley, 1987.

Stevens, L. Robert. *Charles Darwin.* Boston: Twayne, 1978.

Stocking, George W., ed. *A Franz Boas Reader.* Chicago: University of Chicago Press, 1982.

Sykes, Christopher. *No Ordinary Genius: The Illustrated Richard Feynman.* New York: Norton, 1994.

Talbott, John H. *A Biographical History of Medicine.* New York: Grune & Stratton, 1970.

Tanford, Charles, and Reynolds, Jacqueline. *The Scientific Traveler.* New York: Wiley, 1992.

Thackray, Arnold. *John Dalton: Critical Assessments of His Life and Science.* Cambridge, Mass.: Harvard University Press, 1972.

Thoren, Victor. *The Lord of Uraniborg: A Biography of Tycho Brahe.* New York: Cambridge University Press, 1990.

Tinbergen, Nikolaas. "Ethology," pp. 238–68 in *Scientific Thought, 1900–1960,* ed. Rom Harré. Oxford: Oxford University Press, 1969.

Tolstoy, Ivan. *James Clerk Maxwell: A Biography.* Edinburgh: Cannongate, 1981.

Torrey, E. Fuller. *Freudian Fraud: The Malignant Effect of Freud's Theory on American Thought and Culture.* New York: HarperCollins, 1992.

Wear, Andrew. "The Heart and Blood from Vesalius to Harvey," pp. 568–82 in *Companion to the History of Modern Science,* ed. R. C. Olby et al. London: Routledge, 1990.

Weintraub, Pamela. *The Omni Interviews.* New York: Ticknor & Fields, 1984.

Weisskopf, Victor. "Niels Bohr, the Quantum, and the World." *Social Research* 51(3) (1984): 583–96.

White, Michael and Gribbin, John. *Stephen Hawking: A Life in Science.* New York: Viking, 1992.

_____. *Einstein: A Life in Science.* New York: Dutton, 1994.

Wigner, Eugene P. *The Recollections of Eugene P. Wigner, as Told to Andrew Szanton.* New York: Plenum Press, 1992.

Williams, L. Pearce. *Michael Faraday.* New York: Basic Books, 1965.

Williams, Trevor. *A Biographical Dictionary of Scientists,* 2nd ed. New York: Halsted Press, 1974.

_____. *Howard Florey: Penicillin and After.* London: Oxford University Press, 1984.

Wills, Christopher. *Exons, Introns, and Talking Genes.* New York: Basic Books, 1991.

Wilson, David. *Rutherford: Simple Genius.* Cambridge, Mass.: MIT Press, 1983.

Wilson, Edward O. *Sociobiology: The New Synthesis.* Cambridge, Mass.: Harvard University Press, 1975.

_____. *Naturalist.* Washington, D.C.: Island Press, 1994.

Wilson, Leonard G. *Charles Lyell: The Years to 1841.* New Haven: Yale University Press, 1972.

Wolf, Theta H. *Alfred Binet.* Chicago: University of Chicago Press, 1973.

Yoder, Joella. *Unrolling Time: Christiaan Huygens and the Mathematics of Nature.* New York: Cambridge University Press, 1988.

York, Herbert. *The Advisors,* 2nd ed. Stanford, Calif.: Stanford University Press, 1989.

Zilboorg, Gregory. "Psychological Sidelights on Andreas Vesalius." *Bulletin of the History of Medicine* 14(5) (1943): 562–72.

INDEX